$v = \sqrt{600} = \sqrt{6(100)} =$

THE GOLD STANDARD
DAT CHEM

General Chemistry [CHM]
and Organic Chemistry [ORG]

Book II of IV

Gold Standard Contributors
• 4-Book GS DAT Set •

Brett Ferdinand BSc MD-CM
Karen Barbia BS Arch
Brigitte Bigras BSc MSc DMD
Ibrahima Diouf BSc MSc PhD
Amir Durmic BSc Eng
Adam Segal BSc MSc
Da Xiao BSc DMD
Naomi Epstein BEng
Lisa Ferdinand BA MA
Jeanne Tan Te
Kristin Finkenzeller BSc MD
Heaven Hodges BSc
Sean Pierre BSc MD
James Simenc BS (Math), BA Eng
Jeffrey Cheng BSc
Timothy Ruger MSc PhD
Petra Vernich BA
Alvin Vicente BS Arch

DMD Candidates

E. Jordan Blanche BS
[Harvard School of Dental Medicine]
Stephan Suksong Yoon BA
[Harvard School of Dental Medicine]

$ET = Ek + Ep = 1/2mv2 + mgh$

glutamate recept
floating bridges
epithelial-mesenc
subatomic particle

Gold Standard Illustrators
• 4-Book GS DAT Set •

Daphne McCormack
Nanjing Design
· Ren Yi, Huang Bin
· Sun Chan, Li Xin
Fabiana Magnosi
Harvie Gallatiera
Rebbe Jurilla BSc MBA

RuveneCo

The Gold Standard DAT was built for the US DAT.

The Gold Standard DAT is identical to Canadian DAT prep <u>except</u> QR and ORG. Also, you must practice soap carving for the complete Canadian DAT.

The Gold Standard DAT is identical to OAT prep <u>except</u> PAT, which is replaced by OAT Physics; see our Gold Standard OAT book for Physics review and OAT practice test.

Be sure to register at www.DAT-prep.com by clicking on GS DAT Owners and following the directions for Gold Standard DAT Owners. Please Note: benefits are for 1 year from the date of online registration, for the original book owner only and are not transferable; unauthorized access and use outside the Terms of Use posted on DAT-prep.com may result in account deletion; if you are not the original owner, you can purchase your virtual access card separately at DAT-prep.com.

Visit The Gold Standard's Education Center at www.gold-standard.com.

RuveneCo Inc
Gold Standard Multimedia Education
559-334 Cornelia St
Plattsburgh, NY 12901
E-mail: learn@gold-standard.com
Online at www.gold-standard.com

DAT™ is a registered trademark of the American Dental Association (ADA). OAT™ is a registered trademark of the Association of Schools and Colleges of Optometry (ASCO). The Dental Aptitude Test (DAT) program is conducted by the Canadian Dental Association (CDA). Ruveneco Inc and Gold Standard Multimedia Education are neither sponsored nor endorsed by the ADA, ASCO, CDA, nor any of the degree granting institutions that the authors have attended or are attending. Printed in China.

Table of Contents

THE GOLD STANDARD

EXAM SUMMARY

The Dental Admission Test (DAT) consists of 280 multiple-choice questions distributed across quite a diversity of question types in four tests. The DAT is a computer-based test (CBT). This exam requires approximately five hours to complete - including the optional tutorial, break, and post-test survey. The following are the four subtests of the Dental Admission Test:

1. Survey of the Natural Sciences (NS) – 100 questions; 90 min.
   - General Biology (BIO): 40 questions
   - General Chemistry (CHM): 30 questions
   - Organic Chemistry (ORG): 30 questions

2. Perceptual Ability Test (PAT) - 90 questions; 6 subsections; 60 min.
   - Apertures: 15 questions
   - Orthographic or View Recognition: 15 questions
   - Angle Discrimination: 15 questions
   - Paper Folding: 15 questions
   - Cube Counting: 15 questions
   - 3-D Form Development: 15 questions

3. Reading Comprehension (RC) – 50 questions; 3 reading passages; 60 min.

4. Quantitative Reasoning (QR) – 40 questions; 45 min.
   - Mathematics Problems: 30 questions
   - Applied Mathematics/Word Problems: 10 questions

You will get six scores from: (1) BIO (2) CHM (3) ORG (4) PAT (5) QR (6) RC.

You will get two additional scores which are summaries:
  (7) Academic Average (AA) = BIO + CHM + ORG + QR + RC
  (8) Total Science (TS) = BIO + CHM + ORG

Common Formula for Acceptance:

GPA + DAT score + Interview = Dental School Admissions*

*Note: In general, Dental School Admissions Committees will only examine the DAT score if the GPA is high enough; they will only admit or interview if the GPA + DAT score is high enough. Some programs also use autobiographical materials and/or references in the admissions process. Different dental schools may emphasize different aspects of your DAT score, for example: PAT, BIO, TS, AA. The average score for any section is approximately 17/30; the average AA for admissions is usually 18-20 depending on the dental school; the AA for admissions to Harvard is around 22-23; the 100th percentile is usually 25 meaning that virtually 100% of the approximately 13 000 students who take the DAT every year have an AA less than 25. Only a handful of students score 25/30. Our two student contributors scored 27/30 (AA).

The DAT is challenging, get organized.

dat-prep.com/dat-study-schedule

1. How to study:

1. Study the Gold Standard (GS) books and videos to learn
2. Do GS Chapter review practice questions
3. Consolidate: create and review your personal summaries (= Gold Notes) daily

2. Once you have completed your studies:

1. Full-length practice test
2. Review mistakes, all solutions
3. Consolidate: review all your Gold Notes and create more
4. Repeat until you get beyond the score you need for your targeted dental school

3. Full-length practice tests:

1. ADA practice exams
2. Gold Standard DAT exams
3. TopScore Pro exams
4. Other sources if needed

4. How much time do you need?

On average, 3-6 hours per day for 3-6 months

WARNING: Study more or study more efficiently. You choose. The Gold Standard has condensed the content that you require to excel at the DAT. We have had Ivy League dental students involved in the production of the Gold Standard series so that pre-dent students can feel that they have access to the content required to get a score satisfactory at any dental school in the country. To make the content easier to retain, you can also find aspects of the Gold Standard program in other formats such as:

Is there something in the Gold Standard that you did not understand? Don't get frustrated, get online.

dat-prep.com/forum   dat-prep.com/QRchanges-2015

Good luck with your studies!

Gold Standard Team

GOLD STANDARD
MULTIMEDIA EDUCATION

GENERAL
CHEMISTRY

STOICHIOMETRY

Chapter 1

Memorize	Understand	Importance
* Define: molecular weight * Define: empirical/molecular formula * Rules for oxidation numbers * Common redox agents	* Composition by % mass * Mole concept, limiting reactants * Avogadro's number * Calculate theoretical yield * Basic types of reactions * Calculation of ox. numbers * Stoichiometric coefficients, balancing equations, reaction types	**2 to 4 out of the 30 Gen CHM** DAT questions are based on content in this chapter (in our estimation). * Note that between 50% and 85% of the questions in DAT General Chemistry are from 6 chapters: 1, 2, 4, 5, 6 and 9.

DAT-Prep.com

Introduction ▌▌▌▌

Stoichiometry is simply the math behind the chemistry involving products and reactants. The math is quite simple, in part, because of the law of conservation of mass that states that the mass of a closed system will remain constant throughout a chemical reaction.

Additional Resources

Free Online Forum

Video: Online or DVD

Flashcards

1.1 Generalities

Most substances known to us are mixtures of pure compounds. Air, for instance, contains the pure compounds nitrogen (~78%), oxygen (~21%), water vapor and many other gases (~1%). The compositional ratio of air or any other mixture may vary from one location to another. Each pure compound is made up of molecules which are composed of smaller units: the *atoms*. Atoms combine in very specific ratios to form molecules. A molecule is the smallest unit of a compound presenting the properties of that compound. During a chemical reaction molecules break down into individual atoms which then recombine to form new compounds. Stoichiometry establishes relationships between the above-mentioned specific ratios for individual molecules (or moles) or for molecules involved in a given chemical reaction.

1.2 Empirical Formula vs. Molecular Formula

The molecules of oxygen (O_2) are made up of two atoms of the same element. Water molecules on the other hand are composed of two different elements: hydrogen and oxygen in the specific ratio 2:1. Note that water is not a mixture of hydrogen and oxygen since this ratio is specific and does not vary with the location or the experimental conditions. The *empirical formula* of a pure compound is the simplest whole number ratio between the numbers of atoms of the different elements making up the compound. For instance, the empirical formula of water is H_2O (2:1 ratio) while the empirical formula of hydrogen peroxide is HO (1:1 ratio). The *molecular formula* of a given molecule states the exact number of the different atoms that make up this molecule. The empirical formula of water is identical to its molecular formula, i.e. H_2O; however, the molecular formula of hydrogen peroxide, H_2O_2, is different from its empirical formula (both correspond to a 1:1 ratio).

1.3 Mole - Atomic and Molecular Weights

Because of the small size of atoms and molecules chemists have to consider collections of a large number of these particles to bring chemical problems to our macroscopic scale. Collections of tens or dozens of atoms are still too small to achieve this practical purpose. For various reasons the number 6.02 × 10^{23} (Avogadro's number: N_A) was chosen. It is the number of atoms in 12 grams of the most abundant *isotope* of carbon (isotopes are elements which are identical chemically since the number of protons are the same; their masses differ slightly since the number of neutrons differ). A mole of atoms or molecules (or in fact any particles in general) contains an Avogadro number of these particles. The weight in grams of a mole of atoms of a given element is the gram-atomic weight, GAW, of that element (sometimes weight is measured in atomic mass units - *see CHM 11.2, 11.3*). Along the same lines, the weight in grams of a mole of molecules of a given compound is its gram-molecular weight, GMW. Here are some equations relating these concepts in a way that will help you solve some of the stoichiometry problems:

For an element:

$$moles = \frac{weight\ of\ sample\ in\ grams}{GAW}$$

For a compound:

$$moles = \frac{weight\ of\ sample\ in\ grams}{GMW}$$

The GAW of a given element is not to be confused with the mass of a single atom of this element. For instance the mass of a single atom of carbon-12 (GAW = 12 g) is $12/N_A = 1.993 \times 10^{-23}$ grams. Atomic weights are dimensionless numbers based on carbon-12 as the reference standard isotope and are defined as follows:

$$\frac{mass\ of\ an\ atom\ of\ X}{mass\ of\ an\ atom\ of\ Y} =$$
$$\frac{atomic\ weight\ of\ element\ X}{atomic\ weight\ of\ element\ Y}$$

Clearly if the reference element Y is chosen to be carbon-12 (which is the case in standard periodic tables) the GAW of any element X is numerically equal to its atomic weight. In the table of atomic weights, all the elements then have values in which are relative to the carbon-12 isotope. The molecular weight of a given molecule is equal to the sum of the atomic weights of the atoms that make up the molecule. For example, the molecular weight of H_2O is equal to 18.0 amu/molecule (H = 1.008 and O = 16.00). The molar weight (or molar mass) of H_2O is numerically equal to the molecular weight (18.0) however, the units are in grams/mol as the molar weight is based on a mole amount of substance. Thus, molecular weight and molar weight are numerically equivalent however, molecular weight is the weight (amu) per molecule and molar weight is based on the weight (grams) per mole (1 mol = 6.02×10^{23} molecules).

1.4 Composition of a Compound by Percent Mass

The percentage composition of a compound is the percent of the total mass of a given element in that compound. For instance, the chemical analysis of a 100 g sample of pure vitamin C demontrates that there are 40.9 g of carbon, 4.58 g of hydrogen and 54.5 g of oxygen. The percentage composition of pure vitamin C is:

$$\%C = 40.9;\ \%H = 4.58;\ \%O = 54.5$$

The composition of a compound by percent mass is closely related to its empirical formula. For instance, in the case of vitamin

C, the determination of the number of moles of atoms of C, H or O in a 100 g of vitamin C is rather straightforward:

> # moles of atoms of C in a 100 g of
> vitamin C = 40.9/12.0 = 3.41

> # moles of atoms of H in a 100 g of
> vitamin C = 4.58/1.01= 4.53

> # moles of atoms of O in a 100 g of
> vitamin C = 54.5/16.0 = 3.41

[GAW can be determined from the periodic table in Chapter 2]

To deduce the smallest ratio between the numbers above, one follows the simple procedure:

(i) divide each one of the previously obtained numbers of moles by the smallest one of them (3.41 in our case):

> for C: 3.41 mol/3.41 mol = 1.00
> for H: 4.53 mol/3.41 mol = 1.33
> for O: 3.41 mol/ 3.41 mol = 1.00

(ii) multiply the numbers obtained in the previous step by a small number to obtain a whole number ratio. In our case we need to multiply by 3 (in most cases this factor is between 1 and 5) so that :

> for C: $1.00 \times 3 = 3$
> for H: $1.33 \times 3 = 4$ and
> for O: $1.00 \times 3 = 3$

Therefore, in this example, the simplest whole number ratio is 3C:4H:3O and we conclude that the empirical formula for vitamin C is: $C_3H_4O_3$.

In the previous example, instead of giving the composition of vitamin C by percent weight we could have provided the raw chemical analysis data and asked for the determination of that composition.

For instance, this data would be that the burning of a 4.00 mg sample of pure vitamin C yields 6.00 mg of CO_2 and 1.632 mg of H_2O. Since there are 12.0 g of carbon in 44.0 g of CO_2 the number of milligrams of carbon in 6.00 mg of CO_2 (which corresponds to the number of mg of carbon in 4.00 mg of vitamin C) is simply:

6.00 mg $\times$ (12.0 g C/44.0 g CO_2) = 1.636 mg of C in 6.00 mg of CO_2 or 4.00 mg of vitamin C for further clarification.

To convert this number into a percent mass is then trivial. Similarly, the percent mass of hydrogen is obtained from the previous data and bearing in mind that there are 2.02 g of hydrogen (and not 1.01 g) in 18.0 g of water.

Incidentally, "burning" means combustion (CHM 1.5.1, ORG 3.2.1) which takes place in the presence of excess oxygen and results in the production of heat (exothermic), the conversion of the chemical species (new products), and light can be produced (glowing or a flame).

1.5 Description of Reactions by Chemical Equations

The convention for writing chemical equations is as follows: compounds which initially combine or react in a chemical reaction are called *reactants*; they are always written on the left-hand side of the chemical equation. The compounds which are produced during the same process are referred to as the *products* of the chemical reaction; they always appear on the right-hand side of the chemical equation. In the chemical equation:

$$2 \, BiCl_3 + 3 \, H_2O \rightarrow Bi_2O_3 + 6 \, HCl$$

the coefficients represent the relative number of moles of reactants that combine to form the corresponding relative number of moles of products: they are the stoichiometric coefficients of the balanced chemical equation. The law of conservation of mass requires that the number of atoms of a given element remains constant during the process of a chemical reaction.

Balancing a chemical equation is putting this general principle into practice. Chemical equations must be balanced so that there are equal numbers of atoms of each element on both sides of the equation. Many equations are balanced by trial and error however, caution must be practiced when balancing a chemical equation. It is always easier to balance elements that appear only in one compound on each side of the equation; therefore, as a general rule, always balance those elements first and then deal with those which appear in more than one compound last. Thus, a general suggestive procedure for balancing equations would be as follows: (1) count and compare the atoms on both sides of the chemical equation, (2) balance each element one at a time by placing whole number coefficients in front of the formulas resulting in the same number of atoms of each element on each side of the equation. Remember that a coefficient in front of a formula multiplies every atom in the formula (i.e., $2BiCl_3 = 2Bi + 6Cl$). It is best to leave pure elements or metals until the end. Therefore, balance the carbon atoms in both the reactant and product side first. (3) Balance hydrogens in both the reactant and products; and (4) finally, check if all elements are balanced with the smallest possible set of whole number coefficients.

Given the preceding chemical reaction, if H_2O is present in excessive quantity, then $BiCl_3$ would be considered the **limiting reactant.** In other words, since the amount of $BiCl_3$ is relatively small, it is the $BiCl_3$ which determines how much product will be formed. Thus if you were given 316 grams of $BiCl_3$ in *excess* H_2O and you needed to determine the quantity of HCl produced (theoretical yield), you would proceed as follows:

▶ Determine the number of moles of $BiCl_3$ (*see* CHM 1.3) given Bi = 209 g/mol and Cl = 35.5 g/mol, thus $BiCl_3$ = (1 × 209) + (3 × 35.5) = 315.5 or approximately 316 g/mol:

moles $BiCl_3$ = (316 g)/(316 g/mol)
= 1.0 mole of $BiCl_3$.

▶ From the stoichiometric coefficients of the balanced equation:

2 moles of $BiCl_3$: 6 moles of HCl; therefore, 1 mole of $BiCl_3$: 3 moles of HCl

▶ Given H = 1.00 g/mol, thus HCl = 36.5 g/mol, we get:

3 moles × 36.5 g/mol = 110 g of HCl (approx.).

Please note: The theoretical yield is the calculated amount of product that can be predicted from a balanced chemical reaction and is seldom obtained in the laboratory. The actual yield is the actual amount of product produced and recovered in the laboratory. The Percentage yield = Actual yield/Theoretical Yield × 100%.

1.5.1 Categories of Chemical Reactions

Throughout the chapters in General Chemistry we will explore many different types of chemicals and some of their associated reactions. The various chemical reactions may be classified generally as either a redox type (see section 1.6) or as a non-redox type reaction.

The following chart represents a general overview of the chemical reaction classifications or categories followed by a brief description of each of the reaction categories.

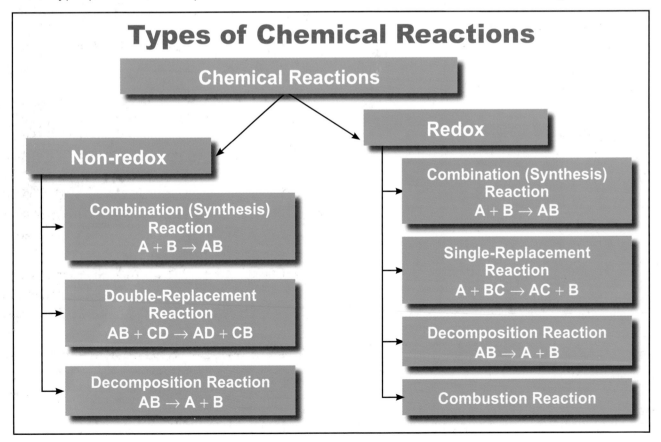

Types of Chemical Reactions

Chemical Reactions

Non-redox

Combination (Synthesis) Reaction
A + B → AB

Double-Replacement Reaction
AB + CD → AD + CB

Decomposition Reaction
AB → A + B

Redox

Combination (Synthesis) Reaction
A + B → AB

Single-Replacement Reaction
A + BC → AC + B

Decomposition Reaction
AB → A + B

Combustion Reaction

Non-redox

Combination (Synthesis) Reaction

General equation: $A + B \rightarrow AB$

Example: $SO_2(g) + H_2O(l) \rightarrow H_2SO_3\ (aq)$

Double-Replacement Reaction (or Metathesis Reaction)

(a) Precipitation Type

General equation: $AB + CD \rightarrow AD + CB$

Example: $CaCl_2(aq) + Na_2CO_3(aq)$
$\rightarrow CaCO_3(s) + 2NaCl(aq)$

(b) Acid-Base Neutralization Type

General equation: $HA + BOH \rightarrow H_2O + BA$
(HA = any H^+ acid & BOH = any OH^- Base)

Example:
$2HCl(l) + Ba(OH)_2(aq) \rightarrow H_2O(l) + BaCl_2(aq)$

(c) Gas Evolution Type Reaction

General equation: $HA + B \rightarrow H_2O + BA$
(HA = H^+ acid & B = special base salt $NaHCO_3$)

Example: $HCl(aq) + NaHCO_3(aq)$
$\rightarrow H_2CO_3(aq)^* + NaCl(aq)$
$\rightarrow H_2O(l) + CO_2(g) + NaCl(aq)$
(*H_2CO_3 is carbonic acid, the "fizz" in sodas, which degrades to $CO_2(g)$ and $H_2O(l)$)

Decomposition Reaction (CHM 4.3.1)

General equation: $AB \rightarrow A + B$

Example: $H_2CO_3(aq) \rightarrow H_2O(l) + CO_2(g)$

Redox

Combination (Synthesis) Reaction

General equation: $A + B \rightarrow AB$

Example: $SO_3(g) + H_2O(l) \rightarrow H_2SO_4(aq)$

Single-Replacement Reaction

General equation: $A + BC \rightarrow AC + B$

Example:
$Zn(s) + CuSO_4(aq) \rightarrow Cu(s) + ZnSO_4(aq)$

Decomposition Reaction

General equation: $AB \rightarrow A + B$

Example: $2NaCl(s) \rightarrow 2Na(l) + Cl_2(g)$
(electrolysis reaction)

Combustion Reaction

Example: $CH_4(g) + 2O_2(g) \rightarrow CO_2(g) + 2H_2O(g)$

Note that compounds in the preceding chart are identified as solid (s), liquid (l), gas (g) or solubilized in water which is an aqueous (aq) solution.

Combination (or synthesis) and decomposition type reactions are classified as both redox and non-redox reactions. Single replacement and combustion type reactions are classified as only redox type reactions; as the oxidation state of at least one atom species changes through electron transfer (oxidation/reduction) on either side of the chemical equation.

The double-replacement type reactions are basically known as precipitation (or solid forming) type reactions or acid-base (neutralization) type reactions. A double replacement type reaction involves ions (CHM 5.2) which exchange partners and may or may not form precipitates depending on the water solubility of the products formed (CHM 5.3). In acid-base (neutralization) type reactions, the usual products formed are both water and a salt (CHM 6.7). Certain acid-base type reactions however are known to form gas products otherwise known as "Gas Evolution type reactions" due to the instability of an intermediate salt product formed as a result of the acid-base reaction (see preceding chart).

When replacement reactions occur, often there are ions known as "spectator ions" that do not undergo any changes and remain ionized in aqueous solutions. These ions can be left out of the end equation known as a "net ionic equation" because it does away with the spectator ions that are consequential to the reaction. Net ionic equations are used to show the actual chemical reaction that occurs during a single or double-replacement type reaction. Thus, it is essential to recognize and familiarize oneself to the various categories of reactions to enable one to further understand chemical reactivity.

1.6 Oxidation Numbers, Redox Reactions, Oxidizing vs. Reducing Agents

A special class of reactions known as *redox* reactions are better balanced using the concept of oxidation state. In a redox reaction, oxidation and reduction must occur simultaneously. Oxidation is defined as either an increase in oxidation number or a loss of one or more electrons and reduction is defined as a decrease in oxidation number or a gain of one or more electrons. This section deals with these reactions in which electrons are transferred from one atom (or a group of atoms) to another.

First of all, it is very important to understand the difference between the ionic charge and the oxidation state of an element. For this let us consider the two compounds sodium chloride (NaCl) and water (H_2O). NaCl is made up of the charged species or ions: Na^+

and Cl^-. During the formation of this ionic compound, one electron is transferred from the Na atom to the Cl atom. It is possible to verify this fact experimentally and determine that the charge of sodium in NaCl is indeed +1 and that the one for chlorine is −1. The elements in the periodic table tend to lose (oxidation) or gain (reduction) electrons to different extents. Therefore, even in non-ionic compounds electrons are always transferred, to different degrees, from one atom to another during the formation of a molecule of the compound. The actual partial charges that result from these partial transfers of electrons can also be determined experimentally. The oxidation state is not equal to such partial charges. It is rather an artificial concept that is used to perform some kind of "electron bookkeeping."

In a molecule like H_2O, since oxygen tends to attract electrons more than hydrogen, one can predict that the electrons that allow bonding to occur between hydrogen and oxygen will be displaced towards the oxygen atom. For the sake of "electron bookkeeping" we assign these electrons to the oxygen atom. The charge that the oxygen atom would have in this artificial process would be -2: this defines the oxidation state of oxygen in the H_2O molecule. In the same line of reasoning one defines the oxidation state of hydrogen in the water molecule as $+1$. The actual partial charges of hydrogen and oxygen are in fact smaller; but, as we will see later, the concept of oxidation state is very useful in stoichiometry.

Here are the general rules one needs to follow to assign oxidation numbers (or oxidation states) to different elements in different compounds:

1. In elementary substances, the oxidation number of an uncombined element regardless of whether it is monatomic (1 atom), diatomic (2 atoms) or polyatomic (multiple atoms), is zero. This is, for instance, the case for N in N_2 or Na in sodium element, O in O_2, or S in S_8.

2. In monatomic ions the oxidation number of the element that make up this ion is equal to the charge of the ion. This is the case for Na in Na^+ ($+1$) or Cl in Cl^- (-1) or Fe in Fe^{3+} ($+3$). Clearly, monatomic ions are the only species for which atomic charges and oxidation numbers coincide.

3. In a neutral molecule the sum of the oxidation numbers of all the elements that make up the molecule is zero. In a polyatomic ion (e.g. SO_4^{2-}) the sum of the oxidation numbers of the elements that make up this ion is equal to the charge of the ion.

4. Some useful oxidation numbers to memorize:

For H: $+1$, except in metal hydrides (general formula XH where X is from the first two columns of the periodic table) where it is equal to -1.

For O: -2 in most compounds. In peroxides (e.g. in H_2O_2) the oxidation number for O is -1, it is $+2$ in OF_2 and $-1/2$ in superoxides (e.g. potassium superoxide: KO_2 which contains the O_2^- ion as opposed to the O^{2-} ion).

For alkali metals (first column in the periodic table): $+1$.

For alkaline earth metals (second column): $+2$.

Aluminium always has an oxidation number of $+3$ in all its compounds. (i.e. chlorides $AlCl_3$, nitrites $Al(NO_2)_3$, etc.)

The oxidation number of each Group VIIA element is -1; however, when it is combined with an element of higher electronegativity, the oxidation number is $+1$. For example, the oxidation number of Cl is -1 in HCl and the oxidation number of Cl is $+1$ in HClO.

An element is said to have been *reduced* during a reaction if its oxidation number decreased during this reaction, it is said to have been oxidized if its *oxidation* number increased. A simple example is:

$$Zn(s) \quad + \quad CuSO_4(aq) \longrightarrow$$

Oxid.#:   0   +2

$$ZnSO_4(aq) \quad + \quad Cu(s)$$

Oxid.#:   +2   0

During this reaction Cu is reduced (oxidation number decreases from +2 to 0) while Zn is oxidized (oxidation number increases from 0 to +2). Since, in a sense, Cu is reduced by Zn, Zn can be referred to as the reducing agent. Similarly, Cu is the oxidizing agent.

The redox titrations will be dealt with in the section on titrations (CHM 6.10). Many of the redox agents in the table below will be explored in the chapters on Organic Chemistry.

Common Redox Agents	
Reducing Agents	**Oxidizing Agents**
* Lithium aluminium hydride ($LiAlH_4$) * Sodium borohydride ($NaBH_4$) * Metals * Ferrous ion (Fe^{2+})	* Iodine (I_2) and other halogens * Permanganate (MnO_4) salts * Peroxide compounds (i.e. H_2O_2) * Ozone (O_3); osmium tetroxide (OsO_4) * Nitric acid (HNO_3); nitrous oxide (N_2O)

1.7 Mixtures

In many stoichiometry problems, it can be assumed that the liquids and solids in the reaction mixtures are pure. Of course, the real world is more complicated since substances are often part of a mixture. A mixture is a material system made up of two or more different substances which are mixed but are not combined chemically. Thus mixtures can be the blending of elements or compounds, without chemical bonding or other chemical change, so that each ingredient substance retains its own chemical properties.

A mixture can be homogeneous (uniform in composition) or heterogeneous (lacks uniformity). In chemistry, a homogeneous mixture means that when dividing the volume in half, the same amount of material is suspended in both halves of the substance. An example of a homogeneous mixture is air. Technically, air can be described as a gaseous solution (oxygen and other gases dissolved in the major component, nitrogen).

Examples of mixtures include alloys, solutions, colloids, and suspensions (coarse dispersion). The following table shows the main properties of three types of mixtures.

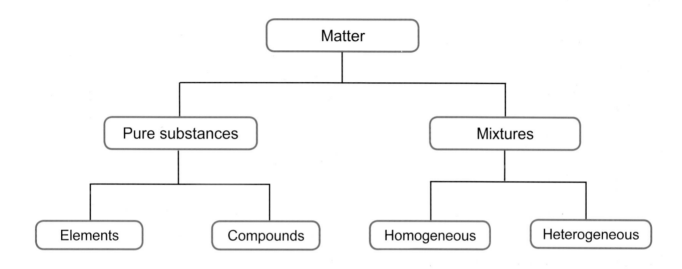

	Solution	Colloid	Suspension
Mixture homogeneity	Homogeneous	Visually homogeneous but microscopically heterogeneous	Heterogeneous
Particle size	< 1 nm	between 1 nm and 1 micrometer	> 1 micrometer
Physical stability	Yes	Yes	No: needs stabilizing agents
Separates in a centrifuge	No	Yes	–
Separates by decantation	No	No	Yes

Decantation is normally performed by pouring off the upper clear portion of a fluid (supernatant) gently, leaving the sediment in the vessel.

An emulsion is a mixture of two or more liquids that are normally immiscible (nonmixable or unblendable). Emulsions are a type of colloid. Vinaigrettes are emulsions.

An alloy is a mixture of two or more metals, or of a metal or metals with a nonmetal. The following are examples:

- steel is an alloy of iron with carbon and, usually, small amounts of a number of other elements;

- stainless steel alloys are a combination of iron, chromium and nickel frequently modified by the presence of other elements. This family of alloys is particularly resistant to corrosion, in contrast to the rusting that can consume ordinary steel;

- pewter is an alloy of tin with minor amounts of copper;

- copper with some zinc makes brass;

- copper with tin forms bronze;

- 18-carat gold is 75% gold, with the balance usually made up of nickel, copper and zinc.

GOLD STANDARD WARM-UP EXERCISES

CHAPTER 1: Stoichiometry

> **Note:** Use the periodic table from the end of Chapter 2 when needed for any Gold Standard Warm-Up Exercises. You will have access to a periodic table for the DAT. Calculators are not permitted for the Natural Sciences.

1) In the manufacture of HCl, 10 grams of chlorine gas were used. If the reaction went to completion and the hydrogen gas was in excess, how many grams of HCl were obtained?

$$H_2 + Cl_2 \rightarrow 2HCl$$

A. 2.5
B. 5.1
C. 10.3
D. 20.0

2) Pig iron consists of iron with about 5% manganese. Which of the following most accurately describes pig iron?

A. It is a colloid.
B. It is a solid solution.
C. It is a complex molecule.
D. It is an alloy.

3) Assume that the composition by volume of air is 80% N_2 and 20% O_2. Which of the following gases are denser than air assuming they are at the same temperature and pressure?

$$CH_4, Cl_2, CO_2, NH_3, NO_2, O_3, SO_2$$

A. CH_4, CO_2, Cl_2, SO_2
B. CO_2, Cl_2, SO_2, NH_3, O_3
C. Cl_2, CO_2, NH_3, NO_2, O_3, SO_2
D. Cl_2, CO_2, NO_2, O_3, SO_2

4) Two moles of a diatomic gas P_2 were mixed with four moles of another diatomic gas Q_2 in a closed vessel. All of the P_2 and Q_2 molecules reacted to yield one triatomic product. Which of the following shows the net reaction between P and Q?

A. $2P_2 + 4Q_2 \rightarrow P_4Q_8$
B. $P_2 + 2Q_2 \rightarrow 2PQ_2$
C. $2P + 4Q \rightarrow P_2Q_4$
D. $P_2 + Q_4 \rightarrow P_2Q_4$

5) What is the oxidation state of the halogen (Hal) in the halate ($HalO_3^-$) molecule?

A. −1
B. −5
C. 1
D. 5

6) What is the oxidation state of chromium in $Cr_2O_7^{2-}$?

A. 6
B. 7
C. 8
D. 12

7) What is the oxidation state of nitrogen in each of the two products in the following reaction, respectively?

$$H_2O + 3NO_2(g) \rightarrow 2HNO_3(aq) + NO(g)$$

A. −5, +2
B. +5, +2
C. +2, +2
D. −2, +2

8) What type of reaction is the following?

$$2MnO_4^- + 16H^+ + 10Cl^- \rightarrow 2Mn^{2+} + 5Cl_2(g) + 8H_2O$$

    A. Lewis acid – Lewis base
    B. Double replacement
    C. Oxidation–reduction
    D. Dissociation

9) When the following equation is balanced, how many moles of water will be produced for each mole of calcium phosphate?

$$\_Ca(OH)_2 + \_H_3PO_4 \rightarrow \_H_2O + \_Ca_3(PO_4)_2$$

    A. 2
    B. 3
    C. 4
    D. 6

10) What would be the approximate ratio between the mass of manganese in the steel sample and the mass of chlorine gas produced?

$$2MnO_4^- + 16H^+ + 10Cl^- \rightarrow 2Mn^{2+} + 5Cl_2(g) + 8H_2O$$

    A. 2:5
    B. 3:2
    C. 3:4
    D. 1:3

2:5

$Mn = 55.0 \text{ g} \times 2$

$Cl_2 = 71.0 \text{ g} \times 5 \Rightarrow 1:3$

GS ANSWER KEY

CHAPTER 1

		Cross-Reference
1.	C	CHM 1.3, 1.5
2.	D	CHM 1.7
3.	D	CHM 1.3
4.	B	CHM 1.5
5.	D	CHM 1.6

		Cross-Reference
6.	A	CHM 1.6
7.	B	CHM 1.6
8.	C	CHM 1.6
9.	D	CHM 1.5
10.	D	CHM 1.3, 1.5

* Explanations can be found at the back of the book.

Go online to DAT-prep.com for additional chapter review Q&A and forum.

ELECTRONIC STRUCTURE AND THE PERIODIC TABLE
Chapter 2

Memorize

* Definitions of quantum numbers
* Shapes of s, p orbitals
* Order for filling atomic orbitals

Understand

* Conventional notation, Pauli, Hund's
* Box diagrams, IP, electronegativity
* Valence, EA
* Variation in shells, atomic size
* Trends in the periodic table

Importance

2 to 4 out of the 30 Gen CHM
DAT questions are based on content in this chapter (in our estimation).
* Note that between 50% and 85% of the questions in DAT General Chemistry are from 6 chapters: 1, 2, 4, 5, 6 and 9.

DAT-Prep.com

Introduction ▌▌▌▌

The periodic table of the elements provides data and abbreviations for the names of elements in a tabular layout. The purpose of the table is to illustrate recurring (periodic) trends and to classify and compare the different types of chemical behavior. To do so, we must first better understand the atom. Please note: more advanced aspects of nuclear (atomic) chemistry will be explored in Chapter 11.

Additional Resources

Free Online Forum

Video: Online or DVD

Flashcards

Special Guest

The modern view of the structure of atoms is based on a series of discoveries and complicated theories that were put forth at the turn of the twentieth century. The atom represents the smallest unit of a chemical element. It is composed of subatomic particles: protons, neutrons and electrons. At the center of the atom is the nucleus composed of protons and neutrons surrounded by electrons forming an electron cloud.

The protons and neutrons have nearly identical masses of approximately 1 amu whereas electrons, by contrast, have an almost negligible mass. Protons and electrons both have electrical charges equal in magnitude but opposite in sign. Protons consist of a single positive (+1) charge, electrons consist of a single negative charge (−1) and neutrons have no charge.

Atoms have equal numbers of protons and electrons unless ionization occurs in which ions are formed. Ions are defined as atoms with either a positive charge (cation) due to loss of one or more valence electrons or negative charge (anion) as a result of a gain in electron(s). An atom's valence electrons are electrons furthest from the nucleus and are responsible for an element's chemical properties and are instrumental in chemical bonding (See CHM 2.2 and 2.3 and Chapter 3).

Atoms of a given element all have an equal number of protons however, may vary in the number of neutrons. Atoms that differ only by neutron number are known as isotopes. Isotopes have the same atomic number but differ in atomic mass due to the differences in their neutron numbers. As they have the same atomic number, isotopes therefore exhibit the same chemical properties.

In the following paragraphs, we will only present the main ideas behind the findings that shaped our understanding of atomic structure. The first important idea is that electrons (as well as any subatomic particles) are in fact waves as well as particles; this concept is often referred to in textbooks as the "dual nature of matter".

Contrary to classical mechanics, in this modern view of matter information on particles is not derived from the knowledge of their position and momentum at a given time but by the knowledge of the wave function (mathematical expression of the above-mentioned wave) and their energy. Mathematically, such information can be derived, in principle, by solving the master equation of quantum mechanics known as the Schrödinger equation. Moreover, the mathematical derivation of atomic orbitals and respective energies comes from solving the equation which includes the total energy profiles for the electrons as well as the wave function describing the wavelike nature of the electrons. Thus, the various solutions to the Schrödinger equation describes the atomic orbitals as complicated wave functions which may alternatively be graphically represented (See Figure III.A.2.1 and Figure III.A.2.2).

In the case of the hydrogen atom, this equation can be solved exactly. It yields the possible states of energy in which the electron can be found within the hydrogen atom and the wave functions associated with these states. The <u>square of the wave function</u> associated with a given state of energy <u>gives</u> the <u>probability to find the electron,</u> which is in that same state of energy, at any given point in space at any given time. These <u>wave functions</u> as well as their geometrical representations are referred to as the *atomic orbitals*. We shall explain further below the significance of these geometrical representations.

Atoms of any element tend to exist toward a minimal energy level (= ground state) unless subjected to an external environmental change. Even for a hydrogen atom there is a large number of possible states in which its single electron can be found (when it is subjected to different external perturbations). A labeling of these states is necessary. This is done using the quantum numbers. Hence, any orbital may be completely described by four quantum numbers; n, l, m_l and m_s. The position and energy of an electron and each of the orbitals are therefore described by its quantum number or energy state. The four quantum numbers are thus described as follows:

(i) n: *the principal quantum number.* This number takes the integer values 1, 2, 3, 4, 5… The higher the value of n the higher the energy of the state labelled by this n. This number defines the atomic shells K (n = 1), L (n = 2), M (n = 3) etc… or the size of an orbital.

(ii) l: *the angular momentum quantum number.* It defines the shape of the atomic orbital in a way which we will discuss further below. For a given electronic state of energy defined by n, l takes all possible integer values between 0 and n – 1. For instance for a state with n = 0 there is only one possible shape of orbital, it is defined by l = 0. For a state defined by n = 3 there are 3 possible orbital shapes with l = 0, 1 and 2.

All orbitals with l = 0 are called "s"-shaped, all with l = 1 are "p"-shaped, those with l = 2 or 3 are "d" or "f"-shaped orbitals respectively. The important shapes to remember are: i) s = spherical, and ii) p = 2 lobes or "dumbbell" (*see the following diagrams*). For values of l larger than 3, which occur with an n greater or equal to 4, the corresponding

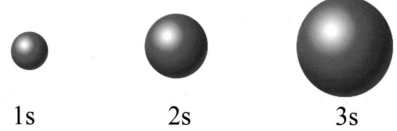

1s   2s   3s

Figure III.A.2.1: Atomic orbitals where l = 0. Notice that the orbitals do not reveal the precise location (position) or momentum of the fast moving electron at any point in time (Heisenberg's Uncertainty Principle). Instead, we are left with a 90% chance of finding the electron somewhere within the shapes described as orbitals.

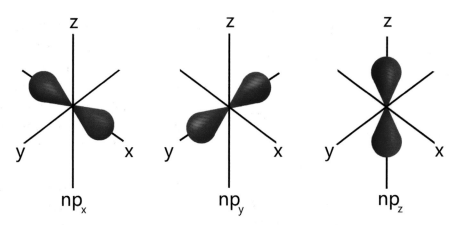

Figure III.A.2.2: Atomic orbitals where $l = 1$.

series of atomic orbitals follows the alphabetical order h, i, j, etc…

(iii) m_l: *the magnetic quantum number.* It defines the orientation of the orbital of a given shape. For a given value of l (given shape), m_l can take any of the $2l + 1$ integer values between $-l$ and $+l$. For instance for a state with $n = 3$ and $l = 1$ (3p orbital in notation explained in the previous paragraph) there are three possible values for m_l: -1, 0 and 1. These 3 orbitals are oriented along x, y or the z axis of a coordinate system with its origin on the nucleus of the atom: they are denoted as $3p_x$, $3p_y$ and $3p_z$. Figure III.A.2.2 shows the representation of an orbital corresponding to an electron in a state ns, np_x, np_y, and np_z. These are the <u>3D volumes where there is 90% chance to find an electron</u> which is in a state ns, np_x, np_y, or np_z, respectively. This type of diagram constitutes the most common geometrical representation of the atomic orbitals (besides looking at the diagrams, consider watching one of the videos if you are having trouble visualizing these facts).

(iv) m_s: *the spin quantum number.* This number takes the values $+1/2$ or $-1/2$ for the electron. Some textbooks present the intuitive, albeit wrong, explanation that the spin angular momentum arises from the spinning of the electron around itself, the opposite signs for the spin quantum number would correspond to the two opposite rotational directions. We do have to resort to such an intuitive presentation because the spin angular moment has, in fact, no classical equivalent and, as a result, the physics behind the correct approach is too complex to be dealt with in introductory courses.

A node is where the probability of finding an electron is zero (the concept behind nodes comes from wave theory which is Physics and not specifically required for the DAT). Nonetheless, the number of nodes is related to the frequency of a wave and therefore its energy. The greater the number of nodes, the greater the energy of the system. In general, with respect to the shapes and the angular or radial nodes of the s, p and d-orbitals, note the following:

s-orbital

The number of radial nodes increases with the principal quantum number n, i.e. 1s orbital has 0 nodes, 2s has 1 node, and 3s has 2 nodes. The s orbital can hold two electrons ($n = 1,2,3$, $l = 0$, $m_l = 0$, $m_s = +1/2, -1/2$).

p-orbital

p orbital starts at the 2nd shell or principal level. The angular momentum quantum number for p orbitals is 1; therefore each orbital has 1 angular node. There are three different magnetic quantum numbers, which give rise to three different orientations of the p orbital. Since each orbital holds two electrons, the three p orbitals hold a total of 6 electrons ($n = 2,3,4$, $l = 1$, $m_l = -1,0,+1$, $m_s = +1/2, -1/2$).

d-orbital

d orbital starts at a principal level of 3 or the 3rd shell. The angular momentum quantum number for d orbitals is 2; therefore each orbital has 2 angular nodes. There are five different magnetic quantum numbers, which give rise to five different orientations of the d orbital. Since each orbital holds two electrons, the three d orbitals hold a total of 10 electrons ($n = 3,4,5$, $l = 2$, $m_l = -2,-1,0,+1,+2$, $m_s = +1/2, -1/2$).

To summarize: the energy of the atom is determined by the number of nodes which is related to the principal quantum number n by: nodes = n−1.

The number of angular nodes is labelled by a letter (s, p, d, f, g, h, i, ...)

s: no angular nodes
p: one angular node
d: two angular nodes
f: three angular nodes, etc...

Note: The number of radial nodes is the total number of nodes minus the number of angular nodes.

2.2 Conventional Notation for Electronic Structure

As described in the previous section, the state of an electron in an atom is completely defined by a set of four quantum numbers (n, l, m_l, m_s). If two electrons in an atom share the same n, l and m_l numbers their m_s have to be of opposite signs: this is known as the Pauli's exclusion principle which states that no two electrons in an atom can have the same four quantum numbers. This principle along with a rule known as Hund's rule which states that electrons fill orbital's singly first until all orbitals of the same energy are filled, constitutes the basis for the procedure that one needs to follow to assign the possible (n, l, m_l, m_s) quantum states to the electrons of a polyelectronic atom. Orbitals are "filled" in sequence, according to an example shown below. When filling a set of orbitals with the same n and l (e.g. the three 2p orbitals: $2p_x$, $2p_y$ and $2p_z$ which differ by their m_l's) electrons are assigned to orbitals with different m_l's first with parallel spins (same sign for their m_s), until each orbital of the given group is filled with one electron, then, electrons are paired in the same orbital with antiparallel spins (opposite signs for m_s). This procedure is illustrated in an example which follows. The <u>electronic configuration</u> which results from orbitals filled in accordance with the previous set of rules corresponds to the atom being in its lowest overall state of energy. This state of lowest energy is referred to as the <u>ground state</u> of the atom.

The restrictions related to the previous set of rules lead to the fact that only a certain number of electrons is allowed for each quantum number:

for a given n (given shell): the maximum number of electrons allowed is $2n^2$. The greater the value of n, the greater the energy level of the shell.

for a given l (s, p, d, f...): this number is $4l + 2$.

for a given m_l (given orbital orientation): a maximum of 2 electrons is allowed.

There is a **conventional notation** for the electronic structure of an atom:

(i) orbitals are listed in the order they are filled (See Figure III.A.2.3)

(ii) generally, in this conventional notation, no distinction is made between electrons in states defined by the same n and l but which do not share the same m_l.

For instance the ground state electronic configuration of oxygen is written as:

$$1s^2\ 2s^2\ 2p^4$$

When writing the electronic configuration of a polyelectronic atom orbitals are filled (with electrons denoted as the superscripts of the configurations) in order of increasing energy: 1s 2s 2p 3s 3p 4s 3d … according to the following figure:

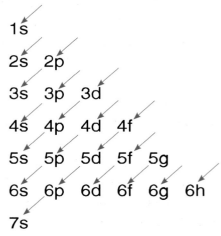

follow the direction of successive arrows moving from top to bottom

Figure III.A.2.3: The order for filling atomic orbitals.

Thus, the electronic configuration or the pattern of orbital filling of an atom generally abides by the following rules or principles:

1. Always fill the lowest energy (or ground state) orbitals first (Aufbau principle)

2. No two electrons in a single atom can have the same four quantum numbers; if n, l, and m_l are the same, m_s must be different such that the electrons have opposite spins. (Pauli exclusion principle) and

3. Degenerate orbitals of the subshell are each occupied singly with electrons of parallel spin before double occupation of the orbitals occurs (Hund's rule).

An alternative way to write the afore-mentioned electronic configuration is based on the avoidance in writing out the inner core electrons. Moreover, this is an abbreviation of the previous longer configuration or otherwise known as a short hand electronic configuration. Here, the core electrons are represented by a prior noble gas elemental symbol within brackets. As an example, calcium may be written in its expanded form or more commonly as a short hand notation represented as $[Ar]4s^2$ shown with the prior noble gas symbol for argon $[Ar]$ written within brackets.

Another illustrative notation is also often used. In this alternate notation orbitals are represented by boxes (hence the referring to this representation as "box diagrams"). Orbitals with the same l are grouped together and electrons are represented by vertical ascending or descending arrows (for the two opposite signs of m_s).

For instance for the series H, He, Li, Be, B, C we have the following electronic configurations:

H: $1s^1$ box diagram: [↑]

He: $1s^2$ box diagram: [↑↓] and not [↑↑]
       (rejected by Pauli's exclusion principle)

Li: $1s^2$ $2s^1$
       [↑↓]   [↑]

Be: $1s^2$ $2s^2$
       [↑↓]   [↑↓]

B: $1s^2$ $2s^2$ $2p^1$
       [↑↓]   [↑↓]   [↑] [ ] [ ]

C: $1s^2$ $2s^2$ $2p^2$

[↑↓]   [↑↓]   [↑] [↑] [ ]

(to satisfy Hund's rule of maximum spin)

To satisfy Hund's rule the next electron is put into a separate 2p "box". The 4th 2p electron (for oxygen) is then put into the first box with an opposite spin.

O: [↑↓]   [↑↓]   [↑↓] [↑] [↑]
    $1s^2$ $2s^2$ $2p^4$

Within a given subshell l, orbitals are filled in such a way to maximize the number of half-filled orbitals with parallel spins. An unpaired electron generates a magnetic field due to its spin. Consequently, when a material is composed of atoms with unpaired electrons, it is said to be *paramagnetic* as it will be attracted to an applied external magnetic field (i.e. Li, Na, Cs). Alternatively, when the material's atoms have paired electrons, it is weakly repelled by an external magnetic field and it is said to be *diamagnetic* (i.e. Cu, molecular carbon, H_2, H_2O). Non-chemists simply call diamagnetic materials "not magnetic". The strongest form of magnetism is a permanent feature of materials like Fe, Ni and their alloys and is said to be *ferromagnetic* (i.e. a fridge magnet).

For the main group elements, the valence electrons of an atom are those that are involved in chemical bonding and are in the outermost principal energy level or shell. For example, for Group IA and Group IIA elements, only electrons from the s subshell are valence electrons. For Group IIIA through Group VIIIA elements, electrons from s and p subshell are valence electrons. Under certain circumstances, elements from Group IIIA through Group VIIA may accept electrons into its d subshell, leading to more than 8 valence electrons.

Finally, as previously mentioned, we should point out that electrons can be promoted to higher unoccupied (or partially occupied) orbitals when the atom is subjected to some external perturbation which inputs energy into the atom. The resulting electronic configuration is then called an excited state configuration (this concept will be explored further in CHM 11.5, 11.6).

2.3 Elements, Chemical Properties and The Periodic Table

Since most chemical properties of the atom are related to their outermost electrons (valence electrons), it is the orbital occupation of these electrons which is most relevant in the complete electronic configuration. The periodic table (there is one at the end of this chapter with a summary of trends) can be used to derive such information in the following way:

(i)   the row or period number gives the "n" of the valence electrons of any given element of the period.

(ii)   the first two columns or groups and helium (He) are referred to as the "s" block. The valence electrons of elements in these groups are "s" electrons.

(iii)   groups 3A to 8A (13th to 18th columns) are the "p" group. Elements belonging to these groups have their ground state electronic configurations ending with "p" electrons.

(iv)   Elements in groups 3B to 2B (columns 3 to 12) are called transition elements. Their electronic configurations end with

$ns^2(n-1)d^x$ where n is the period number and x = 1 for column 3, 2 for column 4, 3 for column 5, etc... Note that these elements sometimes have unexpected or unusual valence shell electronic configurations.

This set of rules should make the writing of the ground-state valence shell electronic configuration very easy. For instance: Sc being an element of the "d" group on the 4th period should have a ground-state valence shell electronic configuration of the form: $4s^23d^x$. Since it belongs to group 3B (column 3) x = 1; therefore, the actual configuration is simply: $4s^23d^1$. However, half-filled (i.e. Cr) and filled (i.e. Cu, Ag, Au) d orbitals have remarkable stability. This stability behavior is essentially related to the closely spaced 3d and 4s energy levels with the stability associated with a half-filled (as in Cr) or completely filled (as in Cu) sublevel. Hence, this stability makes for unusual configurations (i.e. by the rules Cr = $4s^23d^4$, but in reality Cr = $4s^13d^5$ creating a half-filled d orbital). It can be noted that Cr therefore has an electronic configuration of $[Ar]4s^13d^5$, although four d electrons would be expected to be seen instead of five. This is because one electron

→ from s shell, not p shell.

from a s subshell jumps into the d orbital, giving the atom a half filled d subshell. As for Cu, it would have an electronic configuration of $[Ar]4s^2 3d^9$ by the rules. However, the Cu d shell is just one electron away from stability, and therefore, one electron from the s shell jumps into the d shell to convert it into $[Ar]4s^1 3d^{10}$.

Some metal ions form colored solutions due to the transition energies of the d-electrons.

A number of physical and chemical properties of the elements are periodic, i.e. they vary in a regular fashion with atomic numbers. We will define some of these properties and explain their trends:

(A) Ionization Energy

(i) The ionization energy (IE) is defined as the energy required to remove an electron from a gaseous atom or ion. The first ionization energy or potential (1st IE or IP) is the energy required to remove one of the outermost valence electrons from an atom in its gaseous state. The ionization potential increases from left to right within a period and decreases from the top to the bottom of a group or column of the periodic chart. The 1st IP drops sharply when we move from the last element of a period (inert gas) to the first element of the next period. These are general trends, elements located after an element with a half-filled shell, for instance, have a lower 1st IP than expected by these trends.

(ii) The second ionization is the energy or potential (2nd IE or IP) required to remove a second valence electron from the ion to form a divalent ion: the previous trends can be used if one remembers the relationship between 1st and 2nd ionization processes of an atom of element X:

$$X + energy \rightarrow X^+ + 1e^-$$
1st ionization of X
$$X^+ + energy \rightarrow X^{2+} + 1e^-$$
2nd ionization of X

The second ionization process of X can be viewed as the 1st ionization of X^+. With this in mind it is very easy to predict trends of 2nd IP's. For instance, let us compare the 2nd IP's of the elements Na and Al. This is equivalent to comparing the 1st IP's of Na^+ and Al^+. These, in turn, have the same valence shell electronic configurations as Ne and Mg, respectively. Applying the previous general principles on Ne and Mg we arrive at the following conclusions:

• the 1st IP of Ne is greater than the 1st IP of Mg

• the 1st IP of Na^+ is therefore expected to be greater than the 1st IP of Al^+

• the latter statement is equivalent to the final conclusion that the 2nd IP of Na is greater than the 2nd IP of Al.

(B) Electron Affinity

(iii) Electron affinity (EA) is the energy change that accompanies the following process for an atom of element X:

$$X(gas) + 1e^- \rightarrow X^-(gas)$$

Electron affinity

→ This property measures the ability of an atom to accept an electron. The stronger the attraction of a nucleus for electrons, the greater the electron affinity (EA) will be. The electron affinity becomes more negative for non-metals than metals. Thus, halogen atoms (F, Cl, Br...) have a very negative EA because they have a great tendency to form negative ions. On the other hand, alkaline earth metals which tend to form positive rather than negative ions have very large positive EA's. The overall tendency is that EA's become more negative as we move from left to right across a period, they are more negative (less positive) for non-metals than for metals and they do not change considerably within a group or column.

(C) Atomic Radii

(iv) The atomic radius generally decreases from left to right across a period since the effective nuclear charge increases as the number of protons within an atom increases. The effective nuclear charge is the net charge experienced by the valence electrons as a result of the nucleus (ie, protons) and core electrons. Additionally, the atomic radius increases when we move down a group due to the shielding effect of the additional core electrons and the presence of another electron shell.

(D) Electronegativity

(v) Electronegativity is a parameter that measures the ability of an atom, when engaged in a molecular bond, to pull or repel the bond electrons. This parameter is determined from the 1st IE and the EA of a given atom. Electronegativity follows the same general trends as the 1st IE. The greater the electronegativity of an atom, the greater its attraction for bonding electrons. In general, electronegativity is inversely related to atomic size. Moreover, the larger the atom, the less the ability for it to attract electrons to itself in chemical bonding.

In conclusion, as one moves to the right across a row in the periodic table, the atomic radii decreases, the ionization energy (IE) increases and the electronegativity increases. As one moves down along a column within the periodic table, the atomic radii increases, the ionization energy (IE) decreases and electronegativity decreases.

2.3.1 Bond Strength

When there is a big difference in electronegativity between two atoms sharing a covalent bond then the bond is generally weaker as compared to two atoms with little electronegativity difference. This is because in the latter case, the bond is shared more equally and is thus more stable.

Bond strength is inversely proportional to bond length. Thus, all things being equal, a stronger bond would be shorter. Bonds and bond strength is further discussed in ORG 1.3-1.5.1.

2.4 Metals, Nonmetals and Metalloids

The elements of the periodic table belong in three basic categories: metals, nonmetals and metalloids (or semimetals).

Metals – high melting points and densities characterize metals. They are excellent conductors of heat and electricity due to their valence electrons being able to move freely. This fact also accounts for the major characteristic properties of metals: large atomic radius, low ionization energy, high electron affinities and low electronegativity. Groups IA and IIA are the most reactive of all metal species.

[handwritten: Only loses electrons]

[handwritten: cannot become an anion]

Of course, metals tend to be shiny and solid (with the exception of mercury, Hg, a liquid at STP). They are also *ductile* (they can be drawn into thin wires) and *malleable* (they can be easily hammered into very thin sheets).

Nonmetals – Nonmetals have high ionization energies and electronegativities. As opposed to metals, they do not conduct heat or electricity. They tend to gain electrons easily contrarily to metals that readily lose electrons when forming bonds.

Metalloids – The metalloids share properties with both metals and nonmetals. Their densities, boiling points and melting points do not follow any specific trends and are very unpredictable. Ionization energy and electronegativity values vary and can be found in between those of metals and nonmetals. Examples of metalloids are boron, silicon, germanium, arsenic, antimony and tellurium.

Table III A.2.1

*General characteristics of metals, nonmetals and metalloids		
Metals	**Nonmetals**	**Metalloids**
• Hard and Shiny	• Gases or dull, brittle solids	• Appearance will vary
• 3 or less valence electrons	• 5 or more valence electrons	• 3 to 7 valence electrons
• Form + ions by losing e⁻	• Form − ions by gaining e⁻	• Form + and/or − ions
• Good conductors of heat and electricity	• Poor conductors of heat and electricity	• Conduct better than nonmetals but not as well as metals

*These are general characteristics. There are exceptions beyond the scope of the exam.

2.4.1 The Chemistry of Groups

Alkali metals – The alkali metals are found in Group IA and are different than other metals in that they only have one loosely bound electron in their outermost shell. This gives them the largest ionic radius of all the elements in their respective periods. They are also highly reactive (especially with halogens) due to their low ionization energies and low electronegativity and the relative ease with which they lose their valence electron.

b/c they want to lose that electron badly, they pair up with a halogen.

Alkaline Earth metals – The alkaline earth metals are found in Group IIA and also tend to lose electrons quite readily. They have two electrons in their outer shell and experience a stronger effective nuclear charge than alkali metals. This gives them a smaller atomic radius as well as low electronegativity values.

Halogens – The halogens are found in Group VIIA and are highly reactive nonmetals with seven valence electrons in their outer shell. This gives them extremely high electronegativity values and makes them reactive towards alkali metals and alkaline earth metals that seek to donate electrons to form a complete octet. Some halogens are gaseous at Standard Temperature and Pressure (STP; CHM 4.1.1) (F_2 and Cl_2) while others are liquid (Br_2) or solid (I_2).

Noble gases – The noble gases, also called the inert gases, are found in Group VIII and are characterized by being a mostly nonreactive species due to their complete valence shell. This energetically favorable configuration of electrons gives them high ionization energies, low boiling points and no real electronegativities. They are all gaseous at room temperature.

Transition Elements – The transition elements are found in Groups IB to VIIIB and are characterized by high melting points and boiling points. Their key chemical characteristic is their ability to exist in a variety of different oxidation states. For the transition elements, the 4s shell gets filled prior to the 3d shell according to the Aufbau rule. However, electrons are lost from the 4s shell before the 3d shell. Thus, as the d electrons are held only loosely, this contributes to the high electrical conductivity and malleability of transition elements. This is because transition elements can lose electrons from both their s and d orbitals of their valence shell; the d electrons are held more loosely than the s electrons. They display low ionization energies and high electrical conductivities.

PERIODIC TABLE OF THE ELEMENTS

INCREASING IONIZATION ENERGY OR IONIZATION POTENTIAL
INCREASING NEGATIVITY OF ELECTRON AFFINITY

INCREASING ELECTRONEGATIVITY
DECREASING ATOMIC RADIUS

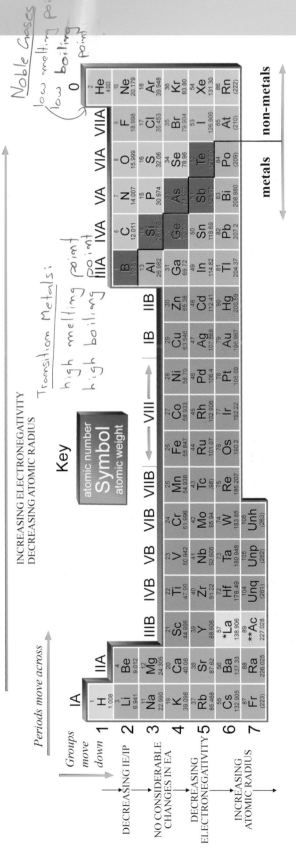

Periods move across

Groups move down

DECREASING IE/IP

NO CONSIDERABLE CHANGES IN EA

DECREASING ELECTRONEGATIVITY

INCREASING ATOMIC RADIUS

(handwritten annotations) Noble Gases: low melting point, low boiling point

Transition Metals: high melting point, high boiling

Key: atomic number / Symbol / atomic weight

non-metals

metals

Element categories in the periodic table

Metals: Alkali metals, Alkaline earth metals, Inner transition elements (Lanthanides, Actinides), Transition elements, Other metals

Metalloids

Nonmetals: Other nonmetals, Halogens

Noble gases

Element	Symbol	Atomic Number
Actinium	Ac	89
Aluminum	Al	13
Americium	Am	95
Antimony	Sb	51
Argon	Ar	18
Arsenic	As	33
Astatine	At	85
Barium	Ba	56
Berkelium	Bk	97
Beryllium	Be	4
Bismuth	Bi	83
Boron	B	5
Bromine	Br	35
Cadmium	Cd	48
Calcium	Ca	20
Californium	Cf	98
Carbon	C	6
Cerium	Ce	58
Cesium	Cs	55
Chlorine	Cl	17
Chromium	Cr	24
Cobalt	Co	27
Copper	Cu	29
Curium	Cm	96
Dysprosium	Dy	66
Einsteinium	Es	99
Erbium	Er	68

Element	Symbol	Atomic Number
Europium	Eu	63
Fermium	Fm	100
Fluorine	F	9
Francium	Fr	87
Gadolinium	Gd	64
Gallium	Ga	31
Germanium	Ge	32
Gold	Au	79
Hafnium	Hf	72
Helium	He	2
Holmium	Ho	67
Hydrogen	H	1
Indium	In	49
Iodine	I	53
Iridium	Ir	77
Iron	Fe	26
Krypton	Kr	36
Lanthanum	La	57
Lawrencium	Lr	103
Lead	Pb	82
Lithium	Li	3
Lutetium	Lu	71
Magnesium	Mg	12
Manganese	Mn	25
Mendelevium	Md	101
Mercury	Hg	80
Molybdenum	Mo	42

Element	Symbol	Atomic Number
Neodymium	Nd	60
Neon	Ne	10
Neptunium	Np	93
Nickel	Ni	28
Niobium	Nb	41
Nitrogen	N	7
Nobelium	No	102
Osmium	Os	76
Oxygen	O	8
Palladium	Pd	46
Phosphorous	P	15
Platinum	Pt	78
Plutonium	Pu	94
Polonium	Po	84
Potassium	K	19
Praseodymium	Pr	59
Promethium	Pm	61
Protactinium	Pa	91
Radium	Ra	88
Radon	Rn	86
Rhenium	Re	75
Rhodium	Rh	45
Rubidium	Rb	37
Ruthenium	Ru	44
Samarium	Sm	62
Scandium	Sc	21

Element	Symbol	Atomic Number
Selenium	Se	34
Silicon	Si	14
Silver	Ag	47
Sodium	Na	11
Strontium	Sr	38
Sulfur	S	16
Tantalum	Ta	73
Technetium	Tc	43
Tellurium	Te	52
Terbium	Tb	65
Thallium	Tl	81
Thorium	Th	90
Thulium	Tm	69
Tin	Sn	50
Titanium	Ti	22
Tungsten	W	74
(Unnilhexium)	(Unh)	106
(Unnilpentium)	(Unp)	105
(Unnilquadium)	(Unq)	104
Uranium	U	92
Vanadium	V	23
Xenon	Xe	54
Ytterbium	Yb	70
Yttrium	Y	39
Zinc	Zn	30
Zirconium	Zr	40

GOLD STANDARD WARM-UP EXERCISES
CHAPTER 2: Electronic Structure and the Periodic Table

1) Which groups of the periodic table comprise the s–block elements?

   A. Groups I, II and III
   B. Groups I and III
   C. Groups II and III
   D. Groups I and II

2) Why do chlorine atoms form anions more easily than they form cations?

   A. The valence electron shell of chlorine contains seven electrons.
   B. Attractive forces between halogen nuclei and valence electrons are weak.
   C. The valence electron shell of chlorine is vacant.
   D. Attractive forces between the valence electrons and the nuclei in halogens are strong.

3) The ability of silver ions to form complexes of many different colors identifies it as being a:

   A. univalent metal.
   B. Group IB element.
   C. Period V element.
   D. transition metal.

4) Why does potassium possess a higher first electron affinity than first ionization energy?

   A. Its valence shells are only partially filled.
   B. The attractive forces between the nucleus and the valence electrons are strong.
   C. It possesses very few inner electron shells.
   D. Its valence electron shell contains only one electron.

5) Carbon is in Group IV of the periodic table, along with such elements as silicon. However, compared with silicon, carbon forms more stable covalent bonds with itself. Why is a C–C bond stronger than a Si–Si bond?

   A. Because carbon is not as good an electrical conductor.
   B. Because carbon has a smaller atomic number.
   C. Because carbon has a smaller atomic radius.
   D. Because carbon has a smaller relative atomic mass.

6) Which of the following energy sublevels can contain the most electrons?

   A. $n = 4, l = 0$
   B. $n = 5, l = 2$
   C. $n = 6, l = 3, m_l = 1$
   D. $n = 4, l = 3$

7) Which of the following electronic configurations is an accurate representation of the electron distribution in a chromium atom?

   A. $1s^2, 2s^2, 2p^6, 3s^2, 3p^6, 3d^6, 4s^0$
   B. $1s^2, 2s^2, 2p^6, 3s^2, 3p^6, 3d^5, 4s^1$
   C. $1s^2, 2s^2, 2p^6, 3s^2, 3p^6, 3d^4, 4s^2$
   D. $1s^2, 2s^2, 2p^6, 3s^2, 3p^6, 3d^3, 4s^2, 4p^1$

8) Which of the following typically has a low melting point?

   A. Metals
   B. Metalloids
   C. Non–metals
   D. Transition metals

9) A researcher tries to determine the ionization energy of iron (Fe) by irradiating the metal with X rays of known energy (E) and then measuring the kinetic energy (K_e) of the emitted electrons. How will she compute the ionization energy from the data obtained?

   A. $E - K_e$
   B. $K_e - E$
   C. $(E)(K_e)$
   D. $(K_e)/(E)$

GS ANSWER KEY

CHAPTER 2

Cross-Reference

1.	D	CHM 2.3
2.	D	CHM 2.3
3.	D	CHM 2.3
4.	D	CHM 2.3
5.	C	CHM 2.3, 2.3.1

Cross-Reference

6.	D	CHM 2.1, 2.2
7.	B	CHM 2.3
8.	C	CHM 2.3
9.	A	CHM 2.3, 11

* Explanations can be found at the back of the book.

Go online to DAT-prep.com for additional chapter review Q&A and forum.

Periodicity

Ionization energy - energy needed to remove the least tightly bounded e^-

$$X \longrightarrow X^+ + e^-$$

E= ? _ ionization potential

$\longrightarrow$ IE increases

• adding to protons & $e-$ $\Rightarrow$ greater interaction
(heavier, but smaller)
$\downarrow$
Smaller radius
$\downarrow$
E required the $e-$ is higher.

$\downarrow$ IE decreases
• adding shells (further & further from the nucleus)

Electronegativity

• pole on an e^-

$\longrightarrow$ EV increases   (F) - greatest electronegativity

$\downarrow$ EV decreases

BONDING

Chapter 3

Memorize	Understand	Importance
* Hybrid orbitals, shapes * Define Lewis: structure, acid, base * Define: octet rule, formal charge	* Ionic, covalent bonds * VSEPR, Resonance * Dipole, covalent polar bonds * Trends in the periodic table	**1 to 3 out of the 30 Gen CHM** DAT questions are based on content in this chapter (in our estimation). * Note that between 50% and 85% of the questions in DAT General Chemistry are from 6 chapters: 1, 2, 4, 5, 6 and 9.

DAT-Prep.com

Introduction ▪▪▪▪

Attractive interactions between atoms and within molecules involve a physical process called chemical bonding. In general, strong chemical bonding is associated with the sharing or transfer of electrons between atoms. Molecules, crystals and diatomic gases are held together by chemical bonds which makes up most of the matter around us.

Additional Resources

Free Online Forum

Video: Online or DVD

Flashcards

Special Guest

3.1 Generalities

Chemical bonds can form between atoms of the same element or between atoms of different elements. Chemical bonds are classified into three groups: ionic, covalent and metallic.

To summarize, if the electronegativity values of two atoms are:

- significantly different...
  - Ionic bonds are formed.
- similar...
  - Metallic bonds form between two metal atoms.
  - Covalent bonds form between two nonmetal atoms (or between metal and nonmetal atoms).
    - Non-polar covalent bonds form when the electronegativity values are very similar.
    - Polar covalent bonds form when the electronegativity values are somewhat further apart.

We will also see in this chapter that many bonds are formed according to the octet rule, which states that an atom tends to form bonds with other atoms until the bonding atoms obtain a stable electron configuration of eight valence electrons in their outermost shells, similar to that of Group VIIIA (noble gas) elements. There are certain exceptions to the octet rule such as, hydrogen forming bonds with two valence electrons; beryllium, which can bond to attain four valence electrons; boron, which can bond to attain six; and elements such as phosphorus and sulfur, which can incorporate d orbital electrons to attain more than eight valence electrons.

3.1.1 The Ionic Bond

Ionic bonds form when there is a complete transfer of one or more electrons between a metal and a nonmetal atom. When an element X with a low ionization potential is combined with an element Y with a large negative electron affinity, one or more electrons are transferred from the atoms of X to the atoms of Y. This leads to the formation of cations X^{n+} and anions Y^{m-}. These ions of opposite charges are then attracted to each other through electrostatic forces which then aggregate to form large stable spatial arrangements of ions: crystalline solids. The bonds that hold these ions together are called ionic bonds.

There exists a large difference in electronegativity between ionically bonded atoms. Electronegativity is defined as the ability of an atom to attract electrons towards its nucleus in bonding and each atomic element is assigned a numerical electronegativity value with a greatest value of 4.0 assigned to the most electronegative element, fluorine. Ionic compounds are known to have high melting and boiling points and high electrical conductivity. In our general example, note that to maintain electrical neutrality the empirical formula of this ionic compound has to be of the general form: $X_m Y_n$ (the total positive charge: $n \times m$ is equal to the total negative charge: $m \times n$ in a unit formula).

For instance, since aluminium tends to form the cation Al^{3+} and oxygen the anion O^{2-} the empirical formula for aluminium oxide is Al_2O_3. Thus, the empirical or simplest formula is written for each of the formula units (Al_2O_3) which are part of a larger crystalline solid. The actual ionic solid lattice formed however, consists of a large and equal number of ions packed together in a manner to allow maximal attraction of all the oppositely charged ions.

H	2.1											
Li	1.0	Be	1.5	B	2.0	C	2.5	N	3.0	O	3.5	F	4.0
Na	0.9	Mg	1.2	Al	1.5	Si	1.8	P	2.1	S	2.5	Cl	3.0
K	0.8	Ca	1.0	Ga	1.6	Ge	1.8	As	2.0	Se	2.4	Br	2.8
Rb	0.8	Sr	1.0	In	1.7	Sn	1.8	Sb	1.9	Te	2.1	I	2.5
Cs	0.7	Ba	0.9	Tl	1.8	Pb	1.9	Bi	1.9	Po	2.0	At	2.2

Table III.A.3.0: Pauling's values for the electronegativity of some important elements. Note that elements in the upper right hand corner of the periodic table have high electronegativities and those in the bottom left hand corner of the table have low electronegativities (CHM 2.3, 2.4.1). Note that Pauling's electronegativity is dimensionless since it measures electron attracting ability on a relative scale.

3.2 The Covalent Bond

Atoms are held together in non-ionic molecules by covalent bonds. In this type of bonding two valence electrons are shared between two atoms. Two atoms sharing one, two or three electron pairs form single, double or triple covalent bonds, respectively. As the number of shared electron pairs increases, the two atoms are pulled closer together, leading to a decrease in bond length and a simultaneous increase in bond strength. As opposed to ionic bonds, atoms in covalent bonds have similar electronegativity. Ionic and covalent bonding are thus considered as the two extremes in bonding types. Covalent bonding is further categorized into the following subclasses; non-polar, polar and coordinate types of covalent bonding.

Non-polar covalent bonding occurs when two bonding atoms have either equal or similar electronegativities or a calculated electronegativity difference of less than 0.4.

Polar covalent bonding occurs when there is a small difference in electronegativity between atoms in the range of approximately 0.4 up to 2.0. When the difference in electronegativity is greater than 2.0, ionic bonding is then known to occur between two atoms. The more electronegative atom will attract the bonding electrons to a larger extent. As a result, the more electronegative atom acquires a partial negative charge and the less electronegative atom acquires a partial positive charge.

Coordinate covalent bonding occurs when the shared electron pair comes from the lone pair of electrons of one of the atoms in the bonding component. Typically coordinate bonds form between Lewis acids (electron acceptors) and Lewis bases (electron donors) as shown below.

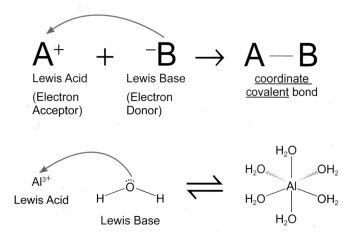

A Lewis structure is a representation of covalent bonding in which shared electrons are shown either as lines or as pairs of dots between two atoms. For instance, let us consider the H_2O molecule. The valence shell electronic configurations of the atoms that constitute this molecule are:

$$O: \quad 2s^2\, 2p^4$$
$$H: \quad 1s^1$$

Since hydrogen has only one electron to share with oxygen there is only one possible covalent bond that can be formed between the oxygen atom and each of the hydrogen atoms. Four of the valence electrons of the oxygen atom do not participate in this covalent bonding, these are called <u>non-bonding electrons or lone pairs</u>. The Lewis structure of

the water molecule is:

$$H\!:\!\ddot{O}\!:\!H \quad \text{or} \quad H\text{-}\ddot{O}\text{-}H$$

Lewis formulated the following general rule known as the <u>octet rule</u> concerning these representations: atoms tend to form covalent bonds until they are surrounded by 8 electrons (with few exceptions such as for hydrogen which can be surrounded by a maximum of only 2 electrons; see CHM 3.1). To satisfy this rule (and if there is a sufficient number of valence electrons), two atoms may share more than one pair of electrons thus forming more than one covalent bond at a time. In such instances the bond between these atoms is referred to as a double or a triple bond depending on whether there are two or three pairs of shared electrons, respectively.

Some molecules cannot fully be described by a single Lewis structure. For instance, for the carbonate ion: CO_3^{2-}, the octet rule is satisfied for the central carbon atom if one of the C…O bonds is double (see the following diagrams). While this leads us to thinking that the three C…O bonds are not equivalent, every piece of experimental evidence concerning this molecule shows that the three bonds are in fact the same (same length, same polarity, etc…). This suggests that in such instances a molecule cannot be described fully by a single Lewis structure. However, a molecule may in fact be represented by two or more valid Lewis structures. Indeed, since there is no particular reason to choose one oxygen atom over another we can write three equivalent Lewis structures for the carbonate ion. These three structures are called <u>resonance structures represented with a double-headed arrow between each resonance structure.</u> The carbonate ion (CO_3^{2-}) actually exists as a hybrid of the three equivalent structures. It is the full set of resonance structures that describe such a molecule. In this picture, the C...O bonds are neither double nor single, they are intermediate and have both a single and a double bonded character (see the following diagrams).

CO_3^{2-}

$$\left[\ddot{:O}-C=\ddot{O} \atop :\ddot{O}: \right]^{2-} \leftrightarrow \left[\ddot{O}=C-\ddot{O}: \atop :\ddot{O}: \right]^{2-} \leftrightarrow \left[:\ddot{O}-C-\ddot{O}: \atop :\ddot{O}: \right]^{2-}$$

The actual structure of the carbonate ion is therefore one which is intermediate between the three resonance structures and is known as a resonance hybrid as shown:

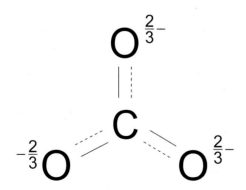

In many molecular structures, all of the respective resonance structures contribute equally to the hybridized representation. However, for some, resonance structures may not all contribute equally. Moreover, the more sta-

ble the resonance structure, the more contribution of that structure to the true hybrid structure based on formal charges.

Thus, based on their stabilities, non-equivalent resonance structures may contribute differently to the true overall hybridized structure representation of a molecule.

It is often interesting to compare the number of valence electrons that an atom possesses when it is isolated and when it is engaged in a covalent bond within a given molecule. This is often quantitatively described by the concept of <u>formal charge</u>.

Generally, a formal charge is a calculated conjured charge assigned to each individual atom within a Lewis structure allowing one to distinguish amongst various possible Lewis structures. The formal charge on any individual atom is calculated based on the difference between the atom's actual number of valence electrons and the number of electrons the atom possesses as part of a Lewis structure.

Moreover, the number of electrons attributed to an atom within a Lewis structure (covalently bonded) is not necessarily the same as the number of valence electrons that would be isolated within that free atom, and the difference is thus referred to as the "formal charge" of that atom. This concept is defined as follows:

Formal charge (of atom X) = Total number of valence electrons in a free atom (V) − [(total number of nonbonding electrons

(N) + ½ total number of bonding electrons (B) in a Lewis structure)].

Where, V is the number of valence electrons of the atom in isolation (atom in ground state); N is the number of non-bonding valence electrons on this atom in the molecule; and B is the total number of bonding electrons shared in covalent bonds with other atoms in the molecule (see structure of CO_3^{2-} in the previous illustrations).

Let us apply this definition to the two previous examples: H_2O and CO_3^{2-}. This process is fairly straightforward in the case of the water molecule:

total # of valence e⁻'s in free O:	6
– total # of non-bonding e⁻'s on O in H_2O:	4
– 1/2 (total # of bonding e⁻'s) on O in H_2O:	2

Formal charge of O in H_2O = 0

In the case of the CO_3^{2-} ion, it is not as obvious. If we consider one of the three equivalent resonance forms, that of the oxygen with a double bond to carbon we have:

total # of valence e⁻'s in free O:	6
- total # of non-bonding e⁻'s on O in the ion:	4
- 1/2 (total # of bonding e⁻) on O in the ion:	2

Formal charge of O of C=O in the ion = 0

Similarly, the calculation of the formal charge for one of the two singly bonded oxygen's of C–O in the same ion leads to the following: $6 - 6 - 1/2(2) = -1$. Considering that CO_3^{2-} is represented by three resonance forms, the actual formal charge of the oxygen atom is $1/3 (-1 -1 + 0) = -2/3$. This value formally reflects the idea that the oxygen atoms are equivalent and that any one of them has a −1 charge in 2 out of three of the resonance forms of this ion. Here are some simple rules to remember about formal charges:

(i) For neutral molecules, the formal charges of all the atoms should add up to zero.

(ii) For an ion, the sum of the formal charges must equal the ion's charge.

The following rules should help you select a plausible Lewis structure:

(i) If you can write more than one Lewis structure for a given neutral molecule; the most plausible one is the one in which the formal charges of the individual atoms are zero.

(ii) Lewis structures with the smallest formal charges on each individual atom are more plausible than the ones that involve large formal charges.

(iii) Out of a range of possible Lewis structures for a given molecule, the most plausible ones are the ones in which negative formal charges are found on the most electronegative atoms and positive charges on the most electropositive ones.

In addition to these rules, remember that some elements have a tendency to form molecules that do not satisfy the octet rule:

(i) When sulfur is the central atom in a molecule or a polyatomic ion, it almost invariably does not fulfill the octet rule.

(ii) The number of electrons around S in these compounds is usually 12 (e.g. SF_6, SO_4^{2-}). This situation (<u>expanded octets</u>) also occurs in other elements in and beyond the third period.

(iii) Molecules that have an element from the 3A group (B, Al, etc...) as their central atom do not generally obey the octet rule. In these molecules there are less than 8 electrons around the central atom (e.g. AlI_3 and BF_3).

(iv) Some molecules with an odd number of electrons can clearly not obey the octet rule (e.g. NO and NO_2).

Formal charge: valence # − (bonded e⁻ + lone pair e⁻).

3.3 Partial Ionic Character

⇒ ★ valence e⁻ − assigned valence (½ bonded e⁻ + lone pairs).

Except for <u>homonuclear molecules</u> (molecules made of atoms of the same element, e.g. H_2, O_3, etc...), bonding electrons are not equally shared by the bonded atoms. Thus a <u>diatomic</u> (= *two atoms*) compound like Cl_2 shares its bonding electrons equally; whereas, a <u>binary</u> (= *two <u>different</u> elements*) compound like CaO (calcium ox<u>ide</u>) or NaCl (sodium chloride) does not. Indeed, for the great majority of molecules, one of the two atoms between which the covalent bond occurs is necessarily more electronegative than the other. This atom will attract the bonding electrons to a larger extent (see CHM 3.2). Although this phenomenon does not lead to the formation of two separate ionic species, it does result in a molecule in which there are partial charges on these particular atoms: the corresponding covalent bond is said to <u>possess partial ionic character</u>. This polar bond will also have a dipole moment given by:

$$D = q \cdot d$$

where q is the absolute value of the partial charge on the most electronegative or the most electropositive bonded atom and d is the distance between these two atoms. To obtain the total dipole moment of a molecule one must add the individual dipole moment vectors present on each one of its bonds. Since this is a vector addition (see ORG 1.5), the overall result may be zero even if the individual dipole moment vectors are very large.

Non-polar bonds are generally stronger than polar covalent and ionic bonds, with ionic bonds being the weakest. However, in compounds with ionic bonding, there is generally a large number of bonds between molecules and this makes the compound as a whole very strong. For instance, although the ionic bonds in one compound are weaker than the non-polar covalent bonds in another compound, the ionic compound's melting point will be higher than the melting point of the covalent compound. Polar covalent bonds have a partially ionic character, and thus the bond strength is usually intermediate between that of ionic and that of non-polar covalent bonds. The strength of bonds generally decreases with increasing ionic character.

3.4 Lewis Acids and Lewis Bases

The Lewis model of acids and bases focuses on the transfer of an electron pair. Generally, a Lewis acid is defined as any substance that may accept an electron pair to form a covalent bond, while a Lewis base, is defined as any substance that donates an electron pair to form a respective covalent bond. Hence, as per the Lewis definition of an acid or base, a substance need not contain a hydrogen as defined by either Arrhenius or Bronsted-Lowry to be an acid, nor is a hydroxyl group (OH^-) needed to be a base (see CHM 6.1). A Lewis acid therefore generally has an empty electronic orbital that can accept an electron pair whereas a Lewis base will contain a full electronic orbital or lone pair of electrons ready to be donated.

In CHM 3.2, we pointed out some exceptions to the Lewis' octet rule. Among these were molecules that had a deficiency of electrons around the central atom as described previously (e.g. BF_3). When such a molecule is put into contact with a molecule with lone pairs (e.g. NH_3) a reaction occurs. Such a reaction can be interpreted as a donation of a pair of electrons from the second type of molecule (Lewis base) to the first type of molecule (Lewis acid), or alternately by an acceptance of a pair of electrons by the first type of molecule. Thus, as previously shown, molecules such as BF_3 are referred to as Lewis acids while molecules such as NH_3 are known as Lewis bases. Thus some examples of Lewis acids are: BF_3, H^+, Cu^{2+}, and Cr^{3+} and Lewis bases are: NH_3, OH^-, and H_2O. {l**E**wis **A**cids: **E**lectron pair **A**cceptors}.

The Lewis acid BF_3 and the Lewis base NH_3. Notice that the green arrows follow the flow of electron pairs.

Bond order   Bond energy

3.5 Valence Shell Electronic Pair Repulsions (VSEPR Models)

One of the shortcomings of Lewis structures is that they cannot be used to predict molecular geometries. In this context a model known as the <u>valence-shell electronic pair repulsion or VSEPR model</u> is very useful. In this model, the geometrical arrangement of atoms or groups of atoms bound to a central atom A is determined by the number of pairs of valence electrons around A. VSEPR procedure is based on the principle that these electronic pairs around the central atom are arranged in such a way that the repulsions between them are minimized. The general VSEPR procedure starts with the determination of the number of electronic pairs around A:

# of valence electrons in a free atom of A
+ # of sigma (or single) bonds involving A
− # of pi (or double) bonds involving A
_____
= (total # of electrons around A)

The division of this total number by 2 yields the total number of electron pairs around A. Note the following important points:

(i)   A single bond counts for 1 sigma bond, a double bond for 1 sigma bond and 1 pi bond and a triple bond for 1 sigma and two pi bonds.

(ii) The general calculation that we have presented is performed for the purposes of VSEPR modeling; its result can be quite different from the one obtained in the corresponding Lewis structure.

(iii) For all practical purposes, one always assigns a double bond (i.e. 1 sigma bond and one pi bond) to a terminal oxygen (an oxygen which is not a central atom and is not attached to any other atom besides the central atom).

(iv) A terminal halogen is always assigned a single bond.

Once the number of pairs around the central atom is determined, the next step is to use Figure III.A.3.1 to predict the geometrical arrangement of these pairs around the central atom.

The next step is to consider the previous arrangement of the electronic pairs and place the atoms or groups of atoms that are attached to the central atom in accordance with such an arrangement. The pairs of electrons which are not involved in the bonding between these atoms and the central atom are known as lone pairs. If we subtract the number of lone pairs from the total number of pairs of electrons, we readily obtain the number of bonding electron pairs. It is the number of bonding electron pairs which ultimately determines the molecular geometry in the VSEPR model according to Table III.A.3.1.

On the other hand, as for the *electronic* geometrical arrangement of a molecule, one is also to consider the free lone pair(s) of electrons. Consequently, a simple molecule such as SO_2 (see Table III.A.3.1) will have a trigonal planar electronic geometry with a bent molecular geometry with the respective differences in geometrical arrangement based solely on the lone pair of the central sulfur atom. Thus, the electron and molecular geometry of a molecule may be different. (Note: electron geometry is based on the geometrical arrangement of electron pairs around a central atom, whereas, molecular geometry is based on the geometrical arrangement of the atoms surrounding a central atom). Let us consider three examples: CH_4, H_2O and CO_2.

1 – CH_4:

# of valence electrons on C:	4
+ # of sigma bonds:	+ 4
– # of pi bonds:	– 0

= 8/2 = 4 pairs

According to Figure III.A.3.1 CH_4 corresponds to a tetrahedral arrangement. Each of these four pairs of electrons corresponds to a H atom bonded each to the central atom of carbon. Therefore, all 4 pairs of electrons are bonding pairs with a tetrahedral molecular and electronic geometry, respectively (due to a lack in lone pairs).

2 – H_2O:

# of valence electrons on O:	6
+ # of sigma bonds on the central O:	+ 2
- # of pi bonds on the central O:	– 0

= 8/2 = 4 pairs

For the H_2O geometry, it also corresponds to a tetrahedral arrangement (i.e. 4 pairs). However, due to lone pairs surrounding each of the oxygen atoms, the molecular geometry is of a bent geometrical shape with a tetrahedral electronic geometrical configuration.

3 – CO_2:

# of valence electrons on C:	4
+ # of sigma bonds for terminal O's:	+ 2
- # of pi bonds for terminal O's:	– 2

= 4/2 = 2 pairs

This total number of pairs corresponds to a linear arrangement. Since both of these electron pairs are used to connect the central C atom to the terminal O's there are no lone pairs left on C. Therefore, the number of bonding pairs is also 2 and both the molecular and electronic geometries are also linear.

Here are some additional rules when applying the VSEPR model:

(i) When dealing with a cation (<u>positive</u> ion) <u>subtract</u> the charge of the ion from the total number of electrons.

(ii) When dealing with an anion (<u>negative</u> ion) <u>add</u> the charge of the ion to the total number of electrons.

(iii) A lone pair repels another lone pair or a bonding pair very strongly. This causes some deformation in bond angles. For instance, the H–O–H angle is smaller than 109.5°.

Table III.A.3.1: Geometry of simple molecules in which the central atom A has one or more lone pairs of electrons (= e^-).

Total number of e^- pairs	Number of lone pairs	Number of bonding pairs	Electron Geometry, Arrangement of e^- pairs	Molecular Geometry (Hybridization State)	Examples
3	1	2	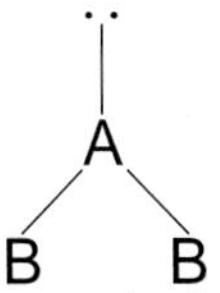 Trigonal planar	Bent (sp^2)	SO_2
4	1	3	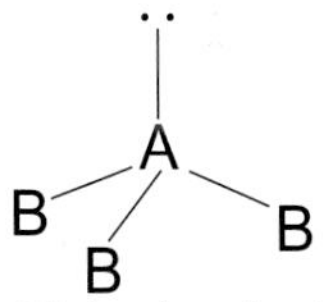 Tetrahedral	Trigonal pyramidal (sp^3)	NH_3
4	2	2	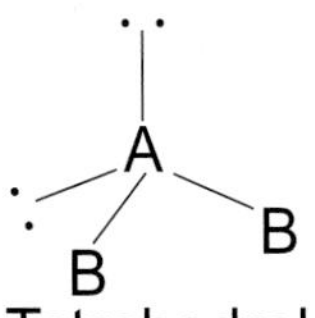 Tetrahedral	Bent (sp^3)	H_2O
5	1	4	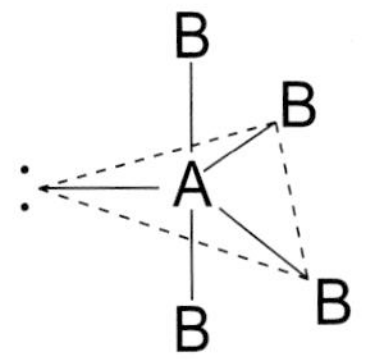 Trigonal bipyramidal	Seesaw (sp^3d)	SF_4
5	2	3	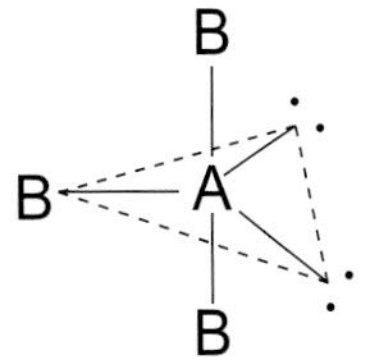 Trigonal bipyramidal	T-shaped (sp^3d)	ClF_3

Note: dotted lines only represent the overall molecular shape and not molecular bonds. In brackets under "Molecular Geometry" is the hybridization, to be discussed in ORG 1.2.

(iv) The previous rule also holds for a double bond. Note that in one of our previous examples (CO_2), the angle is still 180° since there are two double bonds and no lone pairs. Indeed, in this geometry, the strong repulsions between the two double bonds are symmetrical.

(v) The VSEPR model can be applied to polyatomic molecules. The procedure is the same as above except that one can only determine the arrangements of groups of atoms around one given central atom at a time. For instance, you could apply the VSEPR model to determine the geometrical arrangements of atoms around C or around O in methanol (CH_3OH). In the first case the molecule is treated as $CH_3 - X$ (where $-X$ is $-OH$) and in the second it is treated as $HO-Y$ (where $-Y$ is $-CH_3$). The geometrical arrangement is tetrahedral in the first case which gives HCX or HCH

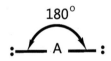

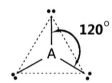

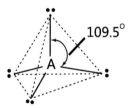

linear arrangement of
2 electron pairs around
central atom A

trigonal planar arrangement
of 3 electron pairs
around central atom A

tetrahedral arrangement
of 4 electron pairs
around central atom A

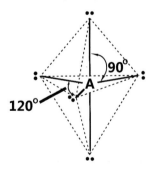

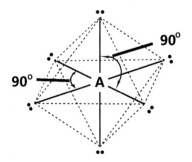

trigonal bipyramidal arrangement
of 5 electron pairs
around central atom A

octahedral arrangement
of 6 electron pairs
around central atom A

Figure III.A.3.1: Molecular arrangement of electron pairs around a central atom A. Dotted lines only represent the overall molecular shape and not molecular bonds.

angles close to 109°. The second case corresponds to a bent arrangement (with two lone pairs on the oxygen) and gives an HOY angle close to 109° as well.This also corresponds to a tetrahedral arrangement,

however only two of these pairs are bonding pairs (connecting the H atoms to the central oxygen atom); therefore, the actual geometry according to Table III.A.3.1 is bent or V-shape geometry.

3.5.1 The AXE Method

The "AXE method" of electron counting can be used when applying the VSEPR model. As we have seen in the previous section, the A signifies the central atom. The X represents the number of sigma bonds between the central atom and outside atoms (see "B" in Table III.A.3.1). Multiple covalent bonds (double, triple, etc.) count as one X. The E is the number of lone pair electrons surrounding A. The sum of X and E, known as the steric number, is also associated with the total number of hybridized orbitals (ORG 1.2). Based on the steric number and the distribution of X's and E's, the VSEPR model makes the predictions in Table III.A.3.2.

Table III.A.3.2: Using the AXE method to determine molecular geometry.

Steric No.	BASIC GEOMETRY			
	0 lone pair	1 lone pair	2 lone pairs	3 lone pairs
2	X—A—X Linear (CO_2)			
3	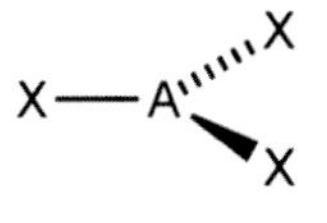 Trigonal planar (BCl_3)	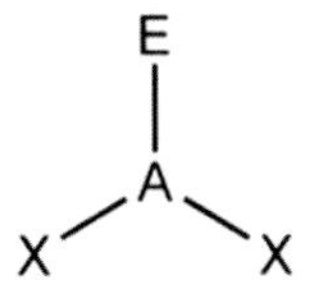 Bent (SO_2)		
4	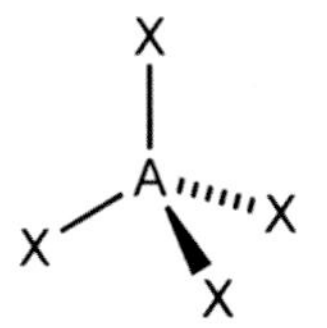 Tetrahedral (CH_4)	 Trigonal pyramidal (NH_3)	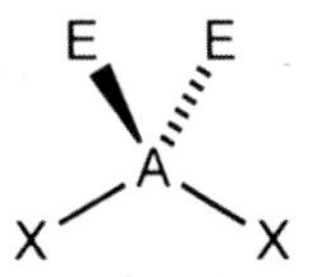 Bent (H_2O)	

Table III.A.3.2: *(continued)*

Steric No.	BASIC GEOMETRY			
	0 lone pair	**1 lone pair**	**2 lone pairs**	**3 lone pairs**
5	 Trigonal bipyramidal (PCl_5)	 Seesaw (SF_4)	 T-shaped (ClF_3)	 Linear (I_3^-)
6	 Octahedral (SF_6)	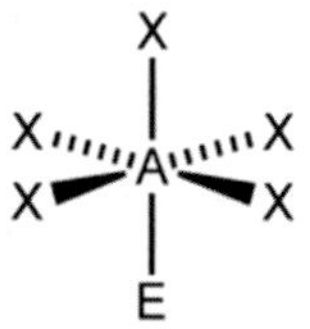 Square pyramidal (BrF_5)	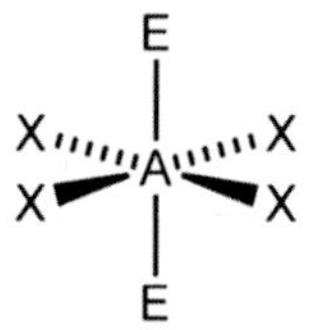 Square planar (XeF_4)	
7	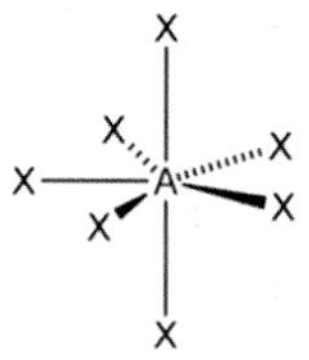 Pentagonal bipyramidal (IF_7)	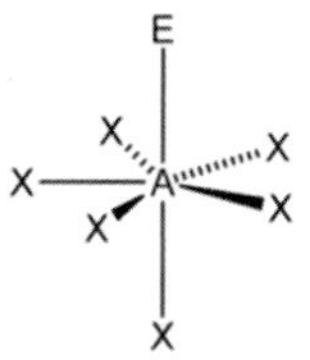 Pentagonal pyramidal ($XeOF_5^-$)	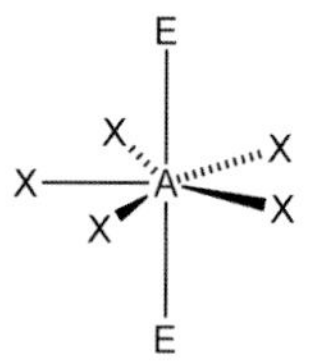 Pentagonal planar (XeF_5^-)	

PLEASE NOTE: Intermolecular bonds is discussed in CHM 4.2.

GOLD STANDARD WARM-UP EXERCISES
CHAPTER 3: Bonding

1) What is the formal charge on the carbon atom in the carbonate ion?

    A. 0
    B. 1
    C. 2
    D. −2

    CO_3^-

    $3(-2) = -6$

2) Diamond consists of tetrahedral arrangements of carbon atoms, with each atom covalently bound to four others to yield a giant molecular structure. What is the hybridization state of carbon in diamond?

    A. It is not hybridized.
    B. sp
    C. sp^2
    D. sp^3

3) Which of the following describes the orbital geometry of an sp^2 hybridized atom?

    A. Trigonal planar
    B. Linear
    C. Tetrahedral
    D. Octahedral

4) In the hypothetical molecule PQ_2, the atom P possesses a lone pair of electrons, what would be the expected shape of the product molecule?

    A. Linear
    B. Bent
    C. Trigonal pyramidal
    D. Tetrahedral

5) Aniline ($C_6H_5NH_2$) acts as a Lewis base because aniline:

    $C_6H_5NH_2 + H_2O \leftrightarrow C_6H_5NH_3^+ + OH^-$

    A. exhibits hydrogen bonding.
    B. has a lone pair of electrons on its nitrogen atom.

C. is an electron pair acceptor.
D. produces OH^- when in solution.

6) Which of the following best summarizes VSEPR?

    A. Hybridized bonds are the key to molecular stability.
    B. The repulsion between bonds helps determine the shapes of covalent molecules.
    C. The repulsion of atomic nuclei helps determine the shapes of covalent molecules.
    D. The repulsion between electrons helps determine the shapes of covalent molecules.

7) Using the VSEPR theory, the shape of PCl_5 is:

    A. pentagonal planar.
    B. octahedral.
    C. trigonal bipyramidal.
    D. square pyramidal.

8) Using the VSEPR theory, the shape of SF_6 is:

    A. octahedral.
    B. tetrahedral.
    C. trigonal bipyramidal.
    D. square pyramidal.

9) Using the VSEPR theory, the shape of ClF_3 is:

    A. trigonal planar.
    B. tetrahedral.
    C. trigonal pyramidal.
    D. T-shaped.

10) Which pair of atoms would most likely form an ionic compound when bonded to each other?

    A. Silicon and nitrogen
    B. Calcium and fluorine
    C. Two sulfur atoms
    D. Carbon and silicon

GS ANSWER KEY

CHAPTER 3

		Cross-Reference
1.	A	CHM 3.2, 3.5
2.	D	CHM 3.5
3.	A	CHM 3.5, ORG 1.2
4.	B	CHM 3.2-3.5
5.	B	CHM 3.4

		Cross-Reference
6.	D	CHM 3.5
7.	C	CHM 3.5
8.	A	CHM 3.5
9.	D	CHM 3.5
10.	B	CHM 2.3, 3.1.1

* Explanations can be found at the back of the book.

Go online to DAT-prep.com for additional chapter review Q&A and forum.

Chemical Bonds

- Intramolecular- within a molecule
- Intermolecular- between " "

(δ^+) e^- (δ^-) $\delta^+ \to \delta^- \; \delta^-$
Br — Br   Br — Br   — dipole-dipole forces too

⊖ ↗
Covalently bonded (sharing e^- equally)

Induced
dipole
(bc it was induced
by an outside (⊖ here)
(harge)

force of
attraction-
intermolecular
bond.

— van der waal's forces (weakest, but important)
— can affect boiling points)

Ionic / Covalent bond

Ionic- complete transfer of e^- $NaCl \to Na^+ + Cl^-$

- melting points are very high
- bonds are strong (fully charged elements)
- conducting substances (charged)

Covalent- complete sharing of e^-

Br_2 or Cl_2

Lewis Dot structure

• most rxn at outermost shell e⁻

$$H\cdot + \overset{..}{\underset{..}{F}}\cdot \longrightarrow H\!:\!\overset{..}{\underset{..}{F}}\!: \qquad (\overset{\delta+}{H}\!\!\rightarrow\!\!\overset{\delta-}{F})$$

7 protons   very stable   Covalent bond with ionic character.
& 7 electrons   (polar bond)

⇓

7 valence e⁻
(also group 7 on periodic table)

hybridization

• changes that occur within an atom

Carbon ("C") ⇒

	1S	2S	2P	
	↑↓	↑↓	↑	↑

$1s^2\ 2s^2\ 2p^2$

Carbon molecule   ↑↓   ↑   ↑ ↑ ↑   more force to push e⁻ apart.

$1s + 3p \Rightarrow 4sp^3$ hybrid

109.5°

C

Hydrogen atom

__CH₄__   ⦂ Tetrahedral; angle 109.5°

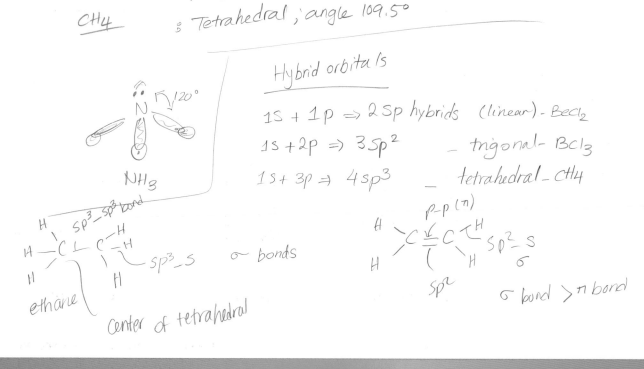

Hybrid orbitals

$1s + 1p \Rightarrow 2sp$ hybrids   (linear) - $BeCl_2$

$1s + 2p \Rightarrow 3sp^2$ — trigonal - BCl_3

$1s + 3p \Rightarrow 4sp^3$ — tetrahedral - CH_4

120°

N

NH₃

H — C — C — H (sp³-sp³ bond)
sp³-s
σ bonds
center of tetrahedral
ethane

p-p (π)
sp^2 - s
σ
sp^2
σ bond > π bond

PHASES AND PHASE EQUILIBRIA
Chapter 4

Memorize	Understand	Importance
* Define: temp. (C, K), gas P and weight * Define: STP, ideal gas, deviation * Define: H bonds, dipole forces	* Kinetic molecular theory of gases * Maxwell distribution plot, H bonds, dipole F. * Deviation from ideal gas behavior * Equations: ideal gas/Charles'/Boyle's * Partial Press., mole fraction, Dalton's * Intermolecular forces, phase change/ diagrams	**4 to 6 out of the 30 Gen CHM** DAT questions are based on content in this chapter (in our estimation). * Note that between 50% and 85% of the questions in DAT General Chemistry are from 6 chapters: 1, 2, 4, 5, 6 and 9.

DAT-Prep.com

Introduction

A phase, or state of matter, is a uniform, distinct and usually separable region of material. For example, for a glass of water: the ice cubes are one phase (solid), the water is a second phase (liquid), and the humid air over the water is the third phase (gas = vapor). The temperature and pressure at which all 3 phases of a substance can coexist is called the triple point.

Additional Resources

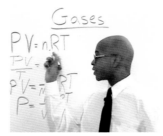

| Free Online Forum | Video: Online or DVD | Flashcards | Special Guest |

Elements and compounds exist in one of three states: <u>the gaseous state, the liquid state or the solid state</u>.

4.1 The Gas Phase

A substance in the gaseous state has neither fixed volume nor fixed shape: it spreads itself <u>uniformly</u> throughout any container in which it is placed.

4.1.1 Standard Temperature and Pressure, Standard Molar Volume

Any given gas can be described in terms of four fundamental properties: mass, volume, temperature and pressure. To simplify comparisons, the volume of a gas is normally reported at 0°C (273.15 K) and 1.00 atm (101.33 kPa = 760 mmHg = 760 torr); these conditions are known as the <u>standard temperature and pressure (STP)</u>. {Note: the SI unit of pressure is the pascal (Pa) and the old-fashioned Imperial unit is the pound per square inch because pressure is defined as force per unit area}

> The volume occupied by one mole of any gas at STP is referred to as the <u>standard molar volume</u> and is equal to 22.4 L.

4.1.2 Kinetic Molecular Theory of Gases (A Model for Gases)

The <u>kinetic molecular theory of gases</u> describes the particulate behavior of matter in the gaseous state. A gas that fits this theory exactly is called an <u>ideal gas</u>. The essential points of the theory are as follows:

1. Gases are composed of <u>extremely small</u> particles (either molecules or atoms depending on the gas) separated by distances that are relatively large in comparison with the diameters of the particles.

2. Particles of gas are in <u>constant motion,</u> except when they collide with one another.

3. Particles of an <u>ideal gas</u> exert no attractive or repulsive force on one another.

4. The collisions experienced by gas particles do not, on the average, slow them down; rather, they cause a <u>change</u> in the direction in which the particles are moving. If one particle loses energy as a result of a collision, the energy is gained by the particle with which it collides. <u>Collisions</u> of the particles of an ideal gas with the walls of the container <u>result in no loss of energy.</u>

5. The <u>average kinetic energy</u> of the particles (KE = 1/2 mv²) <u>increases in direct proportion to the temperature</u> of the gas (KE = 3/2 kT) when the temperature is measured on an absolute scale (i.e. the Kelvin scale) and k is a constant (the Boltzmann constant). The typical speed of a gas particle is directly proportional to the square root of the absolute temperature.

The plot of the distribution of collision energies of gases is similar to that of liquids. However, molecules in liquids require a minimum escape kinetic energy in order to enter the vapor phase (see Figure III.A.4.1 in CHM 4.1.2).

The properties of gases can be explained in terms of the kinetic molecular theory of ideal gases.

Experimentally, we can measure four properties of a gas:

1. The <u>weight</u> of the gas, from which we can calculate the <u>number (N) of molecules or atoms</u> of the gas present;

2. The <u>pressure (P)</u>, exerted by the gas on the walls of the container in which this gas is placed (N.B.: a <u>vacuum</u> is completely devoid of particles and thus has *no* pressure);

3. The <u>volume (V)</u>, occupied by the gas;

4. The <u>temperature (T)</u> of the gas.

In fact, if we know any three of these properties, we can calculate the fourth. So the minimum number of these properties required to fully describe the state of an ideal gas is three.

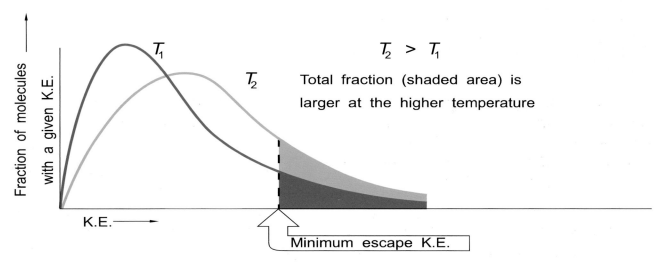

Figure III.A.4.1: The Maxwell Distribution Plot. At a higher temperature T_2, the curve peak is flattened, which means that gas particles within the sample are travelling at a wider range of velocities. Additionally, the larger shaded area at a temperature T_2 means that a greater proportion of molecules will possess the minimum escaping kinetic energy (KE) required to evaporate.

4.1.3 Graham's Law (Diffusion and Effusion of Gases)

Graham's law describes the mean (average) free path of any typical gas particle taken per unit volume. The process taken by such gas particles is known as *diffusion* and its related process *effusion* which are defined as follows:

Diffusion is the flow of gas particles spreading out evenly through random motion. Gas particles diffuse from regions of high concentration to regions of low concentration. The rate at which a gas diffuses is inversely proportional to the square root of its molar mass. The ratio of the diffusion rates of two different gases is inversely proportional to the square root of their respective molar masses. $Rate_1/Rate_2$ and M_1/M_2 represents diffusion rates of gases 1 and 2 and the molar mass of gases 1 and 2. Lighter particles diffuse quicker than heavier particles.

Effusion is the movement of a gas through a small hole or pore into another gaseous region or into a vacuum. If the hole is large enough, the process may be considered diffusion instead of effusion. The rates at which two gases effuse are inversely proportional to the square root of their molar masses, the same as that for diffusion:

$$\frac{Rate_1}{Rate_2} = \sqrt{\frac{M_2}{M_1}}$$

4.1.4 Charles' Law

The volume (V) of a gas is directly proportional to the absolute temperature (expressed in Kelvins) when P and N are kept constant.

$$V = \text{Constant} \times T \quad \text{or} \quad V_1/V_2 = T_1/T_2$$

NOTE: For Charles' Law and all subsequent laws, the subscripts 1 and 2 refer to both initial and final values of all variables for the gas in question.

4.1.5 Boyle's Law

The volume (V) of a fixed weight of gas held at constant temperature (T) varies inversely with the pressure (P).

$$V = \text{Constant} \times 1/P \quad \text{or} \quad P_1V_1 = P_2V_2$$

4.1.6 Avogadro's Law

The volume (V) of a gas at constant temperature and pressure is directly proportional to the number of particles or moles (n) of the gas present.

$$V/n = \text{Constant} \quad \text{or} \quad V_1/n_1 = V_2/n_2$$

4.1.7 Combined Gas Law

For a given constant mass of any gas the product of its pressure and volume divided by its Kelvin temperature is equal to a constant (k). Therefore, by using the combined gas law, one may calculate any of the three variables of a gas exposed to two separate conditions as follows:

This relationship depicts how a change in pressure, volume, and/or temperature of any gas (at constant mass) will be affected as a function of the other quantities (P_2, V_2 or T_2).

$$\frac{P_1 V_1}{T_1} = k = \frac{P_2 V_2}{T_2} \quad \text{(at constant mass)}$$

4.1.8 Ideal Gas Law

The combination of Boyle's law, Charles' law and Avogadro's law yields the "ideal gas law":

$$PV = nRT$$

where R is the <u>universal gas constant</u> and n is the number of moles of gas particles.

R = 0.0821 L-atm/K-mole
= 8.31 kPa-dm³/K-mole

A typical ideal gas problem is as follows: an ideal gas at 27 °C and 380 torr occupies a volume of 492 cm³. What is the number of moles of gas?

Ideal Gas Law problems often amount to mere exercises of unit conversions. The easiest way to do them is to convert the units of the values given to the units of the R gas constant.

$$P = 380 \text{ torr} = \frac{380 \text{ torr}}{(760 \text{ torr/atm})} = 0.500 \text{ atm}$$

$$T = 27\,°C = 273 + 27\,°C = 300 \text{ K}$$

$$V = 492 \text{ cm}^3 = 492 \text{ cm}^3 \times (1 \text{ liter}/1000\text{cm}^3)$$

$$= 0.492 \text{ liter}$$

$$PV = n\text{RT}$$

$$n = PV/R\text{T}$$

$$n = \frac{(0.500 \text{ atm} \times 0.492 \text{ L})}{(0.0821 \text{ L-atm/K-mole} \times 300 \text{ K})}$$

$$n = 0.0100 \text{ mole}$$

Also note that the ideal gas law could be used in the following alternate ways (Mwt = molecular weight):

(i) since n = (mass m of gas sample)/(Mwt M of the gas)

$$PV = (m/M)R T$$

(ii) since m/V is the density (d) of the gas:

$$P = \frac{dRT}{M}$$

4.1.9 Partial Pressure and Dalton's Law

In a mixture of unreactive gases, each gas distributes evenly throughout the container. All particles exert the same pressure on the walls of the container with equal force. If we consider a mixture of gases occupying a total volume (V) at a temperature (T) the term partial pressure is used to refer to the pressure exerted by one component of the gas mixture if it were occupying the entire volume (V) at the temperature (T).

Dalton's law states that the total pressure observed for a mixture of gases is equal to the sum of the pressures that each individual component would exert were it alone in the container.

$$P_T = P_1 + P_2 + \ldots + P_i$$

where P_T is the total pressure and P_i is the partial pressure of any component (i).

The mole fraction (X_i) of any one gas present in a mixture is defined as follows:

$$X_i = n_i/n_{(total)}$$

where n_i = moles of that gas present in the mixture and $n_{(total)}$ = sum of the moles of all gases present in the mixture (see CHM 5.3.1).

Of course, the sum of all mole fractions in a mixture must equal one:

$$\Sigma X_i = 1$$

The partial pressure (P_i) of a component of a gas mixture is equal to:

$$P_i = X_i P_T$$

The ideal gas law applies to any component of the mixture:

$$P_i V = n_i RT$$

4.1.10 Deviation of Real Gas Behavior from the Ideal Gas Law

The particles of an ideal gas have zero volume and no intermolecular forces. It obeys the ideal gas law. Its particles behave as though they were moving points exerting no attraction on one another and occupying no space. Real gases deviate from ideal gas behavior particularly when the gas particles are forced into close proximity under high pressure and low temperature, as follows:

1. They do not obey $PV = nRT$. We can calculate n, P, V and T for a real gas on the assumption that it behaves like an ideal gas but the calculated values will not agree with the observed values.

2. Their particles are subject to intermolecular forces (i.e. forces of attraction between different molecules like Van der Waal forces; CHM 4.2) which are themselves independent of temperature. But the deviations they cause are more pronounced at low temperatures because they are less effectively opposed by the slower motion of particles at lower temperatures. Similarly, an increase in pressure at constant temperature will crowd the particles closer together and reduce the average distance between them. This will increase the attractive force between the particles and the stronger these forces, the more the behavior of the real gas will deviate from that of an ideal gas. Thus, a real gas will act less like an ideal gas at higher pressures than at lower pressures. {Mnemonic: an ideal Plow and Thigh = an ideal gas exists when Pressure is low and Temperature is high}

3. The particles (i.e. molecules or atoms) occupy space. When a real gas is subjected to high pressures at ordinary temperatures, the fraction of the total volume occupied by the particles increases. At moderately high pressure, gas particles are pushed closer together and intermolecular attraction causes the gas to have a smaller volume than would be predicted by the ideal gas law. At extremely high pressure, gas particles are pushed even closer in such a way that the distance between them are becoming insignificant

compared to the size of the particles, therefore causing the gas to take up a smaller volume than would be predicted by the ideal gas law. Under these conditions, the real gas deviates appreciably from ideal gas behavior.

4.   Their size and mass also affect the speed at which they move. At constant temperature, the kinetic energy ($KE = 1/2\ mv^2$) of all particles – light or heavy – is nearly the same. This means that the heavier particles must be moving more slowly than the lighter ones and that the attractive forces between the heavier particles must be exercising a greater influence on their behavior. The greater speed of light particles, however, tends to counteract the attractive forces between them, thus producing a slight deviation from ideal gas behavior. Thus, a heavier particle (molecule or atom) will deviate more widely from ideal gas behavior than a lighter particle. At low temperature, the average velocity of gas particles decreases and the intermolecular attraction becomes increasingly significant, causing the gas to have a smaller volume than would be predicted by the ideal gas law. {The preceding is given by Graham's law, where the rate of movement of a gas (*diffusion* or streaming through a fine hole – *effusion*) is inversely proportional to the square root of the molecular weight of the gas (see CHM 4.1.3)}

4.2 Liquid Phase (Intra- and Intermolecular Forces)

Liquids have the ability to mix with one another and with other phases to form solutions. The degree to which two liquids can mix is called their miscibility. Liquids have definite volume, but no definite shape. As we will discuss, molecules of liquids can be attracted to each other (*cohesion*) as they can be attracted to their surroundings (*adhesion*). The most striking properties of a liquid are its viscosity and surface tension (see CHM 4.2.1, 4.2.2). Liquids also distinguish themselves from gases in that they are relatively incompressible. The molecules of a liquid are also subject to forces strong enough to hold them together. These forces are intermolecular and they are weak attractive forces that is, they are effective over short distances only. Molecules like methane (CH_4) are non-polar and so they are held together by weak intermolecular forces also known as Van der Waal forces (these include forces that are dipole-dipole, dipole-induced dipole and London forces). Whereas, molecules like water have much stronger intermolecular attractive forces because of the hydrogen bonding amongst the molecules. Hence, the most important forces are:

1.   Dipole-dipole forces which depend on the orientation as well as on the distance between the molecules; they are inversely proportional to the fourth power of the distance. In addition to the forces between permanent dipoles, a dipolar molecule induces in a neighboring mol-

ecule an electron distribution that results in another attractive force, the dipole-induced dipole force, which is inversely proportional to the seventh power of the distance and which is relatively independent of orientation.

2. London forces (or Dispersive forces) are attractive forces acting between nonpolar molecules. They are due to the unsymmetrical instantaneous electron distribution which induces a dipole in neighboring molecules with a resultant attractive force. This instantaneous unsymmetrical distribution of electrons causes rapid polarization of the electrons and forma-

tion of short-lived dipoles. These dipoles then interact with neighboring molecules, inducing the formation of more dipoles. Dispersion forces are thus responsible for the liquefaction of noble gases to form liquids at low temperatures (and high pressures).

3. Hydrogen bonds occur whenever hydrogen is covalently bonded to an atom such as O, N or F that attract electrons strongly. Because of the differences in electronegativity between H and O or N or F, the electrons that constitute the covalent bond are closer to the O, N or F nucleus than to the H nucleus leaving

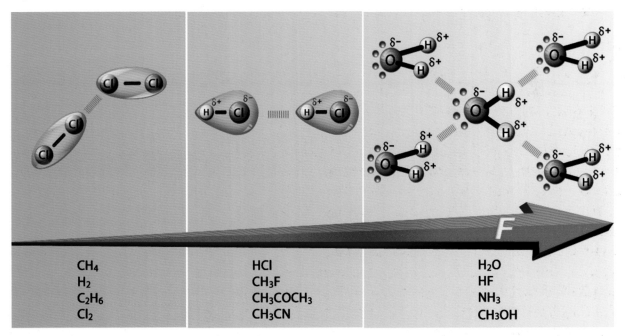

Table III.A.4.1: Van Der Waal's forces (weak) and hydrogen bonding (strong). London forces between Cl_2 molecules, dipole-dipole forces between HCl molecules and H-bonding between H_2O molecules. Note that a partial negative charge on an atom is indicated by δ^- (delta negative), while a partial positive charge is indicated by δ^+ (delta positive). Notice that one H_2O molecule can potentially form 4 H-bonds with surrounding molecules which is highly efficient. The preceding is one key reason that the boiling point of water is higher than that of ammonia, hydrogen fluoride or methanol.

the latter relatively unshielded. The unshielded proton is strongly attracted to the O, N or F atoms of neighboring molecules since these form the negative end of a strong dipole.

The slightly positive charge of the hydrogen atom will then be strongly attracted to the more electronegative atoms of nearby molecules. These forces are weaker than intramolecular bonds, but are much stronger than the other two types of intermolecular forces. Hydrogen bonding is a special case of dipole-dipole interaction. Hydrogen bonds are characterized by unusually strong interactions and high boiling points due to the vast amount of energy required (relative to other intermolecular forces) to break the hydrogen bonds. {Though the H-bonding atoms are often remembered by the mnemonic "Hydrogen is FON!", sulfur is also known to H-bond though far weaker than the more electronegative FON atoms.}

4.2.1 Viscosity

Viscosity is analogous to friction between moving solids. It may, therefore be viewed as the resistance to flow of layers of fluid or liquid past each other. This also means that viscosity, as in friction, results in dissipation of mechanical energy. As one layer flows over another, its motion is transmitted to the second layer and causes this layer to be set in motion. Since a mass m of the second layer is set in motion and some of the energy of the first layer is lost, there is a transfer of momentum between the layers.

The greater the transfer of this momentum from one layer to another, the more energy that is lost and the slower the layers move.

The viscosity (η) is the measure of the efficiency of transfer of this momentum. Therefore the higher the viscosity coefficient, the greater the transfer of momentum and loss of mechanical energy, and thus loss of velocity. The reverse situation holds for a low viscosity coefficient.

Consequently, a high viscosity coefficient substance flows slowly (e.g. molasses), and a low viscosity coefficient substance flows relatively fast (e.g. water). Note that the transfer of momentum to adjacent layers is in essence, the exertion of a force upon these layers to set them in motion.

4.2.2 Surface Tension

Molecules of a liquid exert attractive forces toward each other (cohesive forces), and exert attractive forces toward the surface they touch (adhesive forces). If a liquid is in a gravity free space without a surface, it will form a sphere (smallest area relative to volume).

If the liquid is lining an object, the liquid surface will contract (due to cohesive forces) to the lowest possible surface area. The forces between the molecules on this surface will create a membrane-like effect. Due to the contraction, a potential energy (PE) will present in the surface.

This PE is directly proportional to the surface area (A). An exact relation is formed as follows:

$$PE = \gamma A$$

$\gamma = surface\ tension = PE/A = joules/m^2$

An alternative formulation for the surface tension (γ) is:

$$\gamma = F/l$$

F = force of contraction of surface
l = length along surface

Because of the contraction, a small object which would ordinarily sink in the liquid may float on the surface membrane. For example, a small insect like a "water strider."

The liquid will rise or fall on a wall or in a capillary tube if the adhesive forces are greater than cohesive or vice versa (*see* Figure III.A.4.1b).

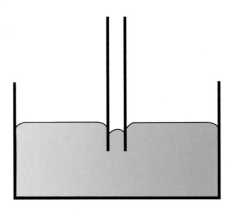

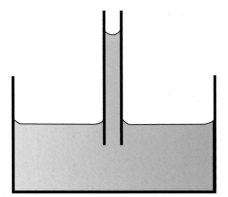

(a) cohesive > adhesive

(b) adhesive > cohesive

Figure III.A.4.1b: Effects of adhesive and cohesive forces. The distance the liquid rises or falls in the tube is directly proportional to the surface tension γ and inversely proportional to the liquid density and radius of the tube. Examples of 2 liquids consistent with the illustrations include: (a) mercury; (b) water.

4.3 Solid Phase

Solids have definite volume and shape and are incompressible under pressure. Intermolecular forces between molecules of molecular solids and electrostatic (i.e. coulombic or "opposite charges attract") interactive forces between ions of ionic solids are strong enough to hold them into a relatively rigid structure. A solid may be crystalline (ordered) or amorphous (disordered). A crystalline solid, such as table salt (NaCl) has a structure with an ordered geometric shape. Its atoms are arranged geometrically with a repeating pattern. It has a specific melting point. An amorphous solid, such as glass, has a molecular structure with no specific shape. It melts over a wide range of temperatures since the molecules require different amounts of energies to break bonds between them.

4.4 Phase Equilibria (Solids, Liquids and Gases)

4.4.1 Phase Changes

Elements and compounds can undergo transitions between the solid, liquid and gaseous states. They can exist in different phases and undergo phase changes which need not involve chemical reactions. Phase changes are reversible with an equilibrium existing between each of the phases. A phase is a homogeneous, physically distinct and mechanically separable part of a system. Each phase is separated from other phases by a physical boundary.

A few examples:

1. Ice/liquid water/water vapor (3 phases)

2. Any number of gases mix in all proportions and therefore constitute just one phase.

3. The system $CaCO_3(s) \rightarrow CaO(s) + CO_2(g)$ (2 phases, i.e. 2 solids: $CaCO_3$ and CaO and a gas: CO_2)

4. A saturated salt solution (3 phases: solution, undissolved salt, vapor)

An example of phase change is the vaporization of water into its vapor state. A system is considered homogeneous when it is uniform throughout its volume so that its properties are the same in all parts. This does not imply a single molecular species: a solution of sodium chloride is homogeneous provided its concentration is the same throughout.

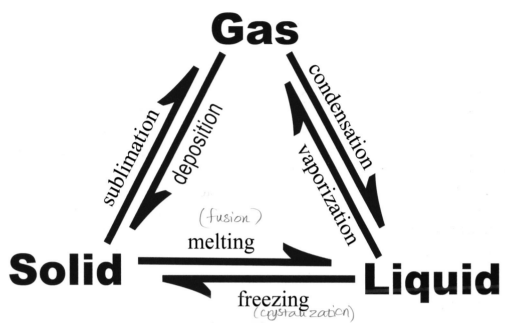

Figure III.A.4.2: Phase Changes

4.4.2 Freezing Point, Melting Point, Boiling Point

The conversion of a liquid to a gas is called <u>vaporization</u>. We can increase the rate of vaporization of a liquid by (i) increasing the temperature (ii) reducing the pressure, or (iii) both. Molecules escape from a liquid because, even though their average kinetic energy is constant, not all of them move at the same speed (*see Figure III.A.4.1*). A fast moving molecule can break away from the attraction of the others and pass into the vapor state. When a tight lid is placed on a vessel containing a liquid, the vapor molecules cannot escape and some revert back to the liquid state. The number of molecules leaving the liquid at any given time equals the number of molecules returning. Equilibrium is reached and the number of molecules in the fixed volume above the liquid remains constant. These molecules exert a constant pressure at a fixed temperature which is called the vapor pressure of the liquid. The vapor pressure is the partial pressure exerted by the gas molecules over the liquid formed by evaporation, when it is in equilibrium with the gas phase condensing back into the liquid phase. The vapor pressure of any liquid is dependent on the intermolecular forces that are present within the liquid and the temperature. Weak intermolecular forces result in volatile substances whereas strong intermolecular forces result in nonvolatile substances.

Boiling and evaporation are similar processes but they differ as follows: the vapor from a boiling liquid escapes with sufficient pressure to push back any other gas present, rather than diffusing through it. Vapor pressure increases as the temperature increases, as more molecules have sufficient energy to break the attraction between each other to escape into the gas phase. The boiling point is therefore the temperature at which the vapor pressure of the liquid equals to the opposing external pressure. Under a lower pressure, the boiling point is reached at a lower temperature. Increased intermolecular interactions (i.e. H_2O see CHM 4.2, alcohol see ORG 6.1, etc.) will decrease the vapor pressure thus raising the boiling point. Other factors being equal, as a molecule becomes heavier (increasing molecular weight), it becomes more difficult to push the molecule into the atmosphere thus the boiling point increases (i.e. alkanes see ORG 3.1.1).

The freezing point of a liquid is the temperature at which the vapor pressure of the solid equals the vapor pressure of the liquid. Increases in the prevailing atmospheric pressure decreases the melting point and increases the boiling point.

When a solid is heated, the kinetic energy of the components increases steadily. Finally, the kinetic energy becomes great enough to overcome the forces holding the components together and the solid changes to a liquid. For pure crystalline solids, there is a fixed temperature at which this transition from solid to liquid occurs. This temperature is called the <u>melting point</u>. Pure solids melt completely at one temperature. Impure solids begin to melt at one temperature but become completely liquid at a higher temperature.

4.4.3 Phase Diagrams

Figure III.A.4.3 shows the temperature of ice as heat is added. Temperature increases linearly with heat until the melting point is reached. At this point, the heat energy added does not change the temperature. Instead, it is used to break intermolecular bonds and convert ice into water. There is a mixture of both ice and water at the melting point. After all of the complete conversion of ice into water, the temperature rises again linearly with heat addition. At the boiling point, the heat added does not change the temperature because the energy is again used to break the intermolecular bonds. After complete conversion of water into gas, the temperature will rise linearly again with heat addition.

Thus, during a phase change, there is no change in temperature. The energy that is added into the system is being used to weaken/break intermolecular forces; in other words, there is an increase in the potential energy of molecules rather than an increase in the average kinetic energy of molecules. The amount of energy to change one mole of substance from solid to liquid or from liquid to gas is called the molar *heat of fusion* and the molar *heat of vaporization* (CHM 8.7) Each

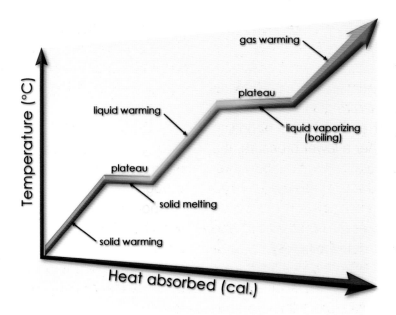

Figure III.A.4.3 Heating curve for H_2O

phase has its own specific heat. Enthalpy of vaporization is greater than that of fusion because more energy is required to break intermolecular bonds (from liquid phase to gas phase) than just to weaken intermolecular bonds (from solid phase to liquid phase).

The temperatures at which phase transitions occur are functions of the pressure of the system. The behavior of a given substance over a wide range of temperature and pressure can be summarized in a <u>phase diagram</u>, such as the one shown for the water system (Fig.III.A.4.4). The diagram is divided into three areas labeled **solid** (ice), **liquid** (water) and **vapor** in each of which only one phase exists. In these areas, *P* and *T* can be independently varied without a second phase appearing. These areas are bounded by curves AC, AD and AB. Line AB represents

sublimation/deposition (sublimation curve). Line AC represents evaporation/condensation (vaporization curve) and Line AD represents melting/freezing (fusion curve). At triple point A, all three phases are known to coexist. At any point on these curves, two phases are in equilibrium. Thus on AC, at a given T, the saturated vapor pressure of water has a fixed value. The boiling point of water (N) can be found on this curve, 100 °C at 760 mmHg pressure. The curve only extends as far as C, the <u>critical point</u>, where the vapor and liquid are indistinguishable. In general, the gas phase is found at high temperature and low pressure; the solid phase is found at low temperatures and high pressure; and the liquid phase is found at high temperatures and high pressure. The temperature at which a substance boils when the pressure is 1 atm is called the normal boiling point.

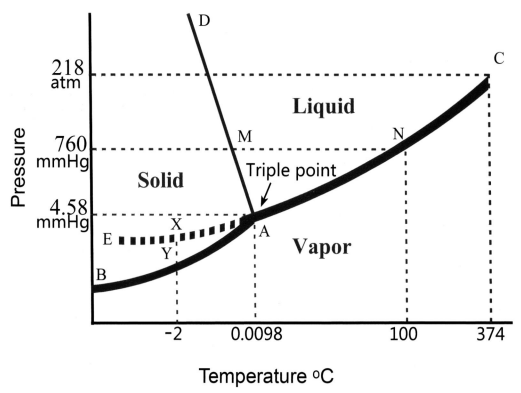

Figure III.A.4.4: Phase diagram for H_2O.

The extension of the curve CA to E represents the <u>metastable equilibrium</u> (*meta* = beyond) between supercooled water and its vapor. If the temperature is slightly raised at point X, a little of the liquid will vaporize until a new equilibrium is established at that higher temperature. Curve AB is the vapor pressure curve for ice. Its equilibria are of lower energy than those of AE and thus more stable.

The slope of line AD shows that an increase in P will lower the melting point of ice. This property is almost unique to water. Because of the negative slope of line AD, an isothermal increase in pressure will compress the solid (ice) into liquid (water). Thus H_2O is unique in that its liquid form is denser than its solid form. The high density of liquid water is due mainly to the cohesive nature of the hydrogen-bonded network of water molecules (see Table III.A.4.1 in CHM 4.2).

Most substances *increase* their melting points with increased pressure. Thus the line AD slants to the right for almost all substances. Point M represents the true melting point of ice, 0.0023 °C at 760 mmHg of pressure. (The 0 °C standard refers to the freezing point of water saturated with air at 760 mmHg). At point A, solid, liquid and vapor are in equilibrium. At this one temperature, ice and water have the same fixed vapor pressure. This is the <u>triple point</u>, 0.0098 °C at 4.58 mmHg pressure.

GOLD STANDARD WARM-UP EXERCISES

CHAPTER 4: Phases and Phase Equilibria

1) Under what conditions would the ideal gas equation be valid?

   A. Volume unknown, pressure high
   B. Average pressure, average volume
   C. Low pressure, high temperature
   D. Normal volume, low temperature

2) If a gas behaved ideally, which of the following would be expected on cooling the gas to 1 K?

   A. It would remain a gas.
   B. It would liquify.
   C. It would solidify.
   D. Cannot be determined from the information given.

3) Reaction I is usually carried out at atmospheric pressure. During the reaction, before equilibrium was reached, the mole fractions of SO_2 (g) and SO_3 (g) were 1/2 and 1/6 respectively. What was the partial pressure of O_2 (g)?

   $$1 - \left(\frac{1}{2} + \frac{1}{6}\right)$$
   $$Total\ n_i$$

   Reaction I

   $$2SO_2(g) + O_2(g) \leftrightarrow 2SO_3(g) \qquad \Delta H = -197 \text{ kJ mol}^{-1}$$

   A. 0.66 atm
   B. 0.16 atm
   C. 0.50 atm
   D. 0.33 atm

4) Assuming ideal conditions, how many liters of oxygen are required to react with 48 liters of ammonia in the reaction below?

   $$4NH_3(g) + 5O_2 \rightarrow 4NO(g) + 6H_2O(g)$$

   A. 48 L
   B. 60 L
   C. 72 L
   D. The answer cannot be determined without knowing the precise densities of the gases.

5) Which of the following is a correct representation of the phase diagram for carbon dioxide?

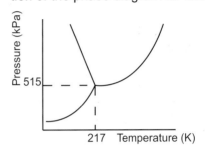

A.

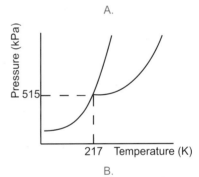

B.

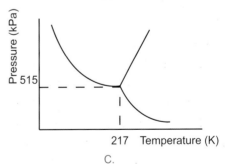

C.

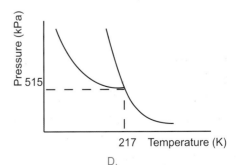

D.

6) Consider the diagram below. The diagram illustrates the effect on the temperature of Substance T–34 undergoing simple transitions from solid to liquid to gas states as heat is added. Which segment of the graph represents fusion of Substance T–34?

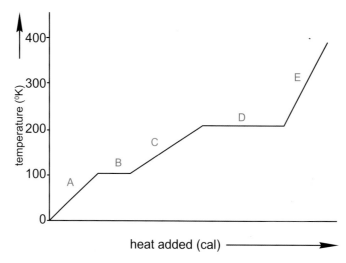

heat added (cal) ⟶

7) Why does "solid" water (ice) float on "liquid" water?

  A. Because it is less dense.
  B. Because it occupies less volume.
  C. Because it exists at lower temperatures.
  D. Because it is a solid.

8) Two identical evacuated flasks are filled with different gases to the same pressure and temperature. The first is filled with hydrogen and the second with propane. The molecular weight of propane is 44 g/mol. Compared with the first flask, the flask filled with propane weighs:

  A. 11 times more.
  B. 22 times more.
  C. the same.
  D. 44 times more.

9) A soccer ball with initial pressure P and initial volume V is inflated with air until the pressure becomes 2P and the volume becomes 1.1V. The temperature being kept constant, the weight of air in the ball has increased by a factor of:

  A. 2.2
  B. 1.1
  C. 1.0
  D. 2.0

10) The density of an unknown gas is determined to be 1.97 g/L at STP. If the gas is known to be one of the following substances, which is most likely?

  A. C_3H_8
  B. HCHO
  C. C_2H_2
  D. CH_3CH_3

11) If the anesthetic mixture is inspired at the rate of 1000 mL/min, what mass of halothane ($CHClBrCF_3$, MW = 197.4) is inspired in one minute if the partial pressure of halothane is 7.6 torr and the temperature is 21 °C? {R = 0.0821 L-atm/K-mole}

  A. 0.08 g
  B. 0.80 g
  C. 1.80 g
  D. 3.36 g

12) A 50–50 (by weight) mixture of He and H_2 exerts a pressure of 600 torr. Approximately what is the partial pressure due to H_2?

  A. 200 torr
  B. 300 torr
  C. 400 torr
  D. 450 torr

Graham's law.

Diffusion / Effusion.

$$\text{rate} = \frac{1}{\sqrt{M}}$$

molecular mass

Maxwell Distribution Plot

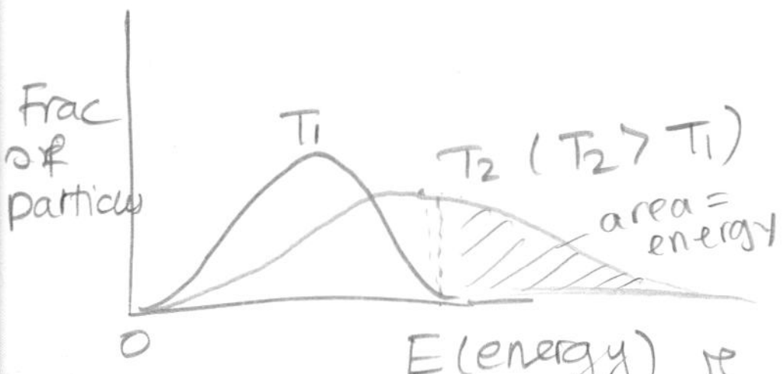

- If increasing T. curve

Bell curve DOES NOT shift to the right.

GS ANSWER KEY

CHAPTER 4

Cross-Reference

1.	C	CHM 4.1.10 (4.1.8)
2.	A	CHM 4.1.2
3.	D	CHM 4.1.9
4.	B	CHM 4.1.6, 4.1.7, 4.1.8, 4.1.9
5.	B	CHM 4.3.3
6.	B	CHM 4.3, 8.7

Cross-Reference

7.	A	CHM 4
8.	B	CHM 4.1.8
9.	A	CHM 4.1.8
10.	A	CHM 4.1.1
11.	A	CHM 4.1.6
12.	C	CHM 4.1.9

* Explanations can be found at the back of the book.

Go online to DAT-prep.com for additional chapter review Q&A and forum.

Gases

P (pressure) $= Nm^{-2} =$ pascal (Pa) unit

1 atm $= 101.3$ KPal $= 760$ torr $= 760$ mmHg

$T: °C \qquad X°C = (X + 273)K$
$\underset{\text{kelvin}}{}$

STP – standard temperature & pressure

for gases: $\left\{ \begin{array}{c} 0°C \\ 273K \end{array} \right. \qquad$ 1 atm $\qquad$ for liquids: $T = 25°$ at STP

PP (partial pressure)

Dalton's law: $\Sigma PP = P_{Tot}$

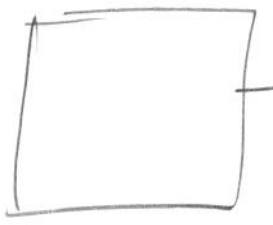

$O_2 + N_2 \qquad \Rightarrow$ Total pressure: 3 atm

1 atm $\qquad (2+1=3)$

pressure of 2 atm

mole fraction of $O_2 = \dfrac{2}{3}$ — for O_2 — total

$N_2 = \dfrac{1}{3}$

＊ Each gas acts indepanda

Avogadro's Law

at STP – $N_A = 6.022 \times 10^{23}$ #of particles (atoms or molecules) / mole

$V = 22.4 L$

(if $V = 44.8 L$

we are dealing with 2 moles)

or if $V = 11.2$

we are dealing with ½ mole)

Equation of State

$$PV = nRT$$
$\qquad (0.08 \text{ (L/atm)})$

$\dfrac{PV}{T} = nR \qquad \Rightarrow \dfrac{P_1 V_1}{T_1} = \dfrac{P_2 V_2}{T_2}$

NOT changing moles
but only P and V or T.

$PV = \dfrac{m}{MW} RT \quad \Rightarrow \quad P = \dfrac{dRT}{MW}$

$\overset{\text{mass}}{}$

$\underset{\substack{\text{molecular} \\ \text{weight}}}{\text{g/mol}} \qquad \underset{\text{density}}{}$

SOLUTION CHEMISTRY

Chapter 5

Memorize	Understand	Importance
Define saturated, supersatured, nonvolatile Common anions and cations in solution Units of concentration Define electrolytes with examples	* Colligative properties, Raoult's law * Phase diagram change due to colligative properties * Bp elevation, fp depression * Osmotic pressure equation * Solubility product, common-ion effect	2 to 4 out of the 30 Gen CHM DAT questions are based on content in this chapter (in our estimation). * Note that between 50% and 85% of the questions in DAT General Chemistry are based on content from 6 chapters: 1, 2, 4, 5, 6 and 9.

DAT-Prep.com

Introduction ▮▮▮

A solution is a homogeneous mixture composed of two or more substances. For example, a solute (salt) dissolved in a solvent (water) making a solution (salt water). In addition, solutions can involve liquids in liquids (i.e. ethanol in water), gases in liquids (i.e. oxygen in water), gases in gases (i.e. nitrogen in air) or even solids in solids (i.e. alloys). Two substances are immiscible if they can't mix to make a solution. Solutions can be distinguished from non-homogeneous mixtures like colloids and suspensions (the differences were discussed in CHM 1.7).

Additional Resources

Free Online Forum

Video: Online or DVD

Flashcards

5.1 Solutions and Colligative Properties

Water (H_2O) is a universal solvent known as a pure substance or a one component system. Pure substances are often mixed together to form solutions. A <u>solution</u> is a sample of matter that is homogeneous but, unlike a pure substance, the composition of a solution can vary within relatively wide limits. Ethanol and water are each pure substances and each have a fixed composition, C_2H_5OH and H_2O, but mixtures of the two can vary continuously in composition from almost 100% ethanol to almost 100% water. Solutions of sucrose in water, however, are limited to a maximum percentage of sucrose - <u>the solubility</u> - which is 67% at 20°C, thus the solution is saturated. If the solution is heated, a higher concentration of sucrose can be achieved (i.e. 70%). Slowly cooling down to 20°C creates a supersaturated solution which may precipitate with any perturbation.

Intermolecular forces (see CHM 4.2) amongst various other parameters may either promote or may prevent the formation of a solution. The formation of solutions primarily involves the breaking of intermolecular forces between solutes and between solvents and the subsequent reformation of new intermolecular interactions amongst the solute and solvent. The initial step in solution formation (i.e. breakage of intermolecular forces amongst the solutes and solvent separately) is endothermic and the second step (i.e. reformation of intermolecular interactions between solute-solvent) is exothermic. If an overall reaction in solution formation is exothermic, the new intermolecular bonds between solute and solvent are more stable and a solution is formed. {Note: "endothermic" - absorbs heat, "exothermic" - releases heat; "enthalpy" is a measure of the total energy; see CHM chapters 7 and 8 for details}

In the energetic requirements of solution formation, the formation of a solution may result in either an increase or a decrease in the enthalpy of solution dependant on the magnitude of interactions between the solute and solvent. Hence, energy changes do occur when a solution forms (i.e exothermic or endothermic). An increase in enthalpy, a positive heat of solution, results in more energy in a system i.e. less stable and weaker bonds. Whereas a decrease in enthalpy, a negative heat of solution, results in less energy in a system i.e. more stable and stronger bonds and thus the respective drive to the formation of a solution.

Lastly, the formation of a solution always results in an increase in entropy or disorder due to the insidious tendency for energy to disperse.

Generally the component of a <u>solution</u> that is stable in the same phase as the solution is called the solvent. If two components of a solution are in the same phase, the component present in the larger amount is called the <u>solvent</u> and the other is called the <u>solute</u>. Many properties of solutions are dependent only on the relative number of molecules (or ions) of the solute and of the solvent. Properties that depend **only** on the number of particles present and not the kind of particles are called colligative properties. For all <u>colligative</u>

properties, a factor known as the Van't Hoff factor (i) is essentially required and defined as, the ratio of moles of particles or ions in a solution to the moles of all undissociated formula units (or molecules) within a solution. The factor (i) is therefore incorporated as a multiple of all the colligative properties equations, respectively (see below). Thus, for non-ionic solutions, the factor (i) is essentially equal to 1 as the particles are undissociated such as for sugar solutions. However, for ionic solutions, the factor (i) is dependent on the number of ions dissociated in solution (i.e., $NaCl = 2$, $CaCl_2 = 3$, etc.). Hence, the most important colligative properties can be found in the following sections.

5.1.1 Vapor-Pressure Lowering (Raoult's Law)

The vapor pressure of the components of an ideal solution behaves as follows:

$$p_i = X_i (p_i)_{pure}$$

where p_i = vapor pressure of component i in equilibrium with the solution

$(p_i)_{pure}$ = vapor pressure of pure component i at the same T

X_i = mole fraction of component i in the liquid.

Thus the vapor pressure of any component of a mixture is lowered by the presence of the other components. Experimentally, it can be observed that when dissolving a solute which cannot evaporate (= *nonvolatile*) into a solvent, the vapor pressure of the resulting solution is lower than that of the pure solvent. The extent to which the vapor pressure is lowered is determined by the mole fraction of the solvent in solution ($X_{solvent}$):

$$P = P°X_{solvent}$$

where P = vapor pressure of solution

$P°$ = vapor pressure of pure solvent (at the same temperature as P).

When rearranged this way, the vapor pressure of a solution is quantified by Raoult's law which states that the lowering of the vapor pressure of the solvent is proportional to the mole fraction of solvent and independent of the chemical nature of the solute.

Hence, to show by how much a solution's vapor pressure is lowered by a solute, we can therefore define the vapor pressure lowering (ΔP) by the following equation; $\Delta P = X_{solute} P°_{solvent}$. Where, $\Delta P = P°_{solvent} - P_{solution}$ and rearranging the differences between the solvent and solution vapor pressures and substituting the solvent mole fraction ($X_{solvent}$) with the solute mole fraction as $X_{solvent} = 1 - X_{solute}$, results in Raoult's law which indicates that the lowering of the vapor pressure is directly proportional to the solute mole fraction as stated previously.

5.1.2 Boiling-Point Elevation and Freezing-Point Depression

When the vapor-pressure curve of a dilute solution and the vapor-pressure curve of the pure solvent are plotted on a phase diagram (see Figure III.A.5.1), it can be seen that a vapor pressure lowering of a solution occurs at all temperatures and that the freezing point and boiling point of a solution must therefore be different from those of the pure liquid.

The freezing point of a pure solvent (water) is lowered or depressed with the addition of another substance; meaning that a solution (solvent + solute) has a lower freezing point than a pure solvent, and this phenomenon is called a "freezing point depression". Alternatively, the boiling point of a pure solvent (water) is elevated when another substance is added; meaning that a solution

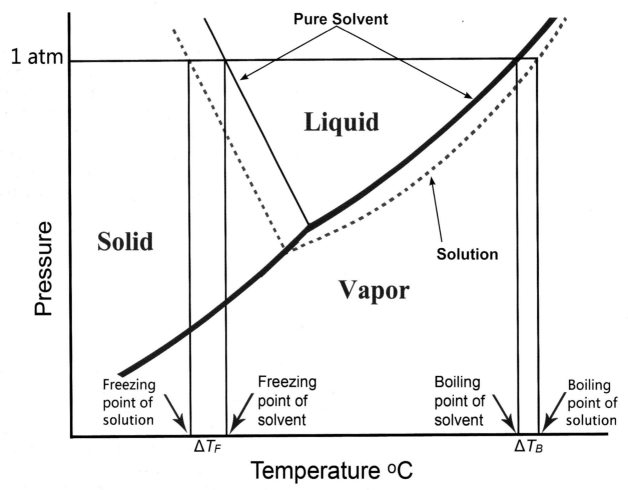

Figure III.A.5.1: Phase diagram of water demonstrating the effect of the addition of a solute.

has a higher boiling point than a pure solvent, and this phenomenon is called "boiling point elevation". The boiling point is therefore higher for the solution than for the pure liquid and the freezing point is lower for the solution than for the pure liquid. Since the decrease in vapor pressure is proportional to the mole fraction (see CHM 5.3.1) of solute, the boiling point elevation (ΔT_B) is also proportional to the mole fraction of solute and:

$$\Delta T_B = i\, K_B{}' X_B = i\, K_B m$$

where $K_B{}'$ = boiling point elevation constant for the solvent

X_B = mole fraction of solute

m = *molality* (moles solute per kilogram of solvent; CHM 5.3.1)

i = Van't Hoff factor

K_B is related to $K_B{}'$ through a change of units.

Similarly, for the freezing point depression (ΔT_F):

$$\Delta T_F = -i\, K_F{}' X_B = -i\, K_F m$$

where $K_F{}'$ = freezing point depression constant for the solvent.

If K_F or K_B is known, it is then possible to determine the molality of a dilute solution simply by measuring the freezing point or the boiling point. These constants can be determined by measuring the freezing point and boiling point of a solution of known molality. If the mass concentration of a solute (in kg solute per kg of solvent) is known and the molality is determined from the freezing point of the solution, the mass of 1 mole of solute can be calculated.

It is important to recall that for a strong electrolyte solution such as NaCl which dissociates to positive and negative ions, the right hand side of the equation is multiplied by the Van't Hoff factor (i) equal to the number of ionic species generated per mole of solute. For NaCl n = 2 but for $MgCl_2$ n = 3. {Remember: colligative properties depend on the **number** of particles present}

5.1.3 Osmotic Pressure

The osmotic pressure (Π) of a solution describes the equilibrium distribution of solvent across semipermeable membranes separated by two compartments. When a solvent and solution are separated by a membrane permeable only to molecules of solvent (a <u>semipermeable</u> membrane), the solvent spontaneously migrates into the solution. The semipermeable membrane allows the solvent to pass but not the solute. Since pure solute cannot pass through the semipermeable membrane into the pure solvent side to equalize the concentrations, the pure solvent begins to then move into the solution side containing the solute. As it does so, the solution level rises and the pressure increases. Eventually a balance is achieved and the increased pressure difference on the solution side is the osmotic pressure. The solvent therefore migrates into the solution across the membrane until a sufficient hydrostatic pressure develops to prevent further migration of solvent. The pressure required to prevent migration of the solvent is therefore the osmotic pressure of the solution and is equal to:

$$\Pi = i\,MRT$$

where R = gas constant per mole
     T = temperature in degrees K and
     M = concentration of solute (mole/liter)
     i = Van't Hoff factor

Note: molarity (M) is used in the osmotic pressure formulation in place of molality as is used for the other respective colligative properties as molarity is temperature dependent and molality is not temperature dependent.

Osmosis and osmotic pressure are also discussed in the context of biology in the following sections: BIO 1.1.1 and 7.5.2.

5.2 Ions in Solution

An important area of solution chemistry involves aqueous solutions. Water has a particular property that causes many substances to split apart into charged species, that is, to dissociate and form <u>ions</u>. Ions that are positively charged are called <u>cations</u> and negatively charged ions are called <u>anions</u>. {Mnemonic: anions <u>a</u>re <u>n</u>egative <u>ions</u>} As a rule, highly charged species (i.e. $AlPO_4$, Al^{3+}/PO_4^{3-}) have a greater force of attraction thus are much less soluble in water than species with little charge (i.e. NaCl, Na^+/Cl^-). The word "aqueous" simply means containing or dissolved in water. All the following ions can form in water.

Common Anions					
F^-	Fluoride	OH^-	Hydroxide	ClO^-	Hypochlorite
Cl^-	Chloride	NO_3^-	Nitrate	ClO_2^-	Chlorite
Br^-	Bromide	NO_2^-	Nitrite	ClO_3^-	Chlorate
I^-	Iodide	CO_3^{2-}	Carbonate	ClO_4^-	Perchlorate
O^{2-}	Oxide	SO_4^{2-}	Sulfate	SO_3^{2-}	Sulfite
S^{2-}	Sulfide	PO_4^{3-}	Phosphate	CN^-	Cyanide
N^{3-}	Nitride	$CH_3CO_2^-$	Acetate	MnO_4^-	Permanganate

Common Cations			
Na^+	Sodium	H^+	Hydrogen
Li^+	Lithium	Ca^{2+}	Calcium
K^+	Potassium	Mg^{2+}	Magnesium
NH_4^+	Ammonium	Fe^{2+}	Iron (II)
H_3O^+	Hydronium	Fe^{3+}	Iron (III)

Table III.A.5.1: Common Anions and Cations.

The DAT does not normally ask Inorganic Chemistry nomenclature (= *naming*) questions but it may be useful to know the International Union of Pure and Applied Chemistry (IUPAC) standard suffixes: (1) Single atom anions are named with an *-ide suffix* (i.e. fluoride); (2) Oxyanions (*polyatomic* or "many atom" anions containing oxygen) are named with *-ite* or *-ate*, for a lesser or greater quantity of oxygen. For example, NO_2^- is nitrite, while NO_3^- is nitrate. The hypo- and per- prefixes can also indicate less oxygen and more oxygen, respectively (see hypochlorite and perchlorate among the Common Anions in Table III.A.5.1). (3) -ium is a very common ending of atoms in the periodic table (CHM 2.3) and it is also common among cations; (4) Compounds with cations: The name of the compound is simply the cation's name (usually the same as the element's), followed by the anion. For example, NaCl is *sodium chloride* and Ca_3N_2 is *calcium nitride*.

5.3 Solubility

The solubility of any substance is generally defined as the amount of the substance (solute) known to dissolve into a particular amount of solvent at a given temperature. The solubility of a solute into a solvent is dependent on the entropy change of solubilization as well as the types of intermolecular forces involved (see CHM 4.2 and 5.1). Solvation or dissolution is the process of interaction between solute and solvent molecules. This process occurs when the intermolecular forces between solute and solvent are stronger than those between solute particles themselves. Generally, ionic and polar solutes are soluble in polar solvents and nonpolar solutes are soluble in nonpolar solvents. Consequently, the expression "like dissolves like" is often used for predicting solubility.

In the following section, the definitions of the various solution concentration units are given with examples.

5.3.1 Units of Concentration

There are a number of ways in which solution concentrations may be expressed.

Molarity (*M*): A one-molar solution is defined as one mole of substance in each liter of solution: M = moles of solute/liter of solution (solution = solute + solvent).

For example: If 55.0g of $CaCl_2$ is mixed with water to make 500.0 ml (0.5 L) of solution, what is the molarity (*M*) of the solution?

$$55.0g \text{ of } CaCl_2 = 55.0 \text{ g}/110.0 \text{ g/mol}$$
$$= 0.500 \text{ mol of } CaCl_2$$

Therefore, the Molarity = 0.500 mol $CaCl_2$/0.5L = 1.00 mol $CaCl_2$/L solution

Normality (*N*): A one-normal solution contains one equivalent per liter. An equivalent is a mole multiplied by the number of reacting units for each molecule or atom; the equivalent weight is the formula weight divided by the number of reacting units.

$$\# \text{ of Equiv.} = \text{mass (in g)/eq. wt. (in g/equiv.)}$$
$$= \text{Normality (in equiv./liter)}$$
$$\times \text{Volume (in liters)}$$

For example, sulfuric acid, H_2SO_4, has two reacting units of protons, that is, there are two equivalents of protons in each mole. Thus:

$$\text{eq. wt.} = 98.08 \text{ g/mole}/2 \text{ equiv./mole}$$
$$= 49.04 \text{ g/equiv.}$$

and the normality of a sulfuric acid solution is twice its molarity. Generally speaking:

$$N = n\,M$$

where *N* is the normality,
  M the molarity,
  n the number of equivalents per unit formula.

Thus for 1.2 M H_2SO_4:

1.2 moles/L × 2 eq/mole = 2.4 eq/L = 2.4 N.

Molality (*m*): A one-molal solution contains one mole/1000g of solvent.

m = moles of solute/kg of solvent.

For example: If 20.0g of NaOH is mixed into 500.0g (0.50 kg) of water, what is the molality of the solution?

$$20.0g \text{ of NaOH} = 20.0 \text{ g}/40.0 \text{ g/mol}$$
$$= 0.500 \text{ mol of NaOH}$$

Therefore, the Molality = 0.500 mol NaOH/0.50 kg water = 1.0 mol NaOH/kg water

Molal concentrations are not temperature-dependent as molar and normal concentrations are (since the solvent volume is temperature-dependent).

Density (ρ): Mass per unit volume at the specified temperature, usually g/ml or g/cm^3 at 20°C.

Osmole (*Osm*): The number of moles of particles (molecules or ions) that contribute to the osmotic pressure of a solution.

Osmolarity: A one-osmolar solution is defined as one osmole in each liter of solution. Osmolarity is measured in osmoles/liter of solution (Osm/L).

For example, a 0.001 M solution of sodium chloride has an osmolarity of 0.002 Osm/L (twice the molarity), because each NaCl molecule ionizes in water to form two ions (Na^+ and Cl^-) that both contribute to the osmotic pressure.

Osmolality: A one-osmolal solution is defined as one osmole in each kilogram of solution. Osmolality is measured in osmoles/kilogram of solution (Osm/kg).

For example, the osmolality of a 0.01 molal solution of Na_2SO_4 is 0.03 Osm/kg because each molecule of Na_2SO_4 ionizes in water to give three ions (2 Na^+ and 1 SO_4^{2-}) that contribute to the osmotic pressure.

Mole Fraction: Is expressed as a mole ratio as the amount of solute (in moles) divided by the total amount of solvent and solute (in moles).

For example: If 110.0g of $CaCl_2$ is mixed with 72.0g water, what are the mole fractions of the two components?

$$72.0g \text{ of } H_2O = 72.0g/18.0 \text{ g/mol}$$
$$= 4 \text{ mol } H_2O$$

$$110.0g \text{ of } CaCl_2 = 110.0g/110 \text{ g/mol}$$
$$= 1 \text{ mol } CaCl_2$$

$$\text{Total mol} = 4 \text{ mol } H_2O + 1 \text{ mol } CaCl_2$$
$$= 5 \text{ mol } (H_2O \text{ and } CaCl_2)$$

Therefore,
X($CaCl_2$) = 1mol $CaCl_2$/5 mol $CaCl_2$ + H_2O = 0.2
and
X(water) = 4 mol H_2O/5 mol H_2O + $CaCl_2$ = 0.8

Dilution: When solvent is added to a solution containing a certain concentration of solute it becomes diluted to produce a solution of a lower solute concentration. The equation representing this is:

$$M_iV_i = M_fV_f$$

Where M = molarity and
V = volume with the initial (i) and final (f) concentrations being measured.

For example: How many ml of a 10.0 mol/L NaOH solution is needed to prepare 500 ml of a 2.00 mol/L NaOH solution?

Given: $M_iV_i = M_fV_f$, where M_i = 10.0 mol/L, M_f = 2.00 mol/L and V_f = 500 ml. Therefore, rearranging the equation gives $V_i = M_f \times V_f/Mi$ and so V_i = (2.00 mol/L)(0.5 L)/(10.0 moL) = 100 mL.

5.3.2 Solubility Product Constant, the Equilibrium Expression

Any solute that dissolves in water to give a solution that contains ions, and thus can conduct electricity, is an *electrolyte*. The solid (s) that dissociates into separate ions surrounded by water is <u>hydrated</u>, thus the ions are aqueous (*aq*).

If dissociation is extensive and irreversible, we have a <u>strong</u> electrolyte:

$$NaCl\ (s) \rightarrow Na^+\ (aq) + Cl^-\ (aq)$$

If dissociation is incomplete and reversible, we have a <u>weak</u> electrolyte:

$$CH_3COOH\ (aq) \rightleftharpoons CH_3COO^-\ (aq) + H^+\ (aq)$$

If dissociation does not occur, we have a nonelectrolyte:

$C_6H_{12}O_6$ (aq) or glucose sugar does NOT dissociate.

<u>Strong electrolytes</u>: salts (NaCl), strong acids (HCl), strong bases (NaOH).

<u>Weak electrolytes</u>: weak acids (CH_3COOH), weak bases (NH_3), complexes ($Fe[CN]_6$), tap water, certain soluble organic compounds, highly charged species (CHM 5.2; $AlPO_4$, $BaSO_4$, exception: AgCl as it is a precipitate in aqueous solutions).

<u>Nonelectrolytes</u>: deionized water, soluble organic compounds (sugars).

The solubility of a solute substance is the maximum amount of solute that can be dissolved in an appropriate solvent at a particular temperature. It can be expressed in units of concentration such as molarity, molality and so on (see CHM 5.3.1). When a maximum amount of solute has been dissolved, the solution is in equilibrium and is said to be saturated. As temperature increases, the solubility of most salts generally increases. However, it is the opposite for gases, as the solubility of gases is known to generally decrease as temperature increases.

When substances have limited solubility and their solubility is exceeded, the ions of the dissolved portion exist in equilibrium with the solid material. When a compound is referred to as insoluble, it is not completely insoluble, but is slightly soluble.

For example, if solid AgCl is added to water, a small portion will dissolve:

$$AgCl\ (s) \rightleftharpoons Ag^+\ (aq) + Cl^-\ (aq)$$

The precipitate will have a definite solubility (i.e. a definite amount in g/liter) or molar solubility (in moles/ liter) that will dissolve at a given temperature.

An overall equilibrium constant can be written for the preceding equilibrium, called the <u>solubility product</u>, K_{sp}, given by the following equilibrium expression:

$$K_{sp} = [Ag^+][Cl^-]$$

The preceding relationship holds regardless of the presence of any undissociated intermediate. In general, each concentration must be raised to the power of that ion's coefficient in the dissolving equation (in our example = 1). A different example would be Ag_2S which would have the following solubility product expression: $K_{sp}= [Ag^+]^2[S^{2-}]$. The calculation of molar solubility s in mol/L for AgCl would simply be: $K_{sp} = [s][s] = s^2$. On the other hand, the expression for Ag_2S would become: $K_{sp} = [2s]^2[s] = 4s^3$.

Knowing K_{sp} at a specified temperature, the molar solubility of compounds can be calculated under various conditions. The amount of slightly soluble salt that dissolves does not depend on the amount of the solid in equilibrium with the solution, as long as there is enough to saturate the solution. Rather, it depends on the volume of solvent. {Note: a low K_{sp} value means little product therefore low solubility and vice-versa}.

The following are examples of problems on solubility product constant and solubility calculations given one or the other.

Another example: The molar solubility of $PbCl_2$ in an aqueous solution is 0.0159 M. What is the K_{sp} for $PbCl_2$?

$$PbCl_2(s) \rightleftharpoons Pb^{2+} (aq) + 2Cl^-(aq)$$
$$K_{sp} = [Pb^{2+}][Cl^-]^2$$

For every mol of $PbCl_2$ that dissociates, one mol of Pb^{2+} and two mol of Cl^- are produced. Since the molar solubility is 0.0159M, $[Pb^{2+}] = 0.0159M$ and $[Cl^-] = 0.0159 \times 2 = 0.0318M$

Therefore,
$$K_{sp} = [0.0159][0.0318]^2 = 1.61 \times 10^{-5}$$

Another example: What are the concentrations of each of the ions in a saturated solution of Ag_2CrO_4 given that solubility product constant K_{sp} is 1.1×10^{-12}?

$$Ag_2CrO_4(s) \rightleftharpoons 2Ag^+ (aq) + CrO_4^{2-} (aq)$$
$$K_{sp} = [Ag^+]^2 [CrO_4^{2-}]$$

For every Ag_2CrO_4 that dissociates, two mol of Ag^+ ion and one mol of CrO_4^{2-} ion are produced.

Let x = concentration of CrO_4^{2-}, then 2x = concentration of Ag^+

Therefore,
$$K_{sp} = [2x]^2 [x]$$
$$1.1 \times 10^{-12} = [2x]^2 [x]$$
solving for x gives; $x = 6.50 \times 10^{-5}$ M

so,
$$[Ag^+] = 1.3 \times 10^{-4} \text{ M and}$$
$$[CrO_4^{2-}] = 6.5 \times 10^{-5} \text{ M}$$

5.3.3 Common-ion Effect on Solubility

If there is an excess of one ion over the other, the concentration of the other is suppressed. This is called the common ion effect. The solubility of the precipitate is decreased and the concentration can still be calculated from the K_{sp}.

For example, Cl^- ion can be precipitated out of a solution of AgCl by adding a slight excess of $AgNO_3$. If a stoichiometric amount of $AgNO_3$ is added, $[Ag^+] = [Cl^-]$. If excess $AgNO_3$ is added, $[Ag^+] > [Cl^-]$ but K_{sp} remains constant. Therefore, $[Cl^-]$ decreases if $[Ag^+]$ is increased. Because the K_{sp} product always holds, precipitation will not take place unless the product of $[Ag^+]$ and $[Cl^-]$ exceeds the K_{sp}. If the product is just equal to K_{sp}, all the Ag^+ and Cl^- ions would remain in solution. Thus, the solubility of an ionic compound in solution containing a common ion is decreased in comparison to the same compound's solubility in water. As another example, the solubility of CaF_2 in water at 25°C would be much larger in comparison to the solubility of the same CaF_2 compound in a solution containing a common ion such as NaF. This decrease in solubility of CaF_2 in a solution containing NaF would be due to the common fluoride (F^-) ion effect on the solubility of CaF_2.

5.3.4 Solubility Product Constant (K_{sp}) vs. Reaction Quotient (Q_{sp})

Solubility product constants are used to describe saturated solutions of ionic compounds of relatively low solubility. A saturated solution is in a state of dynamic equilibrium described by the equilibrium constant (K_{sp}).

$$M_xA_y(s) \leftrightarrow x\ M^{y+}(aq) + y\ A^{x-}(aq)$$

The solubility product constant $K_{sp} = [M^{y+}]^x [A^{x-}]^y$ in a solution at equilibrium (saturated solution). Note that "M" is meant to symbolize the metal and "A" represents the anion.

A reaction quotient is defined by the same formula: $Q_{sp} = [M^{y+}]^x [A^{x-}]^y$ in a solution at any point, not just equilibrium.

K_{sp} therefore represents the ion product at equilibrium while Q_{sp} represents the ion product at any point, not just at equilibrium; and in fact, equilibrium is just a special case of the reaction coefficient as we will see below:

If $Q_{sp} < K_{sp}$, the solution is unsaturated and no precipitate will form.

If $Q_{sp} = K_{sp}$, the solution is saturated and at equilibrium.

If $Q_{sp} > K_{sp}$, the solution is supersaturated and unstable. A solid salt will precipitate until ion product once again equals to K_{sp}.

5.3.5 Solubility Rules

The chemistry of aqueous solutions is such that solubility rules can be established:

1. All salts of alkali metals are soluble.

2. All salts of the ammonium ion are soluble.

3. All chlorides, bromides and iodides are water soluble, with the exception of Ag^+, Pb^{2+}, and Hg_2^{2+}.

4. All salts of the sulfate ion (SO_4^{2-}) are water soluble with the exception of Ca^{2+}, Sr^{2+}, Ba^{2+}, and Pb^{2+}.

5. All metal oxides are insoluble with the exception of the alkali metals and CaO, SrO and BaO.

6. All hydroxides are insoluble with the exception of the alkali metals and Ca^{2+}, Sr^{2+}, Ba^{2+}

7. All carbonates (CO_3^{2-}), phosphates (PO_4^{3-}), sulfides (S^{2-}) and sulfites (SO_3^{2-}) are insoluble, with the exception of the alkali metals and ammonium.

GOLD STANDARD WARM-UP EXERCISES
CHAPTER 5: Solution Chemistry

1) Consider the diagram below. At constant temperature, what is the effect of an increase in pressure on a liquid–gas equilibrium mixture?

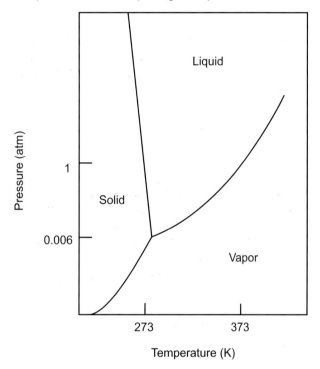

Temperature (K)

A. Change in the slope of the solid–liquid equilibrium
B. Increase in amount of vapor present
C. Increase in amount of solid present
D. Increase in amount of liquid present

2) What was the concentration of sodium sulfate in solution if the sodium ion concentration happens to be 0.02 M?

A. 0.02 M
B. 0.01 M
C. 0.04 M
D. 0.03 M

3) Two moles of sodium chloride, magnesium chloride and aluminium chloride were added to one liter of water in different beakers. Which solution will have the greatest osmolarity assuming that all of the salts are soluble in water?

A. All the solutions will have the same osmolarity.
B. The sodium chloride solution.
C. The magnesium chloride solution.
D. The aluminium chloride solution.

4) The molarity of a dilute solution is approximately equal to its molality when which of the following is true?

A. Under any circumstance
B. When the volume of the solvent in cm^{-3} is equal to its mass in grams
C. When the temperature of the solute is 300 K (i.e. room temperature)
D. When the number of moles of solute in solution is less than one

5) A solution of the sparingly soluble salt $SrCO_3$ in water boils at a higher temperature than pure water. Why is this?

A. $SrCO_3$ increases the density of water.
B. $SrCO_3$ decreases the vapor pressure of the water.
C. $SrCO_3$ has a low solubility in water.
D. $SrCO_3$ decreases the surface tension of the water.

6) What do you expect to happen to the melting point of solid water (ice) if an increased external pressure is applied to the system?

A. The melting point would increase.
B. The melting point would decrease.
C. The melting point would remain at the same value.
D. The direction of change in the value of the

melting point depends on the magnitude of the applied pressure.

7) What is the K_{sp} expression for PbS?

A. $[Pb^{2+}]/[S^{2-}]$
B. $[Pb^{2+}]^2/[S^{2-}]$
C. $[Pb^{2+}][S^{2-}]$
D. $[Pb^{2+}]^2[S^{2-}]$

8) The K_{sp} expression for Bi_2S_3 is:

A. $[Bi_2^{3+}][S_3^{2-}]$
B. $[Bi^{3+}][S^{2-}]$
C. $[Bi^{3+}]^2[S^{2-}]^3$
D. $[2Bi^{3+}]^3[3S^{2-}]^2$

9) Given the solubility of $MgCO_3$ (1.30×10^{-3} mol L^{-1} in H_2O), calculate the solubility product.

A. 1.3×10^{-4}
B. 2.6×10^{-4}
C. 1.7×10^{-6}
D. 6.7×10^{-8}

10) $Ca(OH)_2$ has approximately the same K_{sp} as $CaSO_4$. Which of them has the greater solubility in terms of mol L^{-1}?

A. They both have the same solubility.
B. $Ca(OH)_2$
C. $CaSO_4$
D. It depends on the temperature at the time.

11) A beaker contains equal concentrations of Mn^{2+} and Ni^{2+} ions. It is found that NiS can be selectively precipitated by adding a certain quantity of K_2S to the beaker. If the K_{sp} of NiS is 3.2×10^{-19}, the K_{sp} of MnS must be:

A. less than 3.2×10^{-19}.
B. greater than 3.2×10^{-19}.
C. equal to 3.2×10^{-19}.
D. cannot be determined with the information provided.

12) $MgF_2(s)$ is added to a beaker of water until there is an amount at the bottom that will not dissolve. What is the concentration of F^-? (The K_{sp} of MgF_2 is 6.5×10^{-9})

A. 2.4×10^{-3}M
B. 1.6×10^{-9}M
C. 2.4×10^{-4}M
D. 1.2×10^{-3}M

13) What is the concentration of F^- in the solution of the preceding question if $MgCl_2$ is added to the solution such that the final concentration of Mg^{2+} becomes 0.1 M?

A. 0.05 M
B. 5.0×10^{-4} M
C. 5.0×10^{-3} M
D. 2.5×10^{-4} M

14) A student adds magnesium sulfate to a solution that is 10^{-4} M in each of the ions F^- and CO_3^{2-} until the Mg^{2+} concentration is also 10^{-4} M. Which of the following salts will precipitate from the final mixture? (Data: K_{sp} $MgF_2 = 10^{-8}$; K_{sp} $MgCO_3 = 10^{-5}$)

A. MgF_2 only
B. $MgCO_3$ only
C. Neither MgF_2 nor $MgCO_3$
D. Both MgF_2 and $MgCO_3$

15) Capillaries are much more permeable than most semipermeable membranes. The only plasma constituents they do not allow through them are proteins. Given that the concentration of protein in plasma is roughly 1.5 mmol/L and the concentration of all solutes in plasma is roughly 290 mmol/L, what is the oncotic pressure (i.e. osmotic pressure exerted by proteins) of plasma at 37 °C as far as capillaries are concerned? (Assume the gas constant is 60 L-torr/K-mol.)

A. 43 mmHg
B. 35 mmHg
C. 5400 mmHg
D. 28 mmHg

16) How much ethylene glycol ($C_2H_6O_2$) must be added to 1 kg of water to depress the freezing point to -40 °C?

Assume the K_f of water is 1.9 K/m.

A. 0.9 kg
B. 0.87 kg
C. 130 g
D. 1.3 kg

GS ANSWER KEY

CHAPTER 5

		Cross-Reference
1.	D	CHM 4.3.3, 5.1.2
2.	B	CHM 1.5, 5.2
3.	D	CHM 3.1, 5.2
4.	B	CHM 5.3.1
5.	B	CHM 5.1.1/2
6.	B	CHM 5.1.2
7.	C	CHM 5.3.2
8.	C	CHM 5.3.2

		Cross-Reference
9.	C	CHM 5.3.2
10.	B	CHM 5.3.2
11.	B	CHM 5.3.2, 5.3.3
12.	A	CHM 5.3.2, 5.3.3
13.	D	CHM 5.3.2, 5.3.3
14.	C	CHM 5.3.2, 5.3.3
15.	D	CHM 5.1.3
16.	D	CHM 5.1.2

* Explanations can be found at the back of the book.

Boiling point elevation

$$\underbrace{\Delta T}_{\text{Change in Temp.}} = i B m \underbrace{\quad}_{} \text{molality} \left(\frac{\text{moles}}{\text{kg solvent}} \right)$$

\# of particles   boiling point constant

ex) $NaCl \Rightarrow Na^+ + Cl^-$
(2 particles : 2 = i)

Freezing point depression

$$\Delta T = -i F m$$

Go online to DAT-prep.com for additional chapter review Q&A and forum.

Solution

mole fraction $\Rightarrow$ (X) $\dfrac{\#\text{ of moles of a particle}}{\text{Total }\#\text{ of moles}}$

molality $\Rightarrow$ (m) $\dfrac{\#\text{ of moles of solute}}{1\ kg\ solvent}$

Molarity (M) $=\dfrac{\#\text{ of moles of solute}}{1\ L\ of\ Solution}$

normality (N) $=\dfrac{\#\text{ of equivilance of acid or base}}{1\ L\ of\ Solution}$

$N\overset{?}{V}=C$

normality | Constant
Volume $\quad N_1V_1 = N_2V_2$

HCl $\quad$ 1.2 M

$\dfrac{1\ \text{equivilant of }H^+}{1\ mol} \times \dfrac{1.2\ mol}{1L} = \boxed{1.2N}$ $\dfrac{eq\ of\ acid}{L}$

$\left.\begin{array}{l} NaOH \\ Ca(OH)_2 \end{array}\right\}$ Same calculations depending on their molarity

1.2 M H_2SO_4

$\dfrac{1.2\ mol}{L} \times \dfrac{2\ eq\ acid}{1\ mol} = \boxed{2.4\ N}$

Phase Diagram $\searrow$ eq
P vs. T P $\uparrow$

solid

S and g eq.

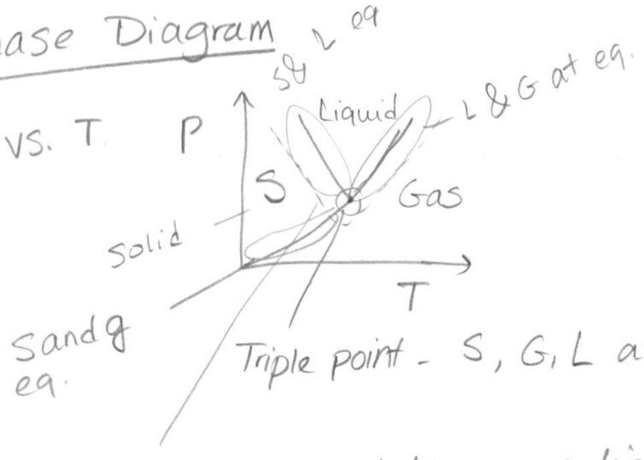

Triple point - S, G, L at equilibrium

Colligitative property - depends on the # of molecules NOT the type

if adding a solute → more liquid ↑B.P. ↓F.p ⌐freezing point

Raoult's law

$P = XP^\circ$ solvent
vapor pressure of

Memorize	Understand	Importance
Define: Bronsted acid, base, pH Examples of strong/weak acids/bases K_w at STP, neutral H_2O pH, conjugate acid/base, zwitterions Equations: K_a, K_b, pK_a pK_b, K_w, pH, pOH Equivalence point, indicator, rules of logarithms	* Calculation of K_a, K_b, pK_a, pK_b, K_w, pH, pOH * Calculations involving strong/weak acids/bases * Salts of weak acids/bases, buffers; indicators * Acid-Base titration/curve, redox titration	**2 to 4 out of the 30 Gen CHM** DAT questions are based on content in this chapter (in our estimation). * Note that between 50% and 85% of the questions in DAT General Chemistry are based on content from 6 chapters: 1, 2, 4, 5, 6 and 9.

DAT-Prep.com

Introduction ▧▨■■

Acids are compounds that, when dissolved in water, give a solution with a hydrogen ion concentration greater than that of pure water. Acids turn litmus paper (an indicator) red. Examples include acetic acid (in vinegar) and sulfuric acid (in car batteries). Bases may have [H⁺] less than pure water and turn litmus blue. Examples include sodium hydroxide (= lye, caustic soda) and ammonia (used in many cleaning products).

Additional Resources

Free Online Forum

Video: Online or DVD

Flashcards

6.1 Acids

A useful definition is given by Bronsted and Lowry: an acid is a proton (i.e. hydrogen ion) donor (cf. Lewis acids and bases, *see* CHM 3.4). A substance such as HF is an acid because it can donate a proton to a substance capable of accepting it. In aqueous solution, water is always available as a proton acceptor, so that the ionization of an acid, HA, can be written as:

$$HA + H_2O \rightleftharpoons H_3O^+ + A^-$$

or:
$$HA \rightleftharpoons H^+ + A^-$$

The equilibrium constant is:

$$K_a = [H^+][A^-]/[HA]$$

Examples of ionization of acids are:

$HCl \rightleftharpoons H^+ + Cl^-$	$K_a = $ infinity
$HF \rightleftharpoons H^+ + F^-$	$K_a = 6.7 \times 10^{-4}$
$HCN \rightleftharpoons H^+ + CN^-$	$K_a = 7.2 \times 10^{-10}$

Acids are generally divided into two categories known as binary acids and oxyacids. The first category is that of acids composed of hydrogen and a nonmetal such as chlorine (HCl). For the halogen containing binary acids, the acid strength increases as a function of the halogen size. Moreover, as the halogen size increases, its bond length increases while its bond strength decreases and as such, its acidity increases. Thus, the acidity of HI > HBr > HCl > HF.

The second category of acids form from oxyanions (anions containing a nonmetal and oxygen such as the hydroxide or nitrate ions, see CHM 5.2) are known as the oxyacids. The oxyacids contain a hydrogen atom covalently bonded to an oxygen atom which is bonded to another central atom X (H-O-X-etc). The more oxygen atoms that are bounded to the central atom, the more acidic the oxyacids. Some examples of oxyacids are listed in Table III.A.6.1.

Note: a diprotic acid (*two protons*, i.e. H_2SO_4) would have K_a values for each of its two ionizable protons: K_{a1} for the first and K_{a2} for the second. Diprotic or any polyprotic acids are known to ionize in successive steps in which each of the steps contain their own dissociation or ionization acid constant, K_a. The first ionization constant (K_{a1}) is typically much larger than the subsequent ionization constants ($K_{a1} > K_{a2} > K_{a3}$, etc...).

Table III.A.6.1: Examples of strong and weak acids.

STRONG	WEAK	STRONG	WEAK
Perchloric $HClO_4$	Hydrocyanic HCN	Sulfuric H_2SO_4	Sulfurous H_2SO_3
Chloric $HClO_3$	Hypochlorous HClO	Hydrobromic HBr	Hydrogen Sulfide H_2S
Nitric HNO_3	Nitrous HNO_2	Hydriodic HI	Phosphoric H_3PO_4
Hydrochloric HCl	Hydrofluoric HF	Hydronium Ion H_3O^+	Benzoic, Acetic and other Carboxylic acids

6.2 Bases

A base is defined as a <u>proton acceptor</u>. In aqueous solution, water is always available to donate a proton to a base, so the ionization of a base B, can be written as:

$$B + H_2O \rightleftharpoons HB^+ + OH^-$$

The equilibrium constant is:

$$K_b = [HB^+][OH^-]/[B]$$

Examples of ionization of bases are:

$$CN^- + H_2O \rightleftharpoons HCN + OH^- \quad K_b = 1.4 \times 10^{-5}$$

$$NH_3 + H_2O \rightleftharpoons NH_4^+ + OH^- \quad K_b = 1.8 \times 10^{-5}$$

$$F^- + H_2O \rightleftharpoons HF + OH^- \quad K_b = 1.5 \times 10^{-11}$$

Strong bases include any hydroxide of the group 1A metals. The most common weak bases are ammonia and any organic amine.

6.3 Conjugate Acid-Base Pairs

The <u>strength</u> of an acid or base is related to the extent that the dissociation proceeds to the right, or to the magnitude of K_a or K_b; the larger the dissociation constant, the stronger the acid or the base. From the preceding K_a values, we see that HCl is the strongest acid (almost 100% ionized), followed by HF and HCN. From the K_b's given, NH_3 is the strongest base listed, followed by CN^- and F^-. Clearly, when an acid ionizes, it produces a base. The acid, HA, and the base produced when it ionizes, A^-, are called a <u>conjugate acid-base</u> pair, so that the couples HF/F^- and HCN/CN^- are conjugate acids and bases.

Thus, an acid that has donated a proton becomes a conjugate base and a base that has accepted a proton becomes a conjugate acid of that base. For example, HCO_3^-/CO_3^{2-} are a conjugate acid/base pair, wherein

HCO_3^- is the acid and CO_3^{2-} is the conjugate base. Both dissociate partially in water and reach equilibrium.

A strong acid (HCl) has a weak conjugate base (Cl^-) and a strong base (NaOH) has a weak conjugate acid (OH^-). Whereas, a weak acid (CH_3COOH) has a strong conjugate base (CH_3COO^-) and a weak base (NH_3) has a related strong conjugate acid (NH_4^+).

Another example of conjugate acid-base pairs is amino acids. Amino acids bear at least 2 ionizable weak acid groups, a carboxyl ($-COOH$) and an amino ($-NH_3^+$) which act as follows:

$$R-COOH \rightleftharpoons R-COO^- + H^+$$

$$R-NH_3^+ \rightleftharpoons R-NH_2 + H^+$$

R–COO⁻ and R–NH₂ are the conjugate bases (i.e. proton acceptors) of the corresponding acids. The carboxyl group is thousands of times more acidic than the amino group. Thus in blood plasma (pH ≈ 7.4) the predominant forms are the carboxylate anions (R–COO⁻) and the protonated amino group (R–NH₃⁺). This form is called a *zwitterion* as demonstrated by the amino acid alanine at a pH near 7:

$$CH_3\text{-}CH\text{-}COO^-$$
$$|$$
$$NH_3{}^+$$
Alanine

The zwitterion bears no net charge.

6.4 Water Dissociation

Water itself can ionize:

$$H_2O + H_2O \rightleftharpoons H_3O^+ + OH^-$$

or:

$$H_2O \rightleftharpoons H^+ + OH^-$$

At STP, $K_w = [H^+][OH^-] = 1.0 \times 10^{-14} = $ <u>ion product constant</u> for water. It increases with temperature and in a neutral solution, $[H^+] = [OH^-] = 10^{-7}$ M. Note that $[H_2O]$ is not included in the equilibrium expression because it is a pure liquid and it is a large constant ($[H_2O]$ is incorporated in K_w).

6.5 The pH Scale

The <u>pH</u> of a solution is a convenient way of expressing the concentration of hydrogen ions $[H^+]$ in solution, to avoid the use of large negative powers of 10. It is defined as:

$$pH = -\log_{10}[H^+]$$

Thus, the pH of a neutral solution of pure water where $[H^+] = 10^{-7}$ is 7.

A similar definition is used for the hydroxyl ion concentration:

$$pOH = -\log_{10}[OH^-]$$

Since, $K_w = [H^+][OH^-]$

And so, $1.0 \times 10^{-14} = [H^+][OH^-]$

And taking the $-$log of both sides gives $-$log $[1.0 \times 10^{-14}] = -log[H^+][OH^-]$

So, $14.0 = -$log$[H^+] + -$log$[OH^-]$

Therefore, $14.0 = pH + pOH$

Finally, at 25°C, $pH + pOH = 14.0$

A pH of 7 is neutral. Values of pH that are greater than 7 are <u>alkaline</u> (basic) and values that are lower are <u>acidic</u>. The pH can be measured precisely with a pH meter (quantitative) or globally with an indicator which will have a different color over different pH ranges (qualitative). For example, *litmus paper* (very common) becomes <u>b</u>lue in <u>b</u>asic solutions and re<u>d</u> in aci<u>d</u>ic solutions; whereas, *phenolphthalein* is colorless in acid and pink in base.

We will see in CHM 6.9 that a weak acid or base can serve as a visual (qualitative) indicator of a pH range. Usually, only a small quantity (i.e. drops) of the indicator is added to the solution as to minimize the risk of any side reactions.

6.5.1 Properties of Logarithms

Many DAT problems every year rely on a basic understanding of logarithms for pH problems, rate law (CHM 9.10) or a 'random' Nernst equation question (BIO 5 Appendix). Here are the rules you must know:

1) $\log_a a = 1$
2) $\log_a M^k = k \log_a M$
3) $\log_a(MN) = \log_a M + \log_a N$
4) $\log_a(M/N) = \log_a M - \log_a N$
5) $10^{\log_{10} M} = M$

For example, let us calculate the pH of 0.001 M HCl. Since HCl is a strong acid, it will completely dissociate into H^+ and Cl^-, thus :

$$[H^+] = 0.001$$
$$-\log[H^+] = -\log(0.001)$$
$$pH = -\log(10^{-3})$$
$$pH = 3 \log 10 \quad \text{(rule \#2)}$$
$$pH = 3 \quad \text{(rule \#1, a = 10)}$$

6.6 Weak Acids and Bases

Weak acids (HA) and bases (B) partially dissociate in aqueous solutions reaching equilibrium following their dissociation. The following is the generic reaction of any weak acid (HA) dissociation in an aqueous solution.

$$HA + H_2O \rightleftharpoons A^- + H_3O^+$$

Now let us begin by taking a closer look at the development of the acid and base equilibrium constants. Like all equilibrium, acid/base dissociation will have a particular equilibrium constant (K_a or K_b) which will determine the extent of the dissociation (CHM 6.3). Thus, from the preceding equation for any generic acid (HA), the acid dissociation constant $K = [H_3O^+][A^-]/[H_2O][HA]$.

Very little water actually reacts and thus the concentration of water during the reaction is constant and can therefore be excluded from the expression for K. Therefore, this gives rise to the acid dissociation constant known as K_a.

Where, $K_a = K[H_2O] = [H_3O^+][A^-]/[HA]$

Likewise for a weak base dissociation in equilibrium,

$$B + H_2O \rightleftharpoons OH^- + BH^+$$

This gives rise to the base dissociation constant known as K_b.

Where, $K_b = K[H_2O] = [OH^-][BH^+]/[B]$

Weak acids and bases are only <u>partially ionized</u>. The ionization constant can be used to calculate the amount ionized, and from this, the pH.

Since weak acids are not completely dissociated, one needs to find the $[H^+]$ from the acid dissociation and then use a method known in most textbooks as the "ICE method". ICE is an acronym used in which, I = Initial acid $[H^+]$ concentration, C = Change in acid $[H^+]$ concentration and E = acid $[H^+]$ concentration at equilibrium. Thus, the acid concentration $[H^+]$ also represented as (x) at equilibrium is then used to calculate the pH. NOTE: the equilibrium concentration x is usually very small as the acid (or base) is weak and partially dissociated (or ionized). The following is an example of the application of the ICE method in solving for the $[H^+] = x$ at equilibrium and subsequently determining the pH of a weak acid solution.

Example: Calculate the pH and pOH of a 10^{-2} M solution of acetic acid (HOAc). K_a of acetic acid at $25°C = 1.75 \times 10^{-5}$.

$$HOAc \rightleftharpoons H^+ + OAc^-$$

The concentrations are:

	[HOAc]	[H⁺]	[OAc⁻]
Initial	10^{-2}	0	0
Change	$-x$	$+x$	$+x$
Equilibrium	$10^{-2} - x$	x	x

$$K_a = [H^+][OAc^-]/[HOAc] = 1.75 \times 10^{-5}$$
$$= (x)(x)/(10^{-2} - x)$$

The solution is a quadratic equation which may be simplified if <u>less than 5%</u> of the acid is ionized by neglecting x compared to the concentration (10^{-2} M in this case). We then have:

$$x^2/10^{-2} = 1.75 \times 10^{-5}$$
$$x = 4.18 \times 10^{-4} = [H^+]$$

And
$$pH = -\log(4.18 \times 10^{-4}) = 3.38$$
$$pOH = 14.00 - 3.38 = 10.62$$

To confirm the 5% criterion one needs to calculate as follows: $(4.18 \times 10^{-4})/(1.00 \times 10^{-2}) \times 100 = 4.18\%$ which is less than 5% and therefore justifies the usage of the 5% criterion.

Similar calculations hold for weak bases. Note that all the preceding can be estimated without a calculator once you know the squares of all numbers between 1 and 15. The root of 1.69 (a fair estimate of 1.75) is thus 1.3 (also *see* CHM 6.6.1 to see how to estimate an answer without a calculator).

6.6.1 Determining pH with the Quadratic Formula

If you need to calculate pH on the DAT, it is very unlikely that you would need to use the quadratic equation; however, you are expected to be familiar with the different ways to calculate pH and that is why it is presented here.

The solutions of the quadratic equation

$$ax^2 + bx + c = 0$$

are given by the formula (QR 4.6, 4.6.2)

$$x = [-b \pm (b^2 - 4ac)^{1/2}]/2a$$

The problem in CHM 6.6 can be reduced to

$$K_a = (x)(x)/(10^{-2} - x) = 1.75 \times 10^{-5}$$

or

$$x^2 + (1.75 \times 10^{-5})X + (-1.75 \times 10^{-7}) = 0$$

Using the quadratic equation where $a = 1$, $b = 1.75 \times 10^{-5}$ and $c = -1.75 \times 10^{-7}$, and doing the appropriate multiplications we get:

$$X = [-1.75 \times 10^{-5} \pm (3.06 \times 10^{-10} + 7.0 \times 10^{-7})^{1/2}]/2$$

Thus $x = [-1.75 \times 10^{-5} \pm (7.00 \times 10^{-7})^{1/2}]/2$
$= [-1.75 \times 10^{-5} \pm 8.37 \times 10^{-4}]/2$

Hence the two possible solutions are

$$X = [-1.75 \times 10^{-5} - 8.37 \times 10^{-4}]/2 = -4.27 \times 10^{-4}$$

Or
$$X = = [-1.75 \times 10^{-5} + 8.37 \times 10^{-4}]/2$$
$$= 4.10 \times 10^{-4}$$

The first solution is a negative number which is physically impossible for [H+], therefore pH $= -\log(4.10 \times 10^{-4}) = 3.39$

Our estimate in CHM 6.6 (pH = 3.38) was valid as it is less than 1% different from the more precise calculation using the quadratic formula.

Given a multiple choice question with the following choices: 2.5, 3.4, 4.3 and 6.8 – the answer can be easily deduced.

$$-\log (4.10 \times 10^{-4}) = -\log 4.10 - \log 10^{-4}$$
$$= 4 - \log 4.10$$

however

$$0 = \log 10^0 = \log 1 < \log 4.10 << \log 10 = 1$$

Thus a number slightly greater than 0 but significantly less than 1 is substracted from 4. The answer could only be 3.4.

6.7 Salts of Weak Acids and Bases

A *salt* is an ionic compound in which the anion is not OH^- or O^{2-} and the cation is not H^+.

Acids and bases react with each other, forming a salt and water in a reaction known as a <u>neutralization reaction</u>. Salts are compounds composed of both a cation and anion (i.e. Na_2SO_4). As salts contain both a cation and anion, salts may therefore form acidic, basic or neutral solutions when dissolved into water. Hence, a salt can react with water to give back an acid or base in a reaction known as <u>salt hydrolysis</u> and thus affect the solution's pH. Moreover, a salt composed of an anion from a weak acid (CH_3COO^-) and a cation from a strong base (Na^+) dissociates and reacts in water to give rise to OH^- ions (a basic solution). Whereas, a salt composed of an anion from a strong acid (Cl^-) and a cation from a weak base (NH_4^+) dissociates and reacts in water to give rise to H^+ (an acidic solution).

Examples:

NaClO dissociates in water:

$$ClO^- + H_2O \rightleftharpoons HClO + OH^- \text{ (Basic)}$$

NH_4NO_3 dissociates in water:

$$NH_4^+ + H_2O \rightleftharpoons H_3O^+ + NH_3 \text{ (Acidic)}$$

The salt of a weak acid is a <u>Bronsted base</u>, which will accept protons. For example,

$$Na^+ OAc^- + H_2O \rightleftharpoons HOAc + Na^+ OH^-$$

The HOAc here is undissociated and therefore does not contribute to the pH. Because it hydrolyzes, sodium acetate is a weak base (the conjugate base of acetic acid). The ionization constant is equal to the basicity constant of the salt. The weaker the conjugate acid, the stronger the conjugate base, that is, the more strongly the salt will combine with a proton.

$$K_H = K_b = [HOAc][OH^-]/[OAc^-]$$

K_H is the <u>hydrolysis constant</u> of the salt. The product of K_a of any weak acid and K_b of its conjugate base is always equal to K_w.

$$K_a \times K_b = K_w$$

For any salt of a weak acid, HA, that ionizes in water:

$$A^- + H_2O \rightleftharpoons HA + OH^-$$
$$[HA][OH^-]/[A^-] = K_w/K_a.$$

The pH of such a salt is calculated in the same manner as for any other weak base.

Similar equations are derived for the salts of weak bases. They hydrolyze in water as follows:

$$BH^+ + H_2O \rightleftharpoons B + H_3O^+$$

B is undissociated and does not contribute to the pH.

$$K_H = K_a = [B][H_3O^+]/[BH^+]$$

And

$$[B][H_3O^+]/[BH^+] = K_w/K_b.$$

In conclusion, there are four types of salts formed based on the reacting acid and base strengths as follows:

(1) Strong acid + strong base:

$$HCl(aq) + NaOH(aq) \rightleftharpoons NaCl(aq) + H_2O(l)$$

Salts in which the cation and anion are both conjugates of a strong base and a strong acid form neutral solutions.

(2) Strong acid + weak base:

$$HCl(aq) + NH_3(aq) \rightleftharpoons NH_4Cl(aq)$$

Salts that are formed based on a strong acid reacting with a weak base form acidic solutions.

(3) Weak acid + strong base:

$$HOAc(aq) + NaOH(aq) \rightleftharpoons NaOAc(aq) + H_2O(l)$$
(note: HOAc = acetic acid = CH_3COOH)

A salt in which the cation is the counterion of a strong base and the anion is the conjugate base of a weak acid results in the formation of basic solutions.

(4) Weak acid + weak base:

$$HOAc(aq) + NH_3(aq) \rightleftharpoons NH_4OAc(aq)$$

A salt in which the cation is a conjugate acid of a weak base and the anion is the anion of a weak acid will form a solution in which the pH will be dependent on the relative strengths of the acid and base.

6.8 Buffers

A <u>buffer</u> is defined as a solution that resists change in pH when a small amount of an acid or base is added or when a solution is diluted. A buffer solution consists of a <u>mixture of a weak acid and its salt or of a weak base and its salt</u>.

For example, consider the acetic acid-acetate buffer. The acid equilibrium that governs this system is:

$$HOAc \rightleftharpoons H^+ + OAc^-$$

Along with the acid equilibrium component of the buffer solution as shown above, the buffer solution must also contain a significant amount of the conjugate base of the acid as a salt. The following equation depicts the conjugate base salt dissociation of the acetic acid-acetate buffer solution:

$$NaOAc \rightarrow Na^+ + OAc^-.$$

Thus, the buffer is made up of two components (1) a weak acid (HOAc) and (2) the conjugate base of the weak acid as a salt (NaAOc) so that both components are part of the buffer system in apt concentrations to make for a fully functional buffer.

When a small amount of NaOH base is added to the acetic acid/acetate buffer solution, the OH^- ions from the base will react with the free H^+ ions present in the buffer solution from the acetic acid dissociation. This will shift the equilibrium of the buffer toward the right which means more dissociation of the acid (HOAc). Thus, an increase in [OH⁻] from the addition of base to the buffer solution does not change pH significantly due to the reaction of the basic OH⁻ ions with the free protons (H⁺) in solution.

The resistance to pH change is also noted with the addition of an acid (H⁺) to the acetic acid/acetate buffer solution. The addition of acidic H⁺ from the acid will react with the acetate ions (HOAc⁻) from the salt dissociation of the buffer and this will also allow for the buffering capacity of the solution. Thus, due to the presence of both a weak acid and a conjugate base from the salt (or common ion), the buffer solution thus is known to maintain a pH within a certain range known as the buffering capacity.

Buffers must contain a significant amount of both a weak acid or weak base and its conjugate salts. A strong acid or strong base would not have any buffering capacity or effect within a buffer system as the dissociation would be irreversible and so the buffer capacity would not be present. In addition, a weak acid or base in itself would also not be able to work as a buffer system regardless of the fact that there is the presence of their conjugates as the concentrations of the conjugate acid or base from the weak acids or bases would not be sufficient to neutralize the addition of acids (H⁺) or bases (OH⁻). Thus, buffers require the addition of a conjugate acid or base as a salt to the weak acid or base component so to increase the salt concentration of the buffer solution.

If we were to add acetate ions into the system (i.e. from the salt), the H⁺ ion concentration is no longer equal to the acetate ion concentration. The hydrogen ion concentration is:

$$[H^+] = K_a \, ([HOAc]/[OAc^-])$$

Taking the negative logarithm of each side, where $-\log K_a = pK_a$, yields:

$$pH = pK_a - \log \, ([HOAc]/[OAc^-])$$
or
$$pH = pK_a + \log([OAc^-]/[HOAc])$$

This equation is referred to as the Henderson-Hasselbach equation. It is useful for calculating the pH of a weak acid solution containing its salt. A general form can be written for a weak acid, HA, that dissociates into its salt, A⁻ and H⁺:

$$HA \rightleftharpoons H^+ + A^-$$
$$pH = pK_a + \log([salt]/[acid])$$

The buffering capacity of the solution is determined by the concentrations of HA and A⁻. The higher their concentrations, the more acid or base the solution can tolerate. The buffering capacity is also governed by the ratios of HA to A⁻. It is maximum when the ratio is equal to 1, i.e. when $pH = pK_a$.

Similar calculations can be made for mixtures of a weak base and its salt:

$$B + H_2O \rightleftharpoons BH^+ + OH^-$$

And

$$pOH = pK_b + \log ([salt]/[base])$$

Many biological reactions of interest occur between pH 6 and 8. One useful series of buffers is that of phosphate buffers (see BIO 20.5, 20.6). By choosing appropriate mixtures of $H_3PO_4/H_2PO_4^-$, $H_2PO_4^-/HPO_4^{2-}$ or HPO_4^{2-}/PO_4^{3-}, buffer solutions covering a wide pH range can be prepared. Another useful clinical buffer is the one prepared from tris(hydroxymethyl) aminomethane and its conjugate acid, abbreviated Tris buffer.

Amphoteric Species: Some substances such as water can act as either an acid or a base (i.e. a dual property). These types of substances are known as amphoteric substances. Water behaves as an acid when reacted with a base (OH⁻) and alternatively, water behaves as a base when reacted with an acid (H⁺). Many metal oxides and hydroxides are also known to be amphoteric substances. Furthermore, molecules that contain both acidic and basic groups such as amino acids are considered to be amphoteric in nature as well (ORG 12.1.2). The following are examples of the amphoteric nature of HCO_3^- reacting with an acid and a base and water (H_2O) reacting with an acid and base.

In acids: $HCO_3^- + H_3O^+ \rightarrow H_2CO_3 + H_2O$
In bases: $HCO_3^- + OH^- \rightarrow CO_3^{2-} + H_2O$
In acids: $H_2O + HCl \rightarrow H_3O^+ + Cl^-$
In bases: $H_2O + NH_3 \rightarrow NH_4^+ + OH^-$

6.9 Acid-base Titrations

The purpose of a titration is usually the determination of concentration of a given sample of acid or base (the analyte) which is reacted with an equivalent amount of a strong base or acid of known concentration (the titrant). The end point or equivalence point is reached when a stoichiometric amount of titrant has been added. This end point is usually detected with the use of an indicator which changes color when this point is reached. Note: the end point is not exactly the same as the equivalence point. The equivalence point is where a reaction is theoretically complete whereas an end point is where a physical change in solution such as a color change is determined by indicators. Regardless, the volume difference between an end point and an equivalence point can usually be ignored.

The end point is determined precisely by measuring the pH at different points of the titration. The curve pH = f(V) where V is the volume of titrant added is called a titration curve. While a strong acid/strong base titration will have an equivalence point at a neutralization pH of 7, the equivalence point of other titrations do not necessarily occur at pH 7. In fact, a weak acid/strong base titration will result in an equivalence point of a pH > 7 and a strong acid/weak base titration results in an equivalence point of a pH < 7. The differential pH effects at the relative equivalence points are due to the conjugate acids and/or bases formed. An indicator for an acid-base titration is a weak acid or base.

The weak acid and its conjugate base should have two different colors in solution. Most indicators require a <u>pH transition range</u> during the titration of about two pH units. An indicator is chosen so that its pK_a is close to the pH of the equivalence point.

6.9.1 Strong Acid versus Strong Base

In the case of a strong acid versus a strong base, both the titrant and the analyte are completely ionized. For example, the titration of hydrochloric acid with sodium hydroxide:

$$H^+ + Cl^- + Na^+ + OH^- \rightarrow H_2O + Na^+ + Cl^-$$

The H^+ and OH^- combine to form H_2O and the other ions remain unchanged, so the net result is the conversion of the HCl to a neutral solution of NaCl. A typical strong-acid-strong base titration curve is shown in Fig. III.A.6.1 (case where the titrant is a base).

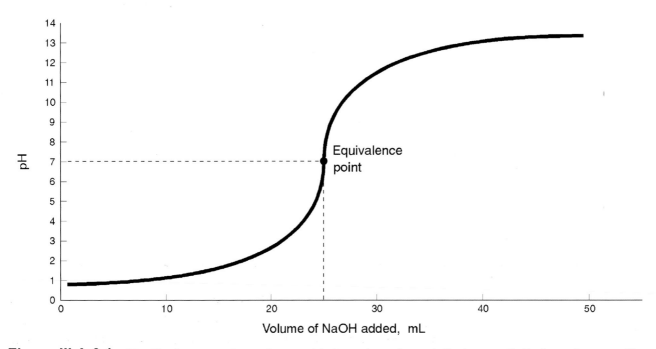

Figure III.A.6.1: The titration curve for a strong acid-strong base is a relatively smooth S-shaped curve with a very steep inclination close to the equivalence point. A small addition in titrant volume near the equivalence point will result in a large change in pH.

If the analyte is an acid, the pH is initially acidic and increases very slowly. When the equivalent volume is reached the pH sharply increases. Midway between this transition jump is the equivalence point. In the case of strong acid-strong base titration the equivalence point corresponds to a neu-tral pH (because the salt formed does not react with water). If more titrant is added the pH increases and corresponds to the pH of a solution of gradually increasing concentration of the titrant base. This curve is simply reversed if the titrant is an acid.

6.9.2 Weak Acid versus Strong Base

The titration of acetic acid with sodium hydroxide involves the following reaction:

$$HOAc + Na^+ + OH^- \rightarrow H_2O + Na^+ + OAc^-$$

The acetic acid is only a few percent ionized. It is neutralized to water and an equivalent amount of the salt, sodium acetate. Before the titration is started, the pH is calculated as described for weak acids. As soon

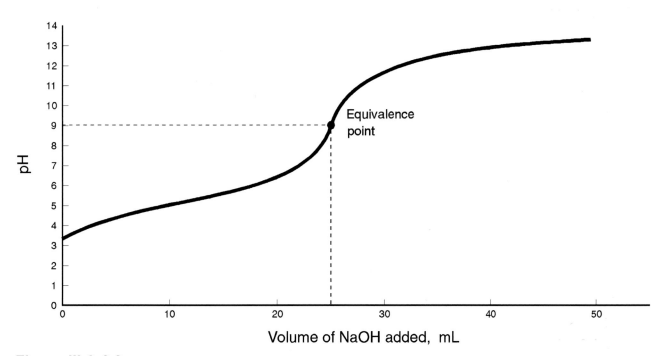

Figure III.A.6.2: The titration curve for a weak acid-strong base or alternatively a strong acid-weak base is somewhat irregular. The pH at the start of the titration prior to base addition is greater than that of a strong acid as the acid is a weak acid. The inclination close to the equivalence point is less significant due to the buffering effect of the solution prior to the equivalence point. A small addition in titrant volume near the equivalence point will therefore result in a small change in pH.

as the titration is started, some of the HOAc is converted to NaOAc and a buffer system is set up. As the titration proceeds, the pH slowly increases as the ratio [OAc⁻]/[HOAc] changes. Halfway towards the equivalence point, $[OAc^-] = [HOAc]$ and the pH is equal to pK_a. At the equivalence point, we have a solution of NaOAc. Since it hydrolyzes, the pH at the equivalence point will be alkaline. The pH will depend on the concentration of NaOAc.

The greater the concentration, the higher the pH. As excess NaOH is added, the ionization of the base, OAc⁻, is suppressed and the pH is determined only by the concentration of excess OH⁻. Therefore, the titration curve beyond the equivalence point follows that for the titration of a strong acid. The typical titration curve in this case is illustrated in Figure III.A.6.2.

6.9.3 Weak Base versus Strong Acid

The titration of a weak base with a strong acid is analogous to the previous case except that the pH is initially basic and gradually decreases as the acid is added (curve in preceding diagram is reversed). Consider ammonia titrated with hydrochloric acid:

$$NH_3 + H^+ + Cl^- \rightarrow NH_4^+ + Cl^-$$

At the beginning, we have NH_3 and the pH is calculated as for weak bases. As soon as some acid is added, some of the NH_3 is converted to NH_4^+ and we are in the buffer region. At the midpoint of the titration, $[NH_4^+]$ $= [NH_3]$ and the pH is equal to $(14 - pK_b)$. At the equivalence point, we have a solution of NH_4Cl, a weak acid which hydrolyzes to give an acid solution. Again, the pH will depend on concentration: the greater the concentration, the lower the pH. Beyond the equivalence point, the free H^+ suppresses the ionization and the pH is determined by the concentration of H^+ added in excess. Therefore, the titration curve beyond the equivalence point will be similar to that of the titration of a strong base. {The midpoint of the titration is the equivalence point of the titration curve}

6.10 Redox Titrations

Redox titrations are based on a redox reaction or reduction-oxidation type reaction between an analyte (or sample) and a titrant. More specifically, redox titrations involve the reaction between an oxidizing agent, which accepts one or more electrons, and a reducing agent, which reduces the other substance by donating one or more electrons (CHM 1.6).

The most useful oxidizing agent for titrations is potassium permanganate - $KMnO_4$. Solutions of this salt are colorful since they contain the purple MnO_4^- ion. On the other hand, the more reduced form, Mn^{++}, is nearly colorless. So here is how this redox titration works: $KMnO_4$ is added to a reaction mixture with a reducing agent (i.e. Fe^{++}). MnO_4^- is quickly reduced to Mn^{++} so the color fades immediately. This will continue until there is no more reducing agent in the mixture. When the last bit of reducing agent has been oxidized (i.e. all the Fe^{++} is converted to Fe^{+3}), the next drop of $KMnO_4$ will make the solution colorful since the MnO_4^- will have nothing with which to react. Thus if the amount of reducing agent was unknown, it can be calculated using stoichiometry guided by the amount of potassium permanganate used in the reaction.

- Lewis acid is a chemical that accepts an e⁻ pair.

GOLD STANDARD WARM-UP EXERCISES
CHAPTER 6: Acids and Bases

1) Sulfuric acid, H_2SO_4, is a polyprotic acid. Consider the following solutions of sulfuric acid and/or its sodium salts.

    Solution I: 0.5 M H_2SO_4
    Solution II: 0.5 M $NaHSO_4$
    Solution III: 0.5 M Na_2SO_4
    Solution IV: A mix of equal volumes of I and II

Which solution has the highest pH?

A. Solution I
B. Solution II
C. Solution III
D. Solution IV

2) The first proton of sulfurous acid (H_2SO_3) ionizes as if from a strong acid while the second ionizes as if from a weak acid ($K_{a2} = 5.0 \times 10^{-6}$). What is the pH of 0.01 M H_2SO_3?

A. 1.0
B. 2.0
C. 3.0
D. 4.0

3) An indicator is usually:

A. a weak acid or base which can form two distinct colors.
B. a weak acid or base which can form one distinct color.
C. a strong acid or base which can form two distinct colors.
D. a strong acid or base which can form one distinct color.

4) A 20.00 mL aliquot of aniline ($C_6H_5NH_2$) was titrated with 0.01 M HCl and a few of the values of the titration are shown in Table 1.

Table 1

Volume of HCl added (mL)	pH
0.0	8.8
15.0	4.6
30.0	2.8

Which of the following graphs accurately depicts the change in pH for the titration of aniline with increasing volumes of hydrochloric acid?

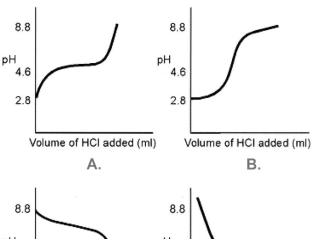

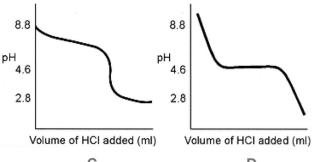

5) The most suitable acid/base indicator for the determination of the end point of the titration in the previous question would probably have a pH range of:

   A. 2.1–3.2.
   B. 3.0–5.0.
   C. 4.8–6.4.
   D. 6.2–7.4.

6) In the aniline-HCl titration, the pH of the reaction mixture drops sharply near the equivalence point of the titration because:

   A. the concentration of $C_6H_5NH_2$ decreases sharply.
   B. the concentration of $C_6H_5NH_3^+$ decreases sharply.
   C. the concentration of H^+ increases sharply.
   D. the concentration of H^+ decreases sharply.

7) Usually, the color change of an indicator occurs over a range of about two pH units. Hydrogen ion concentration must change by at least what factor for the indicator in solution to change color?

   A. 2
   B. 10
   C. 100
   D. 200

8) The conjugate base of sulfuric acid is:

   A. $H_3SO_4^+$
   B. HSO_4^-
   C. HSO_3^-
   D. $H_2SO_3^-$

9) What would the pH of a 0.10 M solution of HCOOH be? $K_a = 1.8 \times 10^{-4}$

   A. 1.0
   B. 2.4
   C. 4.7
   D. 7.0

10) A 0.10 M solution of formic acid (CH_2O_2) has a pH of 2.38. What is the K_a of formic acid?

    A. 1.8×10^{-3}
    B. 1.8×10^{-4}
    C. 1.8×10^{-5}
    D. 1.8×10^{-6}

11) What is the pH of a 0.1 M solution of NH_4Cl?

    (K_b of NH_3 is 1.8×10^{-5})

    A. 3.4
    B. 5.5
    C. 7.0
    D. 9.7

12) H_2SO_4 has $K_{a1} = 1.0 \times 10^3$ and $K_{a2} = 1.2 \times 10^{-2}$. What is the approximate hydrogen ion concentration of 1.0 M H_2SO_4?

    A. 1.00 M
    B. 1.01 M
    C. 1.05 M
    D. 1.10 M

$$K_{a_1} = \frac{[H^+][HSO_4^-]}{[H_2SO_4]} = 10^3$$

$$K_{a_2} = 1.2 \times 10^{-3} = \frac{[H^+][SO_4^{2-}]}{[HSO_4^-]}$$

$$[SO_4^{2-}] = K_{a_2} = 0.012 \, M + 1 = 1.012$$

GS ANSWER KEY

CHAPTER 6

		Cross-Reference
1.	C	CHM 6.1, 6.5
2.	B	CHM 6.5, 6.6
3.	A	CHM 6.5, 6.9
4.	C	CHM 6.9.3
5.	B	CHM 6.5, 6.9
6.	C	CHM 6.9.3

		Cross-Reference
7.	C	CHM 6.5, 6.5.1, 6.9
8.	B	CHM 6.9, 6.9.1/2
9.	B	CHM 6.5, 6.5.1, 6.6
10.	B	CHM 6.5, 6.5.1
11.	B	CHM 6.2, 6.5
12.	B	CHM 6.1

* Explanations can be found at the back of the book.

Go online to DAT-prep.com for additional chapter review Q&A and forum.

Acids & Bases

$$PH = -\log[H^+]$$

K_w (water dissociation constant) $= [H^+][OH^-] = 10^{-14}$

$$Pk_w = PH + POH = 14$$

$$\log(ab) = \log(a) + \log(b)$$

$$-\log(10^{-14}) = 14\log\overset{1}{10} = 14$$

Strong

$HCl \rightleftharpoons H^+ + Cl^-$ proton donor - releases H^+.

H_2SO_4

HNO_3 K_a = acid dissociation constant

$$K_a = \frac{[H^+][Cl^-]}{[HCl]}$$

very high
- a lot of dissolving.

$10^{-3}M \longrightarrow \quad 0 \underline{\qquad} 0$

eventually:

$10^{-3}M\ H^+\ \&\ 10^{-3}M\ Cl^-$

$$PH = -\log(10)^{-3}$$

$$\boxed{PH = 3}$$

weak

$HOAc \rightleftharpoons H^+ + \overset{\ominus}{O}Ac$ $K_a = 1.75 \times 10^{-5}$
acetic acid   small.

I	10^{-3}	0.00	0.00
C	$-X$	$+X$	$+X$
E	$10^{-3}-X$	X	X

$$K_a = \frac{[H^+][OAc^-]}{[HOAc]}$$

$$1.75 \times 10^{-5} = \frac{X^2}{10^{-3}-X} \Rightarrow X = 1.3 \times 10^{-4}$$

ignore (small #)

$$-\log(1.3) + 4 = pH$$

$$pH = 3.\_ \ close\ to\ 4$$

Titration Curve

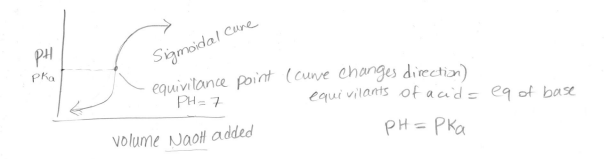

PH
PKa

Sigmoidal curve

equivilance point (curve changes direction)
PH = 7

volume NaOH added

equivilants of acid = eq of base

$$PH = PKa$$

$$HCl + NaOH \rightarrow H_2O + NaCl$$

Solubility product

$$PbCl_{2(s)} \rightleftharpoons Pb^{2+}_{(aq)} + 2Cl^-_{(aq)}$$ conduct electricity ⇒ electrolytes

$$K_{sp} = [Pb^{2+}][Cl^-]^2$$

Concentrations

$$K_{sp} = (S)(2S)^2 = \underline{4S^3}$$

for calculating
solubility of the rxn.

for solubility

THERMODYNAMICS

Chapter 7

Memorize	Understand	Importance
Define: state function Conversion: thermal to mechanical E.	* System vs. surroundings * Law of conservation of energy * Heat transfer * Conduction, convection, radiation	**0 to 2 out of the 30 Gen CHM** DAT questions are based on content in this chapter (in our estimation). * Note that between 50% and 85% of the questions in DAT General Chemistry are based on content from 6 chapters: 1, 2, 4, 5, 6 and 9.

DAT-Prep.com

Introduction ▊▊▊▊

Thermodynamics, in chemistry, refers to the relationship of heat with chemical reactions or with the physical state. Thermodynamic processes can be analyzed by studying energy and topics we will review in the next chapter including entropy, volume, temperature and pressure.

Additional Resources

Free Online Forum

Video: Online or DVD

Flashcards

Special Guest

7.1 Generalities

Thermodynamics deals with fundamental questions concerning energy transfers. One difficulty you will have to overcome is the terminology used. For instance, remember that heat and temperature have more specific meanings than the ones attributed to them in every day life.

A thermodynamic transformation can be as simple as a gas leaking out of a tank or a piece of metal melting at high temperature or as complicated as the synthesis of proteins by a biological cell. To solve some problems in thermodynamics we need to define a "system" and its "surroundings." The system is simply the object experiencing the thermodynamic transformation. The gas would be considered as the system in the first example of transformations. Once the system is defined any part of the universe in direct contact with the system is considered as its surroundings. For instance, if the piece of metal is melted in a high temperature oven: the system is the piece of metal and the oven constitutes its surroundings.

In other instances, the limit between the system and its surroundings is more arbitrary, for example if one considers the energy exchanges when an ice cube melts in a thermos bottle filled with orange juice; the inside walls of the thermos bottle could be considered as part of "the system" or as part of the surroundings. In the first case one would carry out all calculations as though the entire system (ice cube + orange juice + inside walls) is isolated from its surroundings (rest of the universe) and all the energy exchanges take place within the system. In the second case the system (ice cube + orange juice) is not isolated from the surroundings (walls) unless we consider that the heat exchanges with the walls are negligible. There is also no need to include any other part of the universe in the latter case since all exchanges take place within the system or between the system and the inside walls of the thermos bottle.

Some systems may exchange both matter and energy with the surroundings. This is called an "open system". Alternatively, some systems may exchange energy only but not matter with the surroundings. This is called a "closed system". Finally, some systems do not exchange matter or energy with their surroundings. This is called an "isolated system". An isolated system therefore does not interact with its surroundings in any way.

7.2 The First Law of Thermodynamics

Heat, internal energy and work are the first concepts introduced in thermodynamics. Heat is thermal energy (a dynamic property defined during a transformation only), it is not to be confused with temperature (a static property defined for each state of the system). Internal energy is basically the average total mechanical energy (kinetic + potential) of the particles that make up the system. The first law of thermodynamics is often expressed as follows: when a system absorbs an amount of heat Q from the surroundings and does a quantity of work W on the same surroundings its internal energy changes by the amount:

$$\Delta E = Q - W$$

This law is basically the law of conservation of energy for an isolated system. Indeed, it states that if a system does not exchange any energy with its surroundings, its internal energy should not vary. If on the other hand a system does exchange energy with its surroundings, its internal energy should change by an amount corresponding to the energy it takes in from the surroundings.

The sign convention related to the previous mathematical expression of the first law of thermodynamics is:

- heat absorbed by the system: $Q > 0$
- heat released by the system: $Q < 0$
- work done by the system on its surroundings: $W > 0$
- work done by the surroundings on the system: $W < 0$

Caution: Some textbooks prefer a different sign convention: any energy (Q or W) flowing from the system to the surroundings (lost by the system) is negative and any energy flowing from the surroundings to the system (gained by the system) is positive. Within such a sign convention the first law is expressed as:

$$\Delta E = Q + W$$

i.e. the negative sign in the previous equation is incorporated in W.

7.3 Equivalence of Mechanical, Chemical and Thermal Energy Units

The previous equation does more than express mathematically the law of conservation of energy, it establishes a relationship between thermal energy and mechanical energy. Historically thermal energy was always expressed in calories (abbreviated as cal.) defined as the amount of thermal energy required to raise the temperature of 1 g of water by 1 degree Celcius. The standard unit used for mechanical work is the "Joule" (J). This unit eventually became the standard unit

for any form of energy. The conversion factor between the two units is:

$$1 \text{ cal} = 4.184 \text{ J}$$

Chemists often refer to the amount of energies exchanged between the system and its surroundings to the mole, i.e., quantities of energy are expressed in J/mol or cal/mol. To obtain the energy per particle (atom or molecule), you should divide the energy expressed in J or cal by Avogadro's number.

7.4 Temperature Scales

There are three temperature scales in use in science textbooks: the Celsius scale, the absolute temperature or Kelvin scale, and the Farenheit scale. In the Celsius scale the freezing point and the boiling point of water are arbitrarily defined as 0 °C and 100 °C, respectively. The scale is then divided into equal 1/100th intervals to define the degree Celsius or centigrade (from latin centi = 100). The absolute temperature or Kelvin scale is derived from the centigrade scale, i.e., an interval of 1 degree Celsius is equal to an interval of 1 degree Kelvin. The difference between the two scales is in their definitions of the zero point:

$$0 \text{ K} = -273.13 \text{ °C.}$$

Theoretically, this temperature can be approached but never achieved, it corresponds to the point where all motion is frozen and matter is destroyed. The Farenheit scale used in English speaking countries has the disadvantage of not being divided into 100 degrees between its two reference points: the freezing point of water is 32 °F and its boiling point is 212 °F. To convert Farenheit degrees into Celsius degrees you have to perform the following transformation:

$$(X \text{ °F} - 32) \times 5/9 = Y \text{ °C}$$

or

$$°F = 9/5 \text{ °C} + 32.$$

7.5 Heat Transfer

There are three ways in which heat can be transferred between the system and its surroundings:

(a) heat transfer by conduction

(b) heat transfer by convection

(c) heat transfer by radiation

In the first case (a) there is an intimate contact between the system and its surroundings and heat propagates through the entire system from the heated part to the unheated parts. A good example is the heat-ing of a metal rod on a flame. Heat is initially transmitted directly from the flame to one end of the rod through the contact between the metal and the flame. When carrying out such an experiment you would notice at some point that the part of the rod which is not in direct contact with the flame becomes hot as well (please do not attempt!).

In the second case (b), heat is transferred to the entire system by the circulation of a hot liquid or a gas through it. The difference between this mode of transfer and the previous one, is that the entire system or a major part of it is heated up directly by the surroundings and not by propagation of the thermal energy from the parts of the system which are in direct contact with the heating source and the parts which are not.

In the third case (c) there is no contact between the heating source and the system. Heat is transported by radiation. The perfect example is the microwave oven where the water inside the food is heated by the micro-wave source. Most heat transfers are carried out by at least two of the above processes at the same time.

Note that when a metal is heated it expands at a rate which is proportional to the change in temperature it experiences. {For a definition of the coefficient of expansion, OAT students can see PHY 6.3; DAT students can happily ignore that statement since there is no physics on the DAT!}

7.6 State Functions

As previously mentioned, the first law of thermodynamics introduces three fundamen-tal energy functions, i.e., the internal energy E, heat Q, and work W. Let us consider a transformation that takes the system from an initial state (I) to a final state (F) (which can differ by a number of variables such as tem-perature, pressure and volume). The change in the internal energy during this transforma-tion depends only on the properties of the ini-tial state (I) and the final state (F). In other words, suppose that to go from (I) to (F) the system is first subjected to an intermediate transformation that temporarily takes it from state (I) to an intermediate state (Int.) and then to another transformation that brings it from (Int.) to (F), the change in internal energy between the initial state (I) and the final state (F) are independent of the properties of the intermediate state (Int.). The internal energy is said to be a path-independent function or a state function. This is not the case for W and Q. In fact, this is quite conceivable since the amount of W or Q can be imposed by the external operator who subjects the sys-tem to a given transformation from (I) to (F). For instance, Q can be fixed at zero if the operator uses an appropriate thermal insu-lator between the system and its surround-ings. In which case the change in the internal energy is due entirely to the work w ($\Delta E = -w$). It is easy to understand that the same result [transformation from (I) to (F)] could be achieved by supplying a small quantity of heat q while letting the system do more work W on the surroundings so that q – W is equal to –w. In which case we have:

	Work	Heat	Change in internal energy
1st transf.	w	0	$-w$
2nd transf.	$W = w + q$	q	$-w$

and yet in both cases the system is going from (I) to (F).

W and Q are not state functions. They depend on the path taken to go from (I) to (F). If you remember the exact definition of the internal energy you will understand that a system changes its internal energy to respond to an input of Q and W. In other words, contrary to Q and W, the internal energy cannot be directly imposed on the system.

The fact that the internal energy is a state function can be used in three other equivalent ways:

(i) If the changes in the internal energy during the intermediate transformation are known, they can be used to calculate the change for the entire process from (I) to (F): the latter is equal to the sum of the changes in the internal energy for all the intermediate steps.

(ii) If the change in the internal energy to go from a state (I) to a state (F) is $E_{I \to F}$ the change in the internal energy for an opposite transformation that would take the system from (F) to (I) is:

$$\Delta E_{F \to I} = -\Delta E_{I \to F}$$

(iii) If we start from (I) and go back to (I) through a series of intermediate transformations the change in the internal energy for the entire process is zero.

W can be determined experimentally by calculating the area under a pressure-volume curve. The mathematical relation is presented in CHM 8.1.

GOLD STANDARD WARM-UP EXERCISES

CHAPTER 7: Thermodynamics

1) Beaker A has a 100 g sample of water maintained at 25 °C and 1 atm for 24 hours. Beaker B has 100 g of water that was heated to 100 °C from 0 °C over 23 hours and then cooled to 25 °C at 1 atm by the 24th hour. Which of the following is true?
   A. Beaker A has more internal energy than Beaker B.
   B. Beaker B has less internal energy than Beaker A.
   C. Both beakers have the same internal energy.
   D. None of the above.

2) If a system loses 25 kJ of heat at the same time that it is doing 50 kJ of work, what is the change in the internal energy of the system?
   A. –25 kJ
   B. +25 kJ
   C. –75 kJ
   D. +75 kJ

3) Metal foil would aid in preventing heat gain via which of the following processes?
   A. Reflecting radiant energy
   B. Conduction
   C. Convection
   D. Radiation and conduction

4) Hess's law is valid because enthalpy is a state function. Which of the following is not a state function?
   A. Volume
   B. Internal energy
   C. Work
   D. Entropy

5) Down-filled winter clothing reduces heat losses by incorporating pockets of air into the material. Which type of heat transfer process do the air pockets limit?
   A. Radiation
   B. Conduction
   C. Convection
   D. Conduction and convection

GS ANSWER KEY

CHAPTER 7

		Cross-Reference				Cross-Reference
1.	C	CHM 7.6		4.	C	CHM 7.6
2.	C	CHM 7.5		5.	B	CHM 7.5
3.	A	CHM 7.5				

* Explanations can be found at the back of the book.

Go online to DAT-prep.com for additional chapter review Q&A and forum.

Themodynamics

ENTHALPY AND THERMOCHEMISTRY
Chapter 8

Memorize	Understand	Importance
Define: endo/exothermic	* Area under curve: PV diagram * Equations for enthalpy, Hess's law, free E. * Calculation: Hess, calorimetry, Bond diss. E. * 2nd law of thermodynamics * Entropy, free E. and spontaneity	**0 to 3 out of the 30 Gen CHM** DAT questions are based on content in this chapter (in our estimation). * Note that between 50% and 85% of the questions in DAT General Chemistry are based on content from 6 chapters: 1, 2, 4, 5, 6 and 9.

DAT-Prep.com

Introduction ▊▊▊▊

Thermochemistry is the study of energy absorbed or released in chemical reactions or in any physical transformation (i.e. phase change like melting and boiling). Thermochemistry for the DAT includes understanding and/or calculating quantities such as enthalpy, heat capacity, heat of combustion, heat of formation, and free energy.

Additional Resources

Free Online Forum

Video: Online or DVD

Flashcards

8.1 Enthalpy as a Measure of Heat

The application of the general laws of thermodynamics to chemistry lead to some simplifications and adaptations because of the specificities of the problems that are dealt with in this field. For instance, in chemistry it is critical, if only for safety reasons, to know in advance what amounts of heat are going to be generated or absorbed during a reaction. In contrast, chemists are generally not interested in generating mechanical work and carry out most of their chemical reactions at constant pressure. For these reasons, although internal energy is a fundamental function its use is not very adequate in thermochemistry. Instead, chemists prefer to use another function derived from the internal energy: the enthalpy (H). This function is mathematically defined as:

$$\Delta H = \Delta E + P \times (\Delta V)$$

where P and V are respectively the pressure and the volume of the system. Hence, the enthalpy change (ΔH) of any system is the sum of the change in its internal energy (ΔE) and the product of its pressure (P) and volume change (ΔV). As the three components, internal energy, pressure and volume are all state functions, the enthalpy (H) or enthalpy change (ΔH) of a system is therefore also a state function. Thus, enthalpy change depends only on the enthalpies of the initial and final states (ΔH) and not on the path and therefore it is an example of a state function itself. The enthalpy change of a reaction is defined by the following equation $\Delta H = H_{final} - H_{initial}$; where ΔH is the enthalpy change, H_{final} is the enthalpy of the products of a reaction, and $H_{initial}$ is the enthalpy of the reactants of a reaction. A positive enthalpy change ($+\Delta H$) would indicate the flow of heat into a system as a reaction occurs and is called an "endothermic reaction". A cold pack added over an arm swelling would provide for a good example of an endothermic reaction. A negative enthalpy change ($-\Delta H$) would be called an "exothermic reaction" which essentially gives heat energy off from a system into its surroundings. A bunsen burner flame (CHM 12.4.5) would be an appropriate example of an exothermic reaction.

You may wonder about the use of artificially introducing another energy function when internal energy is well defined and directly related to kinetic and potential energy of the particles that make up the system. To answer this legitimate question you need to consider the case of the majority of the chemical reactions where P is constant and where the only type of work that can possibly be done by the system is of a mechanical nature. In this case, since a change in internal energy (ΔE) occurring during a chemical reaction is basically a measure of all the systems energy as heat and work ($Q + W$) exchange with the system's surroundings, therefore, $\Delta E = Q + W$ and since, $W = -P\Delta V$, then, the change in enthalpy during a chemical reaction reduces to: $\Delta H = \Delta E + P \times V = (Q + W) + P \times V = Q + W - W = Q$ In other words, the change in enthalpy during a chemical reaction reduces to:

$$\Delta H = \Delta E + P \times V = (Q + W) + P \times V = Q$$

In other words, the change of enthalpy is a direct measure of the heat that evolves or is absorbed during a reaction carried out at constant pressure.

8.1.1 The Standard Enthalpy of Formation or Standard Heat of Formation (ΔH_f°):

The standard enthalpy of formation, ΔH_f°, is defined as the change of enthalpy that would occur when one mole of a substance is formed from its constituent elements in a standard state reaction. All elements in their standard states (oxygen gas, solid carbon as graphite, etc., at 1 atm and 25°C) have a standard enthalpy of formation of zero, as there is no change involved in their formation. The calculated standard enthalpy of various compounds can then be used to find the standard enthalpy of a reaction. For example, the standard enthalpy of formation for methane (CH_4) gas at 25°C would be the enthalpy of the following reaction:

$$C(s,graphite) + 2H_2(g) \rightarrow CH_4(g),$$

where $\Delta H_f^\circ = -74.6$ KJ/mol. Thus, the chemical

equation for the enthalpy of formation of any compound is always written with respect to the formation of 1 mole of the studied compound.

The standard enthalpy change for a reaction denoted as ΔH°_{rxn}, is the change of enthalpy that would occur if one mole of matter is transformed by a chemical reaction with all reactants and products under standard state. It can be expressed as follows:

$$\Delta H^\circ_{rxn} = \text{(sum of } n_f \Delta H^\circ_f \text{ of products)} \\ - \text{(sum of } n_r \Delta H^\circ_f \text{ of reactants),}$$

where n_r represents the stoichiometric coefficients of the reactants and n_f the stoichiometric coefficients of the products. The ΔH°_f represents the standard enthalpies of formation.

* $C_{graphite} \rightarrow CO_2$ $CO_2 \rightarrow C_{diamond}$

8.2 Heat of Reaction: Basic Principles

As discussed, a reaction during which heat is released is said to be *exothermic* (ΔH is negative). If a reaction requires the supply of a certain amount of heat it is *endothermic* (ΔH is positive).

Besides the basic principle behind the introduction of enthalpy there is a more fundamental advantage for the use of this function in thermochemistry: it is a state function. This is a very practical property. For instance,

consider two chemical reactions related in the following way:

| reaction 1: | $A + B \rightarrow C$ |
| reaction 2: | $C \rightarrow D$ |

If these two reactions are carried out consecutively they lead to the same result as the following reaction:

overall reaction: $A + B \rightarrow D$

Because H is a state function we can apply the same arguments here as the ones we previously used for E. The initial state (I) corresponding to A + B, the intermediate state (Int.) to C, and the final state (F) to the final product D. If we know the changes in the enthalpy of the system for reactions 1 and 2, the change in the enthalpy during the overall reaction is:

$$\Delta H_{OVERALL} = \Delta H_1 + \Delta H_2$$

This is known as Hess's law. Remember that Hess's law is a simple application of the fact that H is a state function.

Thus, since the enthalpy change of a reaction is dependant only on the initial and final states, and not on the pathway that a reaction may follow, the sum of all the reaction step enthalpy changes must therefore be equivalent to the overall reaction enthalpy

change (ΔH). The enthalpy change for a reaction can then be calculated without any direct measurement by using previously determined enthalpies of formation values for each reaction step of an overall equation. Consequently, if the overall enthalpy change is determined to be negative ($\Delta H_{net} < 0$), the reaction is exothermic and is most likely to be of a spontaneous type of reaction and a positive ΔH value would correspond to an endothermic reaction. Thus, Hess's law claims that enthalpy changes are additive and thus the ΔH for any single reaction can be calculated from the difference between the heat of formation of the products and the heat of formation of the reactants as follows:

$$\Delta H^{\circ}_{reaction} = \Sigma \Delta H_f^{\circ}{}_{(products)} - \Sigma \Delta H_f^{\circ}{}_{(reactants)}$$

where the $^{\circ}$ superscript indicates standard state values.

8.3 Hess's Law

Hess's law can be applied in several equivalent ways which we will illustrate with several examples:

Example: assume that we know the following enthalpy changes:

$$2H_2(g) + O_2(g) \rightarrow 2H_2O(l)$$
$$\Delta H_1 = -136.6 \text{ kcal} : R1$$
$$Ca(OH)_2(s) \rightarrow CaO(s) + H_2O(l)$$
$$\Delta H_2 = 15.3 \text{ kcal} : R2$$
$$2CaO(s) \rightarrow 2\,Ca(s) + O_2(g)$$
$$\Delta H_3 = +303.6 \text{ kcal} : R3$$

and are asked to compute the enthalpy change for the following reaction:

$$Ca(s) + H_2(g) + O_2(g) \rightarrow Ca(OH)_2(s) : R$$

It is easy to see that reaction (R) can be obtained by the combination of reactions (R$_1$), (R$_2$) and (R$_3$) in the following way:

$$
\begin{aligned}
-\ 1/2\ (R3):\quad & Ca(s) + 1/2\ O_2(g) \rightarrow CaO(s) \\
+\ 1/2\ (R1):\quad & H_2(g) + 1/2\ O_2(g) \rightarrow H_2O(l) \\
-\quad (R2):\quad & CaO(s) + H_2O(l) \rightarrow Ca(OH)_2(s) \\
\hline
& Ca(s) + H_2(g) + O_2(g) \rightarrow Ca(OH)_2(s)
\end{aligned}
$$

As we previously explained, since H is a state function the enthalpy change for (R) will be given by:

$$\Delta H = -1/2\Delta H_3 + 1/2\Delta H_1 - \Delta H_2$$

Example: assume that we have the following enthalpy changes as shown below:

R1: B_2O_3 (s) + $3H_2O$ (g) → $3O_2$ (g) + B_2H_6 (g)
    (ΔH_1 = 2035 kJ/mol)

R2: H_2O (l) → H_2O (g)   (ΔH_2 = 44 kJ/mol)

R3: H_2 (g) + $(1/2)O_2$ (g) → H_2O (l)
    (ΔH_3 = −286 kJ/mol)

R4: 2B (s) + $3H_2$ (g) → B_2H_6 (g)
    (ΔH_4 = 36 kJ/mol)

and are then asked to find the enthalpy change or ΔH_f of the following reaction (R):

R: 2B (s) + $(3/2)O_2$ (g) → B_2O_3 (s)   (ΔH_f = ?)

After the required multiplication and rearrangements of all step equations (and their respective enthalpy changes), the result is as follows:

(−1) × (R1) B_2H_6 (g) + $3O_2$ (g)
        → B_2O_3 (s) + $3H_2O$ (g)
        (ΔH_1 = −2035 kJ/mol)

(−3) × (R2) $3H_2O$ (g) → $3H_2O$ (l)
        (ΔH_2 = -132 kJ/mol)

(−3) × (R3) $3H_2O$ (l) → $3H_2$ (g) + $(3/2)O_2$ (g)
        (ΔH_3 = 858 kJ/mol)

(+1) × (R4) 2B (s) + $3H_2$ (g) → B_2H_6 (g)
        (ΔH_4 = 36 kJ/mol)

adding the equations while canceling out all common terms, we finally obtain:

2B (s) + $(3/2)O_2$ (g) → B_2O_3 (s)
        (ΔH_f = −1273 kJ/mol)

As noted in the initial example, it is shown that the enthalpy change (ΔH_f) for the final reaction is given by the following:

$$\Delta H_f = (-1)\Delta H_1 + (-3)\Delta H_2 + (-3)\Delta H_3 + (1)\Delta H_4$$

There are no general rules that would allow you to determine which reaction to use first and by what factor it needs to be multiplied. It is important to proceed systematically and follow some simple ground rules:

(i)   For instance, you could start by writing the overall reaction that you want to obtain through a series of reaction additions.

(ii) Number all your reactions.

(iii) Keep in mind as you go along that the reactants of the overall reaction should always appear on the left-hand side and that the products should always appear on the right-hand side.

(iv) Circle or underline the first reactant of the overall reaction. Find a reaction in your list that involves this reactant (as a reactant or a product). Use that reaction first and write it in such a way that this reactant appears on the left-hand side with the appropriate stoichiometric coefficient (i.e., if this reactant appears as a product of a reaction on your list you should reverse the reaction).

(v)   Suppose that in (iv) you had to use the second reaction on your list and that you had to reverse and multiply this reaction by a factor of 3 to satisfy the preceding rule. In your addition, next to this reaction or on top of the arrow write $-3 \times \Delta H_2$.

(vi) Repeat the process for the other reactants and products of the overall reaction

until your addition yields the overall reaction. As you continue this process, make sure to cross out the compounds that appear on the right and left-hand sides at the same time.

8.4 Standard Enthalpies

Hess's law has a very practical use in chemistry. Indeed, the enthalpy change for a given chemical reaction can be computed from simple combinations of known enthalpy changes of other reactions. Because enthalpy changes depend on the conditions under which reactions are carried out it is important to define standard conditions:

(i) Standard pressure: 1 atmosphere pressure (approx. = 1 bar).

(ii) Standard temperature for the purposes of the calculation of the standard enthalpy change: generally 25 °C. The convention is that if the temperature of the standard state is not mentioned then it is assumed to be 25 °C, the standard temperature needs to be specified in all other instances.

(iii) Standard physical state of an element: it is defined as the "natural" physical state of an element under the above standard pressure and temperature. For instance, the standard physical state of water under the standard temperature and pressure of 1 atm and 25 °C is the liquid state. Under the same conditions oxygen is a gas.

Naturally, the standard enthalpy change (notation: $\Delta H°$) for a given reaction is defined as the enthalpy change that accompanies the reaction when it is carried out under standard pressure and temperature with all reactants and products in their standard physical state.

Note that the standard temperature defined here is <u>different from the standard temperature for an ideal gas</u> which is: 0 °C.

8.5 Enthalpies of Formation

The enthalpy of formation of a given compound is defined as the enthalpy change that accompanies the formation of the compound from its constituting elements. For instance,

the enthalpy of formation of water is the $\Delta H_f°$ for the following reaction:

$$H_2 + 1/2\ O_2 \rightarrow H_2O$$

To be more specific the standard enthalpy of formation of water ΔH_f° is the enthalpy change during the reaction:

$$H_2(g) + 1/2 O_2(g) \xrightarrow[\text{1 atm}]{25°C} H_2O(l)$$

where the reactants are in their natural physical state under standard temperature and pressure.

Note that according to these definitions, several of the reactions considered in the previous sections were in fact examples of reactions of formation. For instance, in section 8.3 on Hess's law, reaction (R1) is the reaction of formation of two moles of water, if

reversed reaction (R3) would be the reaction of formation of two moles of CaO and the overall reaction (R) is the reaction of formation of 1 mole Ca(OH)$_2$. Also note that although one could use the reverse of reaction (R2) to form Ca(OH)$_2$, this reaction, even reversed, is not the reaction of formation of Ca(OH)$_2$. The reason is that the constitutive elements of this molecule are: calcium (Ca), hydrogen (H$_2$) and oxygen (O$_2$) and not CaO and H$_2$O. Enthalpies of formation are also referred to as heats of formation. As previously explained, if the reaction of formation is carried out at constant pressure, the change in the enthalpy represents the amount of heat released or absorbed during the reaction.

8.6 Bond Dissociation Energies and Heats of Formation

The bond dissociation energy, also known as the bond dissociation enthalpy, is a measure of bond strength within a particular molecule defined as a standard enthalpy change in the *homolytic* cleavage (= 2 free radicals formed; CHM 9.4) of any studied chemical bond. An example of bond dissociation energies would be the successive homolytic cleavage of each of the C-H bonds of methane (CH$_4$) to give, CH$_3$• + •H, CH$_2$• + •H, CH• + •H and finally C• + •H. The bond dissociation energies for each of the homolytic CH bond cleavage of methane are determined to be as follows: 435 KJ/mol, 444 KJ/mol, 444 KJ/mol and 339 KJ/mol, respectively. The average of these four individual bond dissociation energies is known as the bond

energy of the CH bond and is 414 KJ/mol. Thus, with the exception of all diatomic molecules where only one chemical bond is involved so that bond energy and bond dissociation energy are in this case equivalent, the bond dissociation energy is not exactly the same as bond energy. Bond energy is more appropriately defined as the energy required to sever 1 mole of a chemical bond in a gas and not necessarily the measure of a chemical bond strength within a particular molecule. Bond energy is therefore a measure of bond strength. Moreover as just described, bond energy may be considered as an average energy calculated from the sum of bond dissociation energies of all bonds within a particular compound. Bond energies are always positive values as it always takes energy to break bonds apart.

The difficulty in defining bond dissociation energies in polyatomic molecules is that the amounts of energy required to break a given bond (say an O–H bond) in two different polyatomic molecules (H_2O and CH_3OH, for instance) are different. Bond dissociation energies in polyatomic molecules are approximated to an average value for molecules of the same nature. Within the framework of this commonly made approximation we can calculate the <u>enthalpy change of any reaction</u> using the *sum* of bond energies of the reactants and the products in the following way:

$$\Delta H^\circ_{(reaction)} = \Sigma BE_{(reactants)} - \Sigma BE_{(products)}$$

where BE stands for bond energies.

Standard enthalpy changes of chemical reactions can also be computed using enthalpies of formation in the following way:

$$\Delta H^\circ_{(reaction)} = \Sigma \Delta H_{(bonds\ broken)} + \Sigma \Delta H_{(bonds\ formed)}$$
$$= \Sigma BE_{(reactants)} - \Sigma BE_{(products)}$$

Note how this equation is similar but not identical to the one making use of bond energies. This comes from the fact that a bond energy is defined as the energy required to <u>break</u> (and not to form) a given bond. Also note that the standard enthalpy of formation of a mole of any **element** is zero.

8.7 Calorimetry

Measurements of changes of temperature within a reaction mixture allow the experimental determination of heat absorbed or released during the corresponding chemical reaction. Indeed the amount of heat required to change the temperature of any substance X from T_1 to T_2 is proportional to $(T_2 - T_1)$ and the quantity of X:

$$Q = mC(T_2 - T_1)$$

or

$$Q = nc(T_2 - T_1)$$

where m is the mass of X, n the number of moles. The constant C or c is called the <u>heat capacity</u>. The standard units for C and c are, respectively, the $Jkg^{-1}K^{-1}$ and the $Jmol^{-1}K^{-1}$. C which is the heat capacity per <u>unit mass</u> is also referred to as the <u>specific heat capacity</u>. If you refer back to the definition of the calorie (see CHM 7.3) you will understand that the specific heat of water is necessarily: $1\ cal\ g^{-1}\ {}^\circ C^{-1}$.

Note that heat can be absorbed or released without a change in temperature (CHM 4.3.3). In fact, this situation occurs whenever a phase change takes place for a pure compound. For instance, ice melts at a constant temperature of 0 °C in order to break the forces that keep the water molecules in a crystal of ice we need to supply an amount of heat of 6.01 kJ/mol. There is no direct way of calculating the heat corresponding to a phase change.

Heats of phase changes (heat of fusion, heat of vaporization, heat of sublimation) are generally tabulated and indirectly determined in calorimetric experiments. For instance, if a block of ice is allowed to melt in a bucket of warm water, we can determine the heat of fusion of ice by measuring the temperature drop in the bucket of water and applying the law of conservation of energy. The relevant equation is:

$$Q = m\,L$$

where L is the latent heat which is a constant.

Calorimetry is the science of measuring the heat evolved or exchanged due to a chemical reaction. The thermal energy of a reaction (defined as the system) is measured as a function of its surroundings by observing a temperature change (ΔT) on the surroundings due to the system. The magnitude in temperature change is essentially a measure of a system's or sample's energy content which is measured either while keeping a volume constant (bomb calorimetry) or while keeping a pressure constant (coffee-cup calorimetry).

In a constant volume calorimetry measurement, the bomb calorimeter is kept at a constant volume and there is essentially no heat exchange between the calorimeter and the surroundings and thus, the net heat exchange for the system is zero. The heat exchange for the reaction is then compensated for by the heat change for the water and bomb calorimeter material steel (or surroundings). Thus, $\Delta q_{system} = \Delta q_{reaction} + \Delta q_{water} + \Delta q_{steel} = 0$ in bomb calorimetry, and so $q_{cal} = -q_{reaction}$ in which the temperature change is related to the heat absorbed by the calorimeter (q_{cal}) and if no heat escapes the constant volume calorimeter, the amount of heat gained by the calorimeter then equals that released by the system and so, $q_{cal} = -q_{reaction}$ as stated previously. Note that since $Q = mc\Delta T$ as previously defined, and $q_{reaction} = -(q_{water} + q_{steel})$ therefore, $q_{reaction} = -(m_{water})(c_{water})\Delta T + (m_{steel})(c_{steel})\Delta T$.

For aqueous solutions, a coffee-cup calorimeter is usually used to measure the enthalpy change of the system. This is simply a polystyrene (Styrofoam) cup with a lid and a thermometer. The cup is partially filled with a known volume of water. When a chemical reaction occurs in the coffee-cup calorimeter, the heat of the reaction is absorbed by the water. The change in water temperature is used to calculate the amount of heat that has been absorbed (used to make products, so water temperature decreases) or evolved (lost to the water, so its temperature increases) in the reaction.

8.8 The Second Law of Thermodynamics

The first law of thermodynamics allows us to calculate energy transfers during a given transformation of the system. It does not allow us to predict whether a transformation can or cannot occur spontaneously. Yet our daily observations tell us that certain transformations always occur in a given direction. For instance, heat flows from a hot source to a cold source. We cannot spontaneously transfer heat in the other direction to make the hot source hotter and the cold source colder. The second law of thermodynamics states that entropy (S) of an isolated system will never decrease. In order for a reaction to proceed, the entropy of the system must increase. For any spontaneous process, the entropy of the universe increases which results in a greater dispersal or randomization of the energy ($\Delta S > 0$). The second law of thermodynamics allows the determination of the preferred direction of a given transformation. Transformations which require the smallest amount of energy and lead to the largest disorder of the system are the most spontaneous.

8.9 Entropy

Entropy is regarded as the main driving force behind all the chemical and physical changes known within the universe. All natural processes tend toward an increase in energy dispersal or, in other words, an entropy increase within our universe. Thus, a chemical system or reaction proceeds in a direction of universal entropy increase.

Entropy S is the state function which measures the degree of "disorder" in a system. For instance, the entropy of ice is lower than the entropy of liquid water since ice corresponds to an organized crystalline structure (virtually no disorder). In fact, generally speaking, the entropy increases as we go from a solid to a liquid to a gas. For similar reasons, the entropy decreases when an elastic band is stretched. Indeed, in the "unstretched" elastic band the molecules of the rubber polymer are coiled up and form a disorganized structure. As the rubber is stretched these molecules will tend to line up with each other and adopt a more organized structure.

Entropy has the dimension of energy as a function of temperature as J/K or cal/K. Entropy can therefore be related to temperature and is thus a measure of energy dispersal (in joules) per unit of temperature (in kelvins).

The second law of thermodynamics can be expressed in the alternative form: a spontaneous transformation corresponds to an increase of the entropy of the system plus its surroundings. Hence, a chemical system is known to proceed in a direction that increases the entropy of the universe. As a result, ΔS must be incorporated in an expression that includes both the system and its surroundings so that, $\Delta S_{universe} = \Delta S_{surroundings} + \Delta S_{system} > 0$. When a system reaches a certain temperature equilibrium, it then also reaches its maximal entropy and so, $\Delta S_{universe} = \Delta S_{surroundings} + \Delta S_{system} = 0$. The entropy of the thermodynamic system is therefore a measure of how far the equalization has progressed.

Entropy, like enthalpy, is a state function and is therefore path independent. Hence, a change in entropy depends only on the initial and final states ($\Delta S = S_{final} - S_{initial}$) and not on how the system arrived at that state. Under standard conditions, for any process or reaction, the entropy change for that reaction will be the difference between the entropies of products and reactants as follows:

$$\Delta S°_{reaction} = \Delta S°_{products} - \Delta S°_{reactants}$$

8.10 Free Energy

The Gibbs free energy G is another state function which can be used as a criterion for spontaneity. This function is defined as:

$$G = H - T \cdot S$$

where: H is the enthalpy of the system in a given state,

T is the temperature,

and   S is the entropy of the system.

Consequently, Gibbs Free Energy (G) also determines the direction of a spontaneous change for a chemical system. The derivation for the formulation thus incorporates both the entropy and enthalpy parameters studied in the previous sections. Following various manipulations and derivations, one can then note that Gibbs Free Energy is an

alternative form of both enthalpy and the entropy changes of a chemical process.

The standard Gibbs Free Energy of a reaction ($\Delta G°_{rxn}$), is determined at 25°C and a pressure of 1 atm. For a reaction carried out at constant temperature we can write that the change in the Gibbs free energy is:

$$\Delta G = \Delta H - T \Delta S$$

A reaction carried out at constant pressure is spontaneous if

$$\Delta G < 0$$

It is not spontaneous if:

$$\Delta G > 0$$

and it is in a state of equilibrium (reaction spontaneous in both directions) if:

$$\Delta G = 0.$$

As noted in the previous chapter, the study of thermodynamics generally describes the spontaneity or the direction and extent to which a reaction will proceed. It therefore enables one to predict if a reaction will occur spontaneously or not. Note that non spontaneous processes may turn into spontaneous processes if coupled to another spontaneous process or more specifically by the addition of some external energy.

Thermochemistry then can be used to essentially calculate how much work a system can do or require. Thermodynamics basically then deals with the relative potentials of both the reactants and products of a chemical system. The next chapter will describe the actual rate (or chemical kinetics or speed) of a chemical reaction. In chemical kinetics, the chemical potential of intermediate states of a chemical reaction may also be described and thus enabling one to determine why a reaction may be slow or fast.

GOLD STANDARD WARM-UP EXERCISES

CHAPTER 8: Enthalpy and Thermochemistry

1) If a chemical reaction is at equilibrium, which of the following is true?
   A. The change in entropy is zero.
   B. The number of reacting molecules is zero.
   C. The change in enthalpy is zero.
   D. The change in free energy is zero.

2) In the reaction $N_2(g) + 3H_2(g) \leftrightarrow 2NH_3(g)$, the entropy among the molecules involved:
   A. increases.
   B. remains the same.
   C. decreases.
   D. cannot be determined with the information given.

3) When the reaction $N_2(g) + 3H_2(g) \leftrightarrow 2NH_3(g)$ is at equilibrium, it is "far to the right." The forward reaction must be:
   A. ectoplasmic.
   B. exothermic.
   C. endothermic.
   D. endergonic.

4) A student observes the melting of an ice cube. She concludes that the overall observed process has led to:
   A. the completion of real work.
   B. an increase in the efficiency of the universe.
   C. an increase in the entropy of the universe.
   D. an increase in the total energy of the universe.

5) What would be the expected change in the solubility of a gas when a solution containing the gas is heated and when a solution containing the gas has the pressure over the solution decreased, respectively?
   A. Increase, increase
   B. Increase, decrease
   C. Decrease, increase
   D. Decrease, decrease

6) A phase diagram is a graph showing the thermodynamic conditions of a substance – solid, liquid, gas - at different pressures and temperatures. Which of the following statements is consistent with the triple point of a substance?
   A. The absolute temperature dominates the effect on Gibbs free energy.
   B. The reaction is spontaneous, Gibbs free energy is negative.
   C. The enthalpy change is equal to the effect of the entropy change.
   D. The entropy change is negative because there is more disorder overall.

7) Consider the following data:

$CH_4(g) + 2O_2(g) \rightarrow CO_2(g) + 2H_2O(l)$
$$\Delta H^\circ = -890 \text{ kJ/mol}$$
$H_2O(l) \rightarrow H_2O(g) \quad \Delta H^\circ = 44 \text{ kJ/mol}$

Calculate the enthalpy (ΔH°) of the following reaction:

$$CH_4 + 2O_2(g) \rightarrow CO_2(g) + 2H_2O(g)$$

   A. +846 kJ/mol
   B. −846 kJ/mol
   C. +802 kJ/mol
   D. −802 kJ/mol

8) The standard enthalpies of formation of SO_2 and SO_3 are -297 and -396 kJ/mol, respectively. Calculate the standard enthalpy of reaction for the following:

$$SO_2 + \frac{1}{2}O_2 \rightarrow SO_3.$$

    A. -99 kJ
    B. $+99$ kJ
    C. -396 kJ
    D. $+396$ kJ

9) How much heat is needed to convert a 10-gram ice cube at $0\ °C$ to steam at $100\ °C$?

    Heat of fusion $= 80$ kcal/kg

    Heat of vaporization $= 540$ kcal/kg

    A. 620 cal
    B. 1000 cal
    C. 1620 cal
    D. 7200 cal

10) The total area of the Hubble telescope exposed to the sun is 70 000 m^2. The rate of solar energy incident on the telescope is 120 Wm^{-2}. If a channel covering the entire exposed surface contains water and the temperature of the water must rise by at least $10\ °C$ in order to keep the telescope cool, at what approximate rate must the water be made to flow assuming that energy transfer is instantaneous?

    Specific heat capacity of water $= 4.2$ J $g^{-1}\ °C^{-1}$

    Density of water $= 1000$ kg m^{-3}

    A. 200 L s^{-1}
    B. 3150 L s^{-1}
    C. 2.0×10^5 L s^{-1}
    D. 3.1×10^6 L s^{-1}

GS ANSWER KEY

CHAPTER 8

Cross-Reference

1.	D	CHM 8.10
2.	C	CHM 8.9
3.	B	CHM 8.2, 8.9, 8.10, 9.10
4.	C	CHM 8.8, 8.9
5.	D	CHM 5.3, 8.10, 9.10

Cross-Reference

6.	C	CHM 4.3.3, 8.10
7.	D	CHM 8.5
8.	A	CHM 8.5
9.	D	CHM 8.7
10.	A	CHM 8.7

* Explanations can be found at the back of the book.

Go online to DAT-prep.com for additional chapter review Q&A and forum.

Hess's Law

$$2H_2 + O_2 \longrightarrow 2H_2O \qquad \Delta H_1 = \sim$$

$$Ca(OH)_2 \longrightarrow CaO + H_2O \qquad \Delta H_2 = \sim \rightarrow \text{change sign \& x2}$$
$$\underset{\times 2}{\underleftarrow{\qquad\qquad}}$$

$$2H_2 + O_2 + 2CaO \longrightarrow 2Ca(OH)_2 \quad \text{°} \quad \Delta H_{tot} = \Delta H_1 - \underset{\text{change sign}}{2\Delta H_2}$$

ΔH_f - Heat of formation of a chemical

state function - only depend on initial & final conditions.

Thermochemistry

- chemistry in heat changes

$$Q = mc\Delta T \qquad \overset{\text{Specific heat (constant)}}{}$$

$$Q = mL$$

latent heat - energy that flows in or out due to phase change. _constant temperature._

L_v - latent heat of vaporization

L_f -   "   "   fusion

(normally smaller than L_v.

fusion: solid $\longleftrightarrow$ liquid

Calorimetry   ┌ energy to heat up 1°C water of 1g.

How many **calories** needed to heat **10g** H_2O from $-10°C$ to $120°C$?

- changed phases

$Q = mc\Delta T \qquad (-10°C \rightarrow 0°)$
$Q = (10)(\frac{1}{2})(0+10)$
$\underline{Q = 50 \text{ cal}}$

$Q = mL \atop 80$ (No change in temperature ice $\rightarrow$ liquid) solid
$Q = (10)(\frac{80}{4})$
$\underline{Q = 800 \text{ cal}}$

$Q = mc\Delta T \qquad$ get it to 100°c
$Q = (10)(1)(100-0)$
$Q = 1000 \text{ cal}$

$Q = mL \atop 540$ liquid $\rightarrow$ vapor
$Q = (10)(L_v)$
$\underline{Q = 5400 \text{ cal}}$

$Q = mc\Delta\theta \quad {}_{20}$ vapor $\rightarrow$ 120°
$Q = (10)(\frac{1}{2})(120-100)$
$Q = 100 \text{ cal}$

$Q_{Tot} = 50 + 800 + 1000 + \atop 5400 + \atop 100$
$= \sim \text{ cal}$

(!)
:)

RATE PROCESSES IN CHEMICAL REACTIONS
Chapter 9

Memorize	Understand	Importance
reaction order define: rate determining step generalized potential energy diagrams define: activation energy, catalysis define: saturation kinetics, substrate	* Reaction rates, rate law, determine exponents * Reaction mechanism for free radicals * Rate constant equation; apply Le Chatelier's * Kinetic vs. thermodynamic control * Law of mass action, equations for Gibbs free E., saturation kinetics, Keq	**2 to 4 out of the 30 Gen CHM** DAT questions are based on content in this chapter (in our estimation). * Note that between 50% and 85% of the questions in DAT General Chemistry are based on content from 6 chapters: 1, 2, 4, 5, 6 and 9.

DAT-Prep.com

Introduction ▨▨■■

Rate processes (or chemical kinetics) involve the study of the velocity (speed) and mechanisms of chemical reactions. **Reaction rate** (= *velocity*) tells us how fast the concentrations of reactants change with time. **Reaction mechanisms** show the sequence of steps to get to the overall change. Experiments show that 4 important factors generally influence reaction rates: (1) the nature of the reactants, (2) their concentration, (3) temperature, and (4) catalysis.

Additional Resources

Free Online Forum

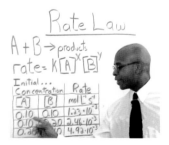

Video: Online or DVD

Flashcards

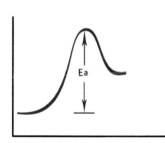

Special Guest

9.1 Reaction Rate

Consider a general reaction

$$2A + 3B \rightarrow C + D$$

The rate or the velocity at which this reaction proceeds can be expressed by one of the following:

(i) rate of disappearance of A: $-\Delta[A]/\Delta t$

(ii) rate of disappearance of B: $-\Delta[B]/\Delta t$

(iii) rate of appearance or formation of C: $\Delta[C]/\Delta t$

(iv) rate of appearance or formation of D: $\Delta[D]/\Delta t$

Where [ ] denotes the concentration of a reactant or a product in moles/liter. Thus, the reaction rate measure is usually expressed as a change in reactant or product concentration ($\Delta_{conc.}$) per unit change in time (Δt).

Since A and B are disappearing in this reaction, [A] and [B] are decreasing with time, i.e. $\Delta[A]/\Delta t$ and $\Delta[B]/\Delta t$ are negative quantities. On the other hand, the quantities $\Delta[C]/\Delta t$ and $\Delta[D]/\Delta t$ are positive since both C and D are being formed during the process of this reaction. By convention: rates of reactions are expressed as positive numbers; as a result, a negative sign is necessary in the first two expressions.

Suppose that A disappears at a rate of 6 (moles/liter)/s. In the same time interval (1s), in a total volume of 1L we have:

(3 mol B/2 mol A) × 6 mol A
= 9 moles of B disappearing
(1 mol C/2 mol A) × 6 mol A
= 3 moles of C being formed
(1 mol D/2 mol A) × 6 mol A
= 3 moles of D being formed

Therefore individual rates of formation or disappearance are not convenient ways to express the rate of a reaction. Indeed, depending on the reactant or product considered the rate will be given by a different numerical value unless the stoichiometric coefficients are equal (e.g. for C and D in our case).

A more convenient expression of the rate of a reaction is the overall rate. This rate is simply obtained by dividing the rate of formation or disappearance of a given reactant or product by the corresponding stoichiometric coefficient, i.e.:

overall rate = $-(1/2)\,\Delta[A]/\Delta t$, or $-(1/3)\,\Delta[B]/\Delta t$,

or $\Delta[C]/\Delta t$, or $\Delta[D]/\Delta t$.

A simple verification on our example will show you that these expressions all lead to the same numerical value for the overall rate: 3 (moles/L)/s. Therefore for a generic equation such as, $aA + bB \rightarrow cC + dD$, a generalization of the overall reaction rate would be as follows:

$$Rate = \frac{-1}{a}\frac{\Delta[A]}{\Delta t} = \frac{-1}{b}\frac{\Delta[B]}{\Delta t} = \frac{+1}{c}\frac{\Delta[C]}{\Delta t} = \frac{+1}{d}\frac{\Delta[D]}{\Delta t}$$

It can be seen from the preceding over-all rate relationship that the rate is the same whether we use one of the reactants or one of the products to calculate the rates. Generally, one can see that knowing the rate of change in the concentration of any one reactant or product at a certain time point allows one to invariably determine the rate of change in the concentration of any other reactant or product at the same time point using the stoichiometri-cally balanced equation.

Whenever the term "rate" is used (with no other specification) it refers to the "overall rate" unless individual and overall rates are equal.

9.2 Dependence of Reaction Rates on Concentration of Reactants

The rate of a reaction (given in moles per liter per second) can be expressed as a function of the concentration of the reactants. In the previous chemical reaction we would have:

$$rate = k \, [A]^m \, [B]^n$$

where [ ] is the concentration of the corre-sponding reactant in moles per liter

k is referred to as the rate constant
m is the order of the reaction with respect to A
n is the order of the reaction with respect to B
m+n is the overall reaction order.

The rate constant k is reaction specific. It is directly proportional to the rate of a reac-tion. It increases with increasing temperature since the proportion of molecules with ener-gies greater than the activation energy E_a of a reaction increases with higher temperatures.

According to the rate law above, the reaction is said to be an (m + n)th order reaction, or, an mth order reaction with respect to A, or, an nth order reaction with respect to B.

The value of the m or nth rate orders of the reaction describes how the rate of the reaction depends on the concentration of the reactant(s).

For example, a zero rate order for reac-tant A (where m = 0), would indicate that the rate of the reaction is independent of the con-centration of reactant A and therefore has a constant reaction rate (this is also applicable to reactant B). The rate equation can therefore be expressed as a rate constant k or the rate = k. The rate probably depends on temperature or other factors excluding concentration.

A first rate order for reactant A (where m = 1) would indicate that the rate of the reac-tion is directly proportional to the concen-tration of the reactant A (or B, where n = 1). Thus, the rate equation can be expressed as follows: rate = $k[A]^1$ or rate = $k[B]^1$.

A second rate order for reactant A ($m = 2$) would indicate that the rate is proportional to the square of the reactant concentration. The rate equation can thus be expressed as follows: rate $= k[A]^2$.

Hence, the rate orders or exponents in the rate law equation can be integers, fractions, or zeros and are not necessarily equal to the stoichiometric coefficients in the given reaction except when a reaction is the rate-determining step (or elementary step). Consequently, although there are other orders, including both higher and mixed orders or fractions that are possible as described, the three described orders (0, 1st and 2nd), are amongst the most common orders studied.

As shown by the graphical representation below, for the zero order reactant, as the concentration of reactant A decreases over time, the slope of the line is constant and thus the rate is constant. Moreover, the rate does not change regardless of the decrease in reactant A concentration over time and thus the zero order rate order. For the first order, the decrease in reactant A concentration is shown to affect the rate of reaction in direct proportion. Thus, as the concentration decreases, the rate decreases proportionally. Lastly, for the second order, the rate of the reaction is shown to decrease proportionally to the square of the reactant A concentration. In fact, the curves for 1st and 2nd order reactions resemble exponential decay.

Reactant Concentration versus Time

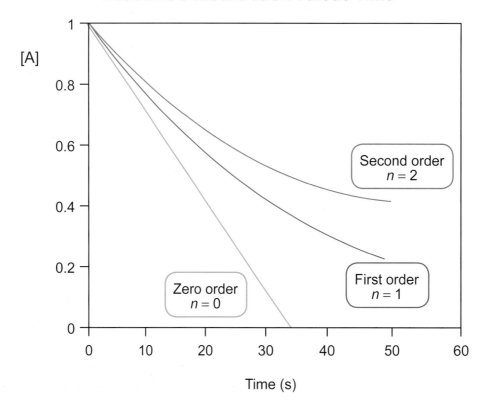

9.2.1 Differential Rate Law vs. Integrated Rate Law (Advanced DAT-30 Topic)

Rate laws may be expressed as differential equations or as integrated rate laws. As differential equations, the relationship is shown between the rate of a reaction and the concentration of a reactant. Alternatively, the integrated rate law expresses a rate as a function of concentration of a reactant or reactants and time.

For example, for a zero order rate, Rate $= k[A]^0 = k$ and since Rate $= -\Delta[A]/\Delta t$, then

$-\Delta[A]/\Delta t = k$ and following the integration of the differential function, the following zero-order integrated rate law is obtained: $[A]_t = -kt + [A]_0$, where $[A]_t =$ is the concentration of A at a particular time point t and $[A]_0$ is the initial concentration of A and k is the rate constant.

The following table summarizes the main rate laws of the 0, 1st and 2nd rate orders and their respective relationships.

Table 9.2.1

Rate Law Summary					
Reaction Order	Rate Law	Units of k	Integrated Rate Law	Straight-Line Plot	Half-Life Equation
0	Rate $= k[A]^0$	$M \cdot s^{-1}$	$[A]_t = -kt + [A]_0$	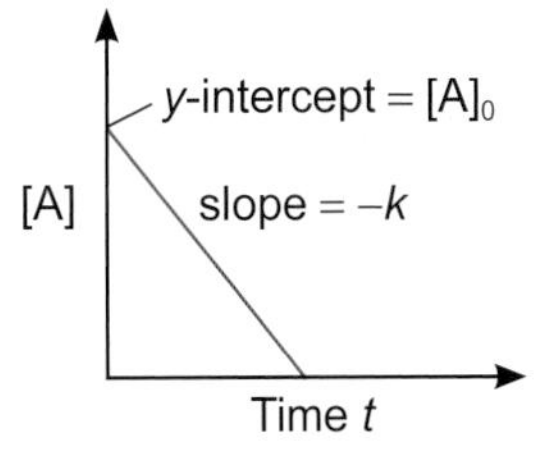 y-intercept $= [A]_0$; slope $= -k$; [A] vs. Time t	$t_{1/2} = \dfrac{[A]_0}{2k} = \dfrac{1}{k}\dfrac{[A]_0}{2}$
1	Rate $= k[A]^1$	s^{-1}	$\ln[A]_t = -kt + \ln[A]_0$ $\ln\dfrac{[A]_t}{[A]_0} = -kt$	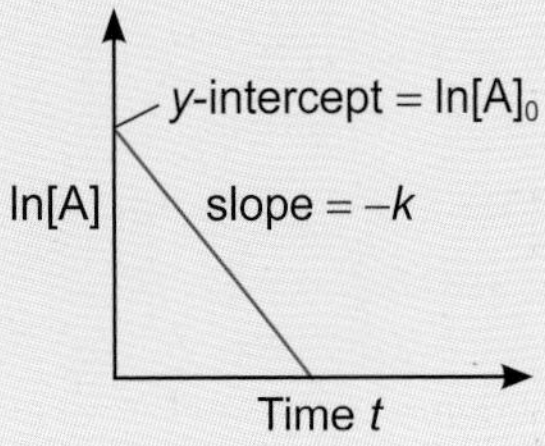 y-intercept $= \ln[A]_0$; slope $= -k$; ln[A] vs. Time t	$t_{1/2} = \dfrac{0.693}{k} = \dfrac{1}{k}(0.693)$
2	Rate $= k[A]^2$	$M^{-1} \cdot s^{-1}$	$\dfrac{1}{[A]_t} = kt + \dfrac{1}{[A]_0}$	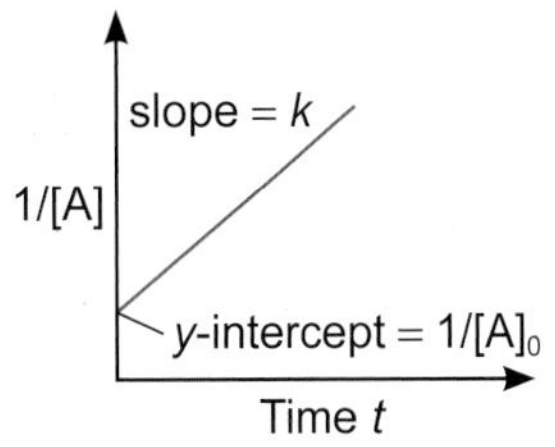 slope $= k$; y-intercept $= 1/[A]_0$; 1/[A] vs. Time t	$t_{1/2} = \dfrac{1}{k[A]_0} = \dfrac{1}{k}\dfrac{1}{[A]_0}$

As depicted by the table, the first and second order rate laws are also derived in a similar manner as the zero order rate law.

Included within the table is also the half-life's of the three described rate laws. The half-life of a reaction is defined as the time needed to decrease the concentration of the reactant to one-half of the original starting concentration (CHM 11.4). Note that each rate order has its own respective half-life.

The rate order of a reactant may be determined experimentally by either the isolation or initial rates method as described in the following section or by plotting concentration, or some function of concentration such as ln[ ] or 1/[ ] of reactant as a function of time. A linear relationship between the dependent concentration variable of reactant and the independent time variable will then delineate the actual order of the reactant. Moreover, if a linear curve is obtained when plotting [reactant] versus time, the order would be zero whereas, if a linear relationship is noted when plotting ln [reactant] versus time, this would be first order and second order would be for a linear relationship between 1/[reactant] versus time.

Therefore, the rate law of a reaction with a multi-step mechanism cannot be deduced from the stoichiometric coefficients of the overall reaction; it must be determined experimentally for a given reaction at a given temperature as will be described in the following section.

9.3 Determining Exponents of the Rate Law

The only way to determine the exponents with certainty is via experimentation. The rate law for any reaction must therefore always be determined by experimentation, often by a method known as the "initial rates method or the isolation method".

In the initial rates method, if there are two or more reactants involved in the reaction, the reactant concentrations are usually varied independent of each other so that, for example, in a two reactant reaction, if one reactant concentration is altered the other reactant concentration would be kept constant and the effect on the initial rate of the reaction would be measured. Consider the following five experiments varying the concentrations of reactants A and B with resulting initial rates of reaction:

$$A + B \rightarrow products$$

In the first three experiments the concentration of A changes but B remains the same. Thus the resultant changes in rate only depend on the concentration of A. Note that when [A] doubles (Exp. 1, 2) the reaction rate doubles, and when [A] triples (Exp. 1, 3) the reaction

Exp. #	Initial Concentration		Initial Rate (mol L^{-1} s^{-1})
	[A]	[B]	
1	0.10	0.10	0.20
2	0.20	0.10	0.40
3	0.30	0.10	0.60
4	0.30	0.20	2.40
5	0.30	0.30	5.40

rate triples. Because it is directly proportional, the exponent of [A] must be 1. Thus the rate of reaction is first order with respect to A.

In the final three sets of experiments, [B] changes while [A] remains the same. When [B] doubles (Exp. 3, 4) the rate increases by a factor of 4 (= 2^2). When [B] triples (Exp. 3, 5) the rate increases by a factor of 9 (= 3^2). Thus the relation is exponential where the exponent of [B] is 2. The rate of reaction is second order with respect to B.

$$\text{initial rate} = k[A]^1[B]^2$$

The overall rate of reaction (n+m) is third order. The value of the rate constant k can be easily calculated by substituting the results from any of the five experiments. For example, using experiment #1:

$$k = \frac{\text{initial rate}}{[A]^1 \, [B]^2}$$

$$k = \frac{0.20 \text{ mol } L^{-1} \text{ s}^{-1}}{(0.10 \text{ mol } L^{-1})(0.10 \text{ mol } L^{-1})^2}$$

$$= 2.0 \times 10^2 \text{ L}^2\text{mol}^{-2}\text{s}^{-1}$$

k is the rate constant for the reaction which includes all five experiments.

Note: The units of the resultant rate constant "k" will differ depending on the overall rate order of a reaction.

9.4 Reaction Mechanism - Rate-determining Step

Chemical equations fail to describe the detailed process through which the reactants are transformed into the products. For instance, consider the reaction of formation of hydrogen chloride from hydrogen and chlorine:

$$Cl_2(g) + H_2(g) \rightarrow 2\ HCl(g)$$

The equation above fails to mention that in fact this reaction is the result of a chain of reactions proceeding in three steps:

Initiation step: formation of free chlorine radicals by photon irradiation or introduction of heat (= *radicals*, the mechanism will be discussed in organic chemistry):

$$1/2\ Cl_2 \rightleftharpoons Cl\cdot$$

The double arrow indicates that in fact some of the Cl free radicals recombine to form chlorine molecules, the whole process eventually reaches a state of equilibrium where the following ratio is constant:

$$K = [Cl\cdot]/[Cl_2]^{1/2}$$

The determination of such a constant will be dealt with in the sub-section on "equilibrium constants."

Propagation step: formation of reactive hydrogen free radicals and reaction between hydrogen free radicals and chlorine molecules:

$$Cl\cdot + H_2 \rightarrow HCl + H\cdot$$

$$H\cdot + Cl_2 \rightarrow HCl + Cl\cdot$$

Termination step: Formation of hydrogen chloride by reaction between hydrogen free radicals and chlorine free radicals.

$$H\cdot + Cl\cdot \rightarrow HCl$$

The detailed chain reaction process above is called the mechanism of the reaction. Each individual step in a detailed mechanism is called an elementary step. Any reaction proceeds through some mechanism which is generally impossible to predict from its chemical equation. Such mechanisms are usually determined through an experimental procedure. Generally speaking each step proceeds at its own rate.

The rate of the overall reaction is naturally limited by the slowest step; therefore, the rate-determining step in the mechanism of a reaction is the slowest step. In other words, the overall rate law of a reaction is basically equal to the rate law of the slowest step. The faster processes have an indirect influence on the rate: they regulate the concentrations of the reactants and products. The chemical equation of an elementary step reflects the exact molecular process that transforms its reactants into its products. For this reason its rate law can be predicted from its chemical equation: in an elementary process, the orders with respect to the reactants are equal to the corresponding stoichiometric coefficients.

In our example, experiments show that the rate-determining step is the reaction between chlorine radicals and hydrogen molecules, all the other steps are much faster. According to the principles stated, the rate law of the overall reaction is equal to the rate law of this rate-determining step. Therefore, the rate of the overall reaction is proportional to the concentration of hydrogen molecules and chlorine radicals but is not directly proportional to the concentration of chlorine molecules. However, since the ratio of concentrations of Cl and Cl_2 is regulated by the initiation step concentration, it can be shown that according to the mechanism provided the rate law is:

$$rate = k[H_2] \bullet [Cl_2]^{1/2}$$

It is important to note that the individual orders of a reaction are generally not equal to the stoichiometric coefficients.

9.5 Dependence of Reaction Rates upon Temperature

Rates of chemical reactions are generally very sensitive to temperature fluctuations. In particular, many reactions are known to slow down by decreasing the temperature or vise versa. How does one therefore explain the temperature dependence on reaction rates? The rate of a reaction is essentially equal to the reactant concentration raised to a reaction order (n) times the rate constant k or rate $= k[A]^x$. From the collision theory of chemical kinetics it was established that the rate constant of a reaction can be expressed as follows:

$$k = A\, e^{-Ea/RT}$$

- A is a constant referred to as the "Arrhenius constant" or the frequency factor which includes two separate components known as, the orientation factor (p) and the collision frequency (z). More specifically, the collision frequency (z) is defined as the number of collisions that molecules acquire per unit time and the orientation factor (p) is defined as the proper orientation reactant molecules require for product formation. Thus, the Arrhenius constant, A, is related to both the frequency of collisions (z) and the proper orientation (p) of the molecular collisions required for final product formation and so $A = pz$.

- e is the base of natural logarithms,
- E_a is the activation energy, it is the energy required to get a reaction started. For reactants to transform into products, the reactants must go through a high energy state or "transition state" which is the minimum energy (activation energy) required for reactants to transform into products. If two molecules of reactants collide with proper orientation and sufficient energy

or force in such a way that the molecules acquire a total energy content surpassing the activation energy, E_a, the collisions will result in a complete chemical reaction and the formation of products. Note: only a fraction of colliding reactant molecules will have sufficient kinetic energy to exceed an activation energy barrier.

- R is the ideal gas constant (1.99 cal mol^{-1} K^{-1})
- T is the absolute temperature.

It can therefore be seen that the rate constant, k, contains the temperature component as an exponent and thus, temperature affects a reaction rate by affecting the actual rate constant k. Note: A rate constant remains constant only when temperature remains constant. The rate constant equation otherwise known as the "Arrhenius equation"

thus describes the relationship between the rate constant (k) and temperature.

Either an increase in temperature or decrease in activation energy will result in an increase in the reaction constant k and thus an increase in the reaction rate. The species formed during an efficient collision, before the reactants transform into the final product(s) is called the activated complex or the transition state.

Within the framework of this theory, when a single step reaction proceeds, the potential energy of the system varies according to Figure III.A.9.1.

The change in enthalpy (ΔH) during the reaction is the difference between the total energy of the products and the reactants.

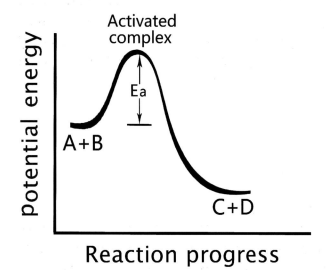
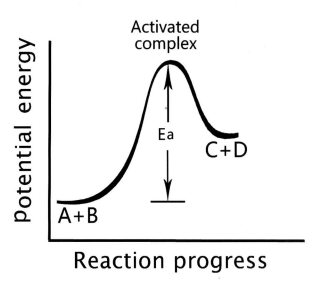

Figure III.A.9.1: Potential energy diagrams: exothermic vs. endothermic reactions.

The left curve of Figure III.A.9.1 shows that the total energy of the reactants is higher than the total energy of the products: this is obviously the case for an exothermic reaction. The right curve of Figure III.A.9.1, shows the profile of an endothermic reaction. A negative enthalpy change indicates an exothermic reaction and a positive enthalpy change depicts an endothermic reaction. The difference in potential energy between the reactant(s) and the activated complex is the activation energy of the forward reaction and the difference between the product(s) and the activated complex is the activation energy of the reverse reaction. Also note that the bigger the difference between the total energy of the reactants and the activated complex, i.e. the activation energy E_a, the slower the reaction.

If a reaction proceeds through several steps one can construct a diagram for each step and combine the single-step diagrams to obtain the energy profile of the overall reaction.

9.6 Kinetic Control vs. Thermodynamic Control

Consider the case where two molecules A and B can react to form either products C or D. Suppose that C has the lowest Gibbs free energy (i.e. the most thermodynamically stable product). Also suppose that product D requires the smallest activation energy and is therefore formed faster than C. If it is product C which is exclusively observed when the reaction is actually performed, the reaction is said to be thermodynamically controlled (i.e. out of a list of possible pathways the reactants choose the one leading to the most stable product). If on the other hand the reactants choose the pathway leading to the product which is produced more quickly it is said to be kinetically controlled.

9.7 Catalysis

A catalyst is a compound that does not directly participate in a reaction (the initial number of moles of this compound in the reaction mixture is equal to the number of moles of this compound once the reaction is completed). Catalysts work by providing an alternative mechanism for a reaction that involves a different transition state, one in which a lower activation energy occurs at the rate-determining step. Catalysts help lower the activation energy of a reaction and help the reaction to proceed. Enzymes are the typical biological catalysts. They are protein molecules with very large molar masses containing one or more active sites (BIO 4.1-4.4). Enzymes are very specialized catalysts. They are generally specific and operate only on certain biological reactants called substrates. They also generally increase the rate of reactions by large factors. The general mechanism of operation of enzymes is as follows:

Enzyme (E) + Substrate (S) → ES (complex)

ES → Product (P) + Enzyme (E)

If we were to compare the energy profile of a reaction performed in the absence of an enzyme to that of the same reaction performed with the addition of an enzyme we would obtain Figure III.A.9.2.

As you can see from Figure III.A.9.2, the reaction from the substrate to the product is facilitated by the presence of the enzyme because the reaction proceeds in two fast steps (low E_a's). Generally, catalysts (or enzymes) stabilize the transition state of a reaction by lowering the energy barrier between reactants and the transition state. Catalysts (or enzymes) do not change the energy difference between reactants and products. Therefore, catalysts do not alter the extent of a reaction or the chemical equilibrium itself. Generally, the rate of an enzyme-catalysed reaction is :

$$rate = k[ES]$$

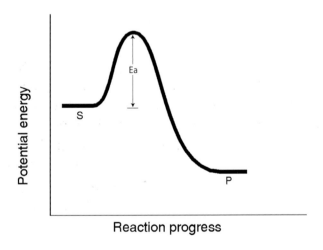
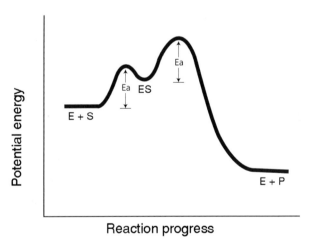

Figure III.A.9.2: Potential energy diagrams: without and with a catalyst.

The rate of formation of the product $\Delta[P]/\Delta t$ vs. the concentration of the substrate $[S]$ yields a plot as in Figure III.A.9.3.

When the concentration of the substrate is large enough for the substrate to occupy all the available active sites on the enzyme, any further increase would have no effect on the rate of the reaction. This is called *saturation kinetics* (BIO 1.1.2).

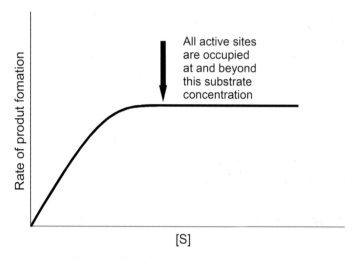

Figure III.A.9.3: Saturation kinetics.

9.8 Equilibrium in Reversible Chemical Reactions

In most chemical reactions once the product is formed, it reacts in such a way to yield back the initial reactants. Eventually, the system reaches a state where there are as many molecules of products being formed as there are molecules of reactants being generated through the reverse reaction. At equilibrium, the concentrations of reactants and products will not necessarily be equal, however, the concentrations remain the same. Hence, the relative concentrations of all components of the forward and reverse reactions become constant at equilibrium. This is called a state of "dynamic equilibrium". It is characterized by a constant K:

$$aA + bB \rightleftharpoons cC + dD$$

where a, b, c and d are the corresponding stoichiometric coefficients:

$$K = \frac{[C]^c \, [D]^d}{[A]^a \, [B]^b}$$

The equilibrium constant K (sometimes symbolized as K_{eq}) has a given value at a given temperature. If the temperature changes the value of K changes. At a given temperature, if we change the concentration of A, B, C or D, the system evolves in such a way as to re-establish the value of K. This is called the law of mass action. {Note: catalysts speed up the rate of reaction without affecting K_{eq}}

The following is an example of how an equilibrium constant K is calculated based on a chemical reaction at equilibrium. Remember that the equilibrium constant K can be directly calculated only when the equilibrium concentrations of reactants and products are known or obtained.

As an example, suppose that initially, 5 moles of reactant X are mixed with 12 moles of Y and both are added into an empty 1 liter container. Following their reaction, the system eventually reaches equilibrium with 4 moles of Z formed according to the following reaction:

$$X (g) + 2Y (g) \rightleftharpoons Z (g)$$

For this gaseous, homogeneous mixture (CHM 1.7), what is the value of the equilibrium constant K?

At equilibrium, 4 moles of Z are formed and therefore, 4 moles of X and 8 moles of Y are consumed based on the mole:mole ratio of the balanced equation. Since 5 moles X and 12 moles Y were initially available prior to equilibrium, at equilibrium following the reaction, there remains 1 mol X and 4 moles Y. Since all of the reaction takes place in a 1 L volume, the equilibrium concentrations are therefore, 1 mol/L for X, 4 mol/L for Y and Z, respectively.

Thus, the equilibrium constant can then be calculated as follows:

$$K = [Z]/[X][Y]^2 = [4]/[1][4]^2 = 0.25.$$

The K value is an indication of where the equilibrium point of a reaction actually

lies, either far to the right or far to the left or somewhere in between. The following is a summary of the significance of the magnitude of an equilibrium constant K and its meaning:

1. If K > 1, this means that the forward reaction is favored and thus, the reaction favors product formation. If K is very large, the equilibrium mixture will then contain very little reactant compared to product.

2. If K < 1, the reverse reaction is favored and so the reaction does not proceed very far towards product formation and thus very little product is formed.

3. If K = 1, neither forward nor reverse directions are favored.

Note: Pure solids and pure liquids do not appear in the equilibrium constant. Thus in heterogeneous equilibria, since the liquid and solid phases are not sensitive to pressure, their "concentrations" remain constant throughout the reaction and so, mathematically, their values are denoted as 1.

Naturally, H_2O is one of the most common liquids dealt with in reactions. Remember to set its activity equal to 1 when it is a liquid but, if H_2O is written as a gas, then its concentration must be considered.

9.8.1 The Reaction Quotient Q to Predict Reaction Direction

The reaction quotient Q is the same ratio as the equilibrium constant K. Q defines all reaction progresses including the K value. In other words, the equilibrium constant K is a special case of the reaction quotient Q.

Thus, the Q ratio has many values dependent on where the reaction lies prior to or subsequent to the concentrations at equilibrium. One may therefore determine if a reaction is going towards an equilibrium by making more products or, alternatively, if a reaction is

moving towards equilibrium by making more reactants. The following is a summary of what Q means in relation to K.

Consider the following reaction:

$$aA + bB \rightleftharpoons cC + dD,$$

$$Q = [C]^c[D]^d/[A]^a[B]^b$$

The reaction quotient Q relative to the equilibrium constant K is essentially a mea-

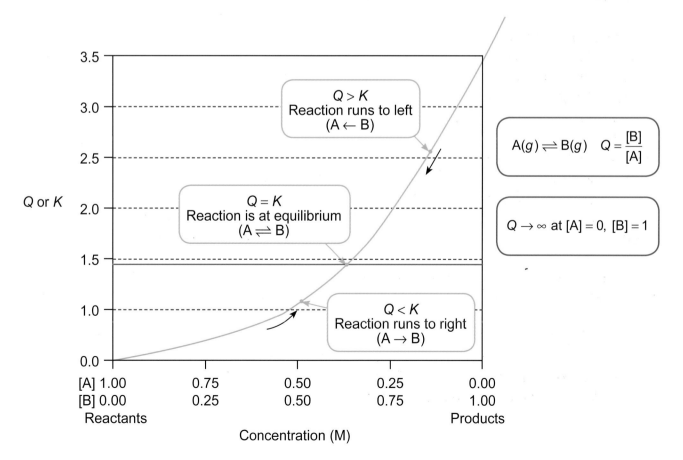

sure of the progress of a reaction toward equilibrium. The reaction quotient Q has many different values and changes continuously as a reaction progresses and depends on the current state of a reaction mixture. However, once all equilibrium concentrations have been reached, Q = K.

If Q = K, the reaction is at equilibrium and all concentrations are at equilibrium. If Q > K, there are more products initially than there are reactants so the reaction proceeds in reverse direction towards a decrease in product concentrations and a simultaneous increase in reactant concentrations until equilibrium is reached. If Q < K, there are more reactants then products and so the reaction proceeds forward towards product formation until equilibrium is reached.

9.9 Le Chatelier's Principle

Le Chatelier's principle states that whenever a perturbation is applied to a system at equilibrium, the system evolves in such a way as to compensate for the applied perturbation. For instance, consider the following equilibrium:

$$N_2 + 3H_2 \rightleftharpoons 2NH_3$$

If we introduce some more hydrogen in the reaction mixture at equilibrium, i.e. if we increase the concentration of hydrogen, the system will evolve in the direction that will decrease the concentration of hydrogen (from left to right). If more ammonia is introduced, the equilibrium shifts from the right-hand side to the left-hand side, while the removal of ammonia from the reaction vessel would do the opposite (i.e. shifts equilibrium from the left-hand side to the right-hand side).

In a similar fashion, an increase in total pressure (decrease in volume) favors the direction which decreases the total number of compressible (i.e. gases) moles (from the left-hand side where there are 4 moles to the right-hand side where there are 2 moles). It can also be said that when there are different forms of a gaseous substance, an increase in total pressure (decrease in volume) favors the form with the greatest density, and a decrease in total pressure (increase in volume) favors the form with the lowest density.

Finally, if the temperature of a reaction mixture at equilibrium is increased, the equilibrium evolves in the direction of the endothermic (heat-absorbing) reaction. For instance, the forward reaction of the equilibrium:

$$N_2O_4(g) \rightleftharpoons 2NO_2(g)$$

is endothermic; therefore, an increase in temperature favors the forward reaction over the backward reaction. In other words, the dissociation of N_2O_4 increases with temperature.

9.10 Relationship between the Equilibrium Constant and the Change in the Gibbs Free Energy

In the "thermodynamics" section we defined the Gibbs free energy. The *standard* Gibbs free energy ($G°$) is determined at 25 °C (298 K) and 1 atm. The change in the standard Gibbs free energy for a given reaction can be calculated from the change in the standard enthalpy and entropy of the reaction using:

$$\Delta G° = \Delta H - T \Delta S°$$

where T is the temperature at which the reaction is carried out. If this reaction happens to be the forward reaction of an equilibrium, the equilibrium constant associated with this equilibrium is simply given by:

$$\Delta G° = -R\, T \ln K_{eq}$$

where R is the ideal gas constant (1.99 cal mol^{-1} K^{-1}) and ln is the natural logarithm (i.e. log to the base e; see QR Appendix).

It is important to remember the sign for Gibbs free energy when the reaction is not spontaneous, spontaneous and at equilibrium (CHM 8.10).

GOLD STANDARD WARM-UP EXERCISES
CHAPTER 9: Rate Processes in Chemical Reactions

1) The reaction $P + 3Q \leftrightarrow R$ was studied and the data in Table 1 were collected.

Table 1

Exp.	[P] in M	[Q] in M	Initial rate of reaction
A	0.30	0.90	5.0×10^{-6}
B	0.30	1.80	1.0×10^{-5}
C	0.90	0.90	4.5×10^{-5}

The rate determining step in this reaction probably involves:

A. two molecules of P and two molecules of Q.
B. three molecules of P and one molecule of Q.
C. one molecule of P and three molecules of Q.
D. two molecules of P and one molecule of Q.

2) This reaction is shifted to the right on the application of heat:

$$3HalO^- \leftrightarrow 2Hal^- + HalO_3^-$$

The ΔH_{rxn} for the reaction is probably:
A. zero.
B. positive.
C. negative.
D. dependent on the temperature at which the reaction occurs.

3) If no catalyst was used in Reaction I, which of the following would experience a change in its partial pressure when the same system reaches equilibrium?

Reaction I

$$2SO_2(g) + O_2(g) \leftrightarrow 2SO_3(g) \qquad \Delta H = -197 \text{ kJ mol}^{-1}$$

A. There will be no change in the partial pressure of any of the reactants.
B. SO_3 (g)
C. SO_2 (g)
D. O_2 (g)

4) If the temperature was decreased in Reaction I of the previous question, which of the following would experience an increase in its partial pressure when the same system reaches equilibrium?

A. There will be no change in the partial pressure of any of the reactants.
B. SO_3 (g)
C. SO_2 (g)
D. O_2 (g) and SO_2 (g)

5) In an experiment carried out at 25 °C, P_2 and Q_2 molecules reacted to yield one triatomic product. This took place spontaneously and was associated with an increase in the temperature of the reaction vessel. If the reaction is an equilibrium type reaction, what does Le Chatelier's Principle predict for a decrease in temperature?

A. Reaction shifts to the right to yield more products
B. Reaction shifts to the left to yield more reactants
C. Reaction equilibrium position is unaffected
D. Depends on whether or not the reaction vessel is connected to a water manometer

6) Which of the following represents the general shape of the potential energy diagram for the following reaction?

$$2NO(g) + O_2(g) \rightarrow 2NO_2(g) \qquad \Delta H° = -116.2 \text{ kJ}$$

A
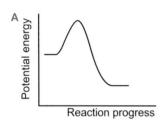

B
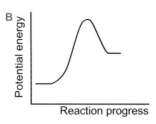

C
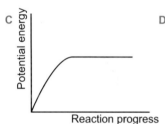

D
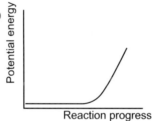

7) The equilibrium shown below was established within the confines of a closed system.

Reaction I

$$4NH_3(g) + 5O_2(g) \rightleftharpoons 4NO(g) + 6H_2O(g)$$
$$\Delta H_{rxn} = -1100 \text{ kJ mol}{-1}$$

What effect will increasing the pressure have on this system?

A. The equilibrium will shift to the left.
B. The equilibrium will shift to the right.
C. The equilibrium position will remain the same.
D. The equilibrium position will depend on whether a catalyst is present or not.

8) Given that $K_{a1}(H_2S) = 9.1 \times 10^{-8}$ and $K_{a2}(H_2S) = 1.2 \times 10^{-15}$, what would be the effect on Reaction I if protons were added to the reaction mixture at equilibrium?

(note: the effect of protons on CN^- is relatively negligible).

Reaction I

$$Ag_2S + 4CN^- \leftrightarrow 2[Ag(CN)_2]^- + S^{2-}$$

A. The equilibrium would shift to the left.
B. The equilibrium would shift to the right.
C. There would be no change in the equilibrium position of the reaction.
D. The change in the equilibrium position cannot be determined from the information given.

9) Consider the following gas phase reaction at equilibrium:

$$H_2 + I_2 \leftrightarrow 2HI$$

ΔH for the forward reaction (production of HI) is negative. Raising the ambient temperature of the reaction would cause:

A. a decrease in entropy.
B. a decrease in pressure.
C. an increase in the concentration of H_2 and I_2.
D. no change in the equilibrium concentrations of reactants and products.

10) Consider the data in Table 1, which pertain to the following reaction:

$$A + B \rightarrow C$$

The equation above may or may not be balanced.

Table 1

Experiment	[A]	[B]	Initial rate of reaction
1	0.10	0.10	4.0×10^{-5}
2	0.10	0.20	4.0×10^{-5}
3	0.20	0.10	16×10^{-5}

The rate law for the reaction is:

A. Rate = k[A][B].
B. Rate = k[A]^2[B].
C. Rate = k[A]^2.
D. Rate = k[A][B]^2.

11) Based on Table 1 in the previous question, the rate constant, k, is:
A. $4.0 \times 10^{-3}\ M^{-1}s^{-1}$
B. $4.0 \times 10^{-3}\ Ms^{-1}$
C. $4.0 \times 10^{-5}\ M^{-1}s^{-1}$
D. $4.0 \times 10^{-5}\ Ms^{-1}$

12) The mechanism of the reaction described in Table 1 from the previous questions most likely involves:
A. a termolecular rate (3 molecules)–determining step.
B. a bimolecular rate–determining step involving two molecules of A, followed by a fast step involving a molecule of B.
C. a fast step involving a molecule of A and a molecule of B, followed by a bimolecular rate-determining step involving another molecule of A.
D. a bimolecular rate–determining step involving a molecule of A and a molecule of B, followed by a fast step involving another molecule of A.

13) Which of the following statements is/are true?
I. k increases with activation energy.
II. k increases with temperature.
III. k decreases with increasing concentrations of products.
A. Only II
B. I and II
C. II and III
D. I, II and III

14) When sucrose is digested, it is hydrolyzed to form glucose and fructose. The following data in Table 1 are collected for the hydrolysis of sucrose in 0.100 M HCl at 35 °C.

Table 1

Concentration of Sucrose (M)	Initial Rate (M/min)
0.500	1.80×10^{-3}
0.400	1.46×10^{-3}
0.200	7.32×10^{-4}

Which of the following might be the rate law for the hydrolysis of sucrose under these conditions?
A. rate $= (1.46 \times 10^{-4}\ min^{-1})$[sucrose]
B. rate $= (1.46 \times 10^{-3}\ min^{-1}M^{-1})$[sucrose]^2
C. rate $= (3.66 \times 10^{-3}\ min^{-1})$[sucrose]
D. rate $= (3.66 \times 10^{-4}\ min^{-1}M^{-1})$[sucrose]^2

15) The graph below represents the exothermic energy changes of the following reaction:

$$A + B \rightarrow C$$

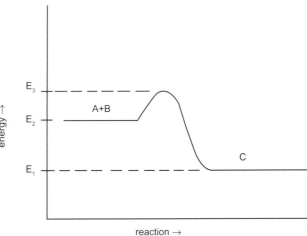

What is the activation energy of this reaction?
A. $E_3 - E_1$
B. $E_2 - E_1$
C. $E_3 - E_2$
D. None of the above

GS ANSWER KEY

CHAPTER 9

		Cross-Reference				Cross-Reference
1.	D	CHM 9.3, 9.4	9.	C	CHM 9.9
2.	B	CHM 8.2, 9.9	10.	C	CHM 9.2, 9.3
3.	A	CHM 9.7, 9.8	11.	A	CHM 9.2, 9.3
4.	B	CHM 9.9	12.	B	CHM 9.2, 9.3
5.	A	CHM 9.9	13.	A	CHM 9.2, 9.3
6.	A	CHM 9.5	14.	C	CHM 9.3
7.	A	CHM 9.9	15.	C	CHM 9.5
8.	B	CHM 5.3.3, 9.9			

* Explanations can be found at the back of the book.

Go online to DAT-prep.com for additional chapter review Q&A and forum.

Rate Law

$A + B \longrightarrow$ products

$rate = K [A]^{x=2} [B]^{y=1}$

Initial ... Concentration		Rate
[A]	[B]	$mol \cdot L^{-1} \cdot s^{-1}$
0.10	0.10	1.23×10^{-3}
0.10	0.20	2.46×10^{-3}
0.20	0.10	4.92×10^{-3}

$\times 2$ $\times 2$ $\Rightarrow$ [B] – first order

$\times 2$

$\times 4 \Rightarrow$ [A] – 2nd order

Potential Energy Diagram

$A + B \longrightarrow C + D$

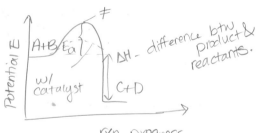

exothermic

$\Delta H = \ominus$

ΔH – difference btw product & reactants.

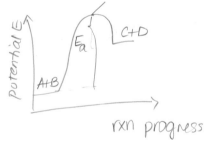

Transition state – bonds created & destroyed ...

Endothermic

$\Delta H \leq \oplus$

Smaller E_a – ↑ spontaneously

larger E_a – less chance "

* Catalyst reduces activation energy

ELECTROCHEMISTRY

Chapter 10

Memorize

efine: anode, cathode, anion, cation
efine: standard half-cell potentials
efine: strong/weak oxidizing/reducing
gents

Understand

* Electrolytic cell, electrolysis
* Calculation involving Faraday's law
* Galvanic (voltaic) cell, purpose of salt bridge
* Half reaction, reduction potentials
* Direction of electron flow

Importance

1 to 3 out of the 30 Gen CHM

DAT questions are based on content in this chapter (in our estimation).
* Note that between 50% and 85% of the questions in DAT General Chemistry are based on content from 6 chapters: 1, 2, 4, 5, 6 and 9.

DAT-Prep.com

Introduction ▌▌▌▌

Electrochemistry links chemistry with electricity (the movement of electrons through a conductor). If a chemical reaction produces electricity (i.e. a battery or galvanic/voltaic cell) then it is an **electrochemical cell**. If electricity is applied externally to drive the chemical reaction then it is **electrolysis**. In general, oxidation/reduction reactions occur and are separated in space or time, connected by an external circuit.

Additional Resources

Free Online Forum

Video: Online or DVD

Flashcards

10.1 Generalities

Electrochemistry is based on oxidation-reduction or redox reactions in which one or more electrons are transferred from one ionic species to another. Recall that oxidation is defined as the loss of one or more electrons and reduction is defined as the gain in electron(s). In a redox reaction, reduction and oxidation must occur simultaneously. Before you read this section you should review the rules that allow the determination of the oxidation state of an element in a polyatomic molecule or ion and the definition of oxidation and reduction processes. We had previously applied the rules for the determination of oxidation numbers in the case of the following overall reaction (see CHM 1.6):

$$CuSO_4(aq) + Zn(s) \rightleftharpoons$$
Oxid.#: +2   0
$$Cu(s) + ZnSO_4(aq)$$
Oxid.#:   0   +2

The reduction and oxidation half-reactions of the forward process are:

reduction half-reaction:
$$Cu^{2+}(aq) + 2e^- \rightarrow Cu(s)$$

oxidation half-reaction:
$$Zn(s) \rightarrow Zn^{2+}(aq) + 2e^-$$

A half reaction does not occur on its own merit. Any reduction half reaction must be accompanied by an associated oxidation half reaction or vise versa, as electrons need to be transferred accordingly from one reactant to another. To determine the number and the side on which to put the electrons one follows the simple rules:

(i) The electrons are always on the left-hand side of a reduction half-reaction.

(ii) The electrons are always on the right-hand side of an oxidation half-reaction.

(iii) For a reduction half-reaction:

# of electrons required = initial oxidation #
                                    – final oxidation #

(iv) For an oxidation half-reaction:
# of electrons required = final oxidation #
                                  – initial oxidation #

The next step is to balance each half-reaction, i.e. the charges and the number of atoms of all the elements involved have to be equal on both sides. The preceding example is very simple since the number of electrons required in the two half-reactions is the same. Consider the following more complicated example:

reduction: $Sn^{2+}(aq) + 2e^- \rightarrow Sn(s)$
oxidation: $Al(s) \rightarrow Al^{3+}(aq) + 3e^-$

to balance the overall reaction you need to multiply the first half-reaction by a factor of 3 and the second by a factor of 2.

Balancing redox reactions in aqueous solutions may not always be as straight forward as balancing other types of chemical reactions. For redox type reactions, both the mass and the charge must be balanced. In addition, when looking at redox reactions occurring in aqueous solutions one must also consider at times if the solution is acidic or basic. The procedure used to balance redox reactions in acidic versus basic solutions is slightly different. Generally, the recommended steps used in balancing redox reactions is as follows and the method used is called the "*half-reaction method of balancing*":

1) Identify all the oxidation states of all elements within the redox reaction.

2) Identify the elements being oxidized and those being reduced.

3) Separate the overall redox reaction into its corresponding oxidation and reduction half reactions.

4) Balance all elements for each half reaction excluding hydrogen and oxygen.

5) Balance oxygen by the addition of water to the side missing the oxygen and balance the oxygen atoms by adding the appropriate coefficients in front of water.

6) Balance hydrogen by the addition of H^+ ion to the side missing the hydrogen atoms until hydrogen is balanced with the appropriate coefficients added. Note that the difference in balancing redox reactions in acidic versus basic aqueous solutions is at this step. In basic solutions, an additional step is required to neutralize the H^+ ions with the addition of OH^- ions so that both may then combine to form water.

7) Balance the half reactions with respect to charge by the addition of electrons on the appropriate side.

8) Balance the number of electrons for each half reaction by multiplying each of the half reactions (if required) with the appropriate coefficient.

9) Add the two half reactions making sure that all electrons are cancelled.

10) Finally, as a check: you should always verify that all elements and charges are balanced on both sides of the overall reaction and that the final overall reaction *never contains any free electrons*.

Example: In acidic solution, balance the following redox reaction:

$$Fe^{2+} (aq) + MnO_4^- (aq) \rightarrow Fe^{3+} (aq) + Mn^{2+} (aq)$$

Step 1: $\quad$ +2 $\qquad$ +7 –2 $\qquad$ +3 $\qquad$ +2

Step 2: Fe is oxidized (+2 to +3)
Mn in MnO_4^- is reduced to Mn^{2+}
(+7 to +2, oxygen will be balanced with water)

Step 3: Oxidation: $Fe^{2+} (aq) \rightarrow Fe^{3+} (aq)$
Reduction: $MnO_4^- (aq) \rightarrow Mn^{2+} (aq)$

Step 4, 5 and 6: Oxidation: $Fe^{2+} (aq) \rightarrow Fe^{3+} (aq)$
Reduction: $8H^+ (aq) + MnO_4^- (aq)$
$\rightarrow Mn^{2+} (aq) + 4H_2O (l)$

Step 7: Oxidation: $Fe^{2+} (aq) \rightarrow Fe^{3+} (aq) + 1e^-$
Reduction: $5e^- + 8H^+ (aq) + MnO_4^- (aq)$
$\rightarrow Mn^{2+} (aq) + 4H_2O (l)$

Step 8: Oxidation: $5[Fe^{2+} (aq) \rightarrow Fe^{3+} (aq) + 1e^-]$
$5Fe^{2+} (aq) \rightarrow 5Fe^{3+} (aq) + 5e^-$
Reduction: $5e^- + 8H^+ (aq) + MnO_4^- (aq)$
$\rightarrow Mn^{2+} (aq) + 4H_2O (l)$

Step 9: Overall: $5Fe^{2+} (aq) + 8H^+ (aq) + MnO_4^- (aq)$
$\rightarrow 5Fe^{3+} (aq) + Mn^{2+} (aq) + 4H_2O (l)$

Step 10: Check if all is balanced.

The oxidation/reduction capabilities of substances are measured by their standard reduction half reaction potentials $E°(V)$. The reduction potential $E°(V)$ is a measure of the tendency of a chemical species to acquire electrons and thereby be reduced. The more positive the reduction potential, the more likely the species is to be reduced. Thus, the species would be regarded as a strong oxidizing agent. These potentials are relative. The reference half-cell electrode chosen to measure the relative potential of all other half cells is known as the **s**tandard **h**ydrogen **e**lectrode or SHE and it corresponds to the following half-reaction:

$$2H^+(1 \text{ molar}) + 2e^- \rightarrow H_2(1 \text{ atm}) \quad E° = 0.00 \text{ (V)}.$$

As the reference SHE cell potential is defined as 0.00 V, any half-cell system that accepts electrons from a SHE cell is reduced and therefore defined by a positive redox potential. Alternatively, any half-cell that donates electrons to a SHE cell is defined by a negative redox potential. Thus, the larger the reduction potential value of a half-cell, the greater the tendency for that half-cell to gain electrons and become reduced. Standard half-cell potentials for other half-reactions have been tabulated and you will see examples to follow, and more in the chapter review Warm-Up Exercises. They are defined for standard conditions, i.e., concentration of all ionic species equal to 1 molar and pressure of all gases involved, if any, equal to 1 atm. The standard temperature is taken as 25 °C. In the case of the Cu^{2+}/Zn reaction the relevant data is tabulated as reduction potentials as follows:

$$Zn^{2+}(aq) + 2e^- \rightarrow Zn(s) \quad E° = -0.76 \text{ volts}$$
$$Cu^{2+}(aq) + 2e^- \rightarrow Cu(s) \quad E° = +0.34 \text{ volts}$$

As shown, it can be seen that the Cu/Cu^{2+} electrode is positive relative to the SHE and that the Zn/Zn^{2+} is negative relative to the SHE. The more positive the $E°$ value, the more likely the reaction will occur spontaneously as written. The strongest reducing agents have large negative $E°$ values. The strongest oxidizing agents have large positive $E°$ values. Therefore, in our example Cu^{2+} is a stronger oxidizing agent than Zn^{2+}. This conclusion can be expressed in the following practical terms:

(i) If you put Zn in contact with a solution containing Cu^{2+} ions a spontaneous redox reaction will occur.

$$Zn(s) \rightarrow Zn^{2+} (aq) + 2e^-; \quad E°(V) = +0.76$$
$$Cu^{2+} (aq) + 2e^- \rightarrow Cu(s); \quad E°(V) = +0.34$$
$$E°_{cell} = E°_{red} + E°_{ox} = +0.34 + 0.76 = + 1.10 \text{ V}.$$

(ii) If you put Cu directly in contact with a solution containing Zn^{2+} ions, no reaction takes place spontaneously.

$$Cu(s) \rightarrow Cu^{2+} (aq) + 2e^-; \quad E°(V) = -0.34$$
$$Zn^{2+} (aq) + 2e^- \rightarrow Zn(s); E°(V) = -0.76$$
$$E°_{cell} = E°_{red} + E°_{ox} = -0.76 + (-0.34) = - 1.10 \text{ V}.$$

Thus for the spontaneous reaction:

$$\textbf{(1)} \ E° = E°_{red} - E°_{ox}$$
$$E° = E°_{red} - E°_{ox} = +0.34 - (-0.76) = 1.10 \text{ V}.$$
$$\text{or } \textbf{(2)} \ E°_{cell} = E°_{red} + E°_{ox} = +0.34 + 0.76 = 1.10 \text{ V}.$$

The positive value confirms the spontaneous nature of the reaction. {The theme of many exam questions: the oxidizing agent is *reduced*; the reducing agent is *oxidized*}

For a cell potential ($E°$) calculation, if one is to calculate it using the formula **(1)** should use the tabulated reduction potentials for both half cell reduction reactions. Alternatively, if one were to calculate the cell potential using the second formula **(2)**, the half cell potential that has the lower potential value or the oxidized half cell (more negative value), needs to be reversed to have it in an oxidized format and therefore the electromotive ($E°$) potential sign itself is also inverted accordingly and the sum of the two half cells is then calculated. Also, note that the stoichiometric factors are <u>not</u> used if one is simply calculating the $E°$ of the cell (because the concentrations are, of course, standard at 1 M).

10.2 Galvanic Cells

As a result of a redox reaction, one may harvest a substantial amount of energy and the energy generated is usually carried out in what is known as an electrochemical cell. There are two types of electrochemical cells: a galvanic (or voltaic) cell and an electrolytic cell. A galvanic cell produces electrical energy from a spontaneous chemical reaction that takes place within an electrochemical cell. On the other hand, an electrolytic cell induces a nonspontaneous chemical reaction within an electrochemical cell by the consumption of electrical energy.

Batteries are self-contained galvanic cells. A <u>galvanic cell</u> uses a <u>spontaneous redox reaction</u> to <u>produce electricity</u>. For instance, one can design a galvanic cell based on the spontaneous reaction:

$$Zn(s) + CuSO_4(aq) \rightarrow Cu(s) + ZnSO_4(aq)$$

An actual view of a galvanic cell is depicted in Figure III.A.10.1a. In addition, Figure III.A.10.1b shows a sketch of a line diagram of the same galvanic cell outlining all the different parts. Note that in Figure III.A.10.1b, Zn is not in direct contact with the Cu^{2+} solution; otherwise electrons will be directly transferred from Zn to Cu^{2+} and no electricity will be produced to an external circuit.

The half-reaction occurring in the left-hand (anode) compartment is the oxidation:

$$Zn(s) \rightarrow Zn^{2+}(aq) + 2e^-$$

The half-reaction occurring in the right-hand (cathode) compartment is the reduction:

$$Cu^{2+}(aq) + 2e^- \rightarrow Cu(s)$$

Therefore, <u>electrons flow</u> out of the compartment where the <u>oxidation</u> occurs to the compartment where the <u>reduction</u> takes place.

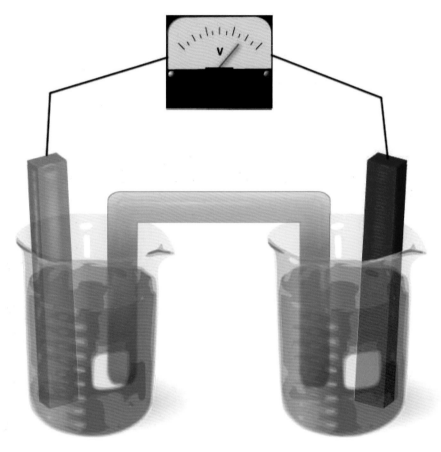

Figure III.A.10.1a: A galvanic (electrochemical) cell. As shown by the displacement in voltage via the voltmeter, the energy of a spontaneous redox reaction is essentially captured within the galvanic cell. A galvanic cell consists mainly of the following parts: **1)** Two separate half cells; **2)** Two solid element electrodes with differing redox potentials; **3)** Two opposing aqueous solutions each in contact with opposing solid electrodes; **4)** One salt bridge with an embedded salt solution; **5)** One ammeter or voltmeter and; **6)** An electrical solid element or wire to allow conductivity of electrons from anode to cathode.

The metallic parts (Cu(*s*) and Zn(*s*) in our example) of the galvanic cell which allow its connection to an external circuit are called electrodes. The electrode <u>out</u> of which <u>electrons flow</u> is the <u>anode</u>, the electrode <u>receiving</u> these <u>electrons</u> is the <u>cathode</u>. In a galvanic cell the <u>oxidation</u> occurs in the <u>anodic compartment</u> and the <u>reduction</u> in the <u>cathodic compartment</u>. The voltage difference between the two electrodes is called the <u>electromotive</u> force (*emf*) of the cell. The voltage is measured by the voltmeter.

All of the participants belonging to each of the half cells are included within their respective half cell. Consequently, one half of the electrochemical cell consists of an appropriate metal (Zn) immersed within a solution containing the ionic form of the same metal ($ZnSO_4$). The other half then contains the complemen-

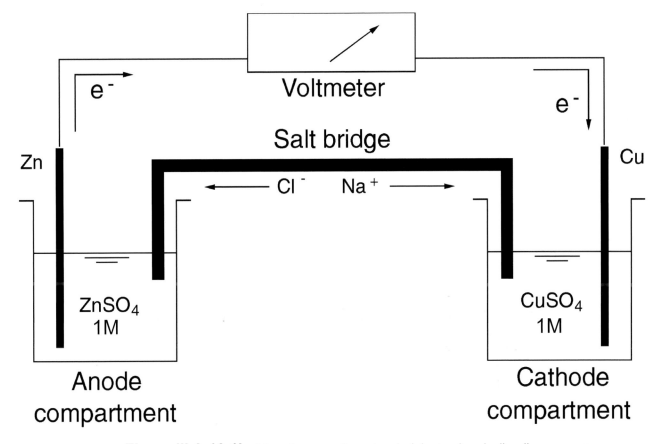

Figure III.A.10.1b: Line diagram of a galvanic (electrochemical) cell.

tary metal (Cu) immersed into an aqueous solution consisting of its metal ion ($CuSO_4$) (Figure III.A.10.1b).

In certain cells, however, the participants involved in the reduction half reaction may all be part of the aqueous solution; in such a case, an inert electrode would replace the respective metal electrode. The inert electrode such as graphite or platinum would act as a conductive surface for electron transfer. An example of such a half-cell would be one where the reduction of manganese (Mn^{7+}) as MnO_4^- occurs in a solution which

also contains manganese as ions (Mn^{2+}). To complete the electrochemical circuit, the two half-cells are then connected with a conducting wire which provides a means for electron flow. Electrons always flow from the anode (oxidation half-cell) to the cathode (reduction half-cell). The electrical energy from the flow of electrons may then be harvested and transformed into some alternative form of energy or mechanical work (as required). In order to prevent an excessive charge build up within each of the half-cell solutions as a result of oxidation and reduction reactions at the anode and cathode, a salt bridge is constructed and used to connect both half-cell solutions.

> **Mnemonic:** LEO is A GERC
> - Lose Electrons Oxidation is Anode
> - Gain Electrons Reduction at Cathode

Electrochemical cells are usually represented as a cell diagram or a compact notation denoting all the parts of the cell. For example, the cell diagram of the cell that was previously discussed in which Zn is oxidized and Cu

reduced would be represented as follows:

$$Zn(s) \mid Zn^{2+}(aq) \parallel Cu^{2+}(aq) \mid Cu(s).$$

The oxidation half reaction is on the left and the reduction half reaction is on the right side of the cell diagram. The single vertical lines represent the substances of each half-cell in different phases (solid and aqueous) and the double vertical line represents the salt bridge.

10.2.1 The Salt Bridge

A salt bridge is a U-shaped tube with a strong electrolyte suspended in a gel allowing the flow of the ions into the half-cell solutions. The salt bridge connects the two compartments chemically (for example, with Na^+ and Cl^-). It has two important functions:

1) Maintenance of Neutrality: As $Zn(s)$ becomes $Zn^{2+}(aq)$, the net charge in the anode compartment becomes positive. To maintain neutrality, Cl^- ions migrate to the anode compartment. The reverse occurs in the cathode compartment: positive ions are lost (Cu^{2+}), therefore positive ions must be gained (Na^+).

2) Completing the Circuit: Imagine the galvanic cell as a circuit. Negative charge leaves the anode compartment via *electrons* in a wire and then returns via *chemicals* (i.e. Cl^-) in the salt bridge. Thus the galvanic cell is an *electrochemical* cell.

As an alternative to a salt bridge, the solutions (i.e. $ZnSO_4$ and $CuSO_4$) can be placed in one container separated by a porous material which allows certain ions to cross (i.e. SO_4^{2-}, Zn^{2-}). Thus it would serve the same functions as the salt bridge.

10.3 Concentration Cell

If the concentration of the ions in one of the compartments of a galvanic cell is not 1 molar, the half-cell potential E is either higher or lower than E°. Therefore, in principle one could use the same substance in both compartments but with different concentrations to produce electricity.

Thus, one may construct a galvanic cell in which both half-cell reactions are the same however, the difference in concentration is the driving force for the flow of current. The emf is equal in this case to the difference between the two potentials E. Such a cell is called a concentration cell.

To determine the direction of electron flow the same rules as previously described are used. The cathodic compartment, in which the reduction takes place is the one corresponding to the largest positive (smallest negative) E.

The electromotive force varies with the differences in concentration of solutions in the half-cells. When the concentration of solution is not equal to 1M, the emf or E_{cell} can be determined by the use of the Nernst equation (BIO Appendix 5) as follows:

$$E_{cell} = E°_{cell} - (RT/nF)(\ln Q)$$

or

$$E_{cell} = E°_{cell} - 0.0592V/n\ (\log Q)$$

where; $E°_{cell}$ is the standard electromotive force, R is the gas constant 8.314J/Kmol, T is the absolute temperature in K, F is the Faraday's constant (CHM 10.5), n is the number of moles of electrons exchanged or transferred in the redox reaction, and Q is the reaction quotient (CHM 9.8.1).

Under standard conditions, Q = 1.00 as all concentrations are at 1.00 M and since log 1 = 0, $E_{cell} = E°_{cell}$.

10.4 Electrolytic Cell

There is a fundamental difference between a galvanic cell or a concentration cell and an electrolytic cell: in the first type of electrochemical cell a spontaneous redox reaction is used to produce a current, in the second type a current is actually imposed on the system to drive a non-spontaneous redox reaction. A cathode is defined as the electrode to which cations flow to and an anode is defined as the electrode to which anions flow. Thus, a similarity between the two cells is that the cathode attracts cations, whereas the anode attracts anions. In both the galvanic cell and the electrolytic cell, reduction occurs always at the cathode and oxidation always occurs at the anode.

Remember the following key concepts:

(i) generally a battery is used to produce a current which is imposed on the electrolytic cell.

(ii) the battery acts as an electron pump: electrons flow into the electrolytic cell at the cathode and flow out of it at the anode.

(iii) the half-reaction occurring at the cathode is a reduction since it requires electrons.

(iv) the half-reaction occurring at the anode is an oxidation since it produces electrons.

In galvanic cells, a spontaneous oxidation reaction takes place at the cell's anode creating a source of electrons. For this reason, the anode is considered the negative electrode. However, in electrolytic cells, a non-spontaneous reduction reaction takes place at the cell's cathode using an external electrical energy as the source of electrons such as a battery. For this reason, the cathode is considered the negative electrode.

An electrolytic cell is composed of three parts: an electrolyte solution and two electrodes made from an inert material (i.e. platinum). The oxidation and reduction half reactions are usually placed in one container.

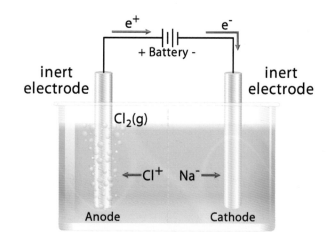

The diagram is a depiction of the electrolysis of molten NaCl. As such, the Na^+ and Cl^- ions are the only species that are present in the electrolytic cell. Thus, the chloride anion (Cl^-) cannot be reduced any further and so it is oxidized at the anode and the sodium cation (Na^+) is therefore reduced. The final products are sodium solid formation at the cathode and chlorine (Cl_2) gas formation at the anode.

Note: the flow of electrons is still from anode to cathode as is for galvanic cells.

10.5 Faraday's Law

Faraday's law relates the amount of elements deposited or gas liberated at an electrode due to current.

We have seen that in a galvanic cell $Cu^{2+}(aq)$ can accept electrons to become $Cu(s)$ which will actually plate onto the electrode. Faraday's Law allows us to calculate the amount of $Cu(s)$. In fact, the law states that the weight of product formed at an electrode is proportional to the amount of electricity transferred at the electrode and to the equivalent weight of the material. Thus we can conclude that 1 mole of $Cu^{2+}(aq)$ + 2 moles of electrons will leave 1 mole of $Cu(s)$ at the electrode. One mole (= Avogadro's number) of electrons is called a *faraday* ($\mathfrak{F}$). A faraday is equivalent to 96 500 coulombs. A coulomb is the amount of electricity that is transferred when a current of one ampere flows for one second ($1C = 1A \cdot S$).

10.5.1 Electrolysis Problem

How many grams of copper would be deposited on the cathode of an electrolytic cell if, for a period of 20 minutes, a current of 2.0 amperes is run through a solution of $CuSO_4$? {The molecular weight of copper is 63.5.}

Calculate the number of coulombs:

$$Q = It = 2.0\,A \times 20\,min \times 60\,sec/min$$
$$= 2400\,C$$

Thus

$$Faradays = 2400\,C \times 1\mathfrak{F}/96\,500\,C$$
$$= 0.025\mathfrak{F}$$

Faradays can be related to moles of copper since

$$Cu^{2+} + 2e^- \rightarrow Cu$$

Since 1 mol Cu: 2 mol e^- we can write

$$0.025\mathfrak{F} \times (1\,mol\,Cu/2\mathfrak{F}) \times (63.5g\,Cu/mol\,Cu)$$
$$= 0.79g\,Cu$$

Electrolysis would deposit 0.79 g of copper at the cathode.

To do the previous problem, you must know the definition of current and charge (CHM 10.5) but the value of the constant (a Faraday) would be given on the exam. You should be able to perform the preceding calculation quickly and efficiently because it involves dimensional analysis.

GOLD STANDARD WARM-UP EXERCISES
CHAPTER 10: Electrochemistry

1) What should happen when a piece of copper is placed in 1M HCl?

Table 1 below shows some Standard State Reduction Potentials.

Reaction	Standard reduction potential (E^o)
$Cu^{2+} + 2e^- \leftrightarrow Cu$	0.34 V
$2H^+ + 2e^- \leftrightarrow H_2$	0.00 V

  A. The copper is completely dissolved by the acid.
  B. The copper is dissolved by the acid with the release of hydrogen gas.
  C. The copper bursts into greenish flames.
  D. Nothing happens.

2) What should happen when a piece of lead is placed in 1M HCl?

Reaction	Standard reduction potential (E^o)
$2H^+ + 2e^- \leftrightarrow H_2$	0.00 V
$Pb^{2+} + 2e^- \leftrightarrow Pb$	−0.13 V

  A. The lead is completely dissolved by the acid.
  B. The lead begins to dissolve with the release of hydrogen gas.
  C. The lead bursts into flames.
  D. Nothing happens.

3) A voltaic cell is set up with F_2/F^- as one half-cell and Br_2/Br^- as the other. What is the voltage of this cell at standard state?

Reaction	Standard reduction potential (E^o)
$F_2 + 2e^- \leftrightarrow 2F^-$	2.87 V
$Br_2 + 2e^- \leftrightarrow 2Br^-$	1.09 V

  A. 3.96 V
  B. 1.78 V
  C. 1.09 V
  D. 1.87 V

4) What is the standard cell potential for the galvanic cell formed using the Cl_2/Cl^- and MnO_4^-/Mn^{2+} half cells given the following?

$$Cl_2 + 2e^- \rightarrow 2Cl^- \qquad E^\circ = +1.36 \text{ V}$$
$$MnO_4^- + 8H^+ + 5e^- \leftrightarrow Mn^{2+} + 4H_2O \qquad E^\circ = +1.51 \text{ V}$$

  A. +0.15 V
  B. +0.83 V
  C. +2.87 V
  D. +5.29 V

5) If a current was passed through a solution of sulfate ions and one mole of sulfur dioxide was obtained, how many moles of chromium metal would be obtained if the same current was passed through a solution of chromium (III) ions in solution?

Table 1

Reaction	Standard reduction potential ($E°$)
$SO_4^{2-} + 4H^+ + 2e \leftrightarrow 2H_2O + SO_2$	+0.17 V
$Cr^{3+} + 3e \leftrightarrow Cr$	−0.74 V

A. 0.33 moles
B. 0.67 moles
C. 1.00 moles
D. 2.00 moles

6) Assume that the standard reduction potential for the reaction

$$A^{3+} + e^- \rightarrow A^{2+}$$

is $E°A$, and the standard reduction potential for the reaction

$$B^+ + e^- \rightarrow B$$

is $E°B$. A solution initially containing 1.0 M A^{3+}, 1.0 M A^{2+} and 1.0 M B^+ is agitated with excess solid B metal. When equilibrium is attained, the solution contains 0.7 M of A^{3+}, 1.3 M of A^{2+} and 1.3 M of B^+. Which of the following can we conclude?

A. $E°A = E°B$
B. $E°A > E°B$
C. $E°A < E°B$
D. $E°A + E°B = 0$

7) In the context of electrochemistry, "standard state" implies that:

A. All solutions are 1 M; all gases have a partial pressure of 1 MPa; the temperature is 273 K.
B. All solutions are 0.1 M; all gases have a partial pressure of 0.1 MPa; temperature is 273 K.
C. All solutions are 0.1 M; all gases have a partial pressure of 0.1 MPa.
D. All solutions are 1 M; all gases have a partial pressure of 0.1 MPa.

8) Which of the halogens will oxidize water to oxygen?

Reactions	Standard reduction potential ($E°$)
$Cl_2 + 2e^- \rightarrow 2Cl^-$	+1.36 V
$ClO_3^- + 6H^+ + 5e^- \rightarrow (½)Cl_2 + 3H_2O$	+1.47 V
$HClO^- + H^+ + e^- \rightarrow (½)Cl_2 + H_2O$	+1.63 V
$BrO_3^- + 6H^+ + 5e^- \rightarrow (½)Br_2 + 3H_2O$	+1.52 V
$F_2 + 2H^+ + 2e^- \rightarrow 2HF$	+3.06 V
$O_2 + 4H^+ + 4e^- \rightarrow 2H_2O$	+1.23 V
$O_3 + 2H^+ + 2e^- \rightarrow O_2 + H_2O$	+2.07 V
$Br_2 + 2e^- \rightarrow 2Br^-$	+1.07 V
$I_2 + 2e^- \rightarrow 2I^-$	+0.62 V

A. All of them
B. fluorine and chlorine
C. fluorine and bromine
D. fluorine, chlorine and bromine

9) The following reaction is spontaneous:

$$Ag^+ + Fe^{2+} \rightarrow Ag + Fe^{3+}$$

If a voltaic cell has one half cell as Ag^+/Ag and the other half cell as Fe^{2+}/Fe^{3+}, the silver electrode will be:

A. the anode and negative.
B. the anode and positive.
C. the cathode and positive.
D. the cathode and negative.

10) For an oxidation–reduction reaction, which of the following is a consistent set of relations?

A. $\Delta G° < 0$, $\Delta E° > 0$, $K_{eq} < 1$
B. $\Delta G° > 0$, $\Delta E° < 0$, $K_{eq} < 1$
C. $\Delta G° < 0$, $\Delta E° < 0$, $K_{eq} < 1$
D. $\Delta G° < 0$, $\Delta E° < 0$, $K_{eq} > 1$

11) A sample of iron was placed in a beaker of water and exposed to the atmosphere for one hour. After this, the iron that remained was removed from the beaker and a current of 0.2 A passed through the beaker which contained only Fe^{2+} in solution. After one hour and twenty minutes, all the iron present had been deposited on the cathode. Given that the Faraday constant F = 96000 C, what was the rate of rusting in grams per hour?

A. 0.209
B. 0.279
C. 0.140
D. 0.450

GS ANSWER KEY

CHAPTER 10

		Cross-Reference
1.	D	CHM 10.1, 10.2, 10.4, 6.1
2.	B	CHM 10.1, 10.2, 10.4, 6.1
3.	B	CHM 10.1, 10.2, 10.4
4.	A	CHM 10.1, 10.2
5.	B	CHM 10.5
6.	B	CHM 10

		Cross-Reference
7.	D	CHM 4.1.1, 10.1
8.	B	CHM 10.1
9.	C	CHM 10.1
10.	B	CHM 1.6, 8.10, 9.10, 10.1
11.	B	CHM 10.5.1

* Explanations can be found at the back of the book.

Go online to DAT-prep.com for additional chapter review Q&A and forum.

Electrolysis

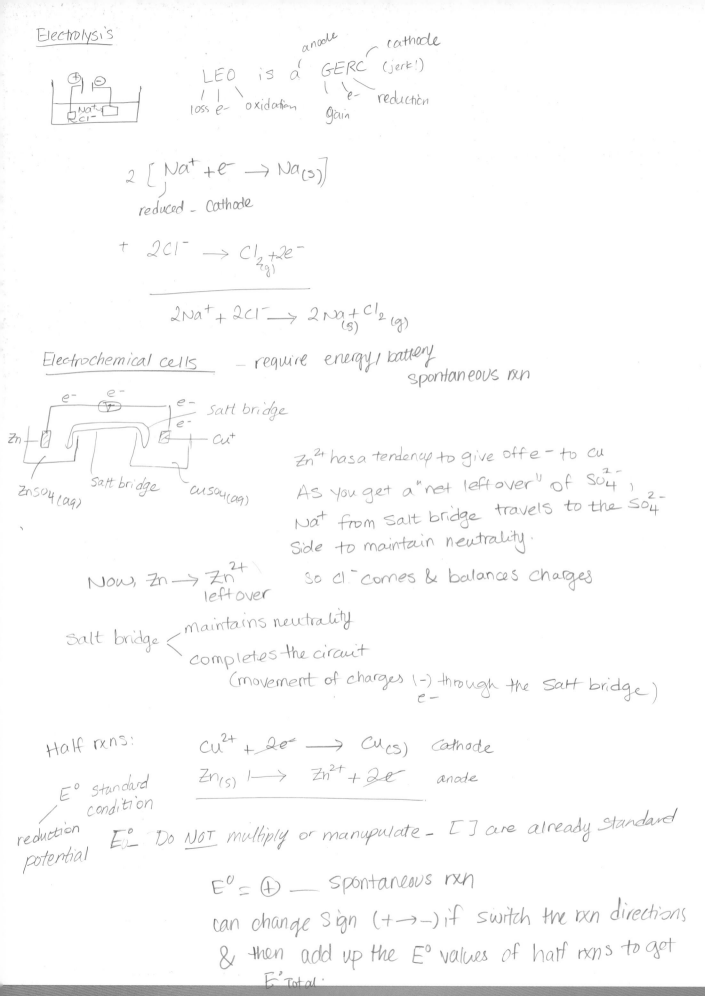

anode ⌐ cathode

LEO is a GERC (jerk!)
 | | \ | \e⁻ reduction
loss e⁻ oxidation gain

$$2 \left[Na^+ + e^- \rightarrow Na_{(s)} \right]$$

reduced - Cathode

$$+ \quad 2Cl^- \rightarrow Cl_{2(g)} + 2e^-$$

$$2Na^+ + 2Cl^- \rightarrow 2Na_{(s)} + Cl_{2 (g)}$$

Electrochemical cells — require energy / battery

spontaneous rxn

Zn | ZnSO₄ (aq)   salt bridge   Cu⁺ | CuSO₄ (aq)

Zn^{2+} has a tendency to give off e⁻ to cu

As you get a "net leftover" of SO_4^{2-}, Na⁺ from salt bridge travels to the SO_4^{2-} side to maintain neutrality.

Now, $Zn \rightarrow Zn^{2+}$ leftover

so cl⁻ comes & balances charges

salt bridge ⟨ maintains neutrality
completes the circuit
(movement of charges (-) through the salt bridge)
                        e⁻

Half rxns: $Cu^{2+} + 2e^- \rightarrow Cu_{(s)}$ Cathode

$Zn_{(s)} \rightarrow Zn^{2+} + 2e^-$ anode

E° standard condition
reduction potential

$E°$ Do NOT multiply or manupulate — [ ] are already standard

$E° = \oplus$ — spontaneous rxn

can change sign (+ → -) if switch the rxn directions
& then add up the E° values of half rxns to get
E° Total.

NUCLEAR CHEMISTRY

Chapter 11

Memorize	Understand	Importance
Equation relating energy and mass; half-life Alpha, beta, gamma particles Equation for maximum number of electrons in a shell Equation relating energy to frequency Equation for the total energy of the electrons in an atom	* Basic atomic structure, amu * Fission, fusion; the Bohr model of the atom * Problem solving for half-life * Quantized energy levels for electrons * Fluorescence	**1 to 3 out of the 30 Gen CHM** DAT questions are based on content in this chapter (in our estimation). * Note that between 50% and 85% of the questions in DAT General Chemistry are based on content from 6 chapters: 1, 2, 4, 5, 6 and 9.

DAT-Prep.com

Introduction

Atomic structure can be summarized as a nucleus orbited by electrons in different energy levels. Transition of electrons between energy levels and nuclear structure (i.e. protons, neutrons) are important characteristics of the atom.

Additional Resources

Free Online Forum

Video: Online or DVD

Flashcards

11.1 Protons, Neutrons, Electrons

Only recently, with high resolution electron microscopes, have large atoms been visualized. However, for years their existence and properties have been inferred by experiments. Experimental work on gas discharge effects suggested that an atom is not a single entity but is itself composed of smaller particles. These were termed elementary particles. The atom appears as a small solar system with a heavy nucleus composed of positive particles and neutral particles: *protons* and *neutrons*. Around this nucleus, there are clouds of negatively charged particles, called *electrons*. The mass of a neutron is slightly more than that of a proton (both $\approx 1.7 \times 10^{-24}$ g); the mass of the electron is considerably less (9.1×10^{-28} g).

Since an atom is electrically neutral, the negative charge carried by the electrons must be equal in magnitude (but opposite in sign) to the positive charge carried by the protons.

Experiments with electrostatic charges have shown that opposite charges attract, so it can be considered that electrostatic forces hold an atom together. The difference between various atoms is therefore determined by their *composition*.

A hydrogen atom consists of one proton and one electron; a helium atom of two protons, two neutrons and two electrons. They are shown in diagram form in Figure III.A.11.1.

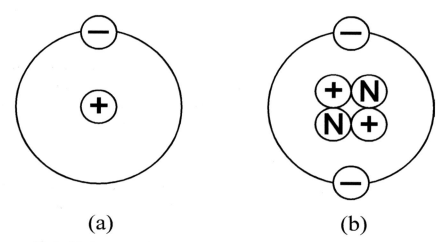

(a)   (b)

Figure III.A.11.1: Atomic structure simplified: (a) hydrogen atom; (b) helium atom.

11.2 Isotopes, Atomic Number, Atomic Weight

A proton has a mass of 1 a.m.u. (*atomic mass unit*) and a charge of +1, whereas, a neutron has a mass of 1 a.m.u. and no charge. The *atomic number* (*AN*) of an atom is the number of protons in the nucleus. In an atom of neutral charge, the atomic number (AN) is also equal to the number of electrons.

The atomic number is conventionally represented by the letter "Z". Each of the chemical elements has a unique number of protons which is identified by its own atomic number "Z". As an example, for the hydrogen H element, Z = 1 and for Na, Z = 11.

An *element* is a group of atoms with the same AN. *Isotopes* are elements which have the same atomic number (Z) but different number of neutrons and hence a different mass number (MN). As an example, the three carbon isotopes differ only in the number of neutrons and therefore have the same number of protons and electrons but differ in mass and are usually represented as follows: C-12, C-13 and C-14 or more specifically as follows: $^{12}_{6}C$, $^{13}_{6}C$ and $^{14}_{6}C$. It is therefore the number of protons that distinguishes elements from each other. The *weighted average* follows the natural abundance of the various isotopic compositions of an element.

The *mass number* (*MN*) of an atom is the number of protons and neutrons in an atom.

The *atomic weight* (*AW*) is the weighted average of all naturally occurring isotopes of an element.

For example: Silicon is known to exist naturally as a mixture of three isotopes (Si-28, Si-29 and Si-30). The relative amount of each of the three different silicon isotopes is found to be 92.2297% with a mass of 27.97693, 4.6832% with a mass of 28.97649 and the remaining 3.0872% with a mass of 29.97377. The atomic weight of silicon is then determined as the weighted average of each of the isotopes as follows:

$$
\begin{aligned}
\text{Si mass} = \ &(27.97693 \times 0.922297) \\
&+ (28.97649 \times 0.046832) \\
&+ (29.97377 \times 0.030872) \\
= \ &28.0854 \text{ g/mol.}
\end{aligned}
$$

It is also important to note that as the number of <u>protons</u> distinguishes *elements* from each other, it is their <u>electronic configuration</u> (CHM 2.1, 2.2, 2.3) that determines their *reactivity*.

The mass of a nucleus is always smaller than the combined mass of its constituent protons and neutrons. The difference in mass is converted to energy (E) which holds protons and neutrons together within the nuclear core.

11.3 Nuclear Forces, Nuclear Binding Energy, Stability, Radioactivity

Coulomb repulsive force (between protons) in the nuclei are overcome by nuclear forces. The nuclear force is a non-electrical type of force that binds nuclei together and is equal for protons and neutrons. The nuclear binding energy (E_b) is a result of the relation between energy and mass changes associated with nuclear reactions,

$$\Delta E = \Delta mc^2$$

in ergs in the CGS system, i.e. m = grams and c = cm/sec; ΔE = energy released or absorbed; Δm = mass lost or gained, respectively; c = velocity of light = 3.0×10^{10} cm/sec.

Conversions:
1 *gram* = 9×10^{20} *ergs*
1 *a.m.u.* = 931.4 *MeV* (*Mev* = 10^6 electron volts)
1 *a.m.u.* = 1/12 the mass of $_6C^{12}$.

The preceding equation is a statement of the law of conservation of mass and energy. The value of E_b depends upon the mass number (MN) as follows, (*see Figure III.A.11.2*):

The peak E_b/MN is at MN = 60. Also, E_b/MN is relatively constant after MN = 20. <u>Fission</u> is when a nucleus splits into smaller nuclei. <u>Fusion</u> is when smaller nuclei combine to form a larger nucleus. Energy is released from a nuclear reaction when nuclei with MN >> 60 undergo fission or nuclei with MN << 60 undergo fusion. Both fusion and fission release energy because the mass difference between the initial and the final nuclear states is converted into energy.

Not all combinations of protons are stable. The most stable nuclei are those with an even number of protons and an even number of neutrons. The least stable nuclei are those with an odd number of protons and an odd number of neutrons. Also, as the atomic number (AN) increases, there are more neutrons (N) needed for the nuclei to be stable.

According to the *Baryon number conservation*, the total number of protons and neutrons remains the same in a nuclear reaction even with the inter-conversions occurring between protons and neutrons.

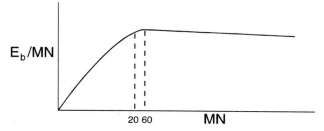

Figure III.A.11.2: Binding Energy per Nucleus. E_b/MN = *binding energy per nucleus; this is the energy released by the formation of a nucleus.*

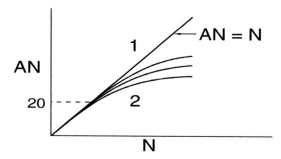

Figure III.A.11.3: Stability of Atoms. AN = atomic number and N = number of neutrons.

Up to AN = 20 (Calcium) the number of protons is equal to the number of neutrons, after this there are more neutrons. If an atom is in region #1 in Figure III.A.11.3, it has too many protons or too few neutrons and must decrease its protons or increase its neutrons to become stable. The reverse is true for region #2. All nuclei after AN = 84 (Polonium) are unstable.

Unstable nuclei become stable by fission to smaller nuclei or by absorption or emission of small particles. Spontaneous fission is rare. Spontaneous radioactivity (emission of particles) is common. The common particles are:

(1) alpha (α) particle = $_2He^4$ (helium nucleus);

(2) beta (β) particle = $_{-1}e^0$ (an electron);

(3) a positron $_{+1}e^0$ (same mass as an electron but opposite charge);

(4) gamma (γ) ray = no mass and no charge, just electromagnetic energy;

(5) orbital electron capture - nucleus takes electrons from K shell and converts a proton to a neutron. If there is a flux of particles such as neutrons ($_0n^1$), the nucleus can absorb these also.

> A neutron walks into a bar and asks the bartender: "How much for a beer?"
> The bartender answers: "For you, no charge." :)

11.4 Nuclear Reaction, Radioactive Decay, Half-Life

Nuclear reactions are reactions in which changes in nuclear composition occur. An example of a nuclear reaction which involves uranium and hydrogen:

$$_{92}U^{238} + {_1}H^2 \rightarrow {_{93}}Np^{238} + 2{_0}n^1$$

for $_{92}U^{238}$: 238 = mass number, 92 = atomic number. The sum of the lower (or higher) numbers on one side of the equation equals the sum of the lower (or higher) numbers on the other side of the equation. Another way of writing the preceding reaction is:

$_{92}U^{238}(_1H^2, 2_0n^1)_{93}Np^{238}$. {# neutrons (i.e. $_{92}U^{238}$) = superscript (238) − subscript (92) = 146}

Radioactive decay is a naturally occurring spontaneous process in which the atomic nucleus of an unstable atom loses energy by the emission of ionizing particles. Such unstable nuclei are known to spontaneously decompose and emit minute atomic sections to essentially gain some stability. The radioactive decay fragments are categorized into alpha, beta and gamma-ray decays. The radioactive decay can result in a nuclear change (*transmutation*) in which the parent and daughter nuclei are of different elements. For example, a C-14 atom may undergo an alpha decay and emit radiation and as a result, transform into a N-14 daughter nucleus. It is also possible that radioactive decay does not result in transmutation but only decreases the energy of the parent nucleus. As an example, a Ni-28 atom undergoing a gamma decay will emit radiation and then transform to a lower energy Ni-28 nucleus. The following is a brief description of the three known types of radioactive decay.

(1) **Alpha (α) decay:** Alpha decay is a type of radioactive decay in which an atomic nucleus emits an alpha particle. An alpha particle is composed of two protons and two neutrons which is identical to a helium-4 nucleus. An alpha particle is the most massive of all radioactive particles. Because of its relatively large mass, alpha particles tend to have the most potential to interact with other atoms and/or molecules and ionize them as well as lose energy. As such, these particles have the lowest penetrating power. If an atomic nucleus of an element undergoes alpha decay, this leads to a transmutation of that element into another element as shown below for the transmutation of Uranium-238 to Thorium-234:

$$^{238}_{92}U \rightarrow {}^{234}_{90}Th + {}^{4}_{2}He^{2+}$$
$$^{238}U \rightarrow {}^{234}Th + \alpha$$

(2) **Beta (β) decay:** Beta decay is a type of decay in which an unstable nucleus emits an electron or a positron. A positron is the antiparticle of an electron and has the same mass as an electron but opposite in charge. The electron from a beta decay forms when a neutron of an unstable nuclei changes into a proton and in the process, an electron is then emitted. The electron in this case is referred to as a beta minus particle or β^-. In beta decays producing positron emissions, it is referred to as beta plus or β^+. For an atomic nucleus undergoing beta decay, the process leads to the transmutation of that element into another as shown for the transmutation of Cesium-137 for beta minus and Na-22 for beta plus emissions:

$$^{137}_{55}Cs \rightarrow {}^{137}_{56}Ba + \beta^-$$
$$^{22}_{11}Na \rightarrow {}^{22}_{10}Ne + \beta^+$$

(3) **Gamma (γ) decay:** Gamma decay is different from the other two types of decays. Gamma decay emits a form of electromagnetic radiation. Gamma rays are high energy photons known to penetrate matter very well and are symbolized by the Greek letter gamma (γ). A source of gamma decay could be a case in which an excited daughter nucleus - following an alpha or beta decay - lowers its energy state further by gamma-ray emission without a change in mass number or atomic number. The following is an example:

$$^{60}Co \rightarrow {}^{60}Ni^* + \beta^-$$

Co-60 decays to an excited Ni*-60 via beta decay and subsequently, the excited Ni*-

60 drops to ground state and emits gamma (γ) rays as follows:

$$^{60}\text{Ni}^* \rightarrow {}^{60}\text{Ni} + \gamma$$

To summarize, a gamma ray has no charge and no mass since it is a form of electromagnetic radiation. As shown, gamma rays are usually emitted in conjunction with other radiation emissions.

Spontaneous radioactive decay is a first order process. This means that the rate of decay is *directly* proportional to the amount of material present:

$$\Delta m / \Delta t = \text{rate of decay}$$

where Δm = change in mass, Δt = change in time.

The preceding relation is equalized by adding a proportionality constant called the decay constant (k) as follows,

$$\Delta m / \Delta t = -km.$$

The minus sign indicates that the mass is decreasing. Also, $k = -(\Delta m/m)/\Delta t$ = fraction of the mass that decays with time.

The *half-life* ($T_{1/2}$) of a radioactive atom is the time required for one half of it to disintegrate. The half-life is related to k as follows,

$$T_{1/2} = 0.693/k.$$

If the number of half-lifes n are known we can calculate the percentage of a pure radioactive sample left after undergoing decay since the fraction remaining = $(1/2)^n$.

For example, given a pure radioactive substance X with $T_{1/2}$ = 9 years, calculating the percentage of substance X after 27 years is quite simple,

$$27 = 3 \times 9 = 3\ T_{1/2}$$

Thus

$$n = 3,\ (1/2)^n = (1/2)^3 = 1/8 \text{ or } 13\%.$$

After 27 years of disintegration, 13% of pure substance X remains. {Similarly, note that *doubling time* is given by $(2)^n$; see BIO 2.2}

Table III.A.11.1: Modes of Radioactive Decay

Decay Mode	Participating particles	Change in (A, Z)	Daughter Nucleus
Alpha decay	α	A = −4, Z = −2	(A − 4, Z − 2)
Beta decay	β^-	A = 0, Z = +1	(A, Z + 1)
Gamma decay	γ	A = 0, Z = 0	(A, Z)
Positron emission	β^+	A = 0, Z = −1	(A, Z − 1)

11.5 Quantized Energy Levels For Electrons, Emission Spectrum

Work by Bohr and others in the early part of the last century demonstrated that the electron orbits are arranged in shells, and that each shell has a defined maximum number of electrons it can contain.

For example, the first shell can contain two electrons, the second eight electrons (see CHM 2.1, 2.2). The maximum number of electrons in each shell is given by:

$$N_{electrons} = 2n^2$$

$N_{electrons}$ designates the number of electrons in shell n.

The state of each electron is determined by the four quantum numbers:

• *principal quantum number n* determines the number of shells, possible values are: 1 (K), 2 (L), 3 (M), etc...

• *angular momentum quantum number l*, determines the subshell, possible values are: 0 (s), 1 (p), 2 (d), 3 (f), n-1, etc...

• *magnetic momentum quantum number m_l*, possible values are: $\pm l, ... , 0$

• *spin quantum number m_s*, determines the direction of rotation of the electron, possible values are: $\pm 1/2$.

Chemical reactions and electrical effects are all concerned with the behavior of electrons in the outer shell of any particular atom. If a shell is full, for example, the atom is unlikely to react with any other atom and

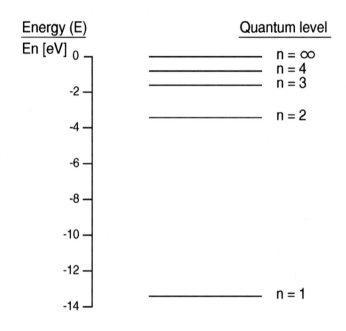

Figure III.A.11.4: Energy levels. The energy E_n in each shell n is measured in electron volts.

is, in fact, one of the noble (inert) gases such as helium.

The energy that an electron contains is not continuous over the entire range of possible energy. Rather, electrons in a atom may contain only discrete energies as they occupy certain orbits or shells. Electrons of each atom are restricted to these discrete energy levels. These levels have an energy below zero.

This means energy is released when an electron moves from infinity into these energy levels.

If there is one electron in an atom, its ground state is n = 1, the lowest energy level available. Any other energy level, n = 2, n = 3, etc., is considered an excited state for that electron. The difference in energy (E) between the levels gives the absorbed (or emitted) energy when an electron moves to a higher orbit (or lower orbit, respectively) and therefore, the frequency (f) of light necessary to cause excitation.

$$E_2 - E_1 = hf$$

where E_1 = energy level one, E_2 = energy level two, h = planck's constant, and f = the frequency of light absorbed or emitted.

Therefore, if light is passed through a substance (e.g., gas), certain wavelengths will be absorbed, which correspond to the energy needed for the electron transition. An *absorption* spectrum will result that has dark lines against a light background. Multiple lines result because there are possible transitions from all quantum levels occupied by electrons to any unoccupied levels.

An *emission* spectrum results when an electron is excited to a higher level by another particle or by an electric discharge, for example. Then, as the electron falls from the excited state to lower states, light is emitted that has a wavelength (which is related to frequency) corresponding to the energy difference between the levels since: $E_1 - E_2 = hf$.

The resulting spectrum will have light lines against a dark background. The absorption and emission spectrums should have the same number of lines but often will not. This is because in the absorption spectrum, there is a rapid radiation of the absorbed light in all directions, and transitions are generally from the ground state initially.

These factors result in fewer lines in the absorption than in the emission spectrum.

The total energy of the electrons in an atom, where KE is the kinetic energy, can be given by:

$$E_{total} = E_{emission} \text{ (or } E_{ionization}) + KE$$

11.6 Fluorescence

Fluorescence is an emission process that occurs after light absorption excites electrons to higher electronic and vibrational levels. The electrons spontaneously lose excited vibrational energy to the electronic states. There are certain molecular types that possess this property, e.g., some amino acids (tryptophan).

The fluorescence process is as follows:

• **Step 1** - absorption of light;

• **Step 2** - spontaneous deactivation of vibrational levels to zero vibrational level for electronic state;

• **Step 3** - fluorescence with light emission (longer wavelength than absorption).

Figure III.A.11.5 shows diagrammatically the steps described above. Step 2 which is not shown in the figure is the intermediate step between light absorption and light emission. See BIO 1.5.1 for fluorescence as applied to microscopy.

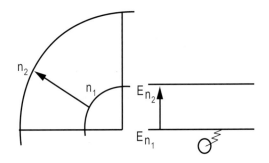 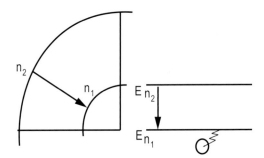

Figure III.A.11.5: The fluorescence process. Represented is an atom with shells n1, n2 and their respective energy levels En.

GOLD STANDARD WARM-UP EXERCISES

CHAPTER 11: Nuclear Chemistry

1) How do gamma rays behave in an electric field?
   A. They are not deflected in any direction.
   B. They are deflected toward the positive plate.
   C. They are deflected toward the negative plate.
   D. They oscillate between plates, that is, they are attracted to one plate and then the other.

2) Why would a neutron be preferred to a proton for bombarding atomic nuclei?
   A. It is smaller than a proton.
   B. It weighs less than a proton.
   C. It has no charge.
   D. It can be obtained from a nucleus.

3) A sample of radioactive substance has a half–life of six months. What percentage of the sample is left undecayed after one year?
   A. 0%
   B. 25%
   C. 50%
   D. 75%

4) Astatine is the last member of Group VII and is radioactive with a half–life of 8 hours. The transport of an astatine sample took 20 hours. What proportion of the sample had undergone radioactive decay?
   A. 0.58
   B. 0.18
   C. 0.82
   D. 0.42

5) Which of the following types of radioactive emissions involves the emission of a helium nucleus?
   A. alpha decay
   B. beta decay
   C. gamma ray
   D. None of the above

6) Given the following reactions, identify X.

$$^{1}_{0}n + {}^{238}_{92}U \rightarrow {}^{239}_{92}U + X$$
$$^{239}_{92}U \rightarrow {}^{239}_{93}Np + {}^{0}_{-1}e$$
$$^{239}_{93}Np \rightarrow {}^{239}_{94}Pu + {}^{0}_{-1}e$$

   A. α – particle
   B. β – particle
   C. γ – ray
   D. proton

7) In a hypothetical radioactive series, Tl–210 undergoes 3 beta decay processes, 1 alpha decay process and 1 gamma ray emission to yield a stable product. What is the product?
   A. $^{214}_{76}Os$
   B. $^{214}_{84}Po$
   C. $^{206}_{86}Rn$
   D. $^{206}_{82}Pb$

8) $^{230}_{90}Th$ undergoes a series of radioactive decay processes, resulting in ^{214}Bi being the final product. What was the sequence of the processes that occurred?
   A. alpha, alpha, alpha, gamma, beta
   B. alpha, alpha, alpha, alpha, beta
   C. alpha, alpha, beta, beta
   D. alpha, beta, beta, beta, gamma

9) Which of the following represents the relative penetrating power of the three types of radio-active emissions in decreasing order?

A. beta > alpha > gamma
B. beta > gamma > alpha
C. gamma > alpha > beta
D. gamma > beta > alpha

10) The beta decay of carbon–14 results in the production of nitrogen, a beta particle and a gamma ray as follows:

$$^{14}_6C \rightarrow {}^X_7N + \beta^- + \gamma$$

The value for X in the formula for nitrogen is equal to:

A. 15.
B. 14.
C. 13.
D. 12.

11) How would you expect a positron will react in an electric field?

A. It would retain its original flight direction.
B. It would be attracted to the positive plate.
C. It would be attracted to the negative plate.
D. It would be attracted to the plate with the greater charge density.

12) A living organism has a C-14 to C-12 ratio of 1/20 during lifetime. Its remains now has a C-14 to C-12 ratio of 1/80. Approximately how old is this organism? Take the half-life of C-14 to be 6000 years.

A. It is 6000 years old.
B. It is 12000 years old.
C. It is 18000 years old.
D. It is 24000 years old.

13) The half-life of one isotope of radium is about 1600 years. In a given sample of this isotope, 15/16 of the radium atoms will decay in a time most nearly equal to:

A. 1500.
B. 3200.
C. 6400.
D. 12800.

14) Tl decays by the emission of beta particles (half-life = 3.1 mins). As a result, Pb is pro-duced. After 9.3 mins, an initially pure sample of Tl contains 7 g of Pb. What was the approxi-mate mass of the original sample?

A. 7 g
B. 8 g
C. 28 g
D. 32 g

15) A radioactive form of phosphorus undergoes β - decay. What would the radioactivity level (R) versus time graph for the decay process look like?

A.
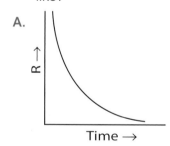

B.
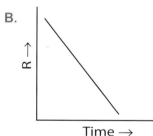

C.
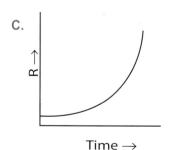

D.
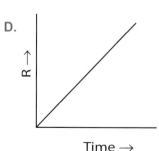

GS ANSWER KEY

CHAPTER 11

		Cross-Reference
1.	A	CHM 11
2.	C	CHM 11.1
3.	B	CHM 11.4
4.	C	CHM 11.4
5.	A	CHM 11.3
6.	C	CHM 11.3, 11.4
7.	D	CHM 11.3, 11.4
8.	B	CHM 11.3, 11.4

		Cross-Reference
9.	D	CHM 11.3, 11.4
10.	B	CHM 11.3, 11.4
11.	C	CHM 11.3
12.	B	CHM 11.4
13.	C	CHM 11.4
14.	B	CHM 11.4
15.	A	CHM 11.4

* Explanations can be found at the back of the book.

Go online to DAT-prep.com for additional chapter review Q&A and forum.

$$^{14}_{6}C \longrightarrow {}^{14}_{7}N + {}^{0}_{-1}e \qquad \beta - decay$$

Element: $T_{1/2} = 10$ years

how much left from a pure sample after 30 years?

3 half years

$$\left(\frac{1}{2}\right)^n = \left(\frac{1}{2}\right)^{\textcircled{3}} = \frac{1}{8}$$

2^n — doupling time

Memorize	**Understand**	**Importance**
Glassware, basic equipment	* Safety * Basic techniques * Equipment: especially glassware * Error and data analysis	**0 to 2 out of the 30 Gen CHM** DAT questions are based on content in this chapter (in our estimation). * Note that between 50% and 85% of the questions in DAT General Chemistry are based on content from 6 chapters: 1, 2, 4, 5, 6 and 9.

DAT-Prep.com

Introduction

The laboratory (or lab) is where scientific research and development is conducted and analyses performed. Some students see a lab as a sterile, boring environment with lots of rules. Others recognize that it is the controlled, uniform environment of a lab - with its many different techniques, instruments and procedures - that has helped produce countless discoveries in chemistry, pharmacy, biotechnology including the human genome project, nanotechnology and much more to come.

Additional Resources

Free Online Forum   Video: Online or DVD   Flashcards   Special Guest

12.1 Introduction

The laboratory is a place in which one may have the opportunity to apply the principles and theories of chemistry. An understanding of laboratory basics is mandatory for anyone studying chemical sciences, biological sciences or the DAT! Despite its potential dangers, the laboratory may be regarded as one of the safest environments.

Good science requires the collection of reliable, accurate and reproducible data. The scientist and/or experimenter must have a working knowledge of applied laboratory techniques as well as an understanding of the equipment used to acquire such data.

12.2 Laboratory Safety

One must be aware of all dangers that may occur in the laboratory and more importantly, one must always take precautionary measures when working in a chemistry laboratory. While in the laboratory, you are not only responsible for your own safety but for the safety of others working with you.

Laboratory Rules and Safety Procedures:

1. Always wear protective eye goggles or glasses. These glasses should be safety grade and made to wrap around the eyes so that no liquids or solids may splash into your eyes.

2. Contact lenses are NEVER to be worn.

3. Always wear a protective lab coat or apron and shoes must completely cover your feet and skin must NEVER be exposed.

4. One must always be made aware of all pertinent safety locations and the proper usage of all available safety equipment such as (amongst others): fire extinguishers, eye wash, safety showers, fire blankets, and all other available equipment.

5. Always tie your hair if worn long and do not wear loose clothing or jewelry while performing any lab work.

6. Your bench top should always be clean and clear of all objects as you perform your lab work. Personal belongings should always be kept away from your work area.

7. One must always keep all stock solutions and solids in a well ventilated and appropriate storage area.

8. Always keep balances and the surrounding area as clean as possible to avoid contamination.

9. Appropriately label all reagent bottles as well as working solutions and all respective materials used should always be appropriately labeled and dated.

10. Always be aware and knowledgeable of all solids, solvents and solutions you are to work with.

11. Never return unused solvents or chemicals back into an initial stock solution or any reagent bottles. This is a major

source of contamination of the entire stock and/or initial solutions.

12. Always dispose of all chemicals and waste as advised by the appropriate and/ or responsible party.

13. Always report all accidents no matter how minor it may seem.

14. Never perform experiments that have not been authorized.

15. Always have some other colleague in the lab working with you and so never be alone in a lab while performing experimental work.

12.3 Laboratory Techniques

12.3.1 Glassware

Chemical glassware forms a staple of basic laboratory equipment in chemistry and is thus a regular question on real DAT tests. It is advisable that you memorize the following types of lab glassware and equipment and know when they are appropriate.

Some items have volumetric graduation or are *graduated for volume* which means, in practical terms, one can measure the volume of the liquid in the container (usually in ml).

A well equipped laboratory generally has various pieces of glassware designed to measure liquid volumes. In the following table, you will find a list of some of the most common glassware in order from least to the most accurate piece of equipment.

A major problem encountered by many when measuring the level of a liquid in a tube is the fact that the surface is not flat due to

Least accurate	Droppers
	Beakers and Erlenmeyer flasks
	Graduated cylinders
Most accurate	Glass Pipettes, burettes and volumetric flasks

adhesive forces or cohesive forces (see CHM 4.2.2). This curved surface is known as a meniscus. Read the level at the midpoint of the meniscus. This point is the bottom for aqueous solutions where the meniscus is curved downwards (concave due to adhesive forces; see image of graduated cylinder); whereas, the midpoint is the top in mercury where the meniscus is curved upwards (convex due to cohesive forces; CHM 4.2.2). In certain instances (highly colored solutions), the meniscus is not clearly defined and this may causes a decrease in accuracy. When reading a liquid level, the eye must be on the same level as the meniscus in order to accurately read the bottom of the curve and avoid making a *parallax* error.

When discussing glassware, "graduated" means that there are marked intervals on the glass for use in measurement.

Glassware is generally marked to indicate the temperature at which the apparatus was calibrated (usually 20 °C), and marked to indicate if it is calibrated to measure either the amount of liquid it may contain (= TC = "to contain") or the amount of liquid that it may deliver (= TD = "to deliver"). There is no real one volume marking that may measure both of these quantities. As suggested by their names, TD, used on burettes and pipets and some graduated cylinders, means that the apparatus is calibrated to accurately deliver or transfer the stated volume to another container. TC, used on volumetric flasks and most graduated cylinders, means that the markings give an accurate measure of the volume contained, but that pouring the liquid into another container will not necessarily deliver the indicated volume.

The following is a short description of each of the major types of glassware:

Droppers, Beakers and Erlenmeyer Flasks

These types of glassware are used for the approximate measurements of volume. The dropper is generally used for volumes of less than or equal to 5 mL. Droppers are known to vary in the volume they deliver (1 mL = 15–20 drops) and contain a high level of uncertainty of approximately ± 10%. Various beakers and Erlenmeyer flasks have approximate volume markings on the outside of the glass with values of ~5% accuracy. When performing precise work, it is not recommended to use any of these glassware pieces.

Graduated Cylinders (TC)

Graduated cylinders contain volume markings used to measure the amount of liquid held by the cylinder with an accuracy of approximately ± 2%. They normally range in size from 10 ml to 1000 ml.

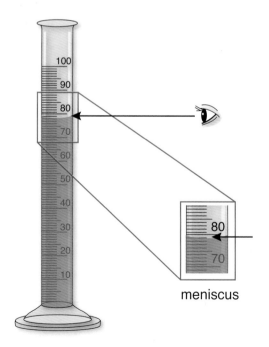

Graduated cylinder

Glass Pipette (also Pipet)

Pipettes are used to deliver measured volumes with an inherent uncertainty of about ± 0.2% and are used mainly for high accuracy work. Generally, there are two types of glass pipettes, volumetric pipettes with one volume mark and graduated pipettes with several markings. In addition to these classes of pipettes, there are also Eppendorf micropipettes and multichannel pipettes that are used for very small volumes ranging from 1.00 µL up to 1000 µL (1 mL). Pipetting requires skill and can be done with a pump or a bulb.

Volumetric flasks (TC)

Volumetric flasks are used to prepare stock solutions of known molar concentra-tions and for dilutions of measured volumes. Volumetric flasks are known to be precise to approximately ± 0.2%. They are characterized by a flat bottomed bulb and a long neck with a single line for measuring a specified volume.

Burette (also Buret)

Burettes are calibrated to measure the volume of liquid delivered. The volume in a burette should be always read to the second decimal place. Burettes can dispense a small measured volume of a liquid, such as in a titration, with extreme precision with volumetric graduation and a stopcock at the bottom. As opposed to most glassware, burettes measure from the top since the liquid is dispensed from the bottom. To properly read a buret, your line of sight should still be level with the bottom of the meniscus.

A typical titration (CHM 6.9) begins with a beaker or Erlenmeyer flask containing a precise volume of the titrand (= the chemical being analyzed) and a small amount of indicator placed underneath a calibrated burette containing the titrant (= titrator reagent prepared as a standard solution).

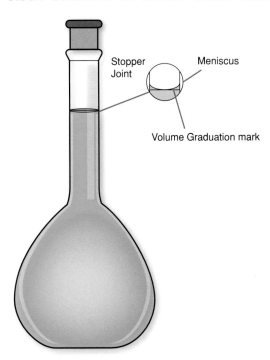

Stopper Joint

Meniscus

Volume Graduation mark

Volumetric flask

Burette

Beaker

Beakers are used to create reactions (i.e. precipitation, electrolysis) and to measure approximate amounts of liquids. It is a graduated container with a spout for pouring.

Beaker

Test tube

The most common of all lab supplies. Holds liquids but does not allow for accurate measurement.

Test tube

Erlenmeyer flask

Used to measure, mix and store liquids. Note that it is a graduated cone-shaped container that usually holds 250 ml or 500 ml of liquid.

Erlenmeyer Flask

Wash bottle

Used especially for cleaning equipment (i.e. pipettes, test tubes). It is normally a flexible plastic (not 'glassware') and it is squeezed lightly to squirt liquid.

Wash bottle

Florence flask

Used mainly for boiling liquids and often as part of a distillation apparatus. Also known as "boiling flask" or "round bottom flask".

Florence Flask

Soxhlet extractor

Used to extract a compound (usually lipids within solids) that has limited solubility in a extracting solvent. Similar to the standard distillation apparatus (CHM 12.7). This setup requires a round-bottom flask at one end and a condenser at the other. In between is the Soxhlet extractor (sections 3, 4, 5, 6 and 7) which is designed to direct the solvent back down via the syphon arms to the round-bottom flask.

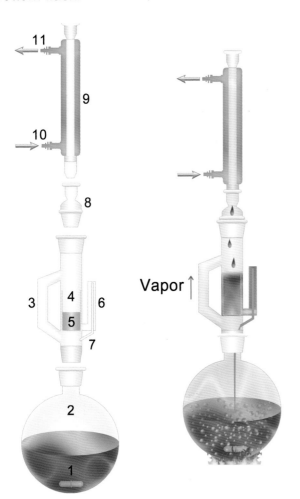

1: Stir bar (or flea, a magnetic bar used to stir liquid) or boiling chip (= boiling stone, anti-bumping granules, ebulliator; ORG 13)

2: Round bottom flask - should not be over-filled with solvent.

3: Distillation path

4: Soxhlet thimble to hold the solid sample for solvent extraction

5: Extraction solid (residue solid) usually to extract lipids

6: Syphon arm inlet

7: Syphon arm outlet

8: Reduction adapter

9: Condenser (also see the diagram in CHM 12.4.4)

10: Cooling water in from the bottom

11: Cooling water out from the top

Flaming can be done using a Bunsen burner or alcohol lamp for sterilization. This is commonly used for small metal or glassware. A variation is to dip the object in 70% ethanol (or a higher concentration) and then touch the object briefly to the Bunsen burner flame. The ethanol will ignite and burn off in a few seconds.

Before starting a titration, the pipette, burette and any required flask are rinsed with deionised water, rather than tap water. Tap water contains ions that may affect the titration result.

Along with the requirements of proper glassware, a well equipped laboratory must also contain the appropriate devices for mass measurements of solids as well as liquids (if densities are to be measured). A sample is generally "massed" in one of two ways. The sample may be added to a clean and dry container and the mass of the container and sample together are then taken and the mass of the two are subsequently subtracted. The second alternative, and more frequently used today, is that in which a container or weighing paper is zeroed (or *tarred*) and the sample is then placed onto the tarred container. For this second method, modern electronic balances are mainly used with a tarring capability.

There are different balances with varying degrees of sensitivities. Laboratory grade range from a "triple-beam balance" which was traditionally used with a sensitivity of approximately ± 0.01g, to the electronic top-loading balance with a sensitivity of ± 0.001g, and finally, to the electronic analytical balance used in most modern laboratories today with a very high sensitivity of approximately ± 0.0001g (= one tenth of a milligram or one ten-thousanth of a gram).

1) Triple beam balance

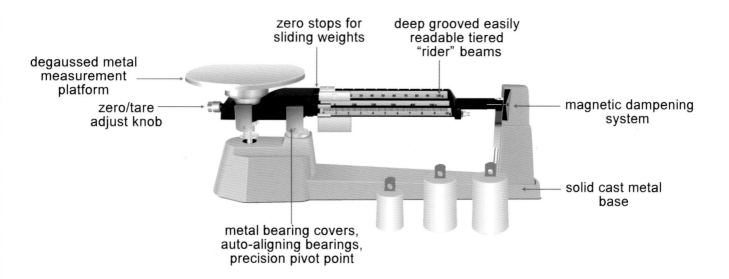

degaussed metal measurement platform

zero stops for sliding weights

deep grooved easily readable tiered "rider" beams

zero/tare adjust knob

magnetic dampening system

solid cast metal base

metal bearing covers, auto-aligning bearings, precision pivot point

2) Top loading electronic balance

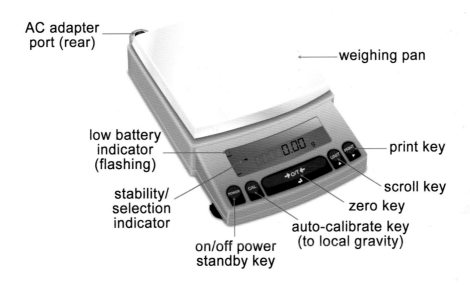

AC adapter port (rear)

weighing pan

low battery indicator (flashing)

print key

stability/ selection indicator

scroll key

zero key

auto-calibrate key (to local gravity)

on/off power standby key

3) Electronic analytical balance

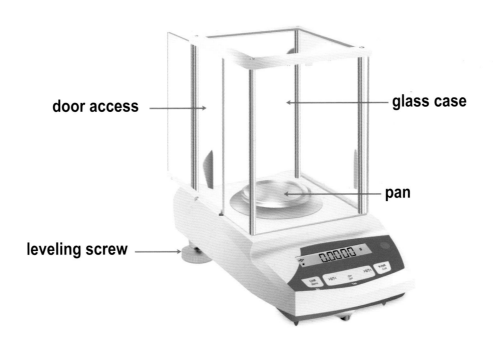

door access

glass case

pan

leveling screw

12.4.1 Scientific Notation

If you have already studied for QR, or if you are already comfortable with math, then you may not need to review this section nor CHM 12.4.2.

Numbers with many zeroes on either side of a decimal can be written in *scientific notation*. For example, a number which is an integer power of ten, the number of zeroes equals the exponent; thus $10^0 = 1$, $10^1 = 10$, $10^2 = 10 \cdot 10 = 100$, $10^3 = 10 \cdot 10 \cdot 10 = 1000$, and so on.

Conversely, the negative exponent corresponds to the number of places to the right of the decimal point; thus $10^{-1} = 1/10 = 0.1$, $10^{-2} = 1/(10 \cdot 10) = 0.01$, $10^{-3} = 1/(10 \cdot 10 \cdot 10) = 0.001$, and so on.

Scientific notation allows us to express a number as a product of a power of ten and a number between 1 and 10. For example, the number 5,478,000 can be expressed as 5.478×10^6; 0.0000723 can be expressed as 7.23×10^{-5}.

12.4.2 Error Analysis

If we divide 2 by 3 on a calculator, the answer on the display would be 0.6666666667. The leftmost digit is the *most significant digit* and the rightmost digit is the *least significant digit*. The number of digits which are really significant depends on the accuracy with which the values 2 and 3 are known.

For example, suppose we wish to find the sum of two numbers *a* and *b* with <u>experimental errors</u> (or *uncertainties*) Δa and Δb, respectively. The uncertainty of the sum c can be determined as follows:

$$c \pm \Delta c = (a \pm \Delta a) + (b \pm \Delta b) = a + b \pm (\Delta a + \Delta b)$$

thus

$$\Delta c = \Delta a + \Delta b.$$

The sign of the uncertainties are not correlated, so the same rule applies to subtraction. Therefore, *the uncertainty of either the sum or difference is the sum of the uncertainties.*

Now we will apply the preceding to significant digits. The number 3.7 has an implicit uncertainty. Any number between 3.65000... and 3.74999... rounds off to 3.7, thus 3.7 really means 3.7 ± 0.05. Similarly, 68.21 really means 68.21 ± 0.005. Adding the two values and their uncertainties we get: $(3.7 \pm 0.05) + (68.21 \pm 0.005) = 71.91 \pm 0.055$. The error is large enough to affect the first digit to the right of the decimal point; therefore, the last digit to the right is not significant. The answer is thus 71.9.

The <u>rule for signiifcant digits</u> states that *the sum or difference of two numbers carries the same number of significant digits to the right of the decimal as the number with the least significant digits to the right of the decimal.* For example, 105.64 − 3.092 = 102.55.

Multiplication and division is somewhat different. Through algebraic manipulation, the uncertainty or experimental error can be determined:

$$c \pm \Delta c = (a \pm \Delta a)(b \pm \Delta b)$$

after some manipulation we get

$$\Delta c/c = \Delta a/a + \Delta b/b.$$

The preceding result also holds true for division. Thus for $(10 \pm 0.5)/(20 \pm 1)$, the fractional error in the quotient is:

$$\Delta c/c = \Delta a/a + \Delta b/b = 0.5/10 + 1/20 = 0.1 \ (10\% \ error)$$

Thus the quotient including its absolute error is $c \pm \Delta c = 0.5(1 \pm 0.1) = 0.5 \pm 0.05$.

The <u>rule for significant digits</u> can be derived from the preceding and it states that *the product or quotient of two numbers has the same number of significant digits as the number with the least number of significant digits.*

12.4.3 Analyzing the Data

When quantitative data is to be properly reported, the data collected as a result of experimentation must reflect the reliability of all equipment and instruments used to make such measurements. It is therefore extremely important to report such data to the correct number of significant figures (also known as significant digits, and often shortened to sig figs or sf) as well as reporting all calculated results to the correct number of significant figures. Significant figures are used to clearly express the precision of such measurements. The number of significant figures obtained as a result of a measurement is equivalent to the number of certain figures in a made measure-

ment plus an additional last figure denoting the uncertainty of the number.

The uncertain figure of a measurement is the last significant figure of the measurement.

Numbers that are known as conversion factors or numbers that define some entity are known as "Exact Numbers". Examples of exact numbers are relationships such as 1 dozen = 12 or 1 foot = 12 inches. Exact numbers have an infinite number of significant figures. Table 12.1 demonstrates how one may distinguish significant figures from non-significant figures.

Table 12.1: Examples of significant figures versus non-significant figures.

Significant	Examples	Non-Significant
Non-zero integers	1.234 (4 sf)	
Zeros between non-zero integers*	1.004 (4 sf)	
Zeros to the right of decimal place AND integers*	1.2000 (5 sf) 0.0041 (2 sf)	Zeros to the right of decimal place BUT to the left of integers
	430 (2 sf)	Zeros to the left of decimal place BUT to the right of integers
	013.2 (3 sf)	Zeros to the left of decimal place AND integers

* Zeros in any number is used to convey either accuracy or magnitude. If a zero is to convey accuracy, then it is known as a significant value and if the zero is used to convey magnitude, then it is non-significant.

When performing mathematical operations on data with a fixed number of significant figures, it is critical to have the correct number of significant figures in the final answer, based upon the number of significant figures in the starting data. The following are examples of such operations:

For Addition and Subtraction:

The answer is limited by the data with the least number of significant figures <u>after the decimal place.</u>

e.g. $23.84 - 1.7 = 22.1$
(2 sf) (1 sf) (1 sf) after decimal place

For Multiplication and Division:

The answer is limited by the data with the least number of significant figures <u>in total</u>.

e.g. $250.00/5.00 = 50.0$
(5 sf) (3 sf) (3 sf)

12.4.4 Basic Lab Techniques

<u>Distillation</u> is the process by which compounds are separated based on differences in boiling points. A classic example of simple distillation is the separation of salt from water. The solution is heated. Water will boil and vaporize at a far lower temperature than salt. Hence the water boils away leaving salt behind. Water vapor can now be condensed into pure liquid water (*distilled water*). As long as one compound is more volatile, the distillation process is quite simple. If the difference between the two boiling points is low, it will be more difficult to separate the compounds by this method. Instead, fractional distillation can

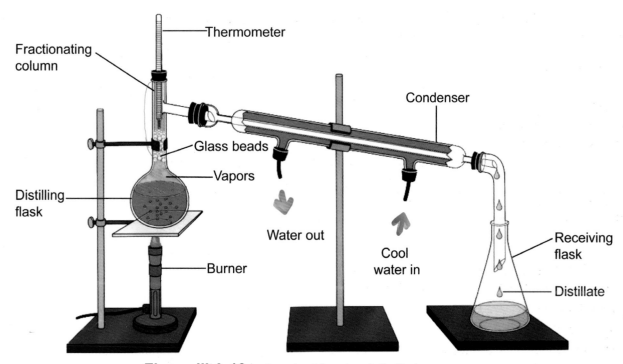

Figure III.A.12.: Standard fractional distillation apparatus

be used in which, for example, a column is filled with glass beads which is placed between the distillation flask and the condenser. The glass beads increase the surface area over which the less volatile compound can condense and drip back down to the distillation flask below. The more volatile compound boils away and condenses in the condenser. Thus the two compounds are separated.

The efficiency of the distillation process in producing a pure product is improved by repeating the distillation process, or, in the case of fractional distillation, increasing the length of the column and avoiding overheating. Overheating may destroy the pure compounds or increase the percent of impurities. Some of the methods which are

used to prevent overheating include boiling slowly, the use of boiling chips (= *ebulliator*, which makes bubbles) and the use of a vacuum which decreases the vapor pressure and thus the boiling point.

Extraction is the process by which a solute is transferred (*extracted*) from one solvent and placed in another. This procedure is possible if the two solvents used cannot mix (= *immiscible*) and if the solute is more soluble in the solvent used for the extraction.

For example, consider the extraction of solute A which is dissolved in solvent X. We choose solvent Y for the extraction since solute A is highly soluble in it and because solvent Y is immiscible with solvent X. We now add solvent Y to the solution involving solute A and solvent X. The container is agitated. Solute A begins to dissolve in the solvent where it is most soluble, solvent Y. The container is left to stand, thus the two immiscible solvents separate. The phase containing solute A can now be removed.

In practice, solvent Y would be chosen such that it would be sufficiently easy to evaporate (= *volatile*) after the extraction so solute A can be easily recovered. Also, it is more efficient to perform several extractions using a small amount of solvent each time, rather than one extraction using a large amount of solvent.

Chromatography is the separation of a mixture of compounds by their distribution between two phases: one stationary and one moving. Molecules are separated based on differences in polarity and molecular weight.

In gas-liquid chromatography, the *stationary phase* is a liquid absorbed to an inert solid. The liquid can be polyethylene glycol, squalene, or others, depending on the polarity of the substances being separated.

The mobile phase is a gas (i.e. He, N_2) which is unreactive both to the stationary phase and to the substances being separated. The sample being analyzed can be injected in the direction of gas flow into one end of a column packed with the stationary phase. As the sample migrates through the column certain molecules will move faster than others. As mentioned the separation of the different types of molecules is dependent on size (*molecular weight*) and charge (*polarity*). Once the molecules reach the end of the column special detectors signal their arrival.

If you are studying for the US DAT or the OAT, then we suggest that you complete your Gold Notes followed by the Warm-Up Exercises in the book and online, and then update your notes and continue to your Organic Chemistry review. It is very important that you review your notes from the beginning on a regular basis. If you are studying for the Canadian DAT, where Organic Chemistry is not required, we suggest that you still review ORG 1.1 to 1.5 because it overlaps General Chemistry, and also review Organic Chemistry Chapter 13 which overlaps this chapter as well as Electrophoresis which is only partly covered at the end of Biology Chapter 15.

Perhaps this is a fair quote to end General Chemistry: "A diamond is merely a lump of coal that did well under pressure." Good luck!

GOLD STANDARD WARM-UP EXERCISES

CHAPTER 12: Laboratory

1) In a titration, a burette is used to:

   A. measure the concentration of the unknown sample.
   B. measure the mass of the unknown sample.
   C. accurately add the indicator.
   D. accurately add the standard reagent.

2) Flaming is a technique used to:

   A. sterilize glassware before use.
   B. colorize a titration.
   C. clean hands after working with bacteria.
   D. clean instruments after use.

3) A student weighs out 0.0127 mol of pure, dry HCl in order to prepare a 0.127 M HCl solution. Of the following pieces of laboratory equipment, which would be most important for preparing the solution?

   A. 100 mL volumetric flask
   B. 100 mL graduated beaker
   C. 100 mL Erlenmeyer flask
   D. 50 mL volumetric pipette

4) The number 0.086030 has how many significant figures?

   A. 4
   B. 5
   C. 6
   D. 7

5) The weight of a metal is 24.7 grams and its volume is 3.3 cm^3. Considering the significant figures in your calculation, the value of the density, in g/cm^3, should be reported as:

   A. 7
   B. 7.5
   C. 7.4
   D. 7.48

Go online to DAT-prep.com for additional chapter review Q&A and forum.

GS ANSWER KEY

CHAPTER 12

		Cross-Reference				*Cross-Reference*
1.	D	CHM 6.9, 12.3.1				
2.	A	CHM 12.3.1	4.	B	CHM 12.4.2, 12.4.3	
3.	A	CHM 12.3.1	5.	B	CHM 12.4.2, 12.4.3	

* Explanations can be found at the back of the book.

CHAPTER REVIEW
SOLUTIONS

Question 1   C

See: CHM 1.3, 1.5

Reaction I shows us that the stoichiometric ratio between Cl_2 and HCl is 1:2.

Using Number of moles Cl_2
  = (Mass used)/(relative molecular mass Cl_2)

Number of moles Cl_2 = 10 g/[(35.5 × 2) g mol^{-1}]
  = 10 g/(71.0 g mol^{-1})

From the ratio above, number of moles HCl produced
  = 2 × number of moles Cl_2

Number of moles HCl = 2 × 10 g/(71.0 g mol^{-1})
Using Number of grams HCl
  = Number of moles HCl × Relative molecular mass of HCl

Number of grams HCl = 2 × 10 g/(71.0 g mol^{-1})
  × (1 + 35.5 g mol^{-1}) approx.
  = 2 × 10 g × 1/2 = 10 g

Question 2   D

See: CHM 1.7

A solid mixture of two or more metals is referred to as an *alloy*.

Question 3   D

See: CHM 1.3

Molecular weight of N_2 = 28
Molecular weight of O_2 = 32
Average molecular weight of air
  = (80% × 28) + (20% × 32)
  = 28.8

Gases denser than air will have a molecular weight greater than 28.8.

  CH_4: Mw = 16
  Cl_2: Mw = 71
  CO_2: Mw = 44
  NH_3: Mw = 17
  NO_2: Mw = 46
  O_3: Mw = 48
  SO_2: Mw = 64

Thus, Cl_2, CO_2, NO_2, O_3, and SO_2 are denser than air.

Question 4   B

See: CHM 1.5

The question indicates that there are 2 moles of P_2 gas and 4 moles of Q_2 gas in the vessel. Next, we learn that all the molecules have reacted to produce a *triatomic* product. Thus the product must have three (*tri*) atoms. Only one answer has a product with three atoms, answer choice B. We know that the product must have a structure P_mQ_n (since both gases have reacted), where m + n = 3. Because there are twice as many Q atoms as P atoms, the overall reaction must be:

  $2P_2 + 4Q_2 \rightarrow 4PQ_2$ or $P_2 + 2Q_2 \rightarrow 2PQ_2$

Question 5   D

See: CHM 1.6

This question is relatively easy. We know that each of the three oxygens has a charge of -2 (total charge -6) and that the overall charge on the molecule is -1. Letting X represent the oxidation state of the halogen, we have:

$$X + (-6) = -1$$
$$X = +5.$$

Question 6   A

See: CHM 1.6

The oxidation state of oxygen is usually -2. Therefore, the total oxidation state due to oxygen = 7 × -2 = -14. The overall charge on the molecule is -2. There are 2 Cr atoms per $Cr_2O_7^{2-}$ molecule, thus:

  2 × oxidation state of Cr + (-14) = -2
    2 × oxidation state of Cr = 12
      Oxidation state of Cr = 12/2 = 6

Question 7   B

See: CHM 1.6

Looking at our answer choices, the oxidation state of N in NO is obviously +2, which makes sense because the oxidation state of oxygen is -2 and the overall charge of NO = 0. For nitric acid, where the charge of H = +1, the charge of O = -2 and the overall charge of the molecule = 0, we obtain:

(1 × H) + (1 × N) + (3 × O) = 0 → (+1) + (N) + (3 × -2) = 0
  (+1) + (N) + (-6) = 0 → N - 5 = 0 → N = +5.

Question 8   C

See: CHM 1.6

The oxidation state of oxygen is -2; therefore, the total oxidation state of the oxygens in MnO_4^- = -2 × 4 = -8. Since the net charge on the ion is -1,

  Oxidation state of Mn + (-8) = -1, thus Mn = -1 + 8 = +7

Since the oxidation state of Mn in Mn^{2+} is +2, there has been a decrease in the oxidation state, that is, a reduction has occurred. {GERC = gain electrons reduction...CHM 10.2}

The oxidation state of Cl in Cl$^-$ is -1 and is 0 in Cl_2 (the oxidation state of an element in naturally occurring form = 0) so an increase in the oxidation state, that is, an oxidation has occurred. {LEO = loss of electrons is oxidation...}

Question 9   D

See: CHM 1.5

Scanning the equation, you should be drawn to Ca in $Ca_3(PO_4)_2$ and you would conclude that you need at least $3Ca(OH)_2$ and thus $2H_3PO_4$ which gives $6H_2Os$.

$$3Ca(OH)_2 + 2H_3PO_4 \rightarrow 6H_2O + Ca_3(PO_4)_2$$

Question 10   D

See: CHM 1.3, 1.5

From the Reaction I, mole ratio between Mn and Cl_2 = 2:5
Relative atomic mass of Mn = 55 approximately (*see the periodic table*)

Relative molecular mass of Cl_2 = 35.5 × 2 = 71.0

Therefore, the mass ratio between Mn and Cl_2
  = (2 × 55):(5 × 71.0)
  = 110:355 = 11:35.5 = 1:3 approximately

Question 1   D
See: CHM 2.3
The s-block elements are those whose s-orbital is the valent orbital.

Question 2   D
See: CHM 2.3
Because the attractive forces between the nuclei and the valence electrons are strong, there is less tendency for electrons to be lost and hence a greater tendency for an electron to be gained in order to attain the more stable noble gas configuration.

Question 3   D
See: CHM 2.3
Colored complexes are a well-known characteristic of most transition metals.

Question 4   D
See: CHM 2.3
Since potassium only has one electron in its outer shell, it is easily removed (i.e. low first ionization potential/energy), thus leaving potassium with the more stable noble gas-like configuration (i.e. Ar). On the other hand, adding an electron to neutral potassium would require much energy (i.e. high first electron affinity) which would leave potassium with two valence electrons which would not be stable.

Noble gases are the most stable elements in the periodic table.

Question 5   C
See: CHM 2.3, 2.3.1
The smaller the atomic radii of the two atoms, the shorter the bond length. Bond **strength** is inversely related to bond **length**. Carbon has the *smaller* atomic radius thus it has the *greater* bond strength. {*This force of attraction is analogous to Coulomb's Law (a physics principle but the basis for 'opposites attract' in general and organic chemistry) where the positive nucleus is attracted to the bond which contains negative electrons*}

Question 6   D
See: CHM 2.1, 2.2
n is the principal quantum number and is irrelevant for this question since each of the choices is broken down to l or m quantum numbers.

l gives the shape of the orbital. 0 indicates s, 1 indicates p, 2 indicates d, 3 indicates f, etc. The maximum number of electrons in each of these is 2, 6, 10, 14, etc., respectively (it is given by the equation $4l + 2$ but most students just memorize the preceding 4 maximum numbers). m gives the spatial orientation of an orbital. At most, only 2 electrons can occupy a single m orbital. Thus:

	Max. no. of electrons
$n = 4, l = 0$	2
$n = 5, l = 2$	10
$n = 6, l = 3, l_m = +1$	2
$n = 4, l = 3$	14

Therefore, the answer is D.

Question 7   B
See: CHM 2.3
In the periodic table, chromium has an atomic number of 24, which means the Cr atom has 24 protons and 24 electrons. To do this problem, refer to CHM 2.2, Figure III.A.2.3, where the arrows show the order for filling atomic orbitals from top to bottom. The diagram shows that the orbital 4s is of lower energy than 3d; however, recall that a half-filled 3d orbital creates a more stable atom [CHM 2.3 (iv)] thus answer choice B. is correct.

Question 8   C
See: CHM 2.3
When you consider non-metals, think of examples: Noble gases, oxygen, nitrogen, etc. They are all gases at room temperature.

Question 9   A
See: CHM 2.3, 11
Ionization energy (or *potential*) is the energy required to remove the least tightly bound electron from an atom. If at the end of the process, that electron has some additional energy (ie. K_e) then that is clearly over and above just the energy required to remove the electron. Thus we can write:

$$Total\ Energy\ E = IE + K_e$$
$$IE = E - K_e$$

Question 1   A CO_3^{-2}
See: CHM 3.2, 3.5
Formal charge is found by dividing the electrons in each bond between the atoms, and then comparing the number of electrons assigned to each atom with the number of electrons on a neutral atom of the element.
In a carbonate ion, we can assign 4 electrons to the C atom, and since C has 4 valence electrons, its formal charge is 0.
Going deeper: note that two of the O's each have a formal charge of -1, and the third O has a formal charge of 0. Thus, the carbonate ion has an overall charge of -2. Or, since each O is equivalent, the charge on each can be considered to be -2/3.

Question 2   D
See: CHM 3.5
The rule is that an atom which exhibits tetrahedral geometry is sp³ hybridized.

Question 3   A
See: CHM 3.5, ORG 1.2
As in ethene and SO_2, the sp² hybridized atom has a trigonal planar orientation.

Question 4   B
See: CHM 3.2-3.5

The question describes a triatomic molecule (PQ_2). The central atom P is thus bonded twice to Q and, according to the question, P also has a lone pair of electrons. Thus P is surrounded by 3 electron pairs (minimum) which is a trigonal planar arrangement leaving a bent molecule (CHM 3.5T).

Question 5   B
See: CHM 3.4

The lone pair of electrons on the nitrogen atom allows it to **donate** a pair of electrons which is the definition of a Lewis base.

Question 6   D
See: CHM 3.5

Valence shell electron pair repulsion (VSEPR) rules predict the shape of individual molecules based on the extent of electron-pair repulsion. Valence electron pairs surrounding an atom repel each other, and thus make an arrangement that minimizes this repulsion producing the molecule's geometry.

Question 7   C
See: CHM 3.5

PCl_5 has 5 valence shell electron pairs. These will arrange themselves in a trigonal bipyramidal shape.

Question 8   A
See: CHM 3.5

SF_6 has 6 valence shell electron pairs. These will arrange themselves in an octahedral shape.

Question 9   D
See: CHM 3.5

ClF_3 has 5 valence shell electron pairs. These would normally arrange themselves in an trigonal bipyramidal fashion. However, since two of the electron pairs are lone pairs, the molecule is consequently T-shaped.

Question 10   B
See: CHM 2.3, 3.1.1

The larger the difference in electronegativity between two atoms involved in a bond, the more ionic (polar) the bond is. Scanning the periodic table, you will notice that Ca is to the far left and F (the most electronegative atom on the periodic table) is to the far right making a great situation for ionic bonding.

CHAPTER REVIEW SOLUTIONS   CHAPTER 4

Question 1   C
See: CHM 4.1.10 (4.1.8)

The ideal gas equation assumes that (1) the volume occupied by the particles of gas is negligible compared to the overall volume of the gas and (2) there are no intermolecular interactions. To closely approximate these assumptions, low pressure is used so that the overall volume of the gas is large (because pressure and volume are inversely related) and high temperature minimizes intermolecular interactions.

{Remember: an ideal Plow and Thigh! (CHM 4.1.10)}

Question 2   A
See: CHM 4.1.2

If a gas is ideal, its particles have absolutely no attractive forces between them. Therefore, it should remain as a gas at all temperatures since liquefaction and solidification are based on mutual electrostatic forces of attraction between particles.

Question 3   D
See: CHM 4.1.9

The sum of the mole fractions of each species present must be unity (=1). Therefore, the partial pressure of O_2 is 1 - (1/6 + 1/2) = 1/3. The partial pressure of a species is given by the product of its mole fraction and the total pressure of the system. Therefore, the answer is given by 1/3 × 1 atm = 0.33 atm, approximately.

Question 4   B
See: CHM 4.1.6, 4.1.7, 4.1.8, 4.1.9

In Reaction 1, 4 moles of NH_3 react with 5 moles of O_2. We are told to assume ideal conditions so that we are dealing with

ideality thus the ideal gas equation applies:

$$PV = nRT$$

If P and T are constant (i.e. at the time the two reactants are exposed to each other) thus:

$$V = n (RT/P) \text{ thus } V = n \text{ (constant)}.$$

{This concept is the basis for molar volume at S.T.P. (CHM 4.1.1); in fact, you can skip the steps above and directly apply Avogadro's Law (CHM 4.1.6)}

Since $V_1/n_1 = \text{constant} = V_2/n_2$ then:

$$48/4 = V(O_2)/5 \text{ thus } 12 = V(O_2)/5$$

Thus

$$V(O_2) = 60 \text{ L}.$$

Question 5   B
See: CHM 4.3.3

Answer choice **B.** is a typical phase diagram for a substance. The exceptions to this rule include substances which exhibit larger intermolecular forces than usual, for example hydrogen bonding. These include water and ammonia, which would yield a phase diagram such as that in answer choice **A.** See the last paragraphs of CHM 4.3.3}

Question 6   B
See: CHM 4.3, 8.7

The latent heat, whether in fusion (solid to liquid transformation) or in vaporization (liquid/vapor transformation), takes place at constant temperature (either B or D). Clearly, fusion must occur at the lower temperature(B).

CHM-212   DAT-prep.com

Question 7   A

See: CHM 4

Less dense solids or liquids float on denser liquids.

Question 8   B

See: CHM 4.1.8

Rearranging the ideal gas equation, we get:

$$n = PV/RT.$$

Since P, V, and T are the same for both gas samples, n is also the same. However, propane has a molecular weight of 44, while H_2 has a molecular weight of 2. Therefore, a molecule of propane weighs 22 times more than a molecule of hydrogen. Consequently, the sample of propane weighs 22 times more than the sample of hydrogen.

Question 9   A

See: CHM 4.1.8

Using n = PV/RT,

$$n_{final} = (2P \times 1.1V)/RT = 2.2 \times n_{initial}.$$

Therefore, the weight of air in the ball is also 2.2 times heavier than initially.

Question 10   A

See: CHM 4.1.1

Molar volume at STP is 22.4 L (CHM 4.1.1).
Use given values and estimate: (2 g/L)(22 L/mol) = 44 g/mol. Taking atomic weights from the periodic table, we find the molecular weight of C_3H_8: $(3 \times 12) + (8 \times 1) = 44$ g/mol.

Question 11   A

See: CHM 4.1.6

PV = nRT, n = PV/RT.
P = (7.6 torr.)(1 atm/760 torr.) = 0.01 atm.
R = 0.08 L * atm/K * mol.
V = (1000 mL/min)(1 min) = 1L.
T = 293 K (approximately 300 K).
n = (.01)(1)/(.08)(300) = 1/2400 mol.

mass = (200 g/mol) (1/2400 moles) = 1/12 = 0.08 grams. (Note: the MW was estimated at 200 instead of 197,4). Remember: check the answers, if they are very close (ie. 0.08, 0.082, 0.083, etc) then clearly you cannot round off figures (estimate). But the answers in this problem are multiples of each other so estimating within reason is logical.

Question 12   C

See: CHM 4.1.9

The partial pressure (pp) is based on the mole fraction (CHM. 4.1.9) not the weight. We must convert the weight into mole fraction, using the atomic weight from the periodic table. Given an arbitrary 200 g of mixture, there is:

H_2: (100 g)/(2 g/mol) = 50 mol of H_2,
He: (100 g)/(4 g/mol) = 25 mol of He.

Mole fraction of H_2: 50/(50 + 25) = 2/3.

Thus, pp of H_2 = 600 (2/3) = 400 torr.

CHAPTER REVIEW SOLUTIONS | CHAPTER 5

Question 1   D

See: CHM 4.3.3, 5.1.2

Simply look at the graph, choose any temperature and then watch what happens as you increase the pressure to infinity: liquid!

Question 2   B

See: CHM 1.5, 5.2

Sodium sulfate dissociates in solution according to the following equation:

$$Na_2(SO_4) \rightarrow 2\,Na^+ + SO_4^{2-}$$

One mole of sodium sulfate dissociates into 2 moles of the sodium ion. Therefore, if the $[Na^+] = 0.02$ M then the $[Na_2(SO_4)]$ is 0.02/2 = 0.01 M.

Question 3   D

See: CHM 3.1, 5.2

Osmolarity, a colligative property (depends on the number of particles, not the nature of the particles; CHM 5.1), is a measure of the amount of solute ions or molecules in solution. Since the three choices in the question are strong electrolytes (i.e. salts), we assume they will dissociate completely into ions according to the following equations:

1. $NaCl \rightarrow Na^+ + Cl^-$ = 2 ions in solution/mole of salt dissolved
2. $MgCl_2 \rightarrow Mg^{+2} + 2Cl^-$ = 3 ions in solution/mole of salt dissolved
3. $AlCl_3 \rightarrow Al^{+3} + 3Cl^-$ = 4 ions in solution/mole of salt dissolved

Since aluminum chloride will dissolve into the most particles, the $AlCl_3$ solution will have the highest osmolarity.

Question 4   B

See: CHM 5.3.1

Molarity = Number of moles per liter [= mol/(1000cm³)]

Molality = Number of moles per 1000 g of solvent
          [= mol/(1000 g)]

Then, if 1000 cm³ = 1000 g,

          Molarity = Molality

Question 5   B

See: CHM 5.1.1/2

A non-volatile solute causes a lowering of the vapor pressure of the solvent and hence an elevation of the boiling point. The preceding is a colligative property.

Question 6   B

See: CHM 5.1.2

The negative slope of the solid-liquid equilibrium curve in the phase diagram depicts that increasing the pressure causes a decrease in the melting point.

Going Deeper:

(1) ideally, you would recognize the shape of the Phase Diagram for Water with its classic features. One of which is the triple point: the point at which solid, liquid and gas exist at equilibrium. The pressure at the triple point is indicated in the graph but the temperature is not. However, you are expected to know that the temperature should be approximately 0 °C (after all, triple point means ice, liquid water and vapor; this is a simplified approximation; details at CHM 5.1.2).

Knowing that the triple point is about 0 °C, now examine the negative slope (upper left part of the graph) which represents the line where solid and liquid exist and equilibrium (melting point). As the pressure P increases, the negative slope demonstrates a decrease in temperature (below 0 °C).

(2) an interesting example: you can't skate on ice! If you have ever skated, you will know about this example. Ice is not very slippery; however, water on ice is VERY slippery. A skate is designed to put a lot of pressure (the weight of the individual) funneled to a very narrow blade. This narrow metal blade literally melts ice by the extreme pressure as the person's skate hits the surface allowing the metal to slide gracefully over the more slippery thin film of water on the ice surface. If the temperature becomes too low for the pressure to have a significant effect, skating becomes too difficult (too much resistance).

Question 7   C

See: CHM 5.3.2

To figure out the K_{sp} expression, it is wise to write the dissociation equation:

$$PbS \leftrightarrow Pb^{2+} + S^{2-}.$$

The K_{sp} is the product of the concentration of each ion raised to the power of the stochiometric coefficient in the equation. In this case,

$$K_{sp} = [Pb^{2+}][S^{2-}].$$

Question 8   C

See: CHM 5.3.2

$$Bi_2S_3 \leftrightarrow 2Bi^{3+} + 3S^{2-}$$
$$K_{sp} = [Bi^{3+}]^2[S^{2-}]^3$$

Question 9   C

See: CHM 5.3.2

Since $MgCO_3 \leftrightarrow Mg^{2+} + CO_3^{2-}$, $K_{sp} = [Mg^{2+}][CO_3^{2-}] = s \times s = s^2$ where s is the solubility. From the information provided, s = 1.30×10^{-3} mol L^{-1}. Thus $K_{sp} = [Mg^{2+}][CO_3^{2-}] = s^2 = (1.30 \times 10^{-3})^2 = 1.69 \times 10^{-6} \approx 1.7 \times 10^{-6}$. {Mathfax: $(13)^2 = 169$ therefore $(1.3)^2 = 1.69$; also, to increase speed you should at least be able to

recognize the squares of numbers between 1-15, i.e. $(12)^2 = 144$; rules of exponents: see QR; of course, you will have a calculator at your disposal but recognizing patterns can make you faster.}

Question 10   B

See: CHM 5.3.2

Consider these two equations:

(i) $CaSO_4 \leftrightarrow Ca^{2+} + SO_4^{2-}$
(ii) $Ca(OH)_2 \leftrightarrow Ca^{2+} + 2OH^-$

On the Surface: for the same K_{sp}, the more ions produced means the more soluble ($Ca(OH)_2$ produces 3 ions as opposed to just 2). Though temperature is indeed related to solubility, it would affect both compounds in a similar way so having 3 ions will still mean that it is more soluble than just 2 ions.

Going Deeper: If $[Ca^{2+}]$ = s = solubility of salt, then:
For (i): $s^2 = K_{sp}$, therefore s = square root of K_{sp} (cf. with previous question/answer)
For (ii): $(2s)^2 \times s = K_{sp}$, therefore s = cube root of $(1/4 \times K_{sp})$

Since K_{sp} is always *less* than 1 for sparingly soluble salts, the value for *s* obtained in (ii) *necessarily* is greater than that obtained in (i). {*For fun(!), work out values for 's' in* (i) *and* (ii) *using any value for* K_{sp} *less than 1*}

Question 11   B

See: CHM 5.3.2, 5.3.3

By adding K_2S, we are essentially adding sulfide anions, which first combine with Ni^{2+} ions to form a NiS precipitate. Since MnS has not yet precipitated, it must be more soluble than NiS. And since both cations (Ni^{2+} and Mn^{2+}) have a charge of +2, their coefficients in their respective dissolution equations must be the same. Thus, MnS must have a higher K_{sp} than NiS; in fact, the K_{sp} of MnS is 3.0×10^{-13}.

Question 12   A

See: CHM 5.3.2, 5.3.3

The balanced equation for the dissolution of $MgF_2(s)$ is:

$$MgF_2(s) \leftrightarrow Mg^{2+}(aq) + 2F^-(aq).$$

$$K_{sp} = [Mg^{2+}][F^-]^2 = 6.5 \times 10^{-9}$$

For convenience, let us denote $[Mg^{2+}]$ as X. Thus:
$$6.5 \times 10^{-9} = X(2X)^2 = X(4X^2) = 4X^3$$
$$X = \text{cube root of } \{(6.5 \times 10^{-9})/4\} = 1.18 \times 10^{-3}$$

Finally, $[F^-] = 2X = 2.35 \times 10^{-3}$.

Question 13   D

See: CHM 5.3.2, 5.3.3

$$K_{sp} = [Mg^{2+}][F^-]^2 = 6.5 \times 10^{-9} = 0.1 [F^-]^2$$

Thus:

$$[F^-] = \text{sq root } (6.5 \times 10^{-9} \times 10) = 2.5 \times 10^{-4} \text{ M}$$

Question 14   C

See: CHM 5.3.2, 5.3.3

$$MgF_2 \rightarrow Mg^{2+} + 2F^-$$
$$Ksp = [Mg^{2+}][F^-]^2 = 10^{-8}$$

Given Ksp = $[10^{-4}][10^{-4}]^2 = 10^{-12}$

Our calculated Ksp (10^{-12}) is much less than the value above which a precipitate is formed (10^{-8}),

$$MgCO_3 \rightarrow Mg^{2+} + CO_3^{2-}$$

$$Ksp = [Mg^{2+}][CO_3^{2-}] = 10^{-5}$$

Given Ksp = $[10^{-4}][10^{-4}] = 10^{-8}$

Again the calculated value is far below the value needed to precipitate (10^{-5}).

Question 15   D

See: CHM 5.1.3

First we should define "osmotic pressure": Osmotic pressure is the hydrostatic (ie. water) pressure produced by a solution in a space divided by a semipermeable membrane (the capillary wall) due to a differential in the concentrations of solute (because we are told that the capillary wall is permeable to everything except proteins then only the proteins constitute the differential concentrations of solute).

$$\Pi = (n/V)RT$$
$$= 0.0015 \times 60 \times 310$$
$$= 27.9 \text{ mmHg or Torr}$$

(The term "oncotic pressure" refers to the osmotic pressure exerted by colloids only (see CHM 1.7). Colloids include proteins and starches in solution.)

Question 16   D

See: CHM 5.1.2

The freezing point of water is 0 °C.

To depress the freezing point to -40 °C,

$$\text{molality of solution} = \Delta T/K_f$$
$$= 40/1.9$$
$$= 21 \text{ m or 21 moles/kg of water}$$

Molecular weight of ethylene glycol = 62
Therefore, mass of ethylene glycol = moles × mw
$$= 21 \times 62$$
$$= 1300 \text{ g}$$
$$= 1.3 \text{ kg}$$

CHAPTER REVIEW SOLUTIONS   CHAPTER 6

Question 1   C

See: CHM 6.1, 6.5

$$pH = -\log_{10}[H^+]$$

The highest pH has the lowest $[H^+]$. Clearly, Na_2SO_4 is the only choice that does not even have dissociable H^+!

Question 2   B

See: CHM 6.5, 6.6

Reaction I

$$H_2SO_3 + H_2O \rightarrow H_3O^+ + HSO_3^- \qquad K_{a1} = \text{very high}$$

Reaction II

$$HSO_3^- + H_2O \leftrightarrow H_3O^+ + SO_3^{2-} \qquad K_{a2} = 5.0 \times 10^{-6}$$

Since we are told to consider the first ionization of H_2SO_3 as if from a strong acid, we assume that the first proton completely dissociates. However, the second proton ionizes as if from a very weak acid. After all, a $K_a \approx 10^{-6}$ means that the product of the reactants is about 1 000 000 (one million!) times greater than the product of the products (which includes the second proton; for K_a see CHM 6.1). The preceding fact combined with the imprecision of the available multiple choice answers means that our answer can be estimated by assuming that H_2SO_3 acts as a strong monoprotic acid like HCl.

Therefore, one proton completely dissociates while the second proton's concentration is relatively negligible; thus $[H^+] = 0.01$ mol dm^{-3} (1 dm^{-3}= 1 L^{-1}, see QR). The pH is equal to the negative logarithm of $[H^+]$ = -log (0.01) = -log (10^{-2}) = 2.

Question 3   A

See: CHM 6.5, 6.9

An indicator is added to titration solutions to detect the pH change associated with the endpoint of a titration. The solution is titrated until a color *change* is observed (eliminating answer choices B. and D.) when a stoichiometric amount of titrant has been added. The indicator consists of a weak acid or base whose undissociated state is a different color than its dissociated (conjugate) state. The indicator chosen should have its pK$_a$ close to the expected pH of the equivalence point.

Question 4   C

See: CHM 6.9.3

HCl is an acid, so one would expect the pH of the reaction mixture to decrease (that is, become more acidic) as increasing volumes of HCl are added. Thus only C. and D. are possible answers. Answer choice D. is wrong because there should be two "plateaus" (*that is, where the slope of a curve approximates 0 in that region*) in this type of graph, there are just regions where the slope approaches infinity (*that is, the slope is almost vertical which is not logical for a titration curve; furthermore, consider the data in Table 1 for pH = 8.8*).

Question 5   B

See: CHM 6.5, 6.9

The range of the indicator should include the range where the graph depicts an almost vertical slope, that is, it should include the *equivalence point* in the middle of that region. This is approximately 4.6 in this instance (*see previous question C.*). Even if you did not know which titration curve was correct in the previous question, all answer choices change the direction of the curve (in math, this is called the point of inflection) around 4.6 which indicates the equivalence point.

Question 6   C

See: CHM 6.9.3

Once the $C_6H_5NH_2$ is depleted (*producing* $C_6H_5NH_3^+$), additional protons from the HCl can no longer be neutralized. Thus the $[H^+]$ increases dramatically, leading to a decrease in pH.

Question 7   C
See: CHM 6.5, 6.5.1, 6.9

Two pH units are equivalent to a 100 fold [H⁺] difference as shown below.

$$pH = -\log(x) = 2$$
$$x = 10^2 = 100$$

The proper interpretation of the answer is: if the pH goes down by 2 units, we have 100 times more hydrogen ion concentration, and if the pH goes up by 2 units, we would have 1/100th of the original hydrogen ion concentration: either an increase or decrease of 100x.

Question 8   B
See: CHM 6.9, 6.9.1/2

Answer choices **A** and **C** are characteristics of a neutral solution, which may not necessarily exist at the equivalence point of a titration.

Question 9   B
See: CHM 6.5, 6.5.1, 6.6

Since formic acid is considered a weak acid (*see* K_a) it will dissociate according to the following equation:

$$HCOOH \leftrightarrow H^+ + HCOO^-$$

The K_a of the reaction must be used to calculate the concentration of protons and the pH:

$$K_a = [H^+][HCOO^-]/[HCOOH]$$

After dissociation, an equal amount X of [H⁺] and [HCOO⁻] will be in solution with a certain concentration of acid left undissociated (0.10 M - X). Substituting these values, we get:

$$K_a = (X)(X)/(0.10\ M - X) = X^2/(0.10\ M - X).$$

Since we expect that $X<<0.10$, we can approximate the denominator to be 0.10 M (*see* CHM 6.6). Substituting the value of K_a, we can calculate the concentration of protons:

$$1.8 \times 10^{-4} = X^2/0.10$$
$$X^2 = 1.8 \times 10^{-5}$$
$$X = (16 \times 10^{-6})^{1/2} = 4 \times 10^{-3}\ approx.$$

Using:

$$pH = -\log[H^+]$$
$$pH = -\log(4 \times 10^{-3}) = -\log(10^{between\ 0\ and\ 1} \times 10^{-3})$$
$$= -(between\ 0\ and\ 1) + 3 = a\ pH\ between\ 2\ and\ 3.$$

Question 10   B
See: CHM 6.5, 6.5.1

$$pH = -\log_{10}[H^+]$$
$$[H^+] = [CHO_2^-]$$
$$= 10^{-pH} = 10^{-2.38}$$
$$Ka = [H^+][CHO_2^-]/[CH_2O_2]$$
$$= (10^{-2.38})^2/0.1$$
$$= 10^{-4.76}/0.1$$
$$= 10^{-3.76}\ (now\ check\ A, B, C, D)$$
$$= (approximately)\ 1.8 \times 10^{-4}$$

Question 11   B
See: CHM 6.2, 6.5

Since K_b of NH_3 is 1.8×10^{-5}, K_a of conjugate acid (NH_4^+) is:

$$10^{-14}/1.8 \times 10^{-5} = (approximately)\ 10^{-10}.$$

Now, K_a of $NH_4^+ = [H^+][NH_3]/[NH_4^+]$,

where $[NH_4^+] = 0.1$ M and $[H^+] = [NH_3]$. Therefore:

$$[H^+] = sq\ rt\ (K_a\ [NH_4^+])$$
$$= sq\ rt\ (10^{-10} \times 0.1)$$
$$= sp\ rt\ 10^{-11}$$
$$= 10^{-5.5}$$
$$pH = -\log_{10}[H^+]$$
$$= 5.5$$

Question 12   B
See: CHM 6.1

First, consider:

$$K_{a1} = [H^+][HSO_4^-]/[H_2SO_4] = 10^3$$
$$[H^+] = [HSO_4^-] = approximately\ 1.0\ M,$$

since K_{a1} is so high and the solution is 1 M H_2SO_4. However, HSO_4^- is also an acid and will dissociate with:

$$K_{a2} = [H^+][SO_4^{2-}]/[HSO_4^-] = 1.2 \times 10^{-2}.$$

Since $[HSO_4^-] = 1.0$ M from the first reaction,

$$[SO_4^{2-}] = K_{a2}$$
$$= 1.2 \times 10^{-2} = 0.012\ M.$$

Thus:

$[H^+]$ generated from the second reaction $= [SO_4^{2-}] = 0.012$ M.

Finally, $[H^+]_{total} = 1 + 0.012 = 1.012$ M.

CHAPTER REVIEW SOLUTIONS   CHAPTER 7

Question 1   C
See: CHM 7.6

The internal energy of the water is a state function and does not depend on the history of the sample.

Question 2   C
See: CHM 7.5

The system is doing work on the surroundings so the work

"w" must have a negative sign since you must always look at the problem from the point of view of the system - not the surroundings. The system is also losing heat to the surroundings so the sign for the heat "q" will also be negative. The energy is the sum of q + w = -25 - 50 = -75

Question 3   A
See: CHM 7.5

Light colors tend to reflect incident electromagnetic radiation including infrared rays, the main type of electromagnetic radiation associated with heat. The answer is easily deduced since there is only one answer which refers to the *reflective* property of the metal foil.

Question 4   C
See: CHM 7.6

A state function is one that depends only on the present state of a system and not the path used to get to the present state. A system's volume, internal energy, and entropy do not depend on

how the system arrived at the current state. However, the work done does depend on the path taken, e.g.: the work done could be as large as we want by taking a path as long as we want.

Question 5   B
See: CHM 7.5

Air is a poor *conductor* of heat. Both radiation and convection typically need air, or some other fluid, as a medium to transmit energy/heat.

Question 1   D
See: CHM 8.10

Answer choice **D** is true for all equilibria.

Question 2   C
See: CHM 8.9

In this reaction, four molecules react to form two molecules, thus increasing the order and decreasing the entropy.

Of course, this is true because we are only examining this one reaction; in truth, there must be some other process driving this reduction in entropy and thus, overall, if we were to include that other process, the entropy of the universe increases.

Example? Put liquid water in your freezer and, indeed, the disorder in the liquid becomes organized water crystals known as ice! Clearly, from the water's point of view, entropy decreased. But, if you were to touch the back of your freezer (we are NOT recommending this!), you will see that it is hot, lots of used and wasted energy creating increased randomness in the universe just to make a few ice cubes!

Question 3   B
See: CHM 8.2, 8.9, 8.10, 9.10

$$\Delta G = \Delta H - T(\Delta S)$$

Since the reaction is spontaneous, $\Delta G < 0$.

Since $\quad\quad\quad\quad \Delta S < 0, -T(\Delta S) > 0$.

Thus, for ΔG to be strictly less than zero, ΔH must be strictly less than zero, which means that the reaction is exothermic.

Question 4   C
See: CHM 8.8, 8.9

Moving from an organized crystalline solid (ice cube) to liquid water is clearly an increase in randomness of water molecules. The Second Law of Thermodynamics suggests that the total entropy (randomness or disorder) increases in any real system.

Question 5   D
See: CHM 5.3, 8.10, 9.10

This is an application of Henry's law. Consider what happens when you open a can of Coke: the carbon dioxide bubbles out of the solution - at times, faster than we want it to - because the pressure within the can is higher than atmospheric pressure. Thus the solubility of the gas decreased as the pressure over the solution was decreased.

The concept that the solubility of a dissolved gas will decrease when the solution is heated sounds a bit backwards since we usually heat up a solvent in order to dissolve something. The can be explained by discussing the overall energy of a system (Gibbs free energy) which is dependent on enthalpy and entropy (CHM 8.10, 9.10). Temperature is associated with entropy or randomness. If you heat up a solution of a gas and the gas escapes, the system becomes more random therefore it is favorable to have a decrease in solubility. Back to the can of Coke: heating up the can before opening it will result in a very rapid escape of gas (please do NOT try this!).

Question 6   C
See: CHM 4.3.3, 8.10

The triple point is where solid, liquid and gas exist at equilibrium and, by definition, ΔG is zero.

$$\Delta G = \Delta H - T\Delta S$$
$$0 = \Delta H - T\Delta S$$
$$\Delta H = T\Delta S$$

Thus the enthalpy change is equal to the effect of the entropy change. One could argue for answer choice A if indeed $\Delta H < T\Delta S$ which is not the case. Note that answer choice B does not apply because the reaction is at equilibrium. Regarding answer choice D, the reverse is theoretically true: an increase in disorder creates a positive change in entropy.

Question 7   D
See: CHM 8.5

Add the two equations to give the third one keeping in mind that the 2nd equation needs to be multiplied through by 2 so that we can cancel $2H_2O(l)$ which is not needed in the final reaction.

$$CH_4(g) + 2O_2(g) \rightarrow CO_2(g) + 2H_2O(l) \quad \Delta H° = -890 \text{ kJ/mol}$$
$$2H_2O(l) \rightarrow 2H_2O(g) \quad\quad\quad\quad \Delta H° = 88 \text{ kJ/mol}$$

Add the equations (note that $2H_2O(l)$ cancels from both sides of the equation) and their enthalpies.

$$CH_4 + 2O_2(l) \rightarrow CO_2(g) + 2H_2O(g) \quad \Delta H° = -802 \text{ kJ/mol}$$

Question 8   A
See: CHM 8.5

Write the equations according to the data given (note the sign of ΔH is reversed because the direction of the equation is reversed; this is done so that when we add the equations, cancellations can occur to produce the desired final reaction):

$$SO_2(g) \rightarrow S(s) + O_2(g) \qquad \Delta H = 297 \text{ kJ}$$
$$S(s) + {}^3/_2 O_2 \rightarrow SO_3 \qquad \Delta H = \text{-396 kJ}$$

Add the two equations to give

$$SO_2(g) + {}^1/_2 O_2 \rightarrow SO_3 \qquad \Delta H = \text{-99 kJ}$$

Question 9   D
See: CHM 8.7

The definition of a calorie is the amount of thermal energy required to raise the temperature of water by 1 degree Celcius (CHM 7.3). Thus it would be normal for you to know that the specific heat "c" of liquid water is 1 cal g^{-1} $°C^{-1}$ (i.e. 1 kcal/kg °C has the same meaning because of dimensional analysis).

1. Heat required to convert 10 grams of ice to 10 grams of water at 0 °C; L = latent heat of fusion.
$$Q = mL = (10)(80) = 800 \text{ cal}$$

2. Heat required to convert 10 grams of water at 0 °C to 10 grams of water at 100 °C.
$$Q = mc\Delta T = 10(1)100 = 1000 \text{ cal}$$

3. Heat required to convert 10 grams of water at 100 °C to 10 grams of steam at 100 °C; L = latent heat of vaporization.

$$Q = mL = (10)(540) = 5400 \text{ cal}$$
$$\text{ADD } (1) + (2) + (3) = 7200 \text{ cal}$$

Question 10   A
See: CHM 8.7

This problem is solved by giving special attention to units (i.e. 1 W = 1 J per s):

Rate of incident solar energy
$$= 70\,000 \text{ m}^2 \times 120 \text{ J s}^{-1} \text{ m}^{-2} = 8\,400\,000 \text{ J s}^{-1}$$

From Quantity of heat (Q)
$$= \text{Mass (m)} \times \text{Specific heat capacity (c)}$$
$$\times \text{ temperature change (T)}$$

Thus in one second:
$$Q = 8\,400\,000 \text{ J} = m \times (4.2 \text{ J g}^{-1} °C^{-1}) \times (10 °C)$$
$$42 \times m = 8\,400\,000; \quad \text{thus } m = 200\,000 \text{ g} = 200 \text{ kg}$$

Using Density = (Mass)/(Volume)
$$\text{Volume} = \text{(Mass)/(Density)} = 200 \text{ kg}/1000 \text{ kg m}^{-3}$$
$$= 0.2 \text{ m}^3 = 0.2 \text{ m}^3 \times 1000 \text{ dm}^3/\text{m}^3$$
$$\text{Volume} = 200 \text{ dm}^3 = 200 \text{ L in one second}$$

Time for a break!

Question 1   D
See: CHM 9.3, 9.4

When [P] is increased by a factor of 3 (Exp A and C, [Q] *is constant*), the initial rate of reaction is increased by a factor of 9 (= 32). Thus the order of reaction with respect to P is 2. When [Q] is increased by a factor of 2 (Exp A and B, [P] *is constant*), the initial rate of reaction is also increased by a factor of 2 (= 21). Therefore, the order of reaction with respect to Q is 1. The order of reaction with respect to a certain component tells you how many molecules of that component are involved in the rate determining step of the reaction which may not be equivalent to the stoichiometric coefficients.

Question 2   B
See: CHM 8.2, 9.9

The question stem indicates that addition of heat to the reaction would shift the reaction to the right. According to Le Chatelier's principle, the addition of a reactant will shift a reaction to the right while the addition of a product has the reverse effect. In this example, we can consider heat as a reactant, which means that the reaction is endothermic and the enthalpy has a positive value.

Question 3   A
See: CHM 9.7, 9.8

Catalysts only affect the rate at which equilibrium is achieved, not the equilibrium position itself.

Question 4   B
See: CHM 9.9

Reaction I is exothermic (ΔH is negative therefore heat is released). The reaction could be written as:

$$2SO_2(g) + O_2(g) \leftrightarrow 2SO_3(g) + \text{Heat}$$

Adding heat (increasing the temperature) adds to the right hand side of the equilibrium forcing a shift to the left in order to compensate. The reverse occurs by decreasing the temperature thus creating a shift to the right which would produce more $SO_3(g)$ and more heat is released. {Note: an increase in pressure would also lead to a right shift; see Le Chatelier's Principle, CHM 9.9}.

Question 5   A
See: CHM 9.9

An easy way to figure out questions involving Le Chatelier's Principle applied to temperature changes is to write out "heat" in the equation as a reactant or a product. In this example, heat is released from the reaction (shown by the temperature rise in the reaction vessel) so it can be considered a product:

$$P_2 + 2Q_2 \rightarrow 2PQ_2 + \text{heat}$$

If we decrease the temperature of the vessel, then we are decreasing the product on the right of the equation and the equilibrium of the reaction will shift towards the right to counteract this, in accordance with Le Chatelier's Principle.

Question 6   A
See: CHM 9.5

As with any potential energy curve of a reaction, we are looking for the shape of a hill because the transition state of the reaction, as a rule, has higher energy than the reactants and the products, eliminating answer choices C. and D. The negative enthalpy of the reaction means that the reaction is exothermic and that the energy of the products (on the right side of the hill) will be lower than the energy of the reactants (on the left side of the hill), as represented by answer choice A.

Question 7   A

See: CHM 9.9

Less particles are on the left side of the equation (9 moles versus 10). Therefore, the increase in pressure favors a shift in the equilibrium position to the left as the reactants occupy less volume (*Le Chatelier's principle*).

Question 8   B

See: CHM 5.3.3, 9.9

Because the acidity constants are small, the undissociated form of the acid tends to predominate in solution, that is, the equilibria $H_2S \leftrightarrow HS^- + H^+$ ($K_{a1} \approx 10^{-7}$) and $HS^- \leftrightarrow H^+ + S^{2-}$ ($K_{a2} \approx 10^{-15}$) both are heavily shifted to the left. According to Le Chatelier's principle, this would lead to Reaction I shifting to the right to counteract the effects of the loss of sulfide anions caused by the addition of protons (H^+).

Question 9   C

See: CHM 9.9

A negative ΔH signifies an exothermic reaction, which means heat (energy) is released.

Thus:
$$H_2 + I_2 \leftrightarrow 2\,HI + heat$$

If you increase the heat (i.e. temperature), the excess heat causes the reverse reaction to occur until equilibrium is again reached (CHM 9.9).

Question 10   C

See: CHM 9.2, 9.3

From the data, it can be seen that changing [B] while holding [A] constant has no effect on the rate. So B should not be a variable in the rate law. Also, it can be seen that doubling [A] leads to the rate quadrupling. So the rate is proportional to $[A]^2$. Thus, the rate law for the reaction is:

$$Rate = k[A]^2.$$

Question 11   A

See: CHM 9.2, 9.3

Let's look at Experiment 1 in Table 1 (this choice is arbitrary).

$$Rate = k[A]^2$$
$$4.0 \times 10^{-5} = k \times 0.1^2$$
$$k = 4.0 \times 10^{-5}/0.01$$
$$= 4.0 \times 10^{-3}$$

Now let's look at the units.

$$Rate = k[A]^2$$
$$M/s = [k] \times M^2$$
$$[k] = (M/s)/M^2$$
$$= M^{-1}s^{-1}$$

Thus, $k = 4.0 \times 10^{-3}\ M^{-1}s^{-1}$.

Question 12   B

See: CHM 9.2, 9.3

For choice A to be correct, the rate law would have to be one of the following, since three molecules would be involved in the rate-determining step.

$$Rate = k[A]^3$$
$$Rate = k[A]^2[B]$$
$$Rate = k[A][B]^2$$
$$Rate = k[B]^3$$

Incidentally, termolecular reactions are extremely rare because of the high improbability of having 3 molecules colliding at their reactive sites simultaneously.

For choice C to be correct, the rate law would have to be:

$$rate = k[A]^2[B].$$

The reason is the following: A and B first quickly react to form, say, AB. AB then reacts slowly with free A to form C. So:

$$rate = k[AB][A].$$

But [AB] is equal to [A][B], therefore:

$$rate = k[A][B][A] = k[A]^2[B].$$
(Note: k is just an arbitrary (nondescript) constant.)

For choice D to be correct, the rate law would have to be:

$$Rate = k[A][B].$$

The actual rate law (rate = $k[A]^2$) tells us however that the rate determining step involves two molecules of A -not one of A and another of B, nor a single one of A, etc. Thus, answer choice B is correct.

Question 13   A

See: CHM 9.2, 9.3

I.   k would decrease if the activation energy were higher since fewer molecules would have the necessary kinetic energy to proceed with the reaction.

II. k does increase with increasing temperature since more molecules would have the necessary kinetic energy to proceed with the reaction.

III. k is unaffected by the concentrations of reactants.

Thus, only statement II is correct.

Question 14   C

See: CHM 9.3

When the concentration of sucrose doubles (i.e. from 0.200 to 0.400M), the rate also doubles (from 7.32×10^{-4} to 1.46×10^{-3}). Therefore:

$$Rate = K\,[sucrose]$$

Now plug in any pair of values, for example:

$$1.80 \times 10^{-3} = K(0.500)$$

Multiply through by 2:

$$3.60 \times 10^{-3} = K$$

Thus: rate = (3.6×10^{-3})[sucrose]

Question 15   C

See: CHM 9.5

The activation energy is the difference between the total energy of the reactants (E_2) and the activated complex (E_3).

Question 1   D
See: CHM 10.1, 10.2, 10.4, 6.1

The relevant reaction is $Cu + 2H^+ \rightarrow Cu^{2+} + H_2$
Using the data provided, E = -0.34 + 0.00 = -0.34 V
Since E < 0, the reaction is not spontaneous.

Question 2   B
See: CHM 10.1, 10.2, 10.4, 6.1

The relevant reaction is $Pb + 2H^+ \rightarrow Pb^{2+} + H_2$
Using the data provided, E = 0.00 - (-0.13) = 0.13 V
Since E > 0, the reaction is spontaneous.

Question 3   B
See: CHM 10.1, 10.2, 10.4

Voltage = 2.87 - 1.09 = 1.78 V

Question 4   A
See: CHM 10.1, 10.2

Galvanic cells use spontaneous redox reactions to produce electricity. Recall that E° = E(reduction) - E(oxidation), and that a positive value of E° means that the reaction is spontaneous. The E° of the reaction for the Cl_2/Cl^- half cell given by the 1st reaction of Table 1 is 1.36 compared to an E° value of 1.51 for Reaction III. In order for the redox reaction to be spontaneous, Reaction III (with the higher E°) will proceed as a reduction (as written) while Cl^- will be oxidized to Cl_2. The overall Eo can be calculated as follows:

E° = E° red - E° ox = 1.51 - 1.36 = 0.15 V.

You should always double check that your overall Eo value is positive for a spontaneous reaction.

Question 5   B
See: CHM 10.5

From Table 1 we can see that each mole of sulfate ions requires *two* moles of electrons for reduction to one mole of sulfur dioxide, but each mole of chromium (III) cations requires *three* moles of electrons for reduction to one mole of chromium metal. Hence, the ratio of the number of moles of electrons available to produce the chromium metal will be 2: 3 producing 0.67 moles of the metal.

Question 6   B
See: CHM 10

Since $[A^{3+}]$ decreases and $[A^{2+}]$ and $[B^+]$ increase, the reaction can be written as:

$$A^{3+} + B \rightarrow A^{2+} + B^+.$$

Clearly, A^{3+} gains an electron from B and is therefore reduced. B loses an electron and is therefore oxidized. A^{3+} is more readily reduced than B^+, therefore:

$$E°A > E°B.$$

Question 7   D
See: CHM 4.1.1, 10.1

1 M is a "nice round number" and 0.1 MPa is approximately the atmospheric pressure (1 atm = 101.3 kPa = 0.101 MPa; conversions in CHM 4.1.1). Note that temperature is sometimes excluded from the definition of standard state. However, for fluids, standard temperature is 25 °C (298 K). When reduction potentials are stated, the temperature is usually cited as well.

Question 8   B
See: CHM 10.1

Table 1 gives us the standard reduction potentials (E°) for the halogens. When comparing 2 reactions, the equation with the highest (E°) will proceed as written (as a reduction) while the reaction with the lowest (E°) will proceed from right to left (as an oxidation reaction). Recall that in a redox reaction, one species is reduced by gaining electrons while the other is oxidized by losing electrons (CHM 1.6, 10.1). In this example, the halogen reactions that have a higher E° than the oxygen/water reaction (the 6th reaction in Table 1) will oxidize water. From Table 1, we see that the relative values of E° are: $Br_2 < O_2 < C_{l2} < F_2$ (1.07 < 1.23 < 1.36 < 3.06). Therefore, the reactions involving fluorine and chlorine will proceed as written when coupled to the oxygen reaction, which will proceed from right to left (i.e. water → oxygen).

Question 9   C
See: CHM 10.1

Since silver gains an electron, it is reduced. By convention, reduction is always at the cathode. Also, since silver gains an electron, electrons must flow through the wire into the Ag^+/Ag half cell. By convention, current flows in the opposite direction to electron flow, so current is flowing from the Ag^+/Ag half cell to the Fe^{2+}/Fe^{3+} half cell.

Thus, also by convention, the silver electrode is *positive*.

Question 10   B
See: CHM 1.6, 8.10, 9.10, 10.1

For a spontaneous redox reaction,

$$\Delta G° < 0$$
$$\Delta E° > 0$$
$$K_{eq} > 1$$

This means that for the reverse reaction, $\Delta G° > 0$, $\Delta E° < 0$, $K_{eq} < 1$
Reminder: Electrolysis is non-spontaneous and as such is viewed as the opposite of galvanic cells (batteries).

Question 11   B
See: CHM 10.5.1

Using Quantity of electricity (Q) = Current(I) × Time(t)

Q = 0.2 A × (80 min × 60 s min^{-1}) = 960 C

Number of faradays required to add 2 moles of electrons to one mole of Fe^{2+} (*to obtain one mole of Fe*) = 2 × F = 2 × 96000 C.

Using Number of moles Fe obtained = Q/(Number of Faradays required to produce 1 mole Fe)

Number of moles Fe = 960 C/(2 × 96000 C) = 1/(100 × 2) = 1/200 mol

Using Number of grams Fe = Number of moles Fe × Relative atomic mass Fe

Number of grams Fe = 1/200 mol × 55.8 g mol^{-1}
Number of grams Fe = (1/200 × 56) g approximately = 7/25 g = 28/100 g = 0.28 g in one hour
{*Nice math!*}

Question 1   A
See: CHM 11

Since gamma rays are uncharged electromagnetic rays, they are not deflected in magnetic or electric fields under normal conditions.

Question 2   C
See: CHM 11.1

Since a neutron has no charge, it would not be impeded in its motion by the positively charged nucleus, unlike the similarly charged proton. {*Note: answer choices A. and B. are false; answer choice D. is true for both a neutron and a proton and is thus an inappropriate answer*}

Question 3   B
See: CHM 11.4

Beware, an entire radioactive sample does not completely decay in two half-lives. Theoretically, it takes forever for every atom of the sample to decay.

Question 4   C
See: CHM 11.4

A half-life of 8 hours means that every 8 hours, half of the sample will undergo radioactive decay. The total number of half-lives undergone by the sample is: 20 hours/(8 hours/half-life) = 5/2 = 2.5. The percentage of the sample leftover after radioactive decay is given by: $(1/2)^n$ where n = number of half lives. After 20 hours, the amount of our sample remaining is: $(1/2)^{2.5} = (1/2)^3$ = 1/8 (approx.). Therefore, the proportion of the sample that has undergone radioactive decay is: 1 - 1/8 = 7/8 = 0.88. Note that the real answer is slightly lower than this value if you take our approximation into account. We could have deduced the answer without the equation by realizing that after 8 hours, 50% (half) of the sample has undergone radiation and after 16 hours, 75 % (half of the half remaining) of the sample has undergone radiation. Thus after 20 hours, the amount must be somewhat more than 75 % leaving only one possible answer (answer choice C.).

Question 5   A
See: CHM 11.3

An alpha particle is defined as a (*doubly positively charged*) helium nucleus.

Question 6   C
See: CHM 11.3, 11.4

The sum of the atomic numbers (*bottom figures or subscripts*) and mass numbers (*top figures or superscripts*) must be the same on both sides of the arrow since matter cannot be destroyed or created (*at least not in DAT Chemistry!*). From this, it is seen that "X" must be (essentially) massless and without charge. Gamma rays fit this description.

Question 7   D
See: CHM 11.3, 11.4

$$^{210}_{81}Th \rightarrow \, ^{x}_{y}Z + 3\,^{0}_{-1}e^{-} + \,^{4}_{2}He^{2+} + gamma \; ray$$

Since the sum of the atomic numbers and mass numbers on either side of the equation must be equal (matter cannot be created or destroyed), we get:

$$210 = \times + (3 \times 0) + 4 + 0 \; ; \; \times = 206$$
$$81 = y + (3 \times -1) + 2 + 0 \; ; \; y = 82$$

You can stop at this point or examine the periodic table for the name of the correct element (answer choice D.). Note that the atomic number and mass number of gamma rays are both zero.

Question 8   B
See: CHM 11.3, 11.4

$$^{230}_{90}Th \rightarrow \, ^{214}_{83}Bi + x\,^{0}_{-1}e^{-} + y\,^{4}_{2}He + z \, (gamma \; ray)$$

Since the sum of the atomic numbers and mass numbers on either side of the equation must be equal (matter cannot be created or destroyed), we get:

$$90 = 83 - \times + 2y \qquad \text{Equation (i)}$$
$$230 = 214 + 4y; \qquad y = 4 \; (\text{i.e. } 4 \; alpha \; decay \; reactions)$$

Substituting for y in Equation (i)

$$90 = 83 - \times + 8; \times = 1 \qquad (\text{i.e. } 1 \; beta \; decay \; reaction)$$

The order of the reactions is irrelevant (i.e. alpha, beta,..). Since gamma rays have no atomic number or mass number, the value of z does not affect this particular calculation.

Question 9   D
See: CHM 11.3, 11.4

Alpha radiation consists of the largest particles (*helium nuclei* with a mass number of 4 thus the greatest inertia) and are the slowest (about 1/3 times the speed of light). Beta radiation consists of smaller (*electrons*, 1/1370 times lighter than a proton), faster particles (about 4/5 times the speed of light). Gamma radiation consists of the smallest particles (*photons*, no mass) which travel at the greatest speed (at the speed of light).

Question 10   B
See: CHM 11.3, 11.4

On the Surface: In radioactive decay, we must have overall conservation of charge and mass. Recall that a beta⁻ particle consists of an electron (charge = -1, mass = negligible) and a gamma (γ) ray is electromagnetic energy (mass = 0, charge = 0). In the equation, the atomic mass on the left of the equation = 14, so the atomic masses on the right must also = 14 to conserve mass: 14 (mass of ^{14}C) = X (mass of ^{x}N) + 0 (mass of β⁻) + 0 (mass of γ) → 14 = X.

Going Deeper: In beta decay, a neutron decays into a proton and an electron (β⁻). Thus on the left-hand side of the equation, there are 8 neutrons and 6 protons. The right-hand side of the equation has 7 neutrons and 7 protons. Thus X must be 14 (to calculate # protons, neutrons).

Question 11   C
See: CHM 11.3

It would be attracted to the plate of opposite charge, negative, since a positron is positively charged.

Question 12   B
See: CHM 11.4

The present amount of C14 to the past amount or C14 is 1/4, corresponding to two half-lives.

Question 13   C
See: CHM 11.4

The amount undecayed is $1/16 = (1/2)^4$ of the original sample, which corresponds to four half-lives: 6400 years.

Question 14   B
See: CHM 11.4

3 half-lives have elapsed (9.3 mins/3.1 mins).
Since the emission of a beta particle results in a neutron turning into a proton, the atomic masses of the Pb and Tl are the same.

If there were initially X g of Tl, after 3.1 mins X/2 g of Pb are formed, after the next 3.1 mins X/4 g of Pb are formed, and after the next 3.1 mins X/8g of Pb are formed. Therefore,

$$X/2 \; X/4 \; X/8 = 7 \text{ g of Pb or, } 4X/8 \; 2X/8 \; X/8 = 7X/8 = 7$$

Thus, X = 8 g

Question 15   A
See: CHM 11.4

This is the shape of the graph for all natural radioactive decay processes (and all first order reactions). If you did not know that then you should at least deduce as follows: (1) radioactivity decreases over time (thus only 2 choices because only 2 graphs have values decreasing over time); and (2) radioactive decay is exponential (so the graph cannot be linear). For fun (!!), compare with the curves and descriptions in CHM 9.2.

CHAPTER REVIEW SOLUTIONS   CHAPTER 12

Question 1   D
See: CHM 6.9, 12.3.1

A typical titration (CHM 6.9) begins with a beaker or Erlenmeyer flask containing a precise volume of the titrand (= the chemical being analyzed) and a small amount of indicator placed underneath a calibrated burette containing the titrant (= titrator reagent prepared as a standard solution). Thus the burette adds the standard reagent.

Question 2   A
See: CHM 12.3.1

Flaming sterilizes glassware using a Bunsen burner or alcohol lamp for sterilization.

Question 3   A
See: CHM 12.3.1

0.0127 mol NaCl x 1 L/0.127 mol = 0.1 L (100 mL)
The most accurate way to measure 0.1 L of solution is to use a volumetric flask. Volumetric flasks are known to be precise to approximately $\pm 0.2\%$.

Question 4   B
See: 12.4.2, 12.4.3

Do not count any zeros to the left of the first non zero integer and then you will be left with 5 digits: 8, 6, 0, 3, 0. If that last 0 to the right was not truly significant then it should not have been reported.

Question 5   B
See: 12.4.2, 12.4.3

The density would be $24.7/3.3 = 7.4848$ g/cm^3. For multiplication and division: the number of significant figures is limited by the data with the least number of significant figures in total. Since the volume only has 2 sig figs, the answer must be rounded off to 2 sig figs so 7.4848 becomes 7.5.

GENERAL CHEMISTRY EQUATION LIST AND TABLES

CHAPTER 1: Stoichiometry

1.3 Mole - Atomic and Molecular Weights

For an element:

$$\text{moles} = \frac{\text{weight of sample in grams}}{\text{GAW}}$$

$1 \text{ mol} = 6.02 \times 10^{23}$ atoms

For a compound:

$$\text{moles} = \frac{\text{weight of sample in grams}}{\text{GMW}}$$

$1 \text{ mol} = 6.02 \times 10^{23}$ molecules

1.5.1 Categories of Chemical Reactions

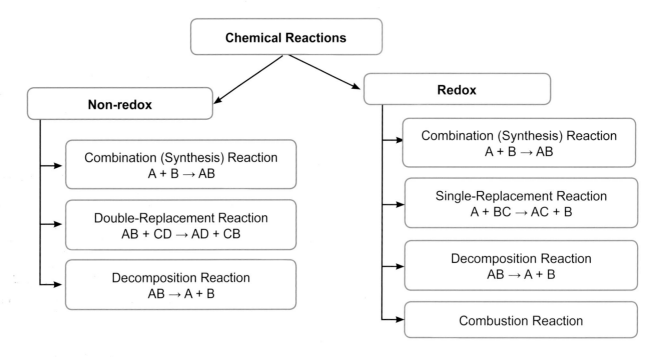

1.6 Oxidation Numbers, Redox Reactions, Oxidizing vs. Reducing Agents

Here are the general rules:

1. In elementary substances, the oxidation number of an uncombined element is zero.
2. In monatomic ions the oxidation number of the element that make up this ion is equal to the charge of the ion.
3. In a neutral molecule the sum of the oxidation numbers of all the elements that make up the molecule is zero.
4. Some useful oxidation numbers to memorize:

   For H: +1, except in metal hydrides where it is equal to -1.

   For O: -2 in most compounds. In peroxides (e.g. in H_2O_2) the oxidation number for O is -1, it is +2 in OF_2 and -1/2 in superoxides.

   For alkali metals +1.

   For alkaline earth metals +2.

   Aluminium always has an oxidation number of +3 in all its compounds.

Common Redox Agents	
Reducing Agents	**Oxidizing Agents**
* Lithium aluminium hydride ($LiAlH_4$) * Sodium borohydride ($NaBH_4$) * Metals * Ferrous ion (Fe^{2+})	* Iodine (I_2) and other halogens * Permanganate (MnO_4) salts * Peroxide compounds (i.e. H_2O_2) * Ozone (O_3); osmium tetroxide (OsO_4) * Nitric acid (HNO_3); nitrous oxide (N_2O)

1.7 Mixtures

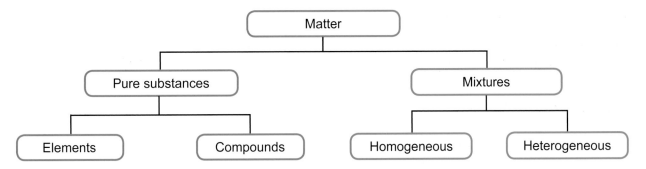

CHAPTER 2: Electronic Structure and the Periodic Table

2.2 Conventional Notation for Electronic Structure

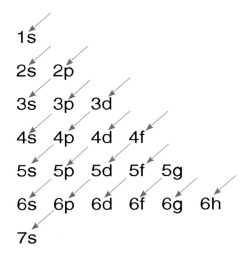

follow the direction of successive arrows moving from top to bottom

Figure III.A.2.3: The order for filling atomic orbitals.

2.4 Metals, Nonmetals and Metalloids

Table III A.2.1

*General characteristics of metals, nonmetals and metalloids		
Metals	**Nonmetals**	**Metalloids**
• Hard and Shiny	• Gases or dull, brittle solids	• Appearence will vary
• 3 or less valence electrons	• 5 or more valence electrons	• 3 to 7 valence electrons
• Form + ions by losing e⁻	• Form – ions by gaining e⁻	• Form + and/or – ions
• Good conductors of heat and electricity	• Poor conductors of heat and electricity	• Conduct better than nonmetals but not as well as metals

*These are general characteristics. There are exceptions beyond the scope of the exam.

CHAPTER 3: Bonding

3.3 Partial Ionic Character

This polar bond will also have a dipole moment given by:

$$D = q \cdot d$$

where q is the charge and d is the distance between these two atoms.

3.4 Lewis Acids and Lewis Bases

The Lewis acid BF_3 and the Lewis base NH_3. Notice that the green arrows follow the flow of electron pairs.

3.5 Valence Shell Electronic Pair Repulsions (VSEPR Models)

Table III.A.3.1a: Geometry of simple molecules in which the central atom A has one or more lone pairs of electrons (= e^-).

Total number of e^- pairs	Number of lone pairs	Number of bonding pairs	Electron Geometry, Arrangement of e^- pairs	Molecular Geometry (Hybridization State)	Examples
3	1	2	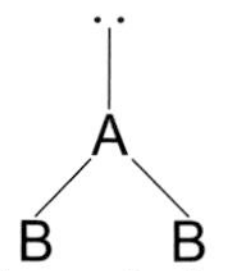 Trigonal planar	Bent (sp^2)	SO_2
4	1	3	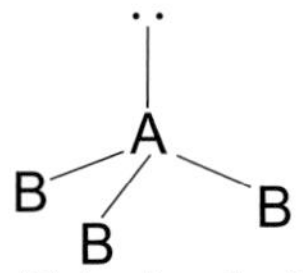 Tetrahedral	Trigonal pyramidal (sp^3)	NH_3
4	2	2	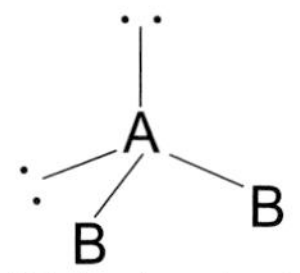 Tetrahedral	Bent (sp^3)	H_2O
5	1	4	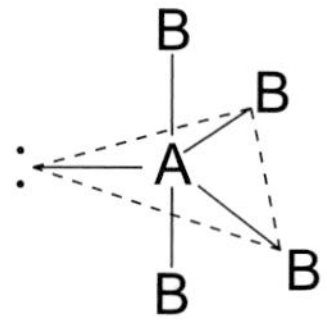 Trigonal bipyramidal	Seesaw (sp^3d)	SF_4
5	2	3	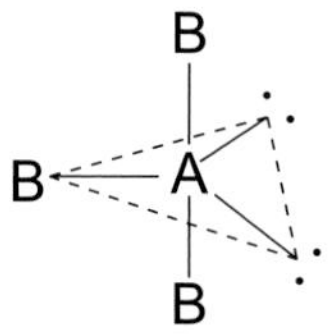 Trigonal bipyramidal	T-shaped (sp^3d)	ClF_3

Note: dotted lines only represent the overall molecular shape and not molecular bonds. In brackets under "Molecular Geometry" is the hybridization, to be discussed in ORG 1.2.

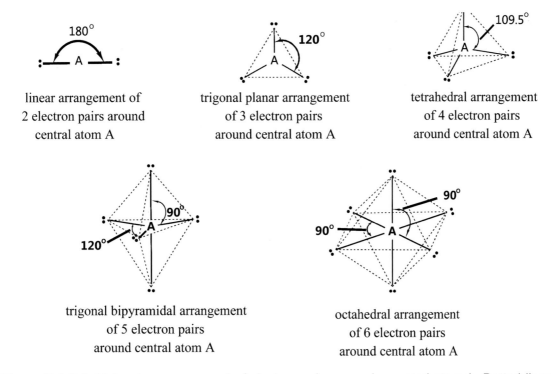

Figure III.A.3.1: Molecular arrangement of electron pairs around a central atom A. Dotted lines only represent the overall molecular shape and not molecular bonds.

CHAPTER 4: Phases and Phase Equilibria

4.1.1 Standard Temperature and Pressure, Standard Molar Volume

0°C (273.15 K) and 1.00 atm (101.33 kPa = 760 mmHg = 760 torr); these conditions are known as the standard temperature and pressure (STP). {Note: the SI unit of pressure is the pascal (Pa).

The volume occupied by one mole of any gas at STP is referred to as the standard molar volume and is equal to 22.4 L.

4.1.2 Kinetic Molecular Theory of Gases (A Model for Gases)

The average kinetic energy of the particles (KE = 1/2 mv^2) increases in direct proportion to the temperature of the gas (KE = 3/2 kT) when the temperature is measured on an absolute scale (i.e. the Kelvin scale) and k is a constant (the Boltzmann constant).

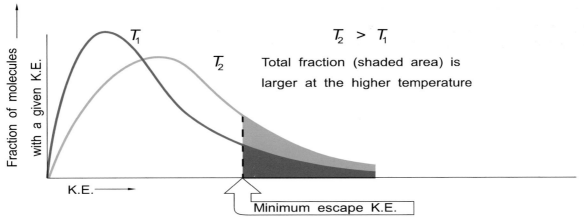

Figure III.A.4.1: The Maxwell Distribution Plot.

4.1.3 Graham's Law (Diffusion and Effusion of Gases)

$$\frac{Rate_1}{Rate_2} = \sqrt{\frac{M_2}{M_1}}$$

4.1.4 Charles' Law

$$V = Constant \times T \quad or \quad V_1/V_2 = T_1/T_2$$

4.1.5 Boyle's Law

$$V = Constant \times 1/P \quad or \quad P_1V_1 = P_2V_2$$

4.1.6 Avogadro's Law

$$V/n = Constant \quad or \quad V_1/n_1 = V_2/n_2$$

4.1.7 Combined Gas Law

$$\frac{P_1V_1}{T_1} = k = \frac{P_2V_2}{T_2} \quad \text{(at constant mass)}$$

4.1.8 Ideal Gas Law

$$PV = nRT$$

since m/V is the density (d) of the gas:

$$P = \frac{dRT}{M}$$

4.1.9 Partial Pressure and Dalton's Law

$$P_T = P_1 + P_2 + \ldots + P_i$$

Of course, the sum of all mole fractions in a mixture must equal one:

$$\Sigma X_i = 1$$

The partial pressure (P_i) of a component of a gas mixture is equal to:

$$P_i = X_i P_T$$

4.2 Liquid Phase (Intra- and Intermolecular Forces)

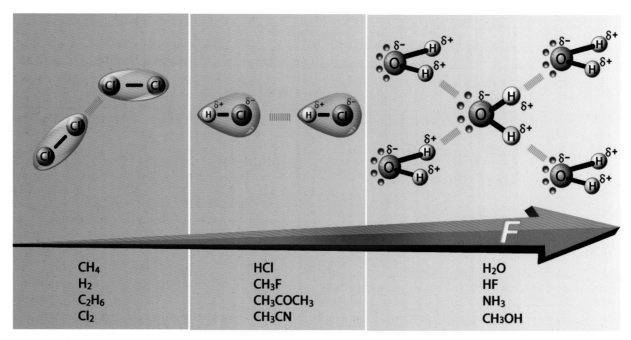

CH₄	HCl	H₂O
H₂	CH₃F	HF
C₂H₆	CH₃COCH₃	NH₃
Cl₂	CH₃CN	CH₃OH

Table III.A.4.1: Van Der Waal's forces (weak) and hydrogen bonding (strong). London forces between Cl_2 molecules, dipole-dipole forces between HCl molecules and H-bonding between H_2O molecules. Note that a partial negative charge on an atom is indicated by δ^- (delta negative), while a partial positive charge is indicated by δ^+ (delta positive). Notice that one H_2O molecule can potentially form 4 H-bonds with surrounding molecules which is highly efficient. The preceding is one key reason that the boiling point of water is higher than that of ammonia, hydrogen fluoride or methanol.

4.2.2 Surface Tension

PE is directly proportional to the surface area (A).

$$PE = \gamma A$$
$$\gamma = surface\ tension$$

$$\gamma = F/l$$

F = force of contraction of surface
l = length along surface

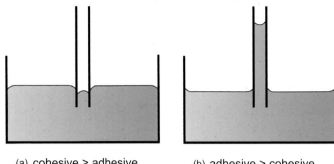

(a) cohesive > adhesive   (b) adhesive > cohesive

4.4.1 Phase Changes

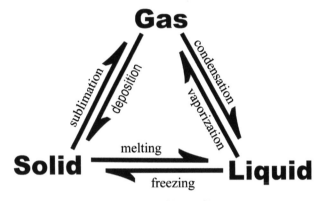

Figure III.A.4.2: Phase Changes

4.4.3 Phase Diagrams

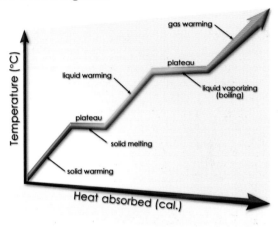

Figure III.A.4.3 Heating curve

CHAPTER 5: Solution Chemistry

5.1.1 Vapor-Pressure Lowering (Raoult's Law)

$$P = P^\circ X_{solvent}$$

where P = vapor pressure of solution
P° = vapor pressure of pure solvent (at the same temperature as P).

5.1.3 Osmotic Pressure

$$\Pi = i\,MRT$$

where R = gas constant per mole
T = temperature in degrees K and
M = concentration of solute (mole/liter)
i = Van't Hoff factor

5.1.2 Boiling-Point Elevation and Freezing-Point Depression

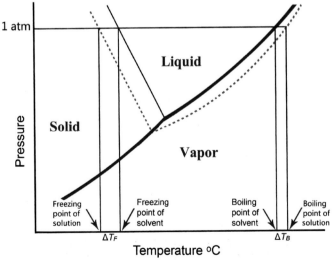

Figure III.A.5.1: Phase diagram of water demonstrating the effect of the addition of a solute.

$$\Delta T_B = i\,K_B m$$
$$\Delta T_F = i\,K_F m$$

5.2 Ions in Solution

Ions that are positively charged are called <u>cations</u> and negatively charged ions are called <u>anions</u>. {Mnemonic: anions are negative ions}

The word "aqueous" simply means containing or dissolved in water.

Common Anions							
F^-	Fluoride	OH^-	Hydroxide	ClO^-	Hypochlorite
Cl^-	Chloride	NO_3^-	Nitrate	ClO_2^-	Chlorite
Br^-	Bromide	NO_2^-	Nitrite	ClO_3^-	Chlorate
I^-	Iodide	CO_3^{2-}	Carbonate	ClO_4^-	Perchlorate
O^{2-}	Oxide	SO_4^{2-}	Sulfate	SO_3^{2-}	Sulfite
S^{2-}	Sulfide	PO_4^{3-}	Phosphate	CN^-	Cyanide
N^{3-}	Nitride	$CH_3CO_2^-$	Acetate	MnO_4^-	Permanganate

Common Cations			
Na^+	Sodium	H^+	Hydrogen
Li^+	Lithium	Ca^{2+}	Calcium
K^+	Potassium	Mg^{2+}	Magnesium
NH_4^+	Ammonium	Fe^{2+}	Iron (II)
H_3O^+	Hydronium	Fe^{3+}	Iron (III)

Table III.A.5.1: Common Anions and Cations.

5.3.1 Units of Concentration

<u>Molarity (*M*)</u>: moles of solute/liter of solution (solution = solute + solvent).

<u>Normality (*N*)</u>: one equivalent per liter.

<u>Molality (*m*)</u>: one mole/1000g of solvent. Molal concentrations are not temperature-dependent as molar and normal concentrations are.

<u>Density (*ρ*)</u>: Mass per unit volume at the specified temperature.

<u>Osmole (*Osm*)</u>: The number of moles of particles (molecules or ions) that contribute to the osmotic pressure of a solution.

<u>Osmolarity</u>: osmoles/liter of solution.

<u>Osmolality</u>: osmoles/kilogram of solution.

<u>Mole Fraction</u>: amount of solute (in moles) divided by the total amount of solvent and solute (in moles).

<u>Dilution</u>: $M_iV_i = M_fV_f$

5.3.2 Solubility Product Constant, the Equilibrium Expression

$$AgCl\ (s) \rightleftharpoons Ag^+\ (aq) + Cl^-\ (aq)$$

$$K_{sp} = [Ag^+][Cl^-]$$

Because the K_{sp} product always holds, precipitation will not take place unless the product of $[Ag^+]$ and $[Cl^-]$ exceeds the K_{sp}.

5.3.5 Solubility Rules

1. All salts of alkali metals are soluble.
2. All salts of the ammonium ion are soluble.
3. All chlorides, bromides and iodides are water soluble, with the exception of Ag^+, Pb^{2+}, and Hg_2^{2+}.
4. All salts of the sulfate ion (SO_4^{2-}) are water soluble with the exception of Ca^{2+}, Sr^{2+}, Ba^{2+}, and Pb^{2+}.
5. All metal oxides are insoluble with the exception of the alkali metals and CaO, SrO and BaO.
6. All hydroxides are insoluble with the exception of the alkali metals and Ca^{2+}, Sr^{2+}, Ba^{2+}
7. All carbonates (CO_3^{2-}), phosphates (PO_4^{3-}), sulfides (S^{2-}) and sulfites (SO_3^{2-}) are insoluble, with the exception of the alkali metals and ammonium.

CHAPTER 6: Acids and Bases

6.1 Acids

$$K_a = [H^+][A^-]/[HA]$$

Table III.A.6.1: Examples of strong and weak acids.

STRONG	WEAK	STRONG	WEAK
Perchloric $HClO_4$ Chloric $HClO_3$ Nitric HNO_3 Hydrochloric HCl	Hydrocyanic HCN Hypochlorous $HClO$ Nitrous HNO_2 Hydrofluoric HF	Sulfuric H_2SO_4 Hydrobromic HBr Hydriodic HI Hydronium Ion H_3O^+	Sulfurous H_2SO_3 Hydrogen Sulfide H_2S Phosphoric H_3PO_4 Benzoic, Acetic and other Carboxylic acids

6.2 Bases

$$K_b = [HB^+][OH^-]/[B]$$

Strong bases include any hydroxide of the group 1A metals. The most common weak bases are ammonia and any organic amine.

6.3 Conjugate Acid-Base Pairs

The acid, HA, and the base produced when it ionizes, A⁻, are called a conjugate acid-base pair.

6.4 Water Dissociation

$$K_w = [H^+][OH^-] = 1.0 \times 10^{-14}$$

6.5 The pH Scale

$$pH = -\log_{10}[H^+]$$

$$pOH = -\log_{10}[OH^-]$$

at 25°C, pH + pOH = 14.0

6.5.1 Properties of Logarithms

1) $\log_a a = 1$
2) $\log_a M^k = k \log_a M$
3) $\log_a(MN) = \log_a M + \log_a N$
4) $\log_a(M/N) = \log_a M - \log_a N$
5) $10^{\log_{10} M} = M$

6.7 Salts of Weak Acids and Bases

$$K_a \times K_b = K_w$$

6.8 Buffers

$$pH = pK_a + \log([salt]/[acid])$$

$$pOH = pK_b + \log([salt]/[base])$$

CHAPTER 7: Thermodynamics

7.2 The First Law of Thermodynamics

$$\Delta E = Q - W$$

- heat <u>absorbed</u> by the system: $Q > 0$
- heat <u>released</u> by the system: $Q < 0$
- work done <u>by the system</u> on its surroundings: $W > 0$
- work done by the surroundings <u>on the system</u>: $W < 0$

7.4 Temperature Scales

$$0\ K = -273.13\ °C.$$

$$(X\ °F - 32) \times 5/9 = Y\ °C$$

7.6 State Functions

	Work	Heat	Change in internal energy
1st transf.	w	0	$-w$
2nd transf.	$W = w + q$	q	$-w$

W can be determined experimentally by calculating the area under a pressure-volume curve.

CHAPTER 8: Enthalpy and Thermochemistry

8.2 Heat of Reaction: Basic Principles

A reaction during which <u>heat</u> is <u>released</u> is said to be *exothermic* (ΔH is negative). If a <u>reaction</u> requires the supply of a certain amount of <u>heat</u> it is *endothermic* (ΔH is positive).

$$\Delta H_{OVERALL} = \Delta H_1 + \Delta H_2$$

$$\Delta H°_{reaction} = \Sigma \Delta H_f°_{(products)} - \Sigma \Delta H_f°_{(reactants)}$$

8.6 Bond Dissociation Energies and Heats of Formation

$$\Delta H^\circ_{(reaction)} = \Sigma\Delta H_{(bonds\ broken)} + \Sigma\Delta H_{(bonds\ formed)}$$
$$= \Sigma BE_{(reactants)} - \Sigma BE_{(products)}$$

8.7 Calorimetry

$$Q = mC(T_2 - T_1)$$

$$Q = mL$$

8.8 The Second Law of Thermodynamics

For any spontaneous process, the entropy of the universe increases which results in a greater dispersal or randomization of the energy ($\Delta S > 0$).

8.9 Entropy

$$\Delta S^\circ_{reaction} = \Delta S^\circ_{products} - \Delta S^\circ_{reactants}$$

8.10 Free Energy

$$\Delta G = \Delta H - T\Delta S$$

A reaction carried out at constant pressure is spontaneous if
$$\Delta G < 0$$

It is not spontaneous if:
$$\Delta G > 0$$

and it is in a state of equilibrium (reaction spontaneous in both directions) if:
$$\Delta G = 0.$$

CHAPTER 9: Rate Processes in Chemical Reactions

9.2 Dependence of Reaction Rates on Concentration of Reactants

$$rate = k\ [A]^m\ [B]^n$$

where [ ] is the concentration of the corresponding reactant in moles per liter

k is referred to as the <u>rate constant</u>

m is the <u>order of the reaction with respect to A</u>

n is the <u>order of the reaction with respect to B</u>

m+n is the <u>overall reaction order</u>.

9.2.1 Differential Rate Law vs. Integrated Rate Law (Advanced DAT-30 Topic)

Table 9.2.1

Rate Law Summary					
Reaction Order	Rate Law	Units of k	Integrated Rate Law	Straight-Line Plot	Half-Life Equation
0	Rate $= k[A]^0$	$M \cdot s^{-1}$	$[A]_t = -kt + [A]_0$	[A]; y-intercept $= [A]_0$; slope $= -k$; Time t	$t_{1/2} = \dfrac{[A]_0}{2k} = \dfrac{1}{k}\dfrac{[A]_0}{2}$
1	Rate $= k[A]^1$	s^{-1}	$\ln[A]_t = -kt + \ln[A]_0$ $\ln\dfrac{[A]_t}{[A]_0} = -kt$	ln[A]; y-intercept $= \ln[A]_0$; slope $= -k$; Time t	$t_{1/2} = \dfrac{0.693}{k} = \dfrac{1}{k}(0.693)$
2	Rate $= k[A]^2$	$M^{-1} \cdot s^{-1}$	$\dfrac{1}{[A]_t} = kt + \dfrac{1}{[A]_0}$	1/[A]; slope $= k$; y-intercept $= 1/[A]_0$; Time t	$t_{1/2} = \dfrac{1}{k[A]_0} = \dfrac{1}{k}\dfrac{1}{[A]_0}$

9.5 Dependence of Reaction Rates upon Temperature

$$k = A\, e^{-Ea/RT}$$

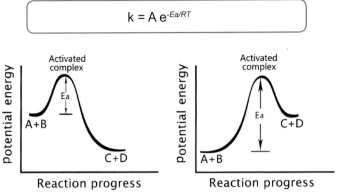

Figure III.A.9.1: Potential energy diagrams: exothermic vs. endothermic reactions.

9.7 Catalysis

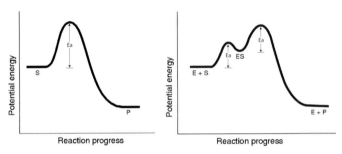

Figure III.A.9.2: Potential energy diagrams: without and with a catalyst.

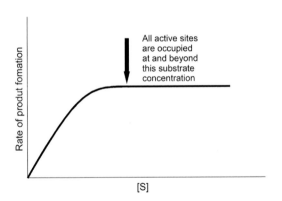

Figure III.A.9.3: Saturation kinetics.

9.8 Equilibrium in Reversible Chemical Reactions

$$aA + bB \rightleftharpoons cC + dD$$

$$K = \frac{[C]^c\,[D]^d}{[A]^a\,[B]^b}$$

{Note: catalysts speed up the rate of reaction without affecting Keq}

9.8.1 The Reaction Quotient Q to Predict Reaction Direction

$$Q = [C]^c[D]^d/[A]^a[B]^b$$

Q > K Reaction runs to left (A ← B)				
Q = K Reaction is at equilibrium (A ⇌ B)				
Q < K Reaction runs to right (A → B)				

Q or K

3.5
3.0
2.5
2.0
1.5
1.0
0.0

[A] 1.00   0.75   0.50   0.25   0.00
[B] 0.00   0.25   0.50   0.75   1.00
Reactants   Products
Concentration (M)

$$A(g) \rightleftharpoons B(g) \quad Q = \frac{[B]}{[A]}$$

$$Q \to \infty \text{ at } [A] = 0,\ [B] = 1$$

9.9 Le Chatelier's Principle

Le Chatelier's principle states that whenever a perturbation is applied to a system at equilibrium, the system evolves in such a way as to compensate for the applied perturbation.

9.10 Relationship between the Equilibrium Constant and the Change in the Gibbs Free Energy

$$\Delta G^\circ = -R\,T\,ln\,K_{eq}$$

CHAPTER 10: Electrochemistry

10.1 Generalities

The more positive the E° value, the more likely the reaction will occur spontaneously as written. The <u>strongest reducing agents</u> have <u>large negative E°</u> values. The <u>strongest oxidizing agents</u> have <u>large positive E°</u> values. The oxidizing agent is *reduced*; the reducing agent is *oxidized*.

10.2 Galvanic Cells

Mnemonic: LEO is A GERC

- Lose Electrons Oxidation is Anode
- Gain Electrons Reduction at Cathode

10.3 Concentration Cell

Nernst equation

$$E_{cell} = E°_{cell} - (RT/nF)(\ln Q)$$

CHAPTER 11: Nuclear Chemistry

11.3 Nuclear Forces, Nuclear Binding Energy, Stability, Radioactivity

$$\Delta E = \Delta mc^2$$

The common particles are:

(1) alpha (α) particle = $_2He^4$ (helium nucleus);
(2) beta (β) particle = $_{-1}e^0$ (an electron);
(3) a positron $_{+1}e^0$ (same mass as an electron but opposite charge); and
(4) gamma (γ) ray = no mass and no charge, just electromagnetic energy.

11.4 Nuclear Reaction, Radioactive Decay, Half-Life

neutrons (i.e. $_{92}U^{238}$)
= superscript (238) – subscript (92)
= 146

$$T_{1/2} = 0.693/k.$$

If the number of half-lifes n are known we can calculate the percentage of a pure radioactive sample left after undergoing decay since the fraction remaining = $(1/2)^n$.

Table III.A.11.1: Modes of Radioactive Decay

Decay Mode	Participating particles	Change in (A, Z)	Daughter Nucleus
Alpha decay	α	A = −4, Z = −2	(A − 4, Z − 2)
Beta decay	β^-	A = 0, Z = +1	(A, Z + 1)
Gamma decay	γ	A = 0, Z = 0	(A, Z)
Positron emission	β^+	A = 0, Z = −1	(A, Z − 1)

10.5 Faraday's Law

Faraday's law relates the amount of elements deposited or gas liberated at an electrode due to current.

One mole (= Avogadro's number) of electrons is called a *faraday* ($\mathfrak{F}$). A faraday is equivalent to 96 500 coulombs. A coulomb is the amount of electricity that is transferred when a current of one ampere flows for one second (1C = 1A . S).

11.5 Quantized Energy Levels For Electrons, Emission Spectrum

The maximum number of electrons in each shell is given by:

$$N_{electrons} = 2n^2$$

$N_{electrons}$ designates the number of electrons in shell n.

The state of each electron is determined by the four quantum numbers:

- *principal quantum number n* determines the number of shells, possible values are: 1 (K), 2 (L), 3 (M), etc...
- *angular momentum quantum number l*, determines the subshell, possible values are: 0 (s), 1 (p), 2 (d), 3 (f), n-1, etc...
- *magnetic momentum quantum number m_l*, possible values are: ±l, ... , 0
- *spin quantum number m_s*, determines the direction of rotation of the electron, possible values are: ±1/2.

$$E_2 - E_1 = hf$$

where E_1 = energy level one, E_2 = energy level two, h = planck's constant, and f = the frequency of light absorbed or emitted.

The total energy of the electrons in an atom, where KE is the kinetic energy, can be given by:

$$E_{total} = E_{emission} \ (or \ E_{ionization}) + KE$$

CHAPTER 12: Laboratory

12.3.1 Glassware

Least accurate	Droppers
	Beakers and Erlenmeyer flasks
	Graduated cylinders
Most accurate	Glass Pipettes, burettes and volumetric flasks

12.4.3 Analyzing the Data

The uncertain figure of a measurement is the last significant figure of the measurement.

Table 12.1: Examples of significant figures versus non-significant figures.

Significant	Examples	Non-Significant
Non-zero integers	1.234 (4 sf)	
Zeros between non-zero integers*	1.004 (4 sf)	
Zeros to the right of decimal place AND integers*	1.2000 (5 sf) 0.0041 (2 sf)	Zeros to the right of decimal place BUT to the left of integers
	430 (2 sf)	Zeros to the left of decimal place BUT to the right of integers
	013.2 (3 sf)	Zeros to the left of decimal place AND integers

* Zeros in any number is used to convey either accuracy or magnitude. If a zero is to convey accuracy, then it is known as a significant value and if the zero is used to convey magnitude, then it is non-significant.

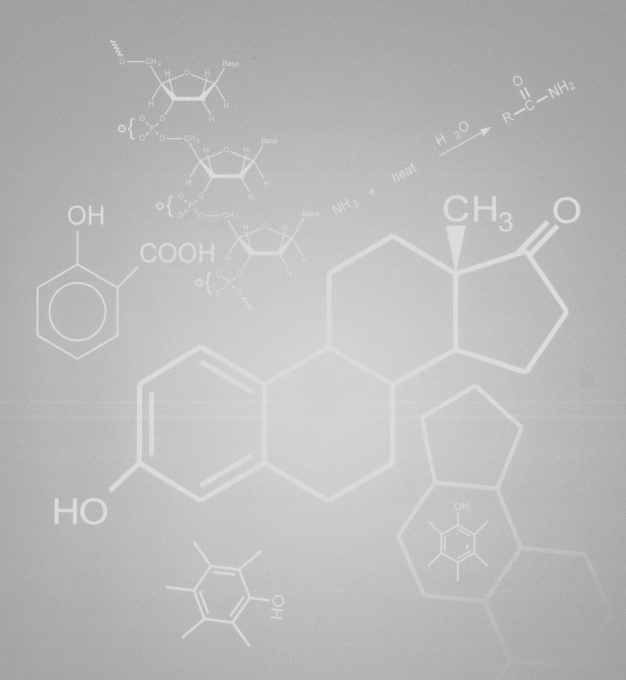

DAT-prep.com

ORGANIC
CHEMISTRY

MOLECULAR STRUCTURE OF ORGANIC COMPOUNDS
Chapter 1

Memorize	Understand	Importance
* Hybrid orbitals and geometries * Periodic table trends * Define: Lewis, dipole moments * Ground rules for reaction mechanisms	* Delocalized electrons and resonance * Multiple bonds, length, energies * Basic stereochemistry * Principles for reaction mechanisms	**2 to 4 out of the 30 ORG** DAT questions are based on content in this chapter (in our estimation). * Note that between 30% and 60% of the questions in DAT Organic Chemistry are based on content from 4 chapters: 1, 2, 5 and 6.

DAT-Prep.com

Introduction

Organic chemistry is the study of the structure, properties, composition, reactions, and preparation (i.e. synthesis) of chemical compounds containing carbon. Such compounds may contain hydrogen, nitrogen, oxygen, the halogens as well as phosphorus, silicon and sulfur. If you master the basic rules in this chapter, you will be able to conquer DAT mechanisms with little or no further memorization.

Additional Resources

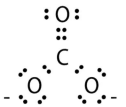

Free Online Q&A + Forum   Video: Online or DVD   Flashcards   Special Guest

Organic chemistry may be defined as the chemistry of the compounds of carbon. Organic chemistry is very important, as living systems are composed mainly of water and organic compounds. Other important organic molecules form essential components of fuels, plastics and other petroleum derivatives.

Carbon (C), hydrogen (H), oxygen (O), nitrogen (N) and the halides (i.e. fluorine – F, chlorine – Cl, bromine – Br, etc.) are the most common atoms found in organic compounds. The atoms in most organic compounds are held together by covalent bonds (*the sharing of an electron pair between two atoms*). Some ionic bonding (*the transfer of electrons from one atom to another*) does exist. Common to both types of chemical bonds is the fact that the atoms bond such that they can achieve the electron configuration of the nearest noble gas, usually eight electrons. This is known as the *octet rule*.

A **carbon** atom has one s and three p orbitals in its outermost shell, allowing it to form 4 single bonds. As well, a carbon atom may be involved in a double bond, where two electron pairs are shared, or a triple bond, where three electron pairs are shared. An **oxygen** atom may form 2 single bonds, or one double bond. It has 2 unshared (lone) electron pairs. A **hydrogen** atom will form only one single bond. A **nitrogen** atom may form 3 single bonds. As well, it is capable of double and triple bonds. It has one unshared electron pair. The **halides** are all able to form only one (single) bond. Halides all have three unshared electron pairs.

Throughout the following chapters we will be examining the structural formulas of molecules involving H, C, N, O, halides and phosphorus (P). However it should be noted that less common atoms often have similar structural formulas within molecules as compared to common atoms. For example, silicon (Si) is found in the same group as carbon in the periodic table; thus they have similar properties. In fact, Si can also form 4 single bonds leading to a tetrahedral structure (i.e. SiH_4, SiO_4). Likewise sulfur (S) is found in the same group as oxygen. Though it can be found as a solid (S_8), it still has many properties similar to those of oxygen. For example, like O in H_2O, sulfur can form a bent, polar molecule which can hydrogen bond (H_2S). We will later see that sulfur is an important component in the amino acid cysteine. {*To learn more about molecular structure, hybrid orbitals, polarity and bonding, review General Chemistry chapters 2 and 3*}

Mnemonic: HONC

H requires 1 more electron in its outer shell to become stable
O requires 2
N requires 3
C requires 4

1.2 Hybrid Orbitals

In organic molecules, the orbitals of the atoms are combined to form **hybrid orbitals**, consisting of a mixture of the s and p orbitals. In a carbon atom, if the one s and three p orbitals are mixed, the result is four hybrid sp^3 orbitals. Three hybridized sp^2 orbitals result from the mixing of one s and two p orbitals, and two hybridized sp orbitals result from the mixing of one s and one p. The geometry of the hybridized orbitals is shown in Figure IV.B.1.1.

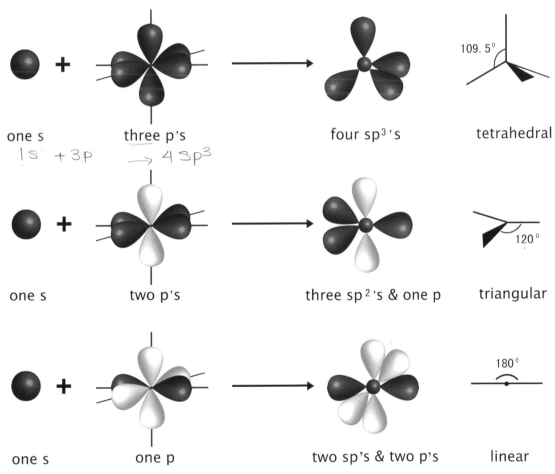

one s   three p's   four sp^3's   tetrahedral

$1s + 3p \rightarrow 4\,sp^3$

one s   two p's   three sp^2's & one p   triangular

one s   one p   two sp's & two p's   linear

Figure IV.B.1.1: Hybrid orbital geometry

NOTE: For details regarding atomic structure and orbitals, see General Chemistry (CHM) sections 2.1, 2.2. For more details regarding hybridized bonds and bond angles (especially for carbon, nitrogen, oxygen and sulfur), see CHM 3.5.

1.3 Bonding

Sigma (or single) bonds are those in which the electron density is between the nuclei. They are symmetric about the axis, can freely rotate, and are formed when orbitals (regular or hybridized) overlap directly. They are characterized by the fact that they are circular when a cross section is taken and the bond is viewed along the bond axis. The electron density in pi bonds overlaps both above and below the plane of the atoms. A single bond is a sigma bond; a double bond is one sigma and one pi bond; a triple bond is one sigma (σ) and two pi (π) bonds.

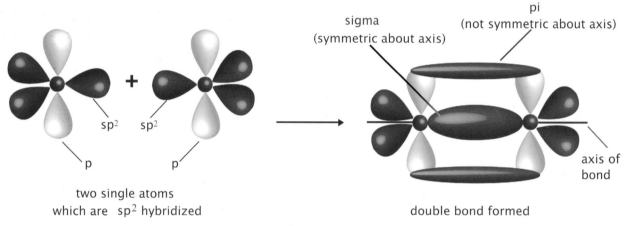

Figure IV.B.1.2: Sigma and pi bonds. The sp^2 hybrids overlap between the nuclei to form a σ bond; the p orbitals overlap above and below the axis between the nuclei to form a π bond.

1.3.1 The Effects of Multiple Bonds

The pi bonds in doubly and triply bonded molecules create a barrier to free rotation about the axis of the bond. Thus multiple bonds create molecules which are much more rigid than a molecule with only a single bond which can freely rotate about its axis.

As a rule, the length of a bond decreases with multiple bonds. For example, the carbon-carbon triple bond is shorter than the carbon-carbon double bond which is shorter than the carbon-carbon single bond.

Bond strength and thus the amount of energy required to break a bond (= *BE, the bond dissociation energy*) varies with the number of bonds. One σ bond has a BE $\approx$ 110 kcal/mole and one π bond has a BE $\approx$ 60 kcal/mole. Thus a single bond (one σ) has a BE $\approx$ 110 kcal/mole while a double bond (one σ + one π) has a BE $\approx$ 170 kcal/mole. Hence multiple bonds have greater bond strength than single bonds.

1.4 Delocalized Electrons and Resonance

Delocalization of charges in the pi bonds is possible when there are hybridized orbitals in adjacent atoms. This delocalization may be represented in two different ways, the molecular orbital (MO) approach or the resonance (*valence bond*) approach. The differences are found in Figure IV.B.1.3.

The MO approach takes a linear combination of atomic orbitals to form molecular orbitals, in which electrons form the bonds. These molecular orbitals cover the whole molecule, and thus the delocalization of electrons is depicted. In the resonance approach, there is a linear combination of different structures with localized pi bonds and electrons, which together depict the true molecule, or **resonance hybrid**. There is no single structure that represents the molecule.

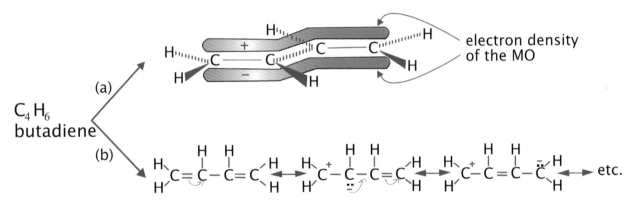

Figure IV.B.1.3: A comparison of MO and resonance approaches. (a) The electron density of the MO covers the entire molecule such that π bonds and p orbitals are not distinguishable. (b) No singular resonance structure accurately portrays butadiene; rather, the true molecule is a composite of all of its resonance structures.

1.5 Lewis Structures, Charge Separation and Dipole Moments

The outer shell (or **valence**) electrons are those that form chemical bonds. **Lewis dot structures** are a method of showing the valence electrons and how they form bonds. These electrons, along with the octet rule (*which states that a maximum of eight electrons are allowed in the outermost shell of an atom*) holds only for the elements in the second row of the periodic table (C,N,O,F). The elements of the third row (Si, P, S, Cl) use d orbitals, and thus can have more than eight electrons in their outer shell.

Let us use CO_2 as an example. Carbon has four valence electrons and oxygen has six. By covalently bonding, electrons are shared and the octet rule is followed,

$$\cdot \ddot{C} \cdot \quad + \quad 2 : \ddot{O} : \quad \longrightarrow$$

$$\ddot{O} :: C :: \ddot{O} \quad \text{or} \quad \ddot{O} = C = \ddot{O}$$

Carbon and oxygen can form resonance structures in the molecule CO_3^{-2}. The −2 denotes two extra electrons to place in the molecule. Once again the octet rule is followed,

In the final structure, each element counts one half of the electrons in a bond as its own, and any unpaired electrons are counted as its own. The sum of these two quantities should equal the number of valence electrons that were originally around the atom.

If the chemical bond is made up of atoms of different electronegativity, there is a **charge separation:**

electron density

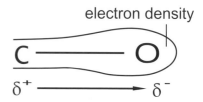

$$\delta^+ \longrightarrow \delta^-$$

There is a slight pulling of electron density by the more electronegative atom (oxygen in the preceding example) from the less electronegative atom (carbon in the preceding example). This results in the C–O bond having **partial ionic character** (i.e. *a polar bond; see* CHM 3.3). The charge separation also causes an underlined{electrical dipole }to be set up in the direction of the arrow. A dipole has a positive end (carbon) and a negative end (oxygen). A dipole will line up in an electric field.

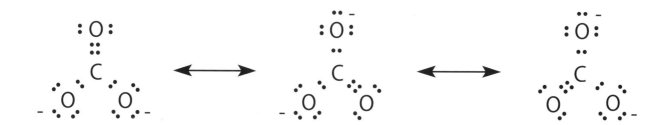

The most electronegative elements (in order, with electronegativities in brackets) are fluorine (4.0), oxygen (3.5), nitrogen (3.0), and chlorine (3.0) [To examine trends, see the periodic table in CHM 2.3]. These elements will often be paired with hydrogen (2.1) and carbon (2.5), resulting in bonds with partial ionic character. The **dipole moment** is a measure of the charge separation and thus, the electronegativities of the elements that make up the bond; the larger the dipole moment, the larger the charge separation.

No dipole moment is found in molecules with no charge separation between atoms (i.e. Cl_2, Br_2), or, when the charge separation is symmetric resulting in a cancellation of bond polarity like vector addition in physics (i.e. CH_4, CO_2).

A molecule where the charge separation between atoms is not symmetric will have a non-zero dipole moment (i.e. CH_3F, H_2O, NH_3 - see ORG 11.1.2). It is important to note that lone pair electrons make large contributions to the overall dipole moment of a molecule.

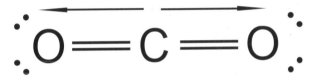

Figure IV.B.1.4: CO_2 - polar bonds but overall it is a non-polar molecule; therefore, CO_2 has a zero dipole moment.

1.5.1 Strength of Polar vs. Non-Polar Bonds

Non-polar bonds are generally stronger than polar covalent and ionic bonds, with ionic bonds being the weakest. However, in compounds with ionic bonding, there is generally a large number of bonds between molecules and this makes the compound as a whole very strong. For instance, although the ionic bonds in one compound are weaker than the non-polar covalent bonds in another compound, the ionic compound's melting point will be higher than the melting point of the covalent compound. Polar covalent bonds have a partially ionic character, and thus the bond strength is usually intermediate between that of ionic and that of non-polar covalent bonds. The strength of bonds generally decreases with increasing ionic character.

Opposites attract. Like charges repel. Such simple statements are fundamental in solving over 90% of mechanisms in organic chemistry. Once you are comfortable with the basics - electronegativity, polarity and resonance - you will not need to memorize the grand majority of outcomes of given reactions. You will be capable of quickly deducing the answer even when new scenarios are presented.

A substance which has a formal positive charge ($^+$) or a partial positive charge ("delta$^+$" or δ^+) is attracted to a substance with a formal negative charge ($^-$) or a partial negative charge (δ^-). In general, a substance with a formal charge would have a greater force of attraction than one with a partial charge when faced with an oppositely charged species. There is an important exception: spectator ions. Ions formed by elements in the first two groups of the periodic table (i.e. Na^+, K^+, Ca^{++}) do not actively engage in reactions in organic chemistry. They simply watch the reaction occur then at the very end they associate with the negatively charged product.

In most carbon-based compounds the carbon atom is bonded to a more electronegative atom. For example, in a carbon-oxygen bond the oxygen is δ^- resulting in a δ^+ carbon (see ORG 1.5). Because opposites attract, a δ^- carbon (which is unusual) could create a carbon-carbon bond with a δ^+ carbon (which is common). There are two important catego-

ries of compounds which can create a carbon-carbon bond; a) alkyl lithiums (RLi) and b) Grignard reagents (RMgBr), because they each have a δ^- carbon. Note that the carbon is δ^- since lithium is to the left of carbon on the periodic table (for electronegativity trends see CHM 2.3).

The expressions "like charges repel" and "opposites attract" are the basic rules of electrostatics. "Opposites attract" is translated in Organic Chemistry to mean "nucleophile attacks electrophile". The nucleophile is "nucleus loving" and so it is negatively charged or partially negative, and we follow its electrons using arrows in reaction mechanisms as it attacks the "electron loving" electrophile which is positively charged or partially positively charged. Sometimes we will use color, or an asterix*, or a "prime" symbol on the letter R (i.e. R vs R' vs R'' vs R'''), during reaction mechanisms to help you follow the movement of atoms. You will better understand the meaning in the pages to follow.

For nucleophiles, the general trend is that the stronger the nucleophile, the stronger the base it is. For example:

$$RO^- > HO^- \gg RCOO^- > ROH > H_2O$$

For information on the quality of leaving groups, see ORG 6.2.4.

Chapter review questions are available online for free. Doing practice questions will help clarify concepts and ensure that you study in a targeted way. We also have an IUPAC nomenclature program that you can use for free.

First, register at DAT-prep.com, then login and click on DAT Textbook Owners in the right column. Your online access continues for one full year from your online registration.

Memorize	Understand	Importance
* Categories of stereoisomers * Define enantiomers, diastereomers * Define ligand, chiral, racemic mixture * IUPAC nomenclature	* Rules for stereochemistry * Identify meso compounds * Assign R/S/E/Z * Fischer projections	**2 to 4 out of the 30 ORG** DAT questions are based on content in this chapter (in our estimation). * Note that between 30% and 60% of the questions in DAT Organic Chemistry are based on content from 4 chapters: 1, 2, 5 and 6.

DAT-Prep.com

Introduction ▮▮▮▮

Stereochemistry is the study of the relative spatial (3 D) arrangement of atoms within molecules. An important branch of stereochemistry, and very relevant to the DAT, is the study of chiral molecules.

Additional Resources

Free Online Q&A + Forum

Video: Online or DVD

Flashcards

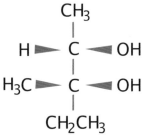

Special Guest

2.1 Isomers

Stereochemistry is the study of the arrangement of atoms in a molecule, in three dimensions. Two *different molecules* with the same number and type of atoms (= *the same molecular formula*) are called isomers. Isomers fall into two main categories: *structural* (constitutional) isomers and *stereoisomers* (spatial isomers). Structural isomers differ by the way their atoms are connected and stereoisomers differ in the way their atoms are arranged in space (enantiomers and diastereomers; see Figure IV.B.2.1.1).

2.1.1 Structural (Constitutional) Isomers

Structural isomers have different atoms and/or bonding patterns in relation to each other like the following *chain* or *skeletal* isomers:

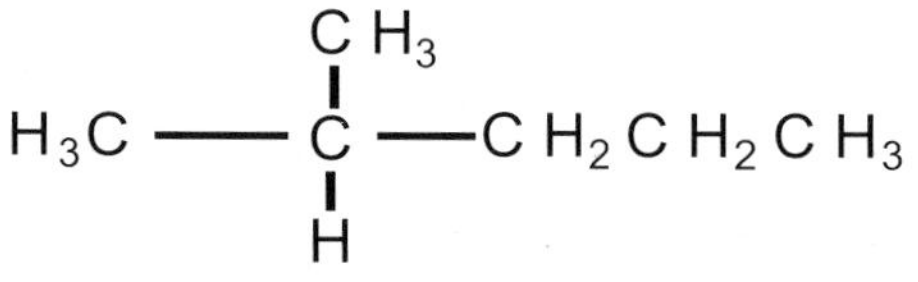

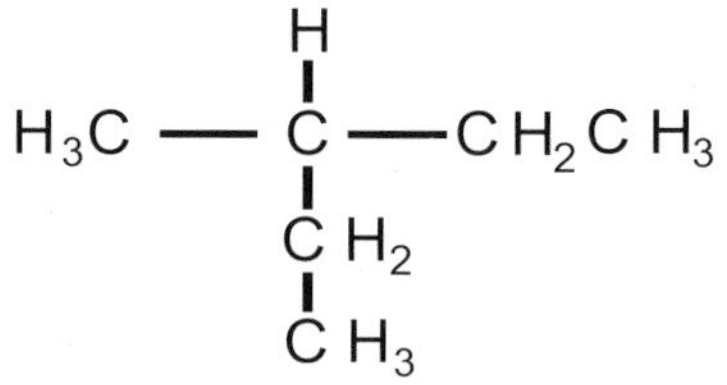

Functional isomers are structural isomers that have the same molecular formula but have different functional groups or *moi*-*eties*. For example, the following alcohol (ORG 6.1) and ether (ORG 10.1):

butan-1-ol
(n-butanol)

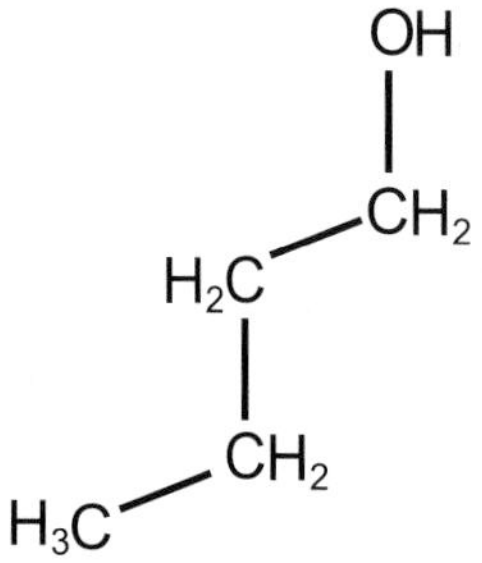

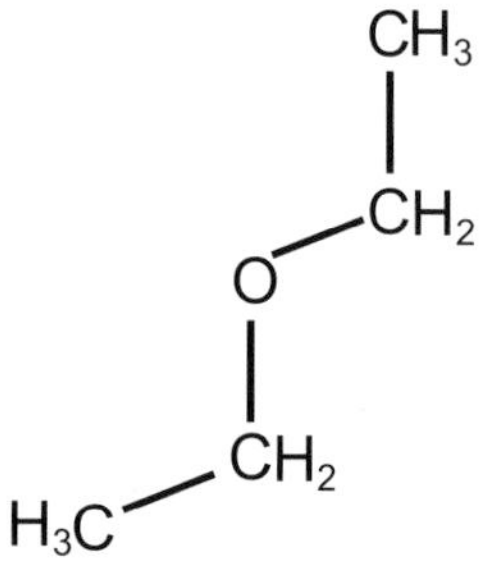

ethoxyethane
(diethyl ether)

Positional or regioisomers are structural isomers where the functional group changes position on the parent structure. For example, the hydroxyl group (-OH) occupying 3 differ-ent positions on the n-pentane (= normal, non-branched alkane with 5 carbons) chain resulting in 3 different compounds:

pentan-1-ol
(1-pentanol)

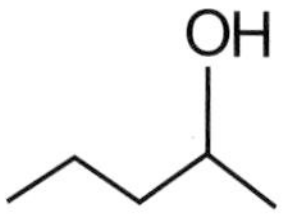

2-pentanol

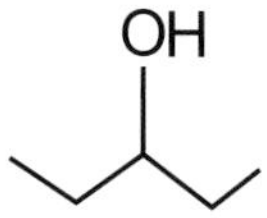

3-pentanol

2.2 Spatial/Stereoisomers

2.2.1 Geometric Isomers *cis/trans*, E/Z

Geometric isomers occur because carbons that are in a ring or double bond structure are *unable* to freely rotate (see conformation of cycloalkane; ORG 3.3, 3.3.1). This results in *cis* and *trans* compounds. When the substituents (i.e. Br) are on the same side of the ring or double bond, it is designated *cis*. When they are on opposite sides, it is designated *trans*. The *trans* isomer is more stable since the substituents are further apart, thus electron shell repulsion is minimized.

cis-dibromoethene   *trans*-dibromoethene

In general, structural and geometric isomers have different reactivity, spectra and physical properties (i.e. boiling points, melting points, etc.). Geometric isomers may have different physical properties but, in general, tend to have similar chemical reactivity.

The E, Z notation is the IUPAC preferred method for designating the stereochemistry of double bonds. E, Z is particularly used for isomeric compounds with 4 different substituent groups bonded to the two *ethenyl* or *vinyl* carbons (i.e. C=C which are sp^2 hybridized carbon atoms). We have just reviewed how to use *cis/trans*. The E, Z notation is used on more complex molecules and, as described, on situations were 4 different substituents are present.

To begin with, each substituent at the double bond is assigned a priority (see 2.3.1 for rules). If the two groups of higher priority are on opposite sides of the double bond, the bond is assigned the configuration E, (from *entgegen*, the German word for "opposite"). If the two groups of higher priority are on the same side of the double bond, the bond is assigned the configuration Z, (from *zusammen,* the German word for "together"). {Generally speaking, learning German is NOT required for the DAT!}

cis-2-bromobut-2-ene
(2 methyl groups on same side)

BUT

(*E*)-2-bromobut-2-ene
(Br is higher priority than methyl)

Mnemonic: Z = Zame Zide; E = Epposites.

2.2.2 Enantiomers and Diastereomers

Stereoisomers are different compounds with the same structure, differing only in the spatial orientation of the atoms (= *configuration*). Stereoisomers may be further divided into enantiomers and diastereomers. Enantiomers must have opposite absolute configurations at each and every chiral carbon.

We will soon highlight the easy way to remember the meaning of a *chiral molecule*, however, the formal definition of chirality is of an object that is not identical with its mirror image and thus exists in two enantiomeric forms. A molecule cannot be chiral if it contains a plane of symmetry. A molecule that has a plane of symmetry must be superimposable on its mirror image and thus must be *achiral*. The most common chirality encountered in organic chemistry is when the carbon atom is bonded to four different groups. Such a carbon lacks a plane of symmetry and is referred to as a *chiral center*. When a carbon atom has only three different substituents, such as the central carbon in methylcyclohexane, it has a plane of symmetry and is therefore achiral.

A stereocenter (= stereogenic center) is an atom bearing attachments such that interchanging any two groups produces a stereoisomer. If a molecule has n stereocenters, then it can have up to 2^n different non-superimposable (non-superposable) structures (= enantiomers).

Enantiomers come in pairs. They are two non-superimposable molecules, which are mirror images of each other. In order to have an enantiomer, a molecule must be chiral. Chiral molecules contain at least one chiral carbon which is a carbon atom that has four different substituents attached. For the purposes of the DAT, the concepts of a chiral carbon, asymmetric carbon and stereocenter are interchangeable.

Enantiomers have the same chemical and physical properties. The only difference is with their interactions with other chiral molecules, and their rotation of plane polarized light.

Conversely, diastereomers are any pair of stereoisomers that are not enantiomers. Diastereomers are both chemically and physically different from each other.

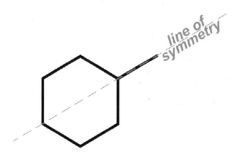

methylcyclohexane

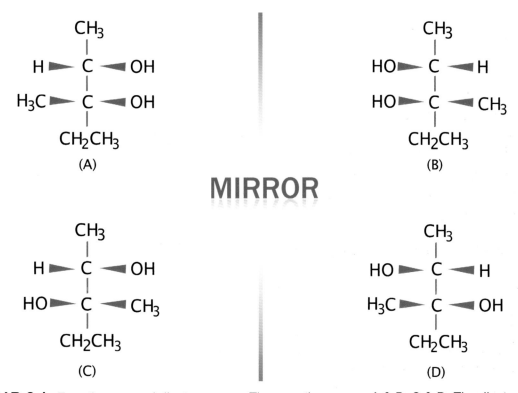

Figure IV.B.2.1: Enantiomers and diastereomers. The enantiomers are A & B, C & D. The diastereomers are A & C, A & D, B & D, B & C. Thus there are 2 pairs of enantiomers. This is consistent with the 2^n equation since each of the structures above have exactly 2 chiral carbons (stereocenters) and thus $2^2 = 4$ enantiomers.

2.3 Absolute and Relative Configuration

Absolute configuration uses the R, S system of naming compounds (*nomenclature; ORG 2.3.1*) and relative configuration uses the D, L system (ORG 2.3.2).

Before 1951, the absolute three dimensional arrangement or <u>configuration</u> of chiral molecules was not known. Instead chiral molecules were compared to an arbitrary standard (*glyceraldehyde*). Thus the *relative* configuration could be determined. Once the actual spatial arrangements of groups in molecules were finally determined, the *absolute* configuration could be known.

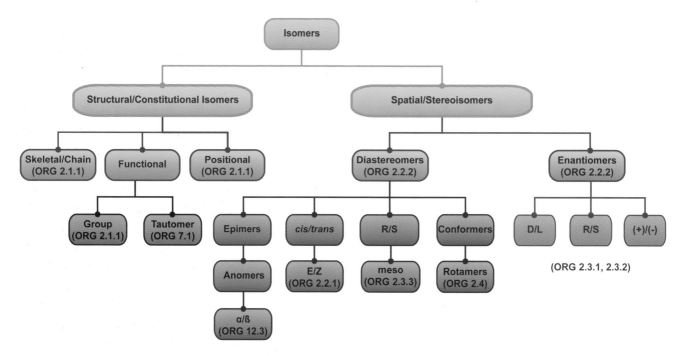

Figure IV.B.2.1.1: Categories of isomers.

2.3.1 The R, S System and Fischer Projections

One consequence of the existence of enantiomers, is a special system of nomenclature: the <u>R, S system</u>. This system provides information about the absolute configuration of a molecule. This is done by assigning a stereochemical configuration at each asymmetric (*chiral*) carbon in the molecule by using the following steps:

1. Identify an asymmetric carbon, and the four attached groups.

2. Assign priorities to the four groups, using the following rules:

i.   Atoms of higher atomic number have higher priority.

ii. An isotope of higher atomic mass receives higher priority.

iii. The higher priority is assigned to the group with the atom of higher atomic number or mass at the first point of difference.

iv. If the difference between the two groups is due to the number of otherwise identical atoms, the higher priority is assigned to the group with the greater number of atoms of higher atomic number or mass.

v. To assign priority of double or triple bonded groups, multiple-bonded atoms are considered as equivalent number of single bonded atoms:

$-CH=CH$ is taken as

$$-\underset{\underset{C}{|}}{CH}-\underset{\underset{C}{|}}{CH}$$

$$\overset{\diagdown}{\underset{\diagup}{C}}=O \quad \text{is taken as} \quad \overset{\diagdown}{\underset{\diagup}{C}}\overset{\diagup O}{\underset{\diagdown O-C}{}}$$

$-CH\equiv CH$ is taken as

$$-\underset{\underset{C}{|}}{\overset{\overset{C}{|}}{C}}-\underset{\underset{C}{|}}{\overset{\overset{C}{|}}{CH}}$$

3. In other words, you must re-orient the molecule in space so that the group of lowest priority is pointing directly back, away from you. The remaining three substituents with higher priority should radiate from the asymmetric carbon atom like the spoke on a steering wheel.

4. Consider the clockwise or counterclockwise order of the priorities of the remaining groups. If they increase in a clockwise direction, the asymmetric carbon is said to have the R configuration. If they decrease in a clockwise direction, the asymmetric carbon is said to have the S configuration {Mnemonic: Clockwise means that when you get to the top of the molecule, you must turn to the Right = R}.

A stereoisomer is named by indicating the configurations of each of the asymmetric carbons.

A Fischer projection is a 2-D way of looking at 3-D structures. All horizontal bonds project toward the viewer, while vertical bonds project away from the viewer. In organic chemistry, Fischer projections are used mostly for carbohydrates (see ORG 12.3.1, 12.3.2). To determine if 2 Fischer projections are superimposable, you can: (1) rotate one projection 180° or (2) keep one substituent in a fixed position and then you can rotate the other 3 groups either clockwise or counterclockwise. Using either technique preserves the 3-D configuration of the molecule.

Assigning R, S configurations to Fischer projections:

1. Assign priorities to the four substituents.

2. If the lowest priority group is on the vertical axis, determine the direction of rotation by going from priority 1 to 2 to 3, and then assign R or S configuration.

3. If the lowest priority group is on the horizontal axis, determine the direction of rotation by going from priority 1 to 2 to 3, obtain the R or S configuration, now the TRUE configuration will be the opposite of what you have just obtained.

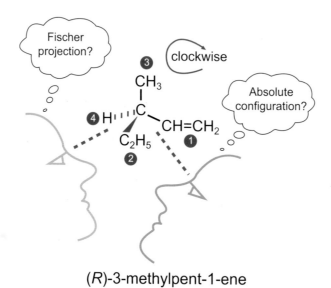

(R)-3-methylpent-1-ene

Figure IV.B.2.2(a): Assigning Absolute Configuration. In organic chemistry, the directions of the bonds are symbolized as follows: a broken line extends away from the viewer (i.e. INTO the page), a solid triangle projects towards the viewer, and a straight line extends in the plane of the paper. According to rule #3, we must imagine that the lowest priority group (H) points away from the viewer.

Fischer Projection

Figure IV.B.2.2(b): Creating the Fischer projection of (R)-3-methyl-1-pentene. Notice that the perspective of the viewer in the image is the identical perspective of the viewer on the left of Figure IV.B.2.2(a). In either case, a perspective is chosen so that the horizontal groups project towards the viewer.

2.3.2 Optical Isomers and the D, L System

Optical isomers are enantiomers and thus are stereoisomers that differ by different spatial orientations about a chiral carbon atom. Light is an electromagnetic wave that contains oscillating fields. In ordinary light, the electric field oscillates in all directions. However, it is possible to obtain light with an electric field that oscillates in only one plane. This type of light is known as **plane polarized light**. When plane polarized light is passed through a sample of a chiral substance, it will emerge vibrating in a different plane than it started. Optical isomers differ only in this rotation. If the light is rotated in a clockwise direction, the compound is dextrorotary, and is designated by a D or (+). If the light is rotated in a counterclockwise direction, the compound is levrorotary, and is designated by an L or (−). All L compounds have the same relative configuration as L-glyceraldehyde.

A racemic mixture will show no rotation of plane polarized light. This is a consequence of the fact that a racemate is a mixture with equal amounts of the D and L forms of a substance.

Specific rotation (α) is an inherent physical property of a molecule. It is defined as follows:

$$\alpha = \frac{\text{Observed rotation in degrees}}{(\text{tube length in dm}) \, (\text{concentration in g/ml})}$$

The observed rotation is the rotation of the light passed through the substance. The tube length is the length of the tube that contains the sample in question. The specific rotation is dependent on the solvent used,

Figure IV.B.2.3: Optical isomers and their Fischer projections. To prove to yourself that the 2 molecules are non-superimposable mirror images (enantiomers), review the rules for Fischer projections (ORG 2.3.1) and compare.

the temperature of the sample, and the wavelength of the light.

It should be noted that there is no clear correlation between the absolute configuration (i.e. R, S) and the direction of rotation of plane polarized light, designated by D/(+) or L (-). Therefore, the direction of optical rotation cannot be determined from the structure of a molecule and must be determined experimentally.

2.3.3 Meso Compounds

Tartaric acid (= 2,3-dihydroxybutanedioic acid which, in the chapters to come, is a compound that you will be able to name systematically = using IUPAC rules) has two chiral centers that have the same four substituents and are equivalent. As a result, two of the four possible stereoisomers of this compound are identical due to a plane of symmetry. Thus there are only three stereoisomeric tartaric acids. Two of these stereoisomers are enantiomers and the third is an achiral diastereomer, called a meso compound. Meso compounds are achiral (optically inactive) diastereomers of chiral stereoisomers.

In a *meso compound*, an internal plane of symmetry exists by drawing a line that will cut the molecule in half. For example, notice that in *meso*-tartaric acid, you can draw a line perpendicular to the vertical carbon chain creating 2 symmetric halves {**MeSo** = **M**irror of **S**ymmetry}.

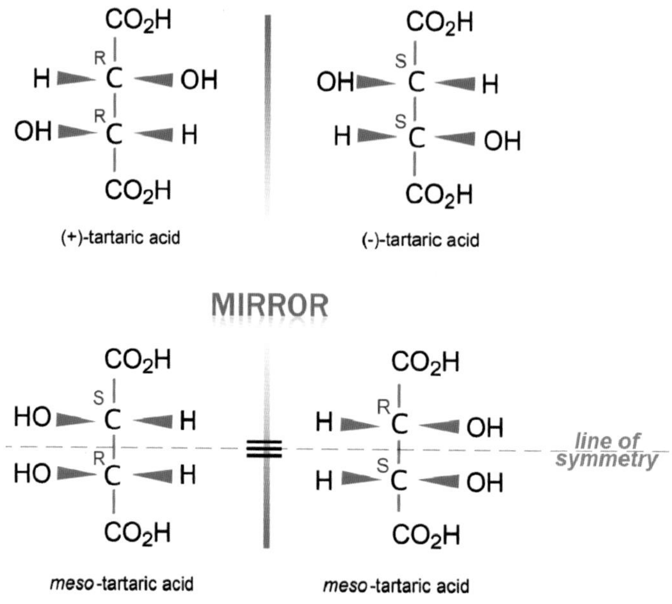

(+)-tartaric acid   (-)-tartaric acid

MIRROR

meso-tartaric acid   *meso*-tartaric acid

2.4 Conformational Isomers

Conformational isomers are isomers which differ only by the rotation about single bonds. As a result, substituents (= *ligands = attached atoms or groups*) can be maximally close (*eclipsed conformation*), maximally apart (*anti or staggered conformation*) or anywhere in between (i.e. *gauche conformation*). Though all conformations occur at room temperature, anti is most stable since it minimizes electron shell repulsion. Conformational isomers are not true isomers. Conformers are different spatial orientations of the same molecules.

Different conformations can be seen when a molecule is depicted from above and from the right, sawhorse projection, or where the line of sight extends along a carbon-carbon bond axis, a Newman projection. The different conformations occur as the molecule is rotated about its axis.

Example 1: Ethane

The lowest energy, most stable conformation, of ethane is the one in which all six carbon-hydrogen bonds are as far away from each other as possible: *staggered*. The reason, of course, is that atoms are surrounded by an outer shell of negatively charged electrons and, the basic rule of electrostatics is that, like charges repel (= electron shell repulsion = **ESR**). The highest energy, or least stable conformation, of ethane is the one in which all six carbon-hydrogen bonds are as close as possible: *eclipsed*. In between these two extremes are an infinite number of possibilities. As we have previously reviewed, when carbon is bonded to four different atoms (i.e. ethane), its bonds are sp^3 hybridized and the carbon atom sits in the center of a tetrahedron (ORG 1.2, CHM 3.5).

normal line: substituent in plane of paper

broken line: substituent going behind plane of paper

heavy line: substituent coming out of plane of paper

skeletal formula (structure)

front carbon

back carbon

sawhorse projection

back carbon

front carbon

Newman projection

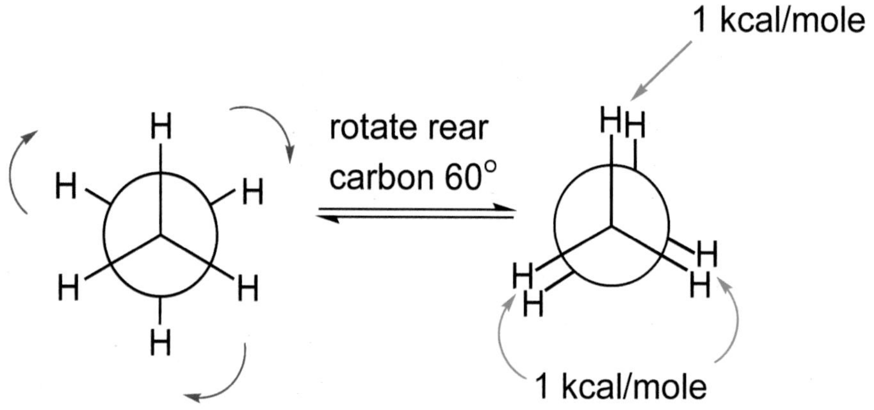

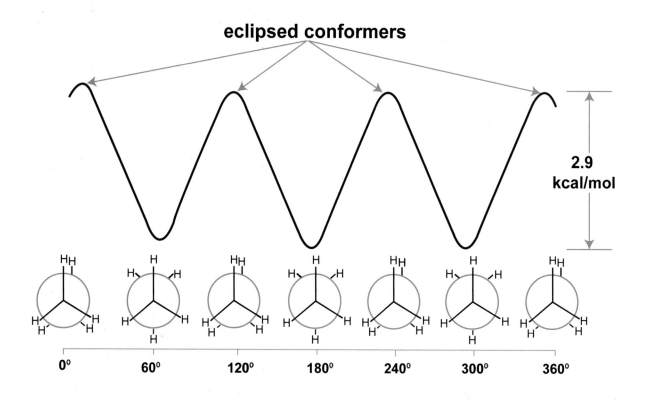

1 kcal/mole

rotate rear
carbon 60°

1 kcal/mole

eclipsed conformers

2.9 kcal/mol

0°   60°   120°   180°   240°   300°   360°

dihedral angle

Example 2: Butane

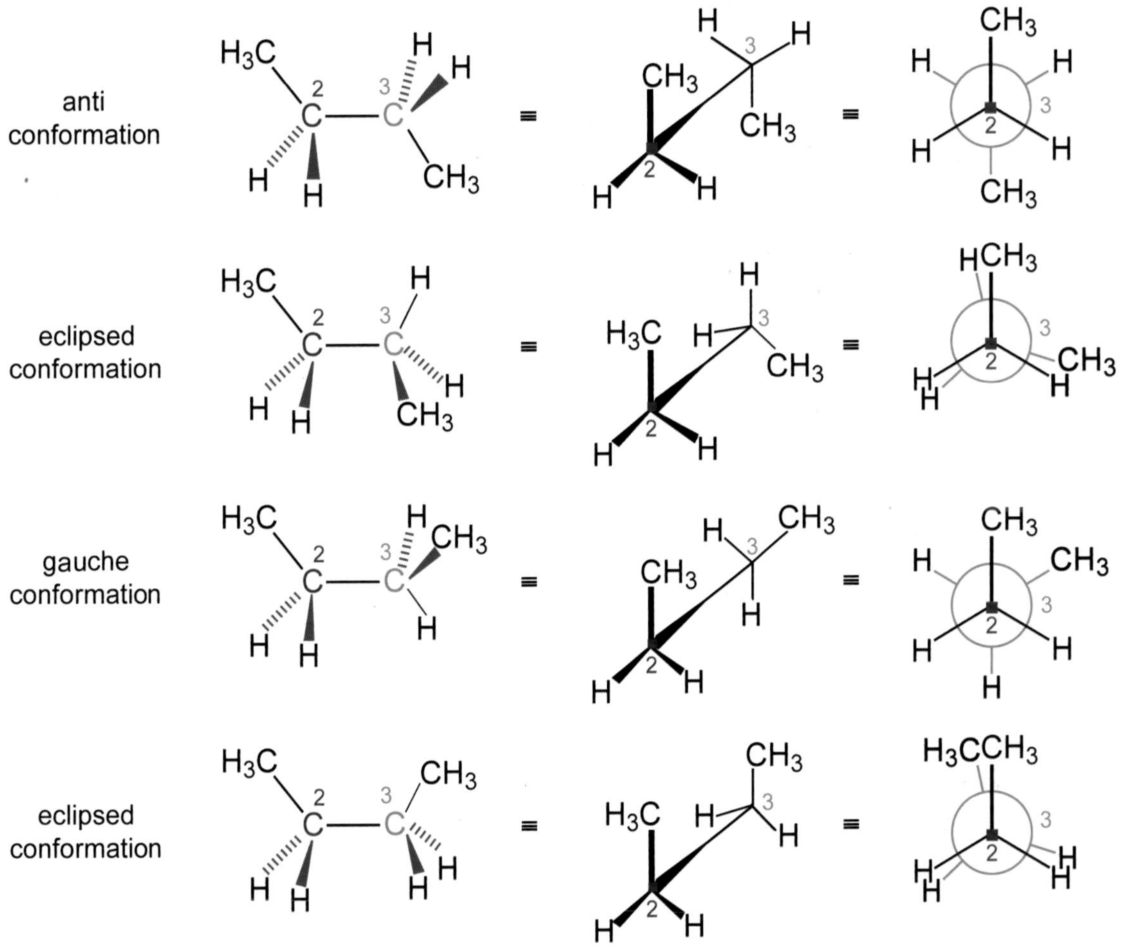

The preceding illustration is a plot of potential energy versus rotation about the C2-C3 bond of butane.

The lowest energy arrangement, the anti conformation, is the one in which two methyl groups (C1 and C4) are as far apart as possible, that is, 180 degrees from each other. When two substituents (i.e. the two methyl groups) are anti and in the same plane, they are *antiperiplanar* to each other.

As rotation around the C2-C3 bond occurs, an eclipsed conformation is reached when there are two methyl-hydrogen interactions and one hydrogen-hydrogen interaction. When the rotation continues, the two methyl groups are 60 degrees apart, thus the gauche conformation. It is still higher in energy than the anti conformation even though it has no eclipsing interactions. The reason, again, is ESR. Because ESR is occurring due to the relative bulkiness (i.e. big size) of the methyl group compared to hydrogens in this molecule, we say that *steric strain* exists between the two close methyl groups.

When two methyl groups completely overlap with each other, the molecule is said to be totally eclipsed and is in its highest energy state (least stable).

At room temperature, these forms easily interconvert: all forms are present to some degree, though the most stable forms dominate.

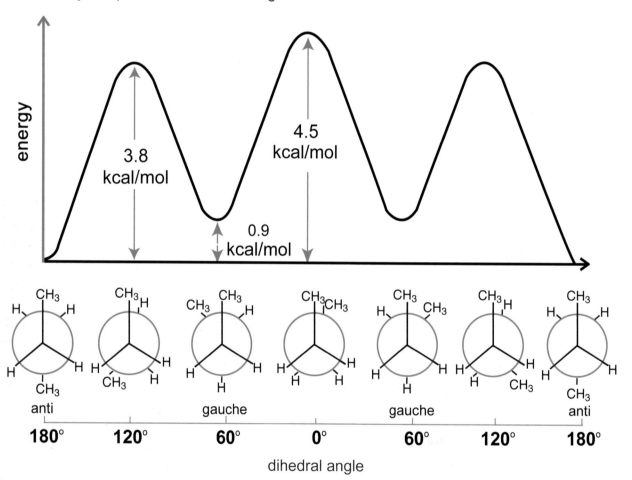

We have seen that conformers rotate about their single bonds. The rotational barrier, or *barrier to rotation*, is the <u>activation energy</u> (CHM 9.5) required to interconvert a subset of the possible conformations called *rotamers*. Butane has three rotamers: two gauche conformers and an anti conformer, where the four carbon centers are coplanar. The three eclipsed conformations with angles between the planes (= *dihedral angles*) of 120°, 0°, and 120° (which is 240° from the first), are not considered to be rotamers, but are instead <u>transition states</u>.

Common Terms

- dihedral angle: torsion (turn/twist) angle
- gauche: skew, synclinal
- **anti**: *trans*, antiperiplanar
- eclipsed: **syn**, *cis*, synperiplanar, torsion angle = 0°

"anti" and "syn" are IUPAC preferred descriptors.

2.5 A Word about IUPAC Nomenclature

IUPAC chemical nomenclature is the set of rules to produce systematic names for chemical compounds. You are responsible for knowing the IUPAC method of naming compounds as there could be 2 questions out of 30 on the DAT which directly rely on nomenclature. IUPAC naming is usually systematic but you will see in upcoming chapters that sometimes the trivial or customary name for a compound is retained as the official IUPAC name.

We have put together this Gold Standard textbook to give you the tools to get an amazing DAT score. However, you will find that sometimes there will be very obscure questions on the DAT, and that can include IUPAC nomenclature. If you will not be satisfied unless you obtain a perfect Organic Chemistry score, then you should review the extensive, detailed rules from the IUPAC website. Fortunately, they have an interactive chart with all the definitions from their fourth major publication, coincidentally named the *Gold Book*, which contains the definitions of a large number of technical terms used in organic chemistry. The extensive summary with interactive map can be found here:

goldbook.iupac.org/Graphs/H02763.3.map.html

We will cover enough nomenclature in our Gold Standard book, and online in our free nomenclature program at dat-prep.com, to get most hard working, insightful students great DAT scores, but if you are aiming for a perfect score, you will also need to review material from the *Gold Book* by IUPAC.

Go online to DAT-prep.com for chapter review Q&A and forum.

<u>Stereochemistry</u>

{ composition- molecular formula
{ constitution- arrangement

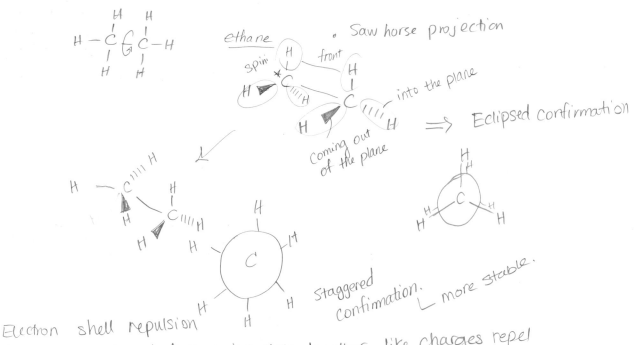

CH₃ ⟶ C=CH₂ , H₃C

CH₃ – CH=CH – CH₃

C_4H_8

Hydrogens can only be implied

} isomers

- Confirmation- ^free rotations with σ bonds.

$H-\overset{H}{\underset{H}{C}} \overset{H}{\underset{H}{C}}-H$ ethane

- Saw horse projection

front   into the plane

⟹ Eclipsed confirmation

Coming out of the plane

Staggered confirmation. └ more stable.

Electron shell repulsion
(To repulsively reject the being close together - like charges repel

– at room temperature, still get the both conformations (but most commonly stable: staggered).

- Configuration- permeanant orientation

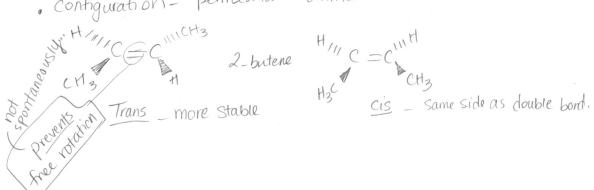

H⁄⁄⁄F C ⇌ C ⁄⁄⁄CH₃   CH₃   H

2-butene

H⁄⁄⁄ C = C ⁄⁄⁄H   H₃C   CH₃

Trans - more stable

cis - Same side as double bond.

not spontaneously
Prevents free rotation

ALKANES

Chapter 3

Memorize	Understand	Importance
* IUPAC nomenclature * Physical properties * Bond angles	* Trends based on length, branching * Ring strain, ESR * Complete combustion * Reactions involving alkenes, alkynes * Technical categorization of "cyclic alkanes" * Mechanisms of reactions * Free radical substitution	**1 to 3 out of the 30 ORG** DAT questions are based on content in this chapter (in our estimation). * Note that between 30% and 60% of the questions in DAT Organic Chemistry are based on content from 4 chapters: 1, 2, 5 and 6.

DAT-Prep.com

Introduction �N�N

Alkanes (a.k.a. paraffins) are compounds that consist only of the elements carbon (C) and hydrogen (H) (i.e. hydrocarbons). In addition, C and H are linked together exclusively by single bonds (i.e. they are saturated compounds). Methane is the simplest possible alkane while saturated oils and fats are much larger.

Additional Resources

Free Online Q&A + Forum

Video: Online or DVD

Flashcards

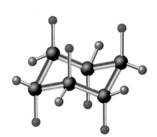

Special Guest

3.1 Description and Nomenclature

<u>Alkanes</u> are hydrocarbon molecules containing only sp^3 hybridized carbon atoms (single bonds). They may be unbranched, branched or cyclic. Their general formula is C_nH_{2n+2} for a straight chain molecule; 2 hydrogen (H) atoms are subtracted for each ring. They contain no functional groups and are fully saturated molecules (= *no double or triple bonds*). As a result, they are chemically unreactive except when exposed to heat or light.

Systematic naming of compounds (= *nomenclature*) has evolved from the International Union of Pure and Applied Chemistry (IUPAC). **The nomenclature of alkanes is the basis of that for many other organic molecules.** The root of the compound is named according to the number of carbons in the longest carbon chain:

C_1 = meth	C_5 = pent	C_8 = oct
C_2 = eth	C_6 = hex	C_9 = non
C_3 = prop	C_7 = hept	C_{10}= dec
C_4 = but		

When naming these as fragments, (alkyl fragments: *the alkane minus one H atom*, symbol: R), the suffix '–yl' is used. If naming the alkane, the suffix '-ane' is used. Some prefixes result from the fact that a carbon with *one* R group attached is a *primary* (normal or n –) carbon, *two* R groups is *secondary* (sec) and with *three* R groups it is a *tertiary* (tert or t –) carbon. Some alkyl groups have special names:

C—C—C—   n-propyl (= propyl)

C—C—C—C—   n-butyl (= butyl)

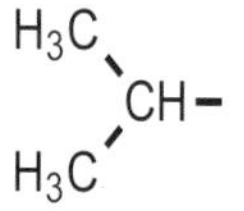

isopropyl
(= 2-propyl or propan-2-yl)

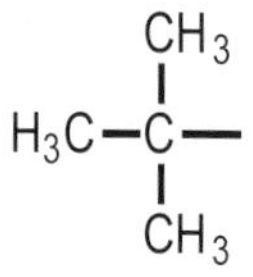

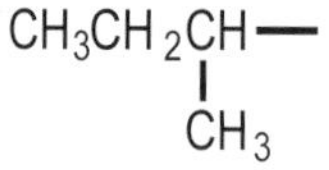

sec-butyl
(= 1-methylpropyl)

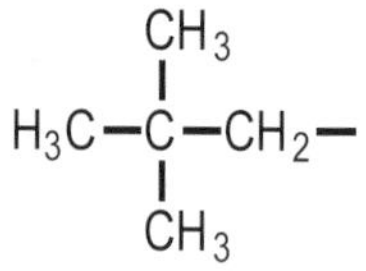

tert-butyl
(= 1,1-dimethylethyl)

neopentyl
(= dimethylpropyl)

Cyclic alkanes are named in the same way (according to the number of carbons), but the prefix 'cyclo' is added. The shorthand for organic compounds is a geometric figure where each corner represents a carbon; hydrogens need not be written, though it should be remembered that the number of hydrogens would exist such that the number of bonds at each carbon is four.

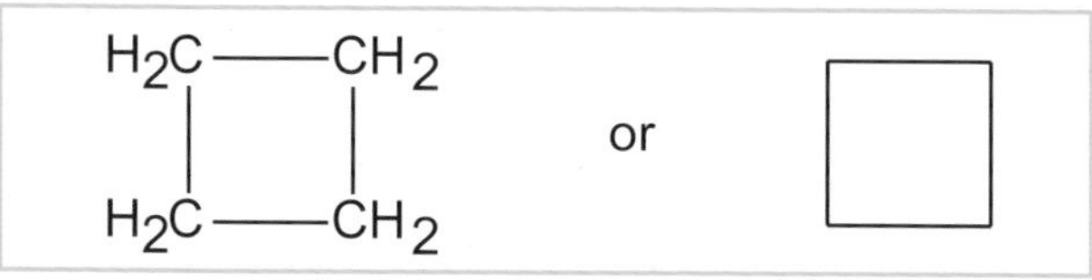

cyclobutane

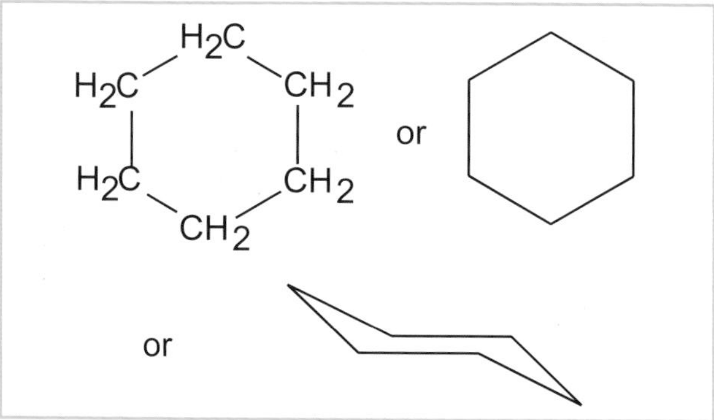

cyclohexane

As mentioned, carbon atoms can be characterized by the number of other carbon atoms to which they are directly bonded. It is very important for you to train your eyes to quickly indentify a primary carbon atom (**1°**), which is bonded to only one other carbon; a secondary carbon atom (**2°**), which is bonded to two other carbons; a tertiary carbon atom (**3°**), which is bonded to three other carbons; and a quaternary carbon atom (**4°**), which is bonded to four other carbons.

The nomenclature for branched-chain alkanes begins by determining the longest straight chain (i.e. *the highest number of carbons attached in a row*). The groups attached to the straight or *main* chain are numbered so as to achieve the lowest set of numbers. Groups are cited in alphabetical order. If a group appears more than once, the prefixes di-(2), tri-(3), tetra-(4) are used. Prefixes such as di-, tri-, tetra- as well as tert-, sec-, n- are not used for alphabetizing purposes. However, cyclo-, iso-, and neo- are considered part of the group name and are used for alphabetizing purposes. If two chains of equal length compete for selection as the main chain, choose the chain with the most substituents.

For example:

4,6-Diethyl-2,5,5,6,7-pentamethyloctane (7 substituents) or 3,5-Diethyl-2,3,4,4,7-pentamethyl octane (a bit better for keeners!) NOT 2,5,5,6-Tetramethyl-4-ethyl-6-isopropyl octane (6 substituents)

Naming cycloalkanes:

1. Use the cycloalkane name as the parent name. The only exception is when the alkyl side chain contains a larger number of carbons than the ring. In that case, the ring is considered as a substituent to the parent alkane.

2. Number the substituents on the ring to arrive at the lowest sum. When two or more different alkyl groups are present, they are numbered by an alphabetical order.

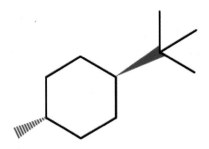

trans-1-tert-butyl-4-methylcyclohexane

3.1.1 Physical Properties of Alkanes

At room temperature and one atmosphere of pressure straight chain alkanes with 1 to 4 carbons are gases (i.e. CH_4 – methane, CH_3CH_3 – ethane, etc.), 5 to 17 carbons are liquids, and more than 17 carbons are solid. Boiling points of straight chain alkanes (= *aliphatic*) show a regular increase with increasing number of carbons. This is because they are nonpolar molecules, and have weak intermolecular forces. Branching of alkanes leads to a dramatic decrease in the boiling point. As a rule, as the number of carbons increase the melting points also increase.

Alkanes are soluble in nonpolar solvents (i.e. benzene, CCl_4 – carbon tetrachloride, etc.), and not in aqueous solvents (= *hydrophobic*). They are insoluble in water because of their low polarity and their inability to hydrogen bond. Alkanes are the least dense of all classes of organic compounds ($<< \rho_{water}$, 1 g/ml). Thus petroleum, a mixture of hydrocarbons rich in alkanes, floats on water.

3.2 Important Reactions of Alkanes

3.2.1 Combustion

Note that the "heat of combustion" is the change in enthalpy of a combustion reaction. Therefore, the higher the heat of combustion, the higher the energy level of the molecule, the less stable the molecule was prior to combustion.

Combustion may be either complete or incomplete. In complete combustion, the hydrocarbon is converted to carbon dioxide (CO_2) and water (H_2O). If there is insufficient oxygen for complete combustion, the reaction gives other products, such as carbon monoxide (CO) and soot (molecular C). This strongly exothermic reaction may be summarized:

$$C_nH_{2n+2} + \text{excess } O_2 \rightarrow nCO_2 + (n+1)H_2O.$$

3.2.2 Radical Substitution Reactions

Radical substitution reactions with halogens may be summarized:

$$RH + X_2 + uv \text{ light}(hf) \text{ or heat} \rightarrow RX + HX$$

The halogen X_2, may be F_2, Cl_2, or Br_2. I_2 does not react. The mechanism of *halogenation* may be explained and summarized by example:

i.   Initiation: This step involves the formation of *free radicals* (highly reactive substances which contain an unpaired electron, which is symbolized by a single dot):

$$Cl\!:\!Cl + uv \text{ light or heat} \rightarrow 2Cl\bullet$$

$$cl\!-\!cl \rightarrow 2cl\bullet$$

ii. Propagation: In this step, the chlorine free radical begins a series of reactions that form new free radicals:

$$CH_4 + Cl\bullet \rightarrow \bullet CH_3 + HCl$$
$$\bullet CH_3 + Cl_2 \rightarrow CH_3Cl + Cl\bullet$$

iii. Termination: These reactions end the radical propagation steps. Termination reactions destroy the free radicals (coupling).

$$Cl\bullet + \bullet CH_3 \rightarrow CH_3Cl$$

$$\bullet CH_3 + \bullet CH_3 \rightarrow CH_3CH_3$$

$$Cl\bullet + Cl\bullet \rightarrow Cl_2$$

Radical substitution reactions can also occur with halide acids (i.e. HCl, HBr) and peroxides (i.e. HOOH – hydrogen peroxide). Chain propagation (step ii) can destroy many organic compounds fairly quick. This step can be inhibited by using a resonance stabilized free radical to "mop up" (*termination*) other destructive free radicals in the medium. For example, BHT is a resonance stabilized free radical added to packaging of many breakfast cereals in order to inhibit free radical destruction of the cereal (= *spoiling*).

The stability of a free radical depends on the ability of the compound to stabilize the unpaired electron. This is analogous to stabilizing a positively charged carbon (= *carbocation*). Thus, in both cases, a tertiary compound is more stable than secondary which, in turn, is more stable than a primary compound.

Please note that the rate law for free radical substitution reactions was discussed in CHM 9.4.

The relative rate of free radical halogenation: $F_2 > Cl_2 > Br_2 > I_2$. Free radical reactions depend not only on the stability of the intermediate, but also on the number of hydrogens present. The following are examples:

1.   When F_2 is treated with UV light and reacted with 2-methylbutane, only one type of product is dominant. Fluorine

radicals are so reactive that it will react mostly with hydrogens type that are most prevalent (hydrogens attached to primary carbons indicated in blue), thus the predominant product will be:

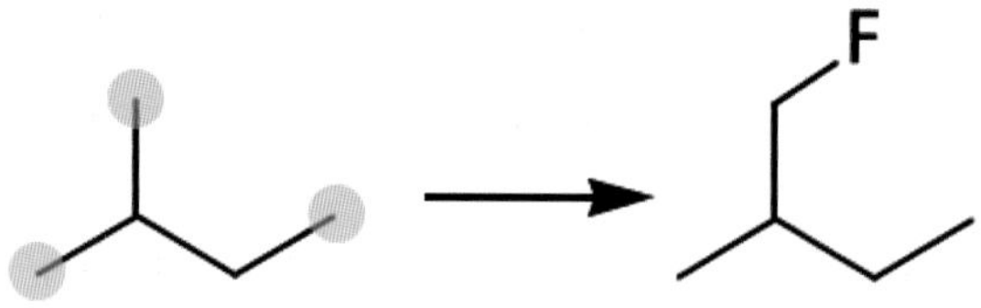

2. When Cl_2 is treated with UV light and reacted with 2-methylbutane, five products are formed. The relative rate of reaction of Br_2 is slower than F_2. Therefore, both abundance of different hydrogens and the relative stability of the primary radical contribute to the types of final products formed.

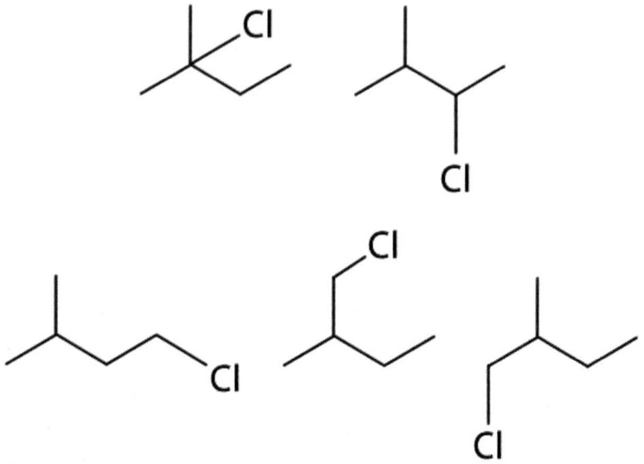

3. When Br_2 is treated with UV light and reacted with 2-methylbutane, only one product is formed because bromine is so selective that it will only react with the most stable ~~primary~~ *tertiary* radical (most substituted carbon atom).

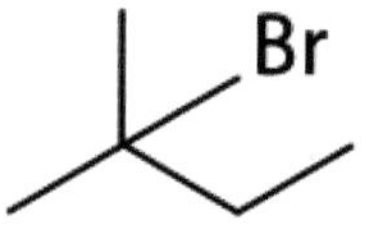

4. I_2 does not react.

The stability of a free radical depends on the ability of the compound to stabilize the unpaired electron. This is analogous to stabilizing a positively charged carbon (= *carbocation*). Thus, in both cases, a tertiary compound is more stable than secondary which, in turn, is more stable than a primary compound.

repeated !!

Also in both cases, the reason for the trend is the same: the charge on the carbon is stabilized by the electron donating effect of the presence of alkyl groups. Alkyl groups are not strongly electron donating, they are normally described as "somewhat" electron donating; however, the combined effect of multiple R groups has an important stabilizing effect that we will see as a critical feature in many reaction types.

$$•CR_3 > •CR_2H > •CRH_2 > •CH_3$$
$$3° > 2° > 1° > \text{methyl}$$

Pyrolysis occurs when a molecule is broken down by heat (*pyro* = fire, *lysis* = separate). C-C bonds are cleaved and smaller chain alkyl radicals often recombine in termination steps creating a variety of alkanes.

3.3 Ring Strain in Cyclic Alkanes

Cyclic alkanes are strained compounds. This **ring strain** results from the bending of the bond angles in greater amounts than normal. This strain causes cyclic compounds of 3 and 4 carbons to be unstable, and thus not often found in nature. The usual angle between bonds in an sp^3 hybridized carbon is 109.5° (= *the normal tetrahedral angle*).

The expected angles in some cyclic compounds can be determined geometrically: 60° in cyclopropane; 90° in cyclobutane and 108° in cyclopentane. Cyclohexane, in the chair conformation, has normal bond angles of 109.5°. The closer the angle is to the normal tetrahedral angle of 109.5°, the more stable the compound. In fact, cyclohexane can be found in a chair or boat conformation or any conformation in between; however, at any given moment, 99% of the cyclohexane molecules would be found in the chair conformation because it is the most stable (lower energy).

Figure IV.B.3.1: The chair and boat conformations of cyclohexane. Some students like to remember that you sit in a chair because a chair is stable. However, a boat can be tippy and so it's less stable.

It is important to have a clear understanding of electron shell repulsion (ESR). Essentially all atoms and molecules are surrounded by an electron shell (CHM 2.1, ORG 1.2) which is more like a cloud of electrons. Because like charges repel, when there are options, atoms and molecules assume the conformation which minimizes ESR.

For example, when substituents are added to a cyclic compound (i.e. Fig. IV.B.3.2), the most stable position is equatorial (equivalent to the anti conformation, ORG 2.1) which minimizes ESR. This conformation is most pronounced when the substituent is bulky (i.e. isopropyl, t-butyl, phenyl, etc.). In other words, a large substituent takes up more space thus ESR has a more prominent effect.

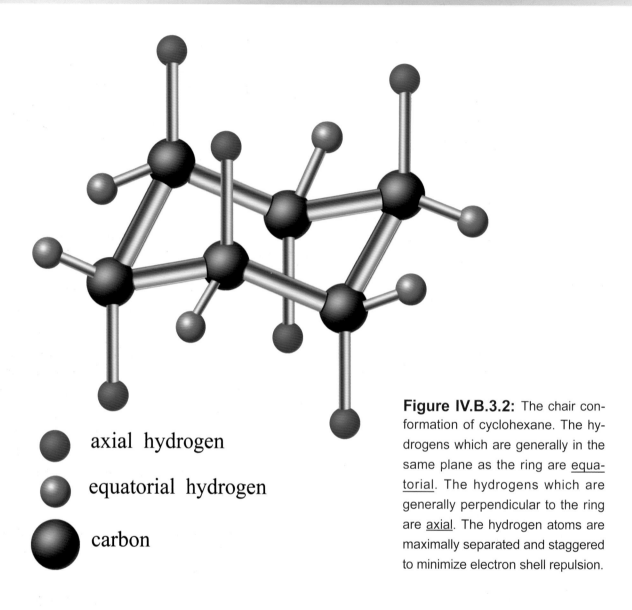

axial hydrogen

equatorial hydrogen

carbon

Figure IV.B.3.2: The chair conformation of cyclohexane. The hydrogens which are generally in the same plane as the ring are equatorial. The hydrogens which are generally perpendicular to the ring are axial. The hydrogen atoms are maximally separated and staggered to minimize electron shell repulsion.

3.3.1 A Closer Look at Ring Strain and Conformations of Cycloalkanes

In cycloalkanes, ring strain comes from three factors: (1) angle strain due to bond angle expansion or compression; (2) torsional strain due to the overlapping of adjacent bonds; and (3) steric strain due to the repulsive interactions when atoms approach too close (ESR).

Because this is the source of many test questions, let's review the two types of hydrogen atoms in cyclohexane: those that are perpendicular to the ring are called *axial hydrogens*, and those that are parallel to the plane of the ring are called *equatorial hydrogens*. Each carbon atom has one axial hydrogen atom and one equatorial hydrogen atom. Every ring has two sides, and each side has an alternating axial-equatorial arrangement. The six axial hydrogen bonds are parallel and have an alternating up-down relationship. The six equatorial hydrogen bonds also have an alternating up-down relationship.

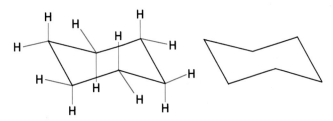

Interconversion of the chair conformations is referred to as *ring flip*, in which each axial and equatorial position becomes interconverted. An axial hydrogen atom in one chair form becomes an equatorial one, and vice versa.

Of course, all conformers between extremes also exist – even if just for a tiny fraction of a second at room temperature. The twist-boat (**C** and **E** in the diagram that follows), the half-chair state (**B**) which is the transition state in the interconversion between the chair (**A**) and twist-boat conformations, and of course, the boat conformer (**D**).

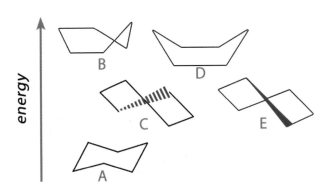

Conformations of mono-substituted cyclohexanes: The two common conformers of a mono-substituted cyclohexane are not equally stable since a substituent is always more stable in an equatorial position than in an axial position. Steric repulsion with other axial substituents (ESR) is present when a substituent is in the axial position, and this is referred to as a *1,3-diaxial interaction*. The axial methyl group on C1 is too close to the axial hydrogens on C3 and C5, resulting in steric strain. Therefore, a bulky substituent can prevent the ring form from adopting certain conformations.

For example, methylcyclohexane has 95% of its conformers with the methyl group at the equatorial position.

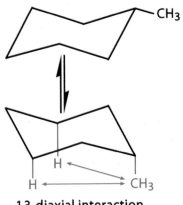

1,3-diaxial interaction

Conformations of di-substituted cyclo-hexanes: The two common conformers of a di-substituted cyclohexane are more complex since 1,2-dimethylcyclohexane has two iso-mers: *cis*-1,2-dimethylcyclohexane and *trans*-1,2-dimethylcyclohexane. In the *cis* isomer, both methyl groups are located on the same side of the ring, and the molecule can exist in either of the following two conformations: each has one axial methyl group and one equatorial methyl group. In the *trans* isomer, methyl groups are located on the opposite side of the ring, and the molecule can exist in

either of the following two conformations: one conformer has both methyl groups axial and the other conformer has both methyl groups equatorial. However, the conformer on the left side (both axial) is less stable and *trans*-1,2-dimethylcyclohexane will exist almost exclusively in the di-equatorial conformation on the right side.

Trans is more stable as it has one conformer with both methyl groups in equatorial positions.

Go online to DAT-prep.com for chapter review Q&A and forum.

Rxn mechanisms

- Nucleophile (nucleus loving) — attracted to Carbon nucleus
  ⟶ w/ protons (+).
  $\ominus$ or $\delta-$ charged

- Electrophile — attracted to e^-.

spectator ion —

break the bond with "I" — polyrized & weaker bond.

$$\underset{\text{Sodium methoxide}}{Na\text{(spectator)}OCH_3} + \underset{\text{methyl Iodide}}{CH_3(I)\text{ leaving group}} \longrightarrow NaI + \underset{\text{dimethyl ether}}{CH_3OCH_3}$$

(just like naming NaOH — Sodium Hydroxide !)

- Spectator ion — 1st & 2nd group of periodic table. Just spectators, not involved. At the end, may associate with whatever is left.

- Nu: $\overset{\ominus}{O}H$ / $\overset{\ominus}{C}N$ / $\overset{\ominus}{N}H_2$ / NH_3 ⟵ Not so strong, though
       $\overset{\ominus}{S}H$ / $\overset{\ominus}{O}R$ /

- Leaving group —
  $Cl^- \gg \overset{\ominus}{O}H \gg \overset{\ominus}{C}H_3$ If you add a Hydrogen and see which one would be
  ↓↓ after adding an "H". a stronger acid → better leaving group.

  $HCl > H_2O > CH_4$

  $- HSO_4^- \overset{+H^+}{\longrightarrow} H_2SO_4$ — Strong acid

good leaving group

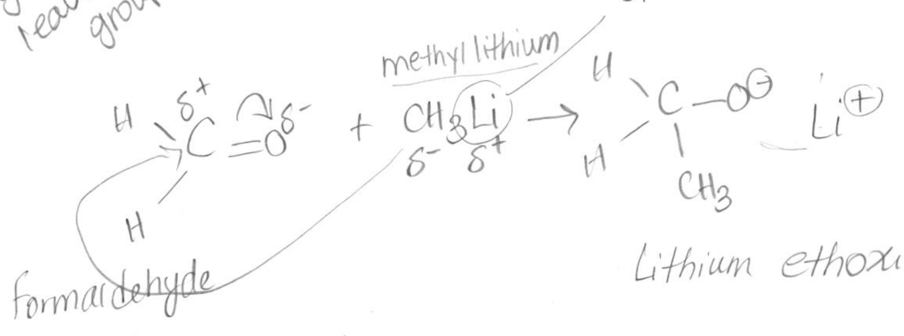

$$\underset{\text{formaldehyde}}{\overset{H}{\underset{H}{>}}C\overset{\delta+}{=}O^{\delta-}} + \underset{\text{methyl lithium}}{CH_3Li} \longrightarrow \overset{H}{\underset{H}{>}}\underset{CH_3}{\overset{|}{C}}-O^{\ominus} \; Li^{\oplus}$$
spectator ion

Lithium ethoxide

$(R\overset{\delta-}{M}\overset{\delta+}{g}X)$ — Grignard reagent

ALKENES

Chapter 4

DAT-Prep.com

Memorize	Understand	Importance
IUPAC nomenclature Properties and hydrogenation reaction catalysts	* Electrophilic addition, Markovnikoff's rule, oxidation * Concept of nucleophile and electrophile * Markovnikoff and anti-Markovnikoff addition * Mechanisms of reactions	**1 to 3 out of the 30 ORG** DAT questions are based on content in this chapter (in our estimation). * Note that between 30% and 60% of the questions in DAT Organic Chemistry are based on content from 4 chapters: 1, 2, 5 and 6.

DAT-Prep.com

Introduction

An alkene (a.k.a. olefin) is an unsaturated chemical compound containing at least one carbon-to-carbon double bond.

Additional Resources

Free Online Q&A + Forum

Video: Online or DVD

Flashcards

Special Guest

4.1 Description and Nomenclature

Alkenes *(olefins)* are unsaturated hydrocarbon molecules containing carbon-carbon double bonds. Their general formula is C_nH_{2n} for a straight chain molecule; 2 hydrogen (H) atoms are subtracted for each ring. The *functional group* in these molecules is the double bond which determines the chemical properties of alkenes. Double bonds are sp^2 hybridized (*see* ORG 1.2, 1.3). The nomenclature is the same as that for alkanes, except that i) the suffix 'ene' replaces 'ane' and ii) the double bond is (are) numbered in the molecule, trying to get the smallest number for the double bond(s). Always select the longest chain that contains the double bond or the greatest number of double bonds as the parent hydrocarbon. For cycloalkenes, the carbons of the double bond are given the 1– and 2– positions.

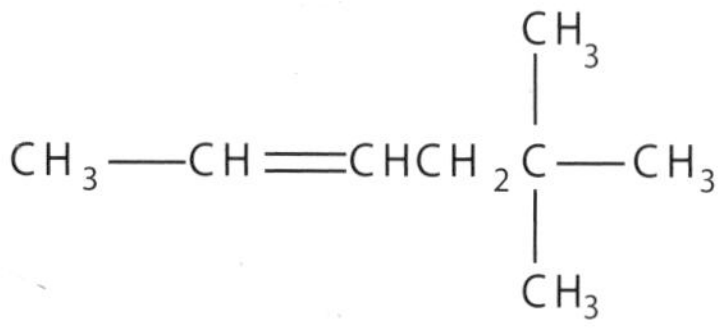

5,5-Dimethyl-2-hexene

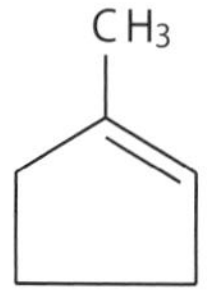

1-methylcyclopentene

Two frequently encountered groups are sometimes named as if they were substituents.

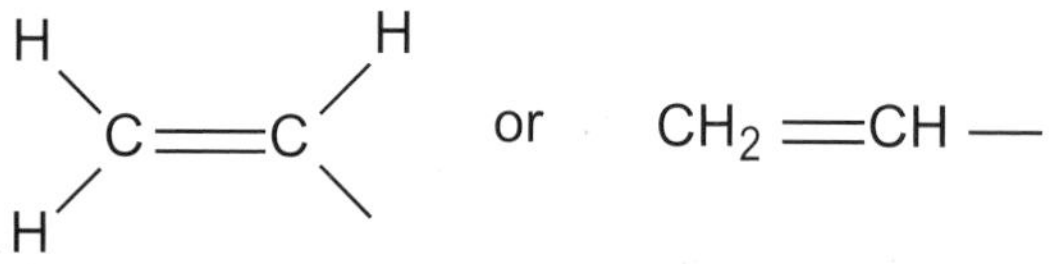

the vinyl group

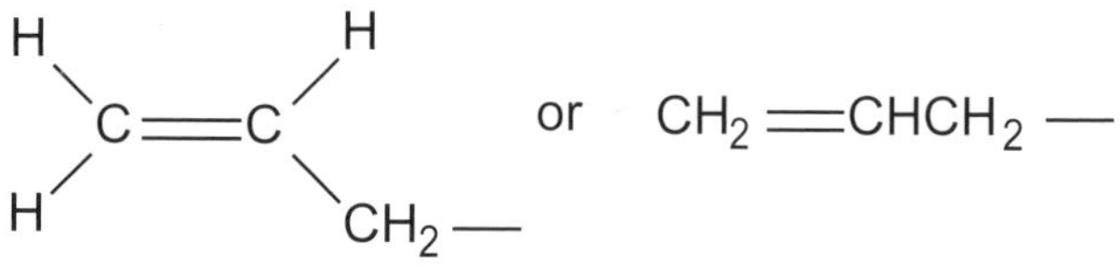

the allyl group

Alkenes have similar physical properties to alkanes. *Trans* compounds tend to have higher melting points (due to better symmetry), and lower boiling points (due to less polarity) than its corresponding *cis* isomer. Alkenes, however, due to the nature of the double bond may be polar. The dipole moment is oriented from the electropositive alkyl group toward the electronegative alkene.

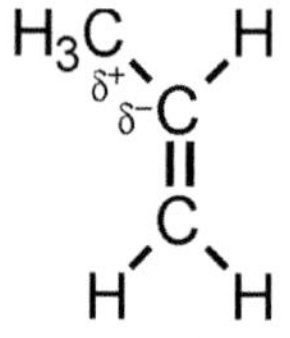

has a small dipole moment

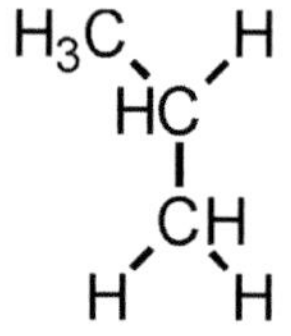

has no dipole moment

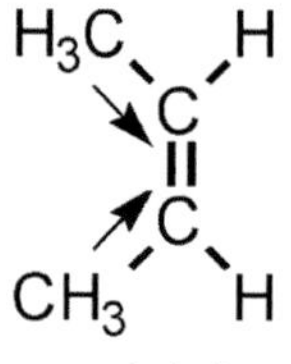

(cis)
small dipole moment

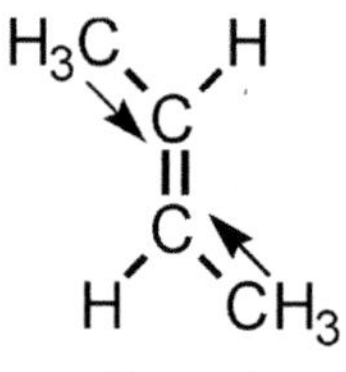

(trans)
no dipole moment

The greater the number of attached alkyl groups (i.e. *the more highly substituted the double bond*), the greater is the alkene's stability. The reason is that <u>alkyl</u> groups are somewhat electron donating, thus they stabilize the double bond.

An alkene with 2 double bonds is a diene, 3 is a triene. A diene with one single bond in between is a conjugated diene. Conjugated dienes are more stable than non-conjugated dienes primarily due to resonance stabilization (see the resonance stabilized conjugated molecule 1,3-butadiene in ORG 1.4). Alkenes, including polyenes (multiple double bonds), can engage in addition reactions (ORG 4.2.1). The notable exceptions include aromatic compounds (conjugated double bonds in a ring; ORG 5.1) which cannot engage in addition reactions which will be discussed in the next chapter.

• Synthesis of Alkenes: The two most common alkene-forming reactions involve elimination reactions of either HX from an alkyl halide or H_2O from alcohol. Dehydrohalogenation occurs by the reaction of an alkyl halide with a strong base. Dehydration occurs

by reacting an alcohol with a strong acid.

We will discuss elimination reactions (E1 and E2), which can be used to synthesize alkenes, in the chapter reviewing alcohols (ORG 6.2.4).

4.2 Important Chemical Reactions

4.2.1 Electrophilic Addition

The chemistry of alkenes may be understood in terms of their functional group, the double bond. When <u>electrophiles</u> (*substances which seek electrons*) add to alkenes, carbocations (= *carbonium ions*) are formed. An important electrophile is H^+ (i.e. in HBr, H_2O, etc.). A <u>nucleophile</u> is a molecule with a free pair of electrons, and sometimes a negative charge, that seeks out partially or completely positively charged species (i.e. a carbon nucleus). Some important nucleophiles are OH^- and CN^-.

E = electrophile   carbocation (intermediate)

Nu = nucleophile

Note that the carbon-carbon double bond is electron rich (nucleophilic) and can donate a pair of electrons to an electrophile (= "electron loving") during reactions. Electrons from the π bond attack the electrophile. As the π bond is weaker than the σ bond, it can be broken without breaking the σ bond. As a result, the carbon skeleton can remain intact. Electrophilic addition to an unsymmetrically substituted alkene gives the more highly substituted carbocation (i.e. the most stable intermediate). We will soon see that Markovnikoff's rule (or Markovnikov's rule) is a guide to determine the outcome of addition reactions.

Another important property of the dou-

ble bond is its ability to stabilize carbocations, carbanions or radicals attached to adjacent carbons (*allylic carbons*). Note that all the following are resonance stabilized:

carbocation

carbanion

carbon radical

The stability of the intermediate carbocation depends on the groups attached to it, which can either stabilize or destabilize it. As well, groups which place a partial or total positive charge adjacent to the carbocation withdraw electrons inductively, by sigma bonds, to destabilize it. More highly substituted carbocations are more stable than less highly substituted ones.

These points are useful in predicting which carbon will become the carbocation, and to which carbon the electrophile and nucleophile will bond. The intermediate carbocation formed must be the most stable. **Markovnikoff's rule** is a result of this, and it states: *the nucleophile will be bonded to the most substituted carbon* (fewest hydrogens attached) *in the product. Equivalently, the electrophile will be bonded to the least sub-*

stituted carbon (most hydrogens attached) *in the product*. An example of this is:

$$H_3C, H_3C \;C{=}C\; CH_3, H \quad + HBr$$

(1) (2)

$$\xrightarrow{H^+} \; H_3C, H_3C \;\overset{+}{C}{-}\overset{CH_3}{\underset{H}{C}}{-}H$$

(1) (2)

$$\xrightarrow{Br^-} \; H_3C{-}\overset{Br}{\underset{CH_3}{C}}{-}\overset{CH_3}{\underset{H}{C}}{-}H$$

(1) (2)

H^+ = electrophile
Br^- = nucleophile
(1) most substituted carbon
(2) least substituted carbon
(1) forms the most stable carbonium ion.

The product, 2-bromo-2-methyl butane, is the more likely or major product (*the Markovnikoff product*). Had the H+ added to the most substituted carbon (which has a much lower probability of occurrence) the less likely or minor product would be formed (*the anti-Markovnikoff product*). {Memory guide for Markovnikoff's rule: "Hydrogen prefers to add to the carbon in the double bond where most of its friends are" (this works because the least substituted carbon has the most bonds to hydrogen atoms)}

Carbocation intermediate rearrangement: In both *hydride shift* and *alkyl group shift*, H or CH_3 moves to a positively charged

carbon, taking its electron pair with it. As a result, a less stable carbocation rearranges to a more stable one (more substituted).

secondary carbocation → tertiary carbocation

secondary carbocation → tertiary carbocation

Markovnikoff's rule is true for the ionic conditions presented in the preceding reaction. However, for radical conditions the reverse occurs. Thus *anti-Markovnikoff* products are the major products under free radical conditions.

• Addition of halogens: This is a simple and rapid laboratory diagnostic tool to test for the presence of unsaturation (C=C). Immediate disappearance of the reddish Br_2 color indicates that the sample is an alkene. The general chemical formula of the halogen addition reaction is:

$$C{=}C + X_2 \longrightarrow X{-}C{-}C{-}X$$

The π electron pair of the double bond attacks the bromine, or X_2 molecule, setting up an induced dipole and then displacing the bromide ion. The intermediate forms a cyclic bromonium ion R_2Br , which is then attacked by Br-, giving the di-bromo addition product.

Since the intermediate is a bromonium ion, the bromide anion can only attack from the opposite side, yielding an anti product.

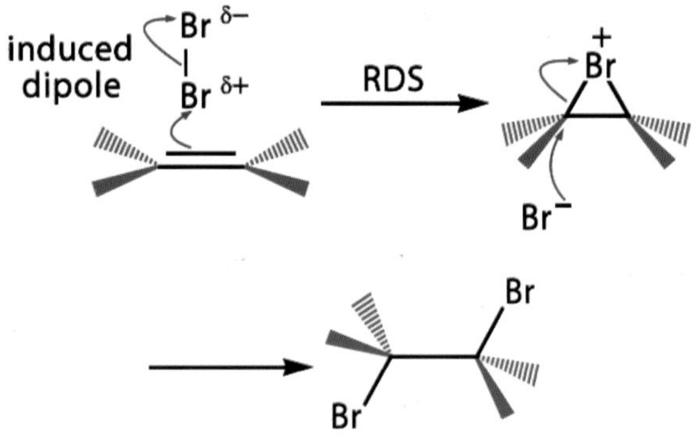

RDS = rate determining step (CHM 9.4)

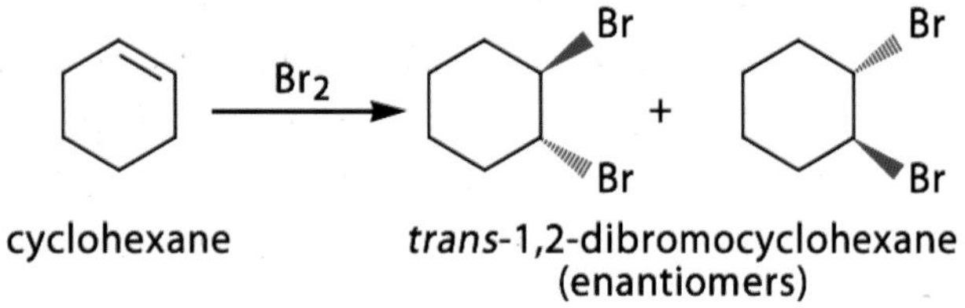

cyclohexane

trans-1,2-dibromocyclohexane
(enantiomers)

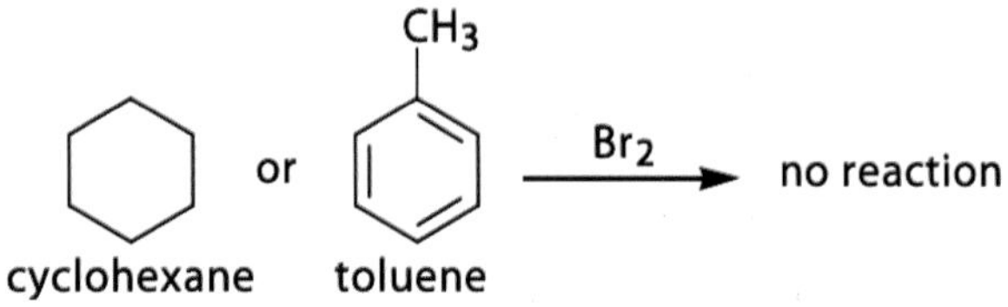

cyclohexane   toluene

Halogen addition does not occur in saturated hydrocarbons (i.e. cyclohexane) which lack the electron rich double bond, nor do the reactions occur within an aromatic ring because of the increased stability afforded by conjugation in a ring system due to resonance.

• Halohydrin formation reaction: A halohydrin (or haloalcohol) is a functional group where one carbon atom has a halogen substituent and an adjacent carbon atom has a hydroxyl substituent. This addition, which produces a halohydrin, is done by reacting an alkene with a halogen X_2 in the presence of water. The intermediate forms a cyclic bromonium ion R_2Br. The water molecule competes with the bromide ion as a nucleophile and reacts with the bromonium ion to form the halohydrin. The net effect is the addition of HO-X to the alkene.

In practice, the bromohydrin reaction is carried out using a reagent called NBS. Markovnikoff regiochemistry and anti addition is observed.

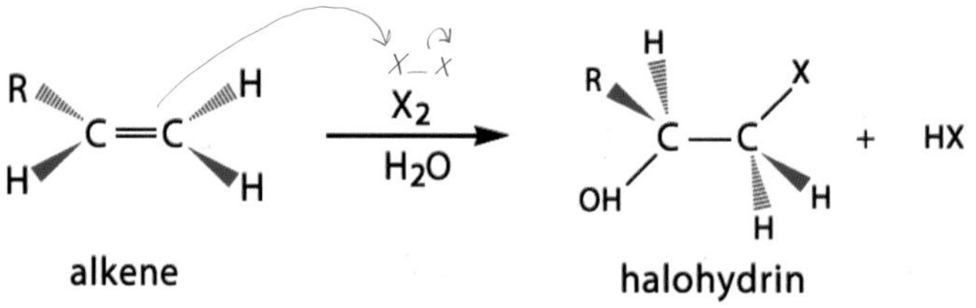

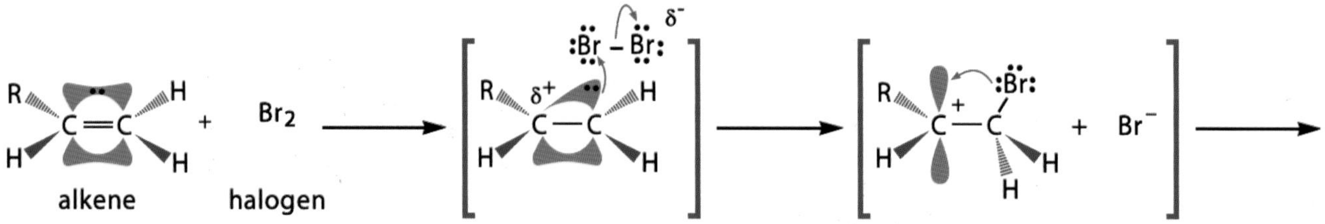

alkene   halohydrin

alkene   halogen

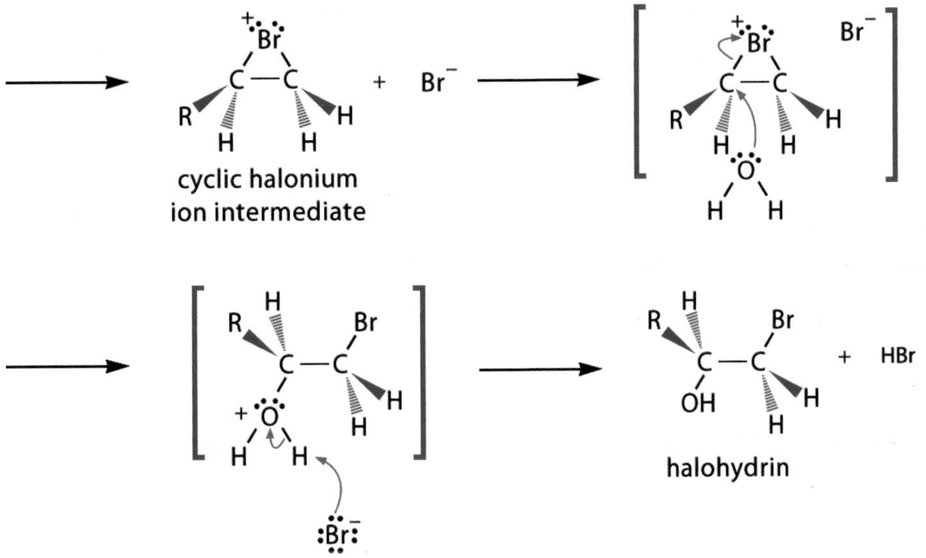

cyclic halonium
ion intermediate

halohydrin

•   Addition of water by oxymercuration: When an alkene is treated with mercuric acetate $Hg(OAc)_2$, electrophilic addition to the alkene occurs and an alcohol is produced. Instead of forming a bromonium ion as in halohydrin formation, an intermediate mercurinium ion is formed. A nucleophilic attack of the water molecule to the intermediate ion yields the final alcohol product: the hydroxyl group attaches to the more substituted carbon atom. Markovnikoff regiochemistry is observed.

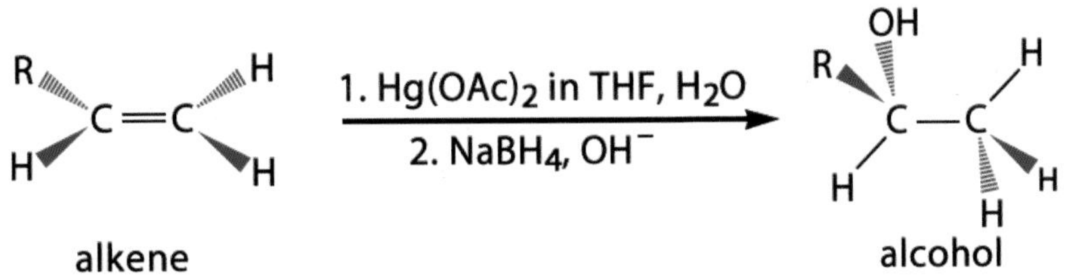

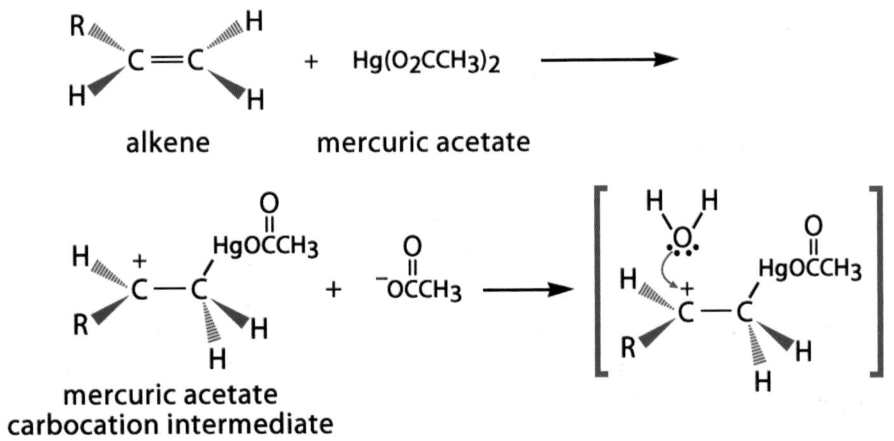

alkene   alcohol

alkene   mercuric acetate

mercuric acetate
carbocation intermediate

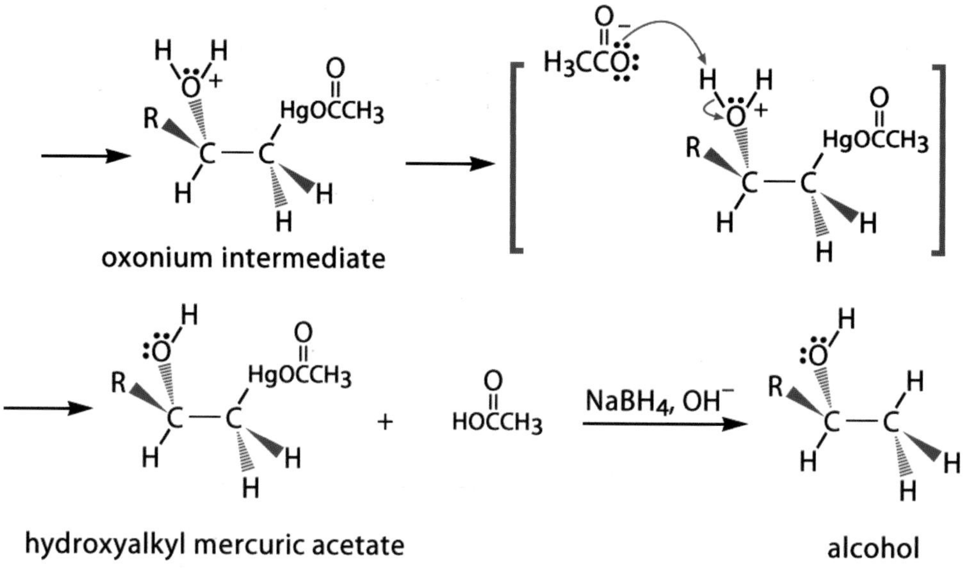

oxonium intermediate

hydroxyalkyl mercuric acetate   alcohol

•   Addition of HX: As we have seen earlier in this section, this reaction occurs via a carbocation intermediate. The halide ion then combines with the carbocation to give an alkyl halide. The proton will add to the less substituted carbon atom, yielding a more substituted (stabilized) carbocation. Markovnikoff regiochemistry is observed. This can be seen in the first two mechanisms shown in this section (ORG 4.2.1).

•   Free radical addition of HBr to alkenes: Once a bromine free radical has formed in an initiation step (ORG 3.2.2), it adds to the alkene double bond, yielding an alkyl radical. The regiochemistry of this free radical addition is determined in the first propagation step because, instead of H attacking first in electrophilic addition, the bromine radical adds first to the alkene. Thus anti-Markovnikoff addition is observed.

    The stability order of radicals is identical to the stability order of carbocations, tertiary being the most stable and methyl the least.

    Notice that the free radical reaction mechanism that follows uses single headed arrows to follow the movement of single electrons, as opposed to the normal arrows that we have seen which follow the movement of electron pairs.

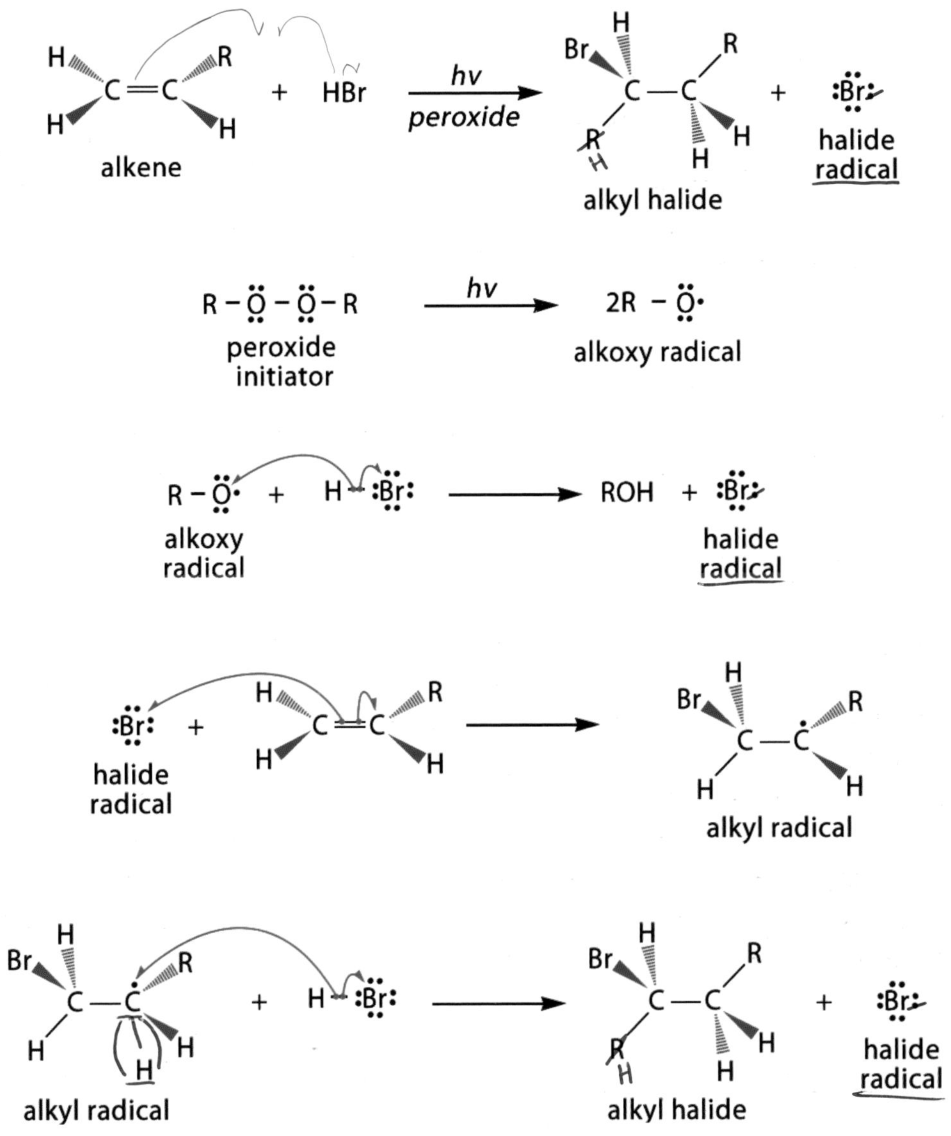

alkene + HBr → (hv, peroxide) → alkyl halide + halide radical

peroxide initiator → (hv) → 2R – Ö· alkoxy radical

alkoxy radical + H–Br → ROH + halide radical

halide radical + alkene → alkyl radical

alkyl radical + H–Br → alkyl halide + halide radical

4.2.2 Oxidation

Alkenes can undergo a variety of reactions in which the carbon-carbon double bond is oxidized. Using potassium permanganate ($KMnO_4$) under mild conditions (*no heat*), or osmium tetroxide (OsO_4), a glycol (= *a dialcohol*) can be produced.

In the following chapters, you will learn how to derive systematic nomenclature (these are names of compounds based on rules as opposed to "common" names often based on tradition). IUPAC (official) nomenclature is usually systematic (i.e. ethane-1,2-diol) but sometimes it is not (i.e. acetic acid). Knowing both the common and the systematic names is the safest way to approach the DAT.

The first reaction that follows is the oxidation of ethene (= ethylene) under mild conditions and the second is the oxidation of 2-butene under abrasive conditions.

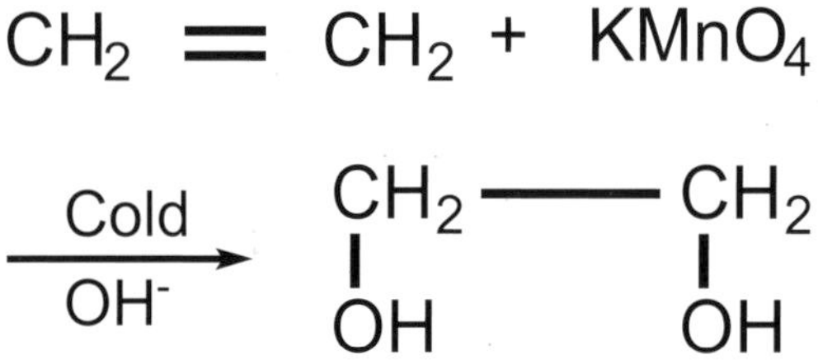

$$CH_2 = CH_2 + KMnO_4$$

$$\xrightarrow[OH^-]{Cold}$$

CH$_2$——CH$_2$
| |
OH   OH

Ethylene glycol
(1,2-ethanediol or ethane-1,2-diol)

Using $KMnO_4$ under more abrasive conditions leads to an oxidative cleavage of the double bond:

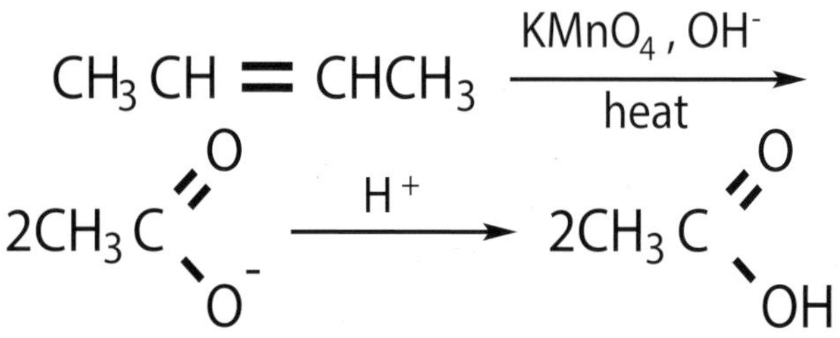

$$CH_3CH = CHCH_3 \xrightarrow[heat]{KMnO_4, OH^-}$$

$2CH_3C \overset{O}{\underset{O^-}{\diagup}}$ $\xrightarrow{H^+}$ $2CH_3C \overset{O}{\underset{OH}{\diagup}}$

Acetate ion   Acetic acid
(ethanoate ion)   (ethanoic acid)

Specifically, cold dilute $KMnO_4$ produces 1,2-diols with the syn orientation. Hot, basic $KMnO_4$ leads to oxidative cleavage of the double bonds with the double bond being replaced with a C=O bond and an O atom added to each H atom.

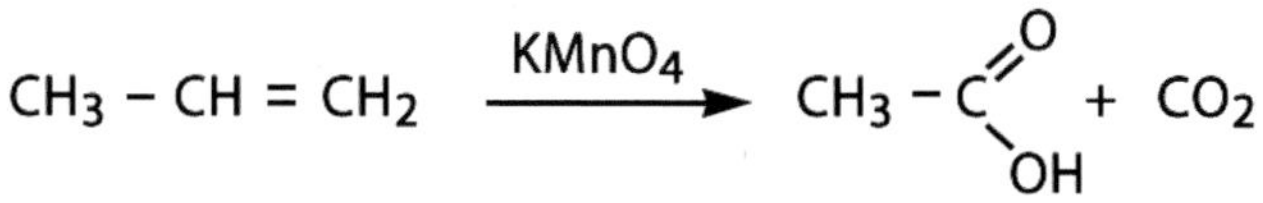

$$CH_3 - CH = CH_2 \xrightarrow{KMnO_4} CH_3 - C\overset{O}{\underset{OH}{\diagup}} + CO_2$$

acetic acid

$$CH_3 - CH = C\overset{CH_3}{\underset{CH_3}{\diagup}} \xrightarrow{KMnO_4}$$

$CH_3 - C\overset{O}{\underset{OH}{\diagup}}$ + $O = C\overset{CH_3}{\underset{CH_3}{\diagdown}}$

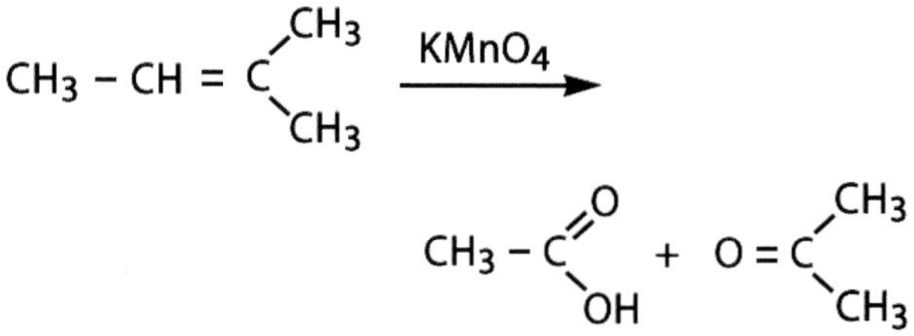

acetic acid   acetone

$$CH_2 = CH - CH = CH_2 \xrightarrow{KMnO_4} CO_2 \text{ only}$$

Ozone (O_3) reacts vigorously with alkenes. The reaction (= *ozonolysis*) leads to an oxidative cleavage of the double bond which can produce a ketone and an aldehyde:

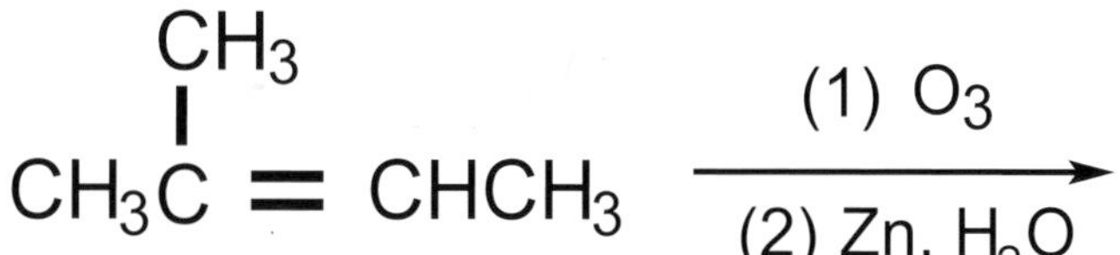

$$CH_3\overset{CH_3}{\overset{|}{C}} = CHCH_3 \xrightarrow[(2) Zn, H_2O]{(1) O_3}$$

2-Methyl-2-butene

$$CH_3\overset{CH_3}{\overset{|}{C}} = O + CH_3\overset{O}{\overset{||}{C}}H$$

Acetone   Acetaldehyde
(propanone)   (ethanal)

Note that the second step in the reaction uses a reducing agent such as zinc metal. If the starting alkene has a tetra-substituted double bond (i.e. 4 R groups), two ketones will be formed. If it has a tri-substituted double bond, a ketone and an aldehyde will be formed as in the reaction shown. If it has a di-substituted double bond, two aldehydes will be formed.

The hydroboration–oxidation reaction is a two-step organic reaction that converts an alkene into an alcohol by the addition of water across the double bond. The hydrogen and hydroxyl group are added in a syn addition leading to *cis* stereochemistry. Hydroboration–oxidation is an anti-Markovnikoff reaction since the hydroxyl group (not the hydrogen) attaches to the less substituted carbon.

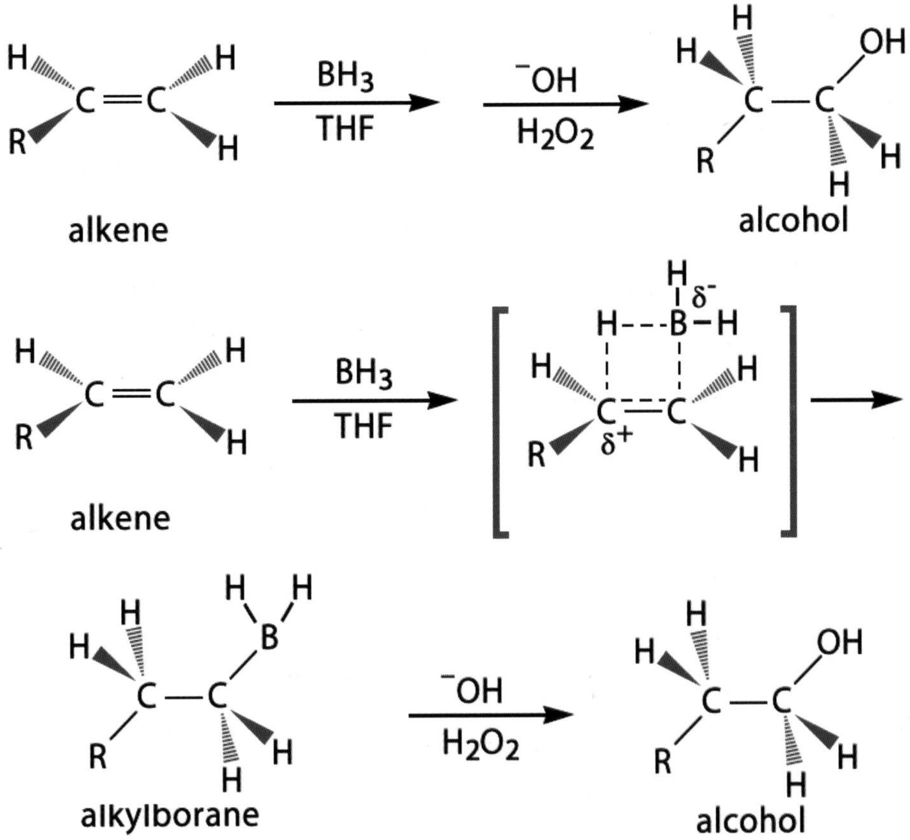

alkene → BH₃ THF → ⁻OH H₂O₂ → alcohol

alkene → BH₃ THF → [intermediate] →

alkylborane → ⁻OH H₂O₂ → alcohol

•   Epoxide Formation: Alkenes can be oxidized with peroxycarboxylic acids (i.e. CH_3CO_3H or mCPBA). The product is an oxirane (discussed in ORG 10.1.1, ethers).

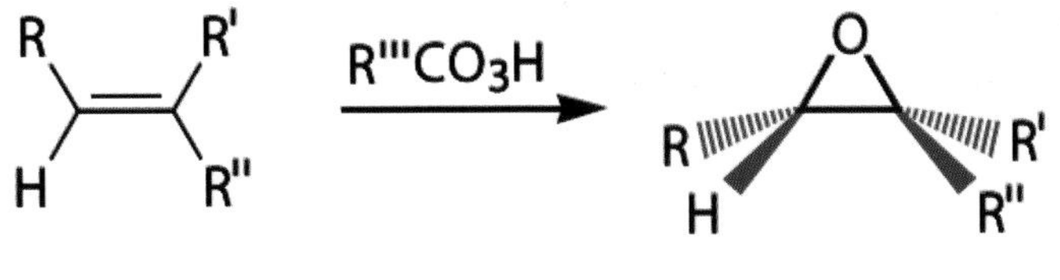

4.2.3 Hydrogenation

Alkenes react with hydrogen in the presence of a variety of metal catalysts (i.e. Ni – nickel, Pd – palladium, Pt – platinum). The reaction that occurs is an *addition* reaction since one atom of hydrogen adds to each carbon of the double bond (= *hydrogenation*). Both hydrogens add to the double bond from the same metal catalyst surface, thus syn addition is observed. Since there are two phases present in the process of hydrogenation (the hydrogen and the metal catalyst), the process is referred to as a heterogenous catalysis.

A carbon with multiple bonds is not bonded to the maximum number of atoms that potentially that carbon could possess. Thus it is *unsaturated*. Alkanes, which can be formed by hydrogenation, are *saturated* since each carbon is bonded to the maximum number of atoms it could possess (= *four*). Thus hydrogenation is sometimes called the process of saturation.

$$CH_3CH = CH_2 + H_2 \longrightarrow CH_3CH_2 - CH_3$$

Alkenes are much more reactive than other functional groups towards hydrogenation. As a result, other functional groups such as ketones, aldehydes, esters and nitriles are usually unchanged during the alkene hydrogenation process.

4.2.4 The Diels–Alder Reaction

The Diels–Alder reaction is a cycloaddition reaction between a conjugated diene and a substituted alkene (= the dienophile) to form a substituted cyclohexene system.

> Diene + Dienophile = Cyclohexene

All Diels-Alder reactions have four common features: (1) the reaction is initiated by heat; (2) the reaction forms new six-membered rings; (3) three π bonds break and two new C-C σ bonds and one new C-C π bond are formed; (4) all bonds break and form in a single step.

The Diels Alder diene must have the two double bonds on the same side of the single bond in one of the structures, which is called the s-*cis* conformation (s-*cis*: *cis* with respect to the single bond). If double bonds are on the opposite sides of the single bond in the Lewis structure, this is called the s-*trans* conformation (s-*trans*: *trans* with respect to the single bond).

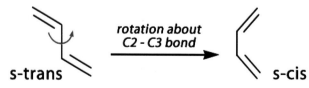

s-trans   *rotation about C2 - C3 bond* →   s-cis

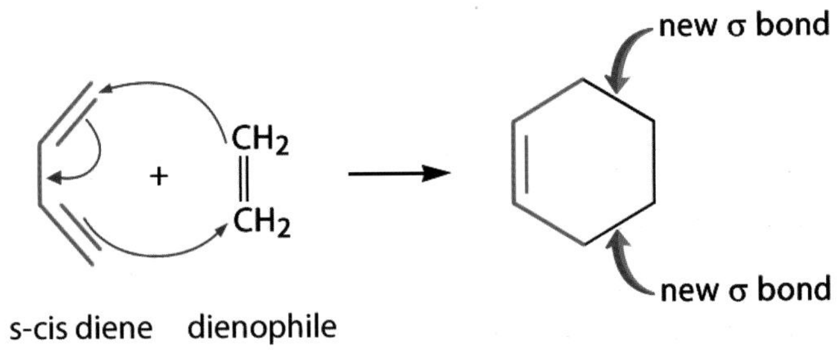

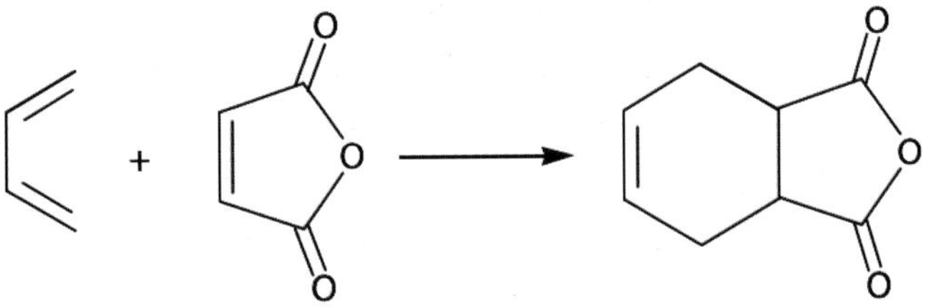

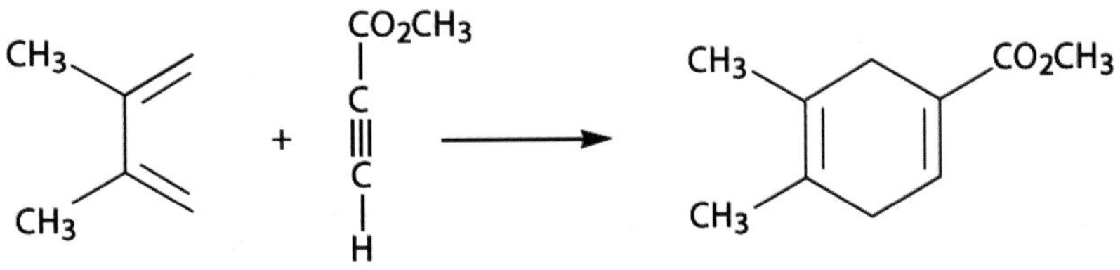

s-cis diene   dienophile

new σ bond

new σ bond

The Diels-Alder reaction is useful because it sometimes creates stereocenters, it always forms a ring, and the reaction is stereospecific (i.e. the reaction mechanism dictates the stereoisomers). For example, a *cis* dienophile generates a ring with *cis* substitution, while a *trans* dienophile generates a ring with *trans* substitution.

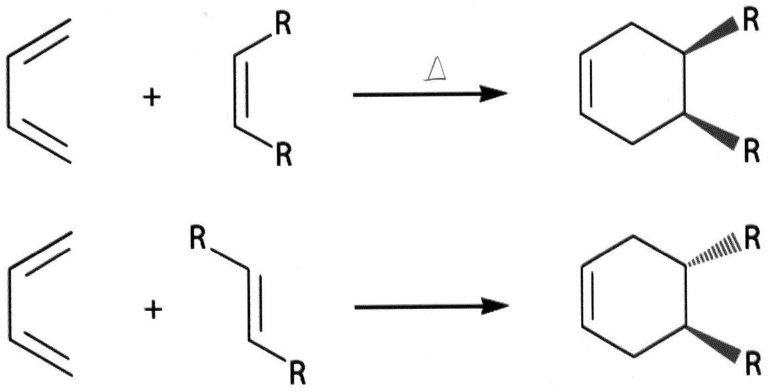

Diels-Alder reactions are reversible (= "Retro-Diels-Alder"). by adding (H+)

4.2.5 Resonance Revisited

General Chemistry section 3.2 and Organic Chemistry section 1.4 are important to review before you move on to the next chapter on Aromatics. Many exam questions rely on your understanding of resonance and how it affects stability and reactions. It is helpful to remember that the only difference between different resonance forms is the placement of π or non-bonding electrons. The atoms themselves do not change positions, create new bonds nor are they "resonating" back and forth. The resonance hybrid with its electrons delocalized is more stable than any single resonance form. The greater the numbers of authentic resonance forms possible, the more stable the molecule.

4.3 Alkynes

Alkynes are unsaturated hydrocarbon molecules containing carbon-carbon triple bonds. The nomenclature is the same as that for alkenes, except that the suffix 'yne' replaces 'ene'. Alkynes have a higher boiling point than alkenes or alkanes. Internal alkynes, where the triple bond is in the middle of the compound, boil at higher temperatures than terminal alkynes. Terminal alkynes are relatively acidic.

Basic reactions such as reduction, electrophilic addition, free radical addition and hydroboration proceed in a similar manner to alkenes. Oxidation also follows the same rules and uses the same reactants and catalysts. However, unlike alkenes, alkynes can be partially hydrogenated yielding alkenes with just one equivalent of H_2. The reaction with palladium in Lindlar's catalyst produces the *cis* alkene while sodium or lithium in liquid ammonia will produce the *trans* alkene via a free radical mechanism.

Go online to DAT-prep.com for chapter review Q&A and forum.

○ Carbonyl group

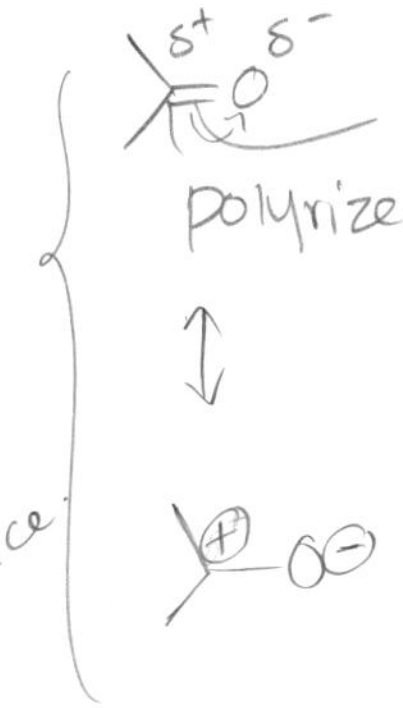

$$\sigma \ \& \ \pi \text{ bonds}$$

polarized bond

$\updownarrow$

increased stability with resonance.

• which reacts fastest with NaCN? — Spectator ion

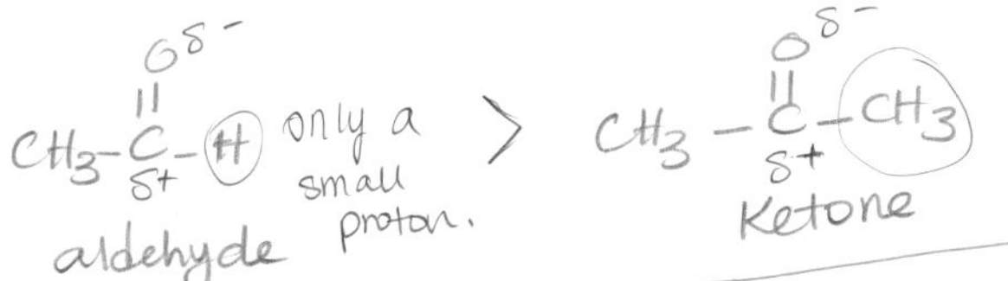

$$CH_3-\overset{O^{\delta-}}{\underset{\delta+}{\overset{\|}{C}}}-H \quad \text{only a small proton.} \quad > \quad CH_3-\overset{O^{\delta-}}{\underset{\delta+}{\overset{\|}{C}}}-CH_3$$

aldehyde

Ketone

Steric hinderance — bulkiness of the molecule.

NaCN

unstable bond btween 2 C−C $\delta+$.

So e⁻ can come back down and kick out the $CF_3^{(-)}$.

most electronegative, making adjacent Carbon more $\delta+$, more Susceptible to Nu: attacks

$$CF_3 - \overset{O}{\overset{\|}{C}} - H \quad > \quad CH_3 - \overset{O}{\overset{\|}{C}} - H$$

AROMATICS

Chapter 5

Memorize	Understand	Importance
IUPAC nomenclature Hückel's rule for identifying aromatic compounds	* Activating and deactivating groups * Importance of resonance * Substituent effects on the ring	**2 to 4 out of the 30 ORG** DAT questions are based on content in this chapter (in our estimation). * Note that between 30% and 60% of the questions in DAT Organic Chemistry are based on content from 4 chapters: 1, 2, 5 and 6.

DAT-Prep.com

Introduction

Aromatics are cyclic compounds with unusual stability due to cyclic delocalization and resonance.

Additional Resources

Free Online Q&A + Forum

Video: Online or DVD

Flashcards

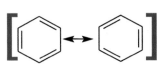

Special Guest

5.1 Description and Nomenclature

Aromatic compounds are cyclic and have their π electrons delocalized over the entire ring and are thus stabilized by π-electron delocalization. Benzene is the simplest of all the aromatic hydrocarbons. The term *aromatic* has historical significance in that many well known fragrant compounds were found to be derivatives of benzene. Although at present, it is known that not all benzene derivatives have fragrance, the term remains in use today to describe benzene derivatives and related compounds.

Benzene is known to have only one type of carbon-carbon bond, with a bond length of ≈ 1.4 Å (angstroms, 10^{-10}m) somewhere between that of a single and double bond. Benzene is a hexagonal, flat symmetrical molecule. All C-C-C bond angles are 120° and all C-C bonds are of equal length - a value between a normal single and double bond length; all six carbon atoms are sp^2 hybridized; and, all carbons have a p orbital perpendicular to the benzene ring, leading to six π electrons delocalized around the ring. The benzene molecule may thus be represented by two different resonance structures, showing it to be the average of the two:

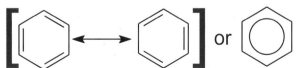

Many monosubstituted benzenes have common names by which they are known.

Others are named by substituents attached to the aromatic ring. Some of these are:

OH — phenol

CH_3 — toluene

NH_2 — aniline

NO_2 — nitrobenzene

CO_2H — benzoic acid

Disubstituted benzenes are named as derivatives of their primary substituents. In this case, either the usual numbering or the ortho-meta-para system may be used. Ortho (*o*) substituents are at the 2nd position from the primary substituent; meta (*m*) substituents are at the 3rd position; para (*p*) substituents are at the 4th position. If there are more than two substituents on the aromatic ring, the numbering system is used. Some examples are:

CH_3 ... NO_2

m - Nitrotoluene

NO_2 NO_2

o - Dinitrobenzene

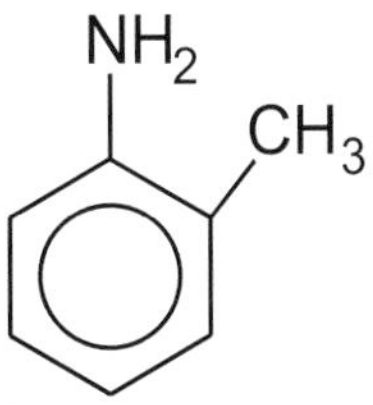

o- Methylaniline
o- Aminotoluene

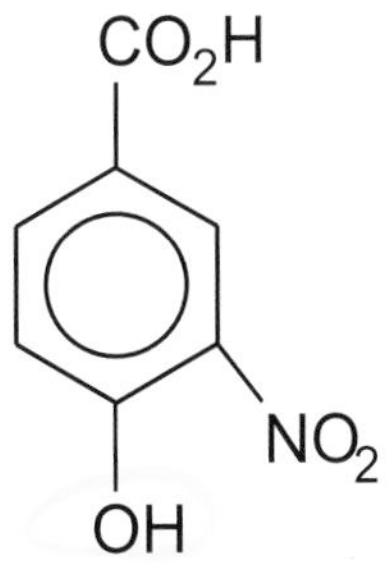

3 - nitro - 4 -
hydroxybenzoic acid

When benzene is a substituent, it is called a *phenyl or aryl group*. The shorthand for phenyl is Ph. Toluene without a hydrogen on the methyl substituent is called a *benzyl group*.

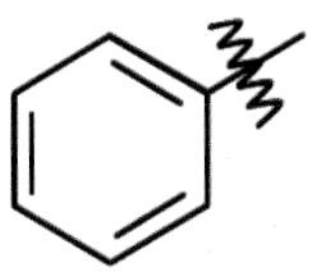

phenyl group

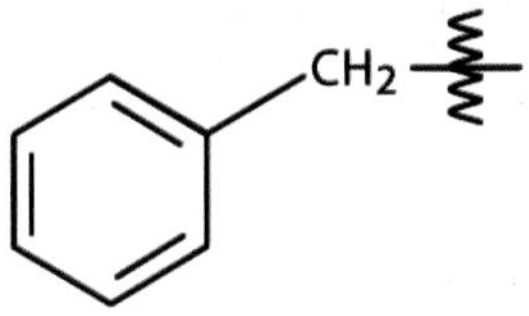

benzyl group

Benzene undergoes substitution reactions that retain the cyclic conjugation as opposed to electrophilic addition reactions.

5.1.1 Hückel's Rule

If a compound does not meet all the following criteria, it is likely not aromatic.

non-aromatic
1. The molecule is cyclic.
2. The molecule is planar.
3. The molecule is fully conjugated (i.e. p orbitals at every atom in the ring; ORG 1.4).

anti-aromatic
4. The molecule has 4n + 2 π electrons.

If rules 1., 2. and/or 3. are broken, then the molecule is non-aromatic. If rule 4. is broken then the molecule is antiaromatic.

Notice that the number of π delocalized electrons must be even but NOT a multiple of 4. So 4n + 2 number of π electrons, where n = 0, 1, 2, 3, and so on, is known as Hückel's Rule. Thus the number of pi electrons can be 2, 6, 10, etc. Of course, benzene is aromatic (6 electrons, from 3 double bonds), but cyclobutadiene is not, since the number of π delocalized electrons is 4. Note that a cyclic molecule with conjugated double bonds in a monocyclic (= 1 ring) hydrocarbon is called an annulene. So cyclobutadiene can be called [4] annulene.

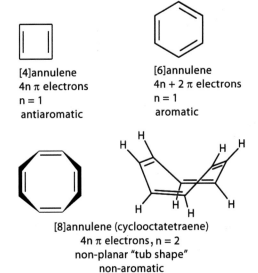

[4]annulene
4n π electrons
n = 1
antiaromatic

[6]annulene
4n + 2 π electrons
n = 1
aromatic

[8]annulene (cyclooctatetraene)
4n π electrons, n = 2
non-planar "tub shape"
non-aromatic

The number of p orbitals and the number of π electrons can be different, which means, whether a molecule is neutral, a cation or an anion, it can be aromatic. Note that aliphatic describes all compounds that are aromatic. A cyclic compound containing only 4n electrons is said to be anti-aromatic.

- Cyclopentadienide anion:

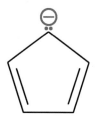

Because of the lone pair, there are 6 π electrons, which meets Hückel's number, so it is aromatic. Thus you can see that if an electron pair is added, or subtracted, a molecule can then become aromatic by fulfilling Hückel's rule. Therefore, if 2 electrons are added to [8]annalene, it will then become a more stable molecule. Specifically, the cyclooctatetraenide dianion ($C_8H_8^{2-}$) is aromatic (thus it has increased stability), and planar, like the cyclopentadienide anion, and both fulfill Hückel's rule.

- Cycloheptatrienyl cation:

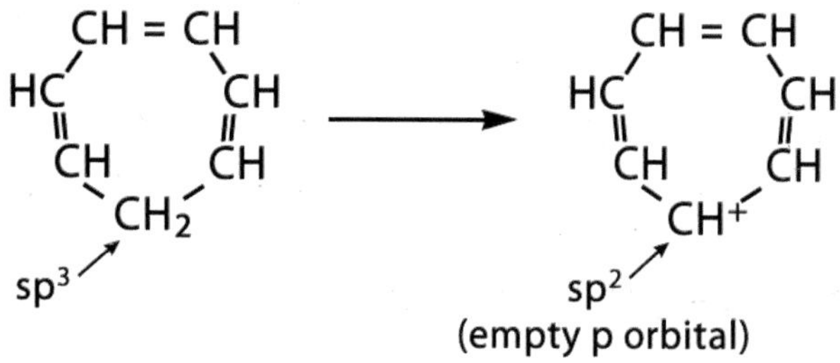

6 π electrons with conjugation through resonance because of the cation, meets Hückel's number, so it is aromatic.

Heterocyclic compounds can be aromatic as well.

- Pyridine:

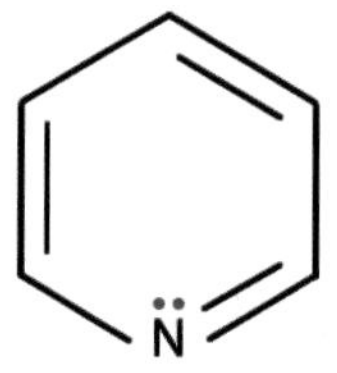

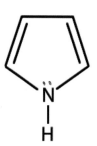

Each sp^2 hybridized carbon atom has a p orbital and contains one π electron. The nitrogen atom is also sp^2 hybridized and has one electron in the p orbital, bringing the total to six π electrons. The nitrogen nonbonding electron pair is in a sp^2 orbital perpendicular to other p orbitals and is not involved with the π system. Thus pyridine is aromatic.

- Pyrrole:

Each sp^2 hybridized carbon atom has a p orbital and contains one π electron. The nitrogen atom is also sp^2 hybridized with its nonbonding electron pair sitting in the p orbital, bringing the total to six π electrons. Thus pyrrole is aromatic.

5.2 Electrophilic Aromatic Substitution

One important reaction of aromatic compounds is known as electrophilic aromatic substitution, which occurs with electrophilic reagents. The reaction is similar to a S_N1 mechanism in that an addition leads to a rearrangement which produces a substitution. However, in this case it is the electrophile (*not a nucleophile*) which substitutes for an atom in the original molecule. The reaction may be summarized:

Note that the intermediate positive charge is stabilized by resonance.

It is important to understand that the electrophile used in electrophilic aromatic substitution must always be a powerful electrophile. After all, the resonance stabilized aromatic ring is resistant to many types of routine chemical reactions (i.e. oxidation with $KMnO_4$ – ORG 4.2.2, electrophilic addition with acid - ORG 4.2.1, and hydrogenation - ORG 4.2.3). Remembering that Br, a halide, is already very electronegative (CHM 2.3), Br^+ is an example of a powerful electrophile. In a reaction called bromination, $Br_2/FeBr_3$ is used to generate the Br^+ species which adds to the aromatic ring. Similar reactions are performed to "juice up" other potential substituents (i.e. alkyl, acyl, iodine, etc.) to become powerful electrophiles to add to the aromatic ring.

• Aromatic halogenation: The benzene ring with its 6 π electrons in a conjugated system acts as an electron nucleophile (electron donor) in most chemical reactions. It reacts with bromine, chlorine or iodine to produce mono-substituted products. Fluorine is too reactive and tends to produce multi-substituted products. Therefore, the electrophilic substitution reaction is characteristic of aromaticity and can be used as a diagnostic tool to test the presence of an aromatic ring.

benzene + X_2 $\xrightarrow[\text{or } FeX_3]{Fe}$ halobenzene — X + HX hydrogen halide

halogen (X = Cl or Br)

• **Aromatic nitration**: The aromatic ring can be nitrated when reacted with a mixture of nitric and sulfuric acid. The benzene ring reacts with the electrophile in this reaction, the nitronium ion NO_2^+, yielding a carbocation intermediate in a similar way as the aromatic halogenation reaction.

$+ HNO_3$ $\xrightarrow[50\,°C]{H_2SO_4 \text{ catalyst}}$ NO_2

• **Aromatic sulfonation**: Aromatic rings can react with a mixture of sulfuric acid and sulfur trioxide (H_2SO_4/SO_3) to form sulfonic acid. The electrophile in this reaction is either HSO_3 or SO_3.

$\xrightarrow[-H_2O]{H_2SO_4/SO_3}$ SO_3H

• **Friedel-Crafts alkylation**: This is an electrophilic aromatic substitution in which the benzene ring is alkylated when it reacts with an alkyl halide. The benzene ring attacks the alkyl cation electrophile, yielding an alkyl-substituted benzene product.

There are several limitations to this reaction:

1. The reaction does not proceed on an aromatic ring that has a strong deactivating substituent group.

2. Because the product is attacked even faster by alkyl carbocations than the starting material, poly-alkylation is often observed.

3. Skeletal rearrangement of the alkyl group sometimes occurs. A hydride shift or an alkyl shift may produce a more stable carbocation.

$R-Cl + FeCl_3 \longrightarrow R^+ + FeCl_4^-$

$\xrightarrow[\text{catalyst regenerated}]{- HCl}$

• **Friedel-Crafts acylation**: An electrophilic aromatic substitution in which the benzene ring is acylated when an acyl group is introduced to the ring. The mechanism is similar to that of Friedel-Crafts alkylation. The electrophile is an acyl cation generated by the reaction between the acyl halide and $AlCl_3$. Because the product is less reactive than the starting material, only mono-substitution is observed.

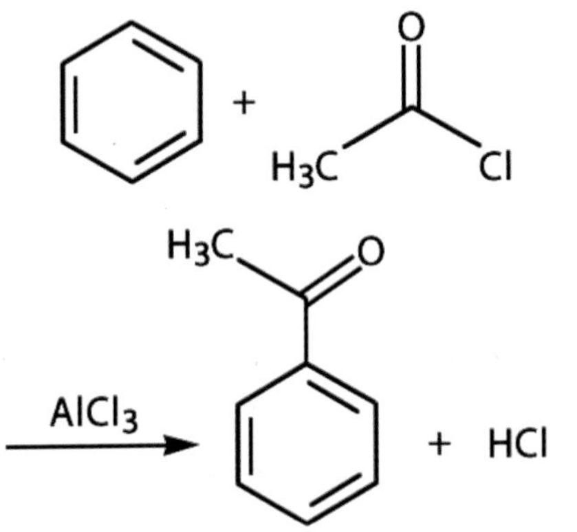

When groups are attached to the aromatic ring, the intermediate charge delocalization is affected. Thus nature of first substituent on the ring determines the position of the second substituent. Substituents can be classified into three classes: ortho-para (o-p) directing activators, ortho-para directing deactivators, and meta-directing deactivators. As implied, these groups indicate where most of the electrophile will end up in the reaction.

5.2.1 O-P Directors

If a substituted benzene reacts more rapidly than a benzene alone, the substituent group is said to be an _activating group_. Activating groups can *donate* electrons to the ring.

Thus the ring is more attractive to an electrophile. All activating groups are o/p directors. Some examples are $-OH, -NH_2, -OR, -NR_2$, $-OCOR$ and alkyl groups.

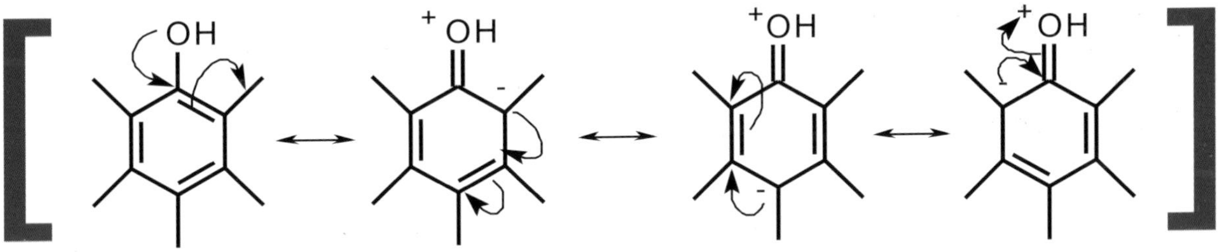

Note that the partial electron density (δ^-) is at the ortho and para positions, so the electrophile favors attack at these positions. Good stabilization results with a substituent at the ortho or para positions:

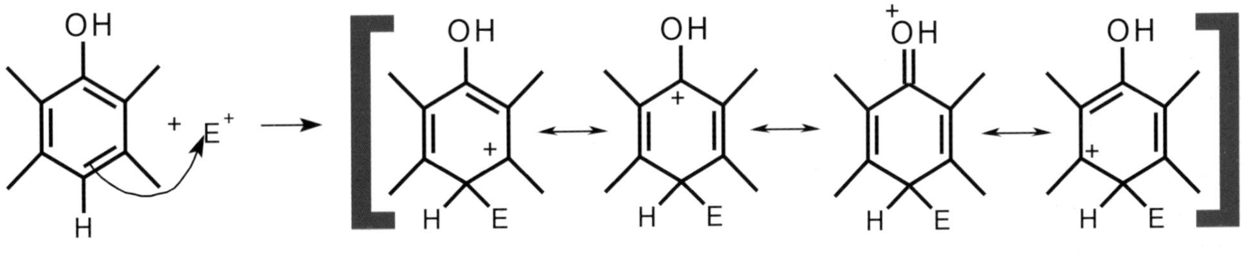

When there is a substituent at the meta position, the −OH can no longer help to delocalize the positive charge, so the o-p positions are favored over the meta:

Note that even though the substituents are o-p directors, probability suggests that there will still be a small percentage of the electrophile that will add at the meta position.

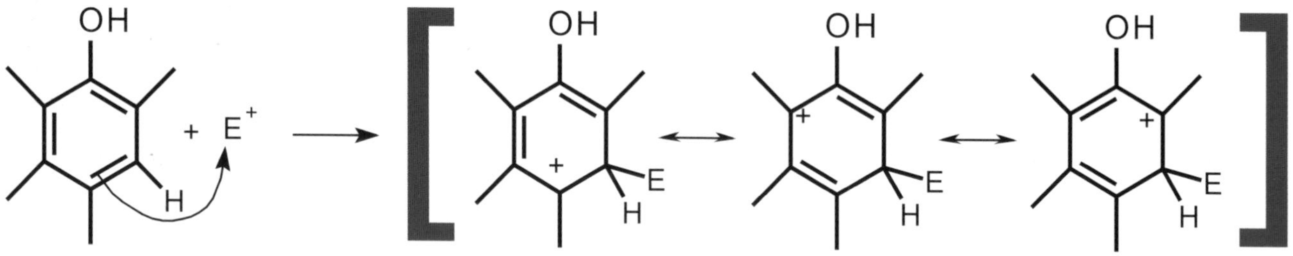

5.2.2 Meta Directors

If a substituted benzene reacts more slowly than the benzene alone, the substituent group is said to be a deactivating group. Deactivating groups can *withdraw* electrons from the ring. Thus the ring is less attractive to an electrophile. All deactivating groups are meta directors, with the exception of the weakly deactivating halides which are o−p directors (-F, -Cl, -Br, -I). Some examples of meta direc-

tors are −NO$_2$, −SO$_2$, −CN, -SO$_3$H, -COOH, -COOR, -COR, CHO.

Without any substituents, the partial positive charge density (δ^+) will be at the o−p positions. Thus the electrophile avoids the positive charge and favors attack at the meta position:

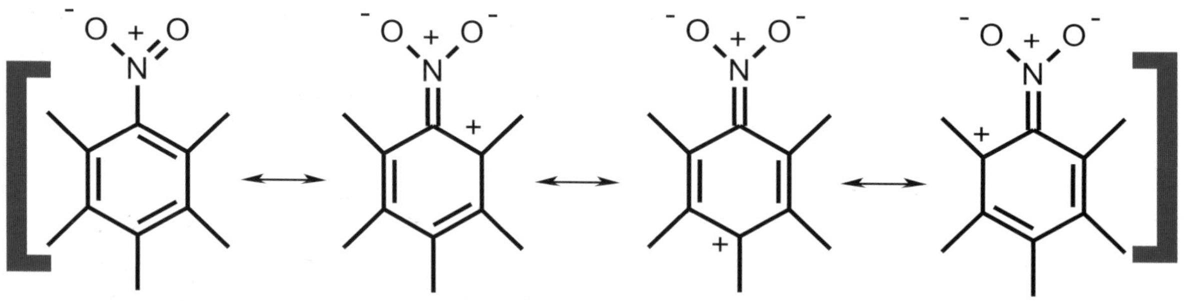

If you are seeking another way to learn, consider logging into your DAT-prep.com account and clicking on Videos to choose the Aromatic Chemistry videos.

With a substituent at the meta position:

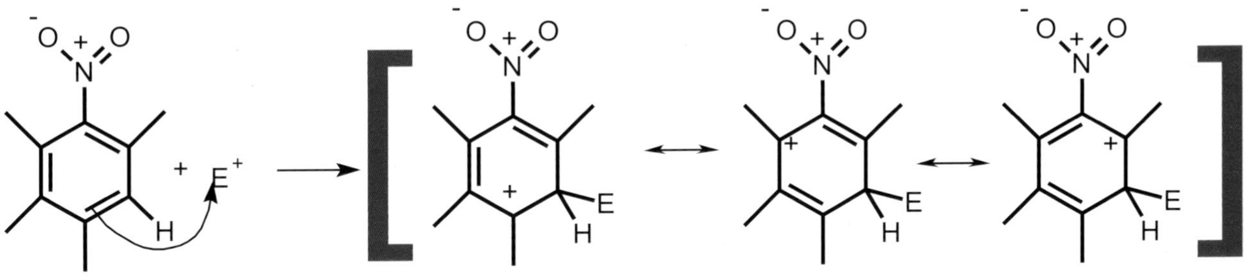

Note that even though the substituents are meta directors, probability suggests that there will still be a smaller percentage of the electrophile that will add at the o–p positions.

5.2.3 Reactions with the Alkylbenzene Side Chain

• Oxidation: Alkyl groups on the benzene ring react rapidly with oxidizing agents and are converted into a carboxyl group. The net result is the conversion of an alkylbenzene into benzoic acid.

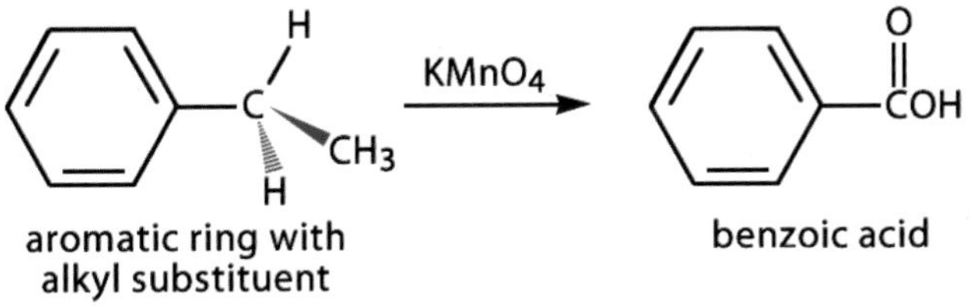

aromatic ring with
alkyl substituent

benzoic acid

• Bromination: NBS (N-bromosuccinimide) reacts with alkylbenzene through a radical chain mechanism (ORG 3.2.2): the benzyl radical generated from NBS in the presence of benzoyl peroxide reacts with Br_2 to yield the final product and bromine radical, which will cycle back into the reaction to act as a radical initiator. The reaction occurs exclusively at the benzyl position because the benzyl radical is highly stabilized through different forms of resonance.

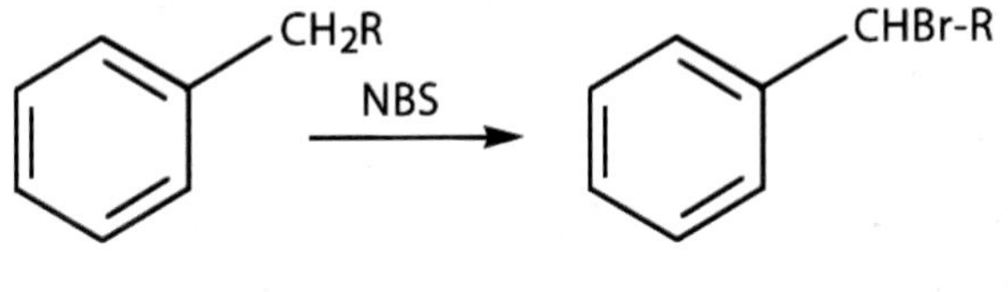

• Reduction: Reductions of aryl alkyl ketones in the presence of H_2 and Pd/C can be used to convert the aryl alkyl ketone generated by the Friedel-Crafts acylation reaction into an alkylbenzene.

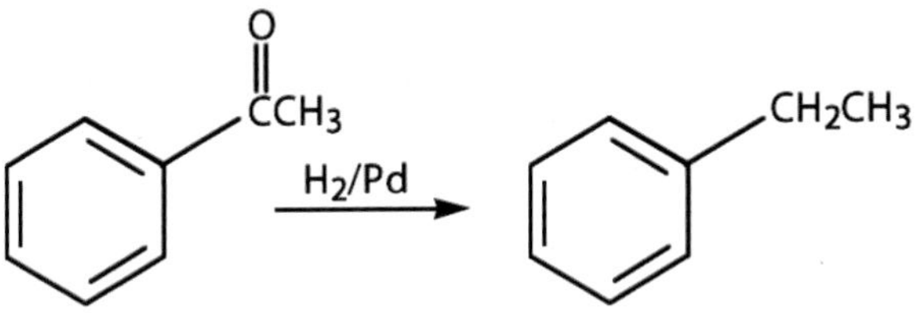

Go online to DAT-prep.com for chapter review Q&A and forum.

ALCOHOLS

Chapter 6

Memorize	Understand	Importance
* IUPAC nomenclature * Physical properties * Products of oxidation * Define: steric hindrance	* Trends based on length, branching * Effect of hydrogen bonds * Mechanisms of reactions * Nucleophilic substitution	**4 to 6 out of the 30 ORG** DAT questions are based on content in this chapter (in our estimation). * Note that between 30% and 60% of the questions in DAT Organic Chemistry are based on content from 4 chapters: 1, 2, 5 and 6.

DAT-Prep.com

Introduction ▧▦▧█

An alcohol is any organic compound in which a hydroxyl group (-OH) is bound to a carbon atom of an alkyl or substituted alkyl group.

Additional Resources

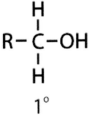

Free Online Q&A + Forum　　Video: Online or DVD　　Flashcards　　Special Guest

6.1 Description and Nomenclature

The systematic naming of alcohols is accomplished by replacing the −e of the corresponding alkane with −ol.

Alcohols are compounds that have hydroxyl groups bonded to a saturated carbon atom with the general formula ROH. It can be thought of as a substituted water molecule, with one of the water hydrogens replaced with an alkyl group R. Alcohols are classified as primary (1°), secondary (2°) or tertiary (3°):

$$
\begin{array}{ccc}
\text{H} & \text{H} & \text{R} \\
| & | & | \\
\text{R}-\text{C}-\text{OH} & \text{R}-\text{C}-\text{OH} & \text{R}-\text{C}-\text{OH} \\
| & | & | \\
\text{H} & \text{R} & \text{R} \\
1° & 2° & 3°
\end{array}
$$

As with alkanes, special names are used for branched groups:

$$
\begin{array}{cc}
\text{OH} & \text{OH} \\
| & | \\
\text{CH}_3-\text{CH}-\text{CH}_3 & \text{CH}_3-\text{C}-\text{CH}_3 \\
 & | \\
 & \text{CH}_3
\end{array}
$$

IUPAC: propan-2-ol
- Isopropanol
- Isopropyl alcohol

IUPAC: 2-methylpropan-2-ol
- 2-methyl-2-propanol
- tert-butanol

The alcohols are always numbered to give the carbon with the attached hydroxy (−OH) group the lowest number (choose the longest carbon chain that contains the hydroxyl group as the parent):

$$
\begin{array}{c}
\text{OH} \\
| \\
\text{CH}_3\text{CH}_2\text{CH}_2\text{CHCH}_2\text{CH}_3
\end{array}
$$

3-hexanol NOT 4-hexanol

$$
\begin{array}{ccc}
\text{CH}_3 & \text{OH} & \text{CH}_3 \\
| & | & | \\
\text{CH}_3\text{CH}_2\text{CH}_2\,\text{CHCH}_2\,\text{CHCH}_2\,\text{CHCH}_3
\end{array}
$$

2,6-dimethyl-4-nonanol

The shorthand for methanol is MeOH, and the shorthand for ethanol is EtOH. Alcohols are weak acids ($K_a \approx 10^{-18}$), being weaker acids than water. Their conjugate bases are called alkoxides, very little of which will be present in solution:

$$C_2H_5OH + OH^- \rightleftharpoons C_2H_5O^- + H_2O$$

ethanol   *ethoxide*

The acidity of an alcohol decreases with increasing number of attached carbons. Thus CH_3OH is more acidic than CH_3CH_2OH; and CH_3CH_2OH (a primary alcohol) is more acidic than $(CH_3)_2CHOH$ (a secondary alcohol), which is, in turn, more acidic than $(CH_3)_3COH$ (a tertiary alcohol).

Alcohols have higher boiling points and a greater solubility than comparable alkanes, alkenes, aldehydes, ketones and alkyl halides. The higher boiling point and greater solubility is due to the greater polarity and hydrogen bonding of the alcohol. In alcohols, hydrogen bonding is a weak association of the −OH proton of one molecule, with the oxygen of another. To form the hydrogen bond, both a donor, and an acceptor are required:

$$
\begin{array}{c}
\text{donor} \qquad\qquad\qquad \text{H} \quad \text{acceptor} \\
\\
\text{O}-\text{H}----\text{O} \\
| \qquad\quad {}_{\delta^+} \quad {}_{\delta^-} \quad | \\
\text{CH}_3 \qquad\qquad\qquad\qquad \text{CH}_3
\end{array}
$$

Sometimes an atom may act as both a donor and acceptor of hydrogen bonds. One example of this is the oxygen atom in an alcohol:

hydrogen bonds

As the length of the carbon chain (= R) of the alcohol molecule increases, the nonpolar chain becomes more meaningful, and the alcohol becomes less water soluble. The hydroxyl group of a primary alcohol is able to form hydrogen bonds with molecules such as water more easily than the hydroxyl group of a tertiary alcohol. The hydroxyl group of a tertiary alcohol is crowded by the surrounding methyl groups and thus its ability to participate in hydrogen bonds is lessened. As well, in solution, primary alcohols are more acidic than secondary alcohols, and secondary alcohols are more acidic than tertiary alcohols. In the gas phase, however, the order of acidity is reversed.

6.1.1 Acidity and Basicity of Alcohols

Alcohols are both weakly acidic and weakly basic. Alcohols can dissociate into a proton and its conjugate base, the alkoxy ion (alkoxide, RO^-), just as water dissociates into a proton and a hydroxide ion. As weak acids, alcohols act as proton donors, thus $ROH + H_2O \rightarrow RO^- + H_3O^+$. As weak bases, alcohols act as proton acceptors, thus $ROH + HX \rightarrow ROH_2^+ + X^-$.

Substituent effects are important in determining alcohol acidity. The more easily the alkoxide ion is accessible to a water molecule, the easier it is stabilized through solvation (CHM 5.3), the more its formation is favored, and the greater the acidity of the alcohol molecule. For example $(CH_3)_3COH$ is less acidic than CH_3OH.

Inductive effects are also important in determining alcohol acidity. Electron-withdrawing groups stabilize an alkoxide anion by spreading out the charge, thus making the alcohol molecule more acidic. Vice versa, electron-donating groups destabilize an alkoxide anion, thus making the alcohol molecule less acidic. For example $(CH_3)_3COH$ is less acidic than $(CF_3)_3OH$.

Since alcohols are weak acids, they do not react with weak bases. However, they do react with strong bases such as NaH, $NaNH_2$, or sodium or potassium metal.

$$CH_3CH_2OH + NaH \rightarrow CH_3CH_2O^-Na^+ + H_2$$

$$CH_3CH_2OH + NaNH_2 \rightarrow CH_3CH_2OH + NH_3$$

$$2CH_3CH_2OH + 2Na \rightarrow 2CH_3CH_2O^-Na^+ + H_2$$

6.1.2 Synthesis of Alcohols

1. **Hydration of alkenes:** Alcohols can be prepared through the hydration of alkenes: **(1)** Halohydrin (one carbon with a halogen and an adjacent carbon with a hydroxyl substituent) formation yields a Markovnikoff hydration product with anti stereospecificity (i.e. the OH nucleophile adds to the most substituted carbon but *opposite* to the halide); **(2)** Hydroboration-oxidation yields a syn stereospecific anti-Markovnikoff hydration product (the OH adds to the least substituted carbon); **(3)** Oxymercuration-reduction yields a Markovnikoff hydration product.

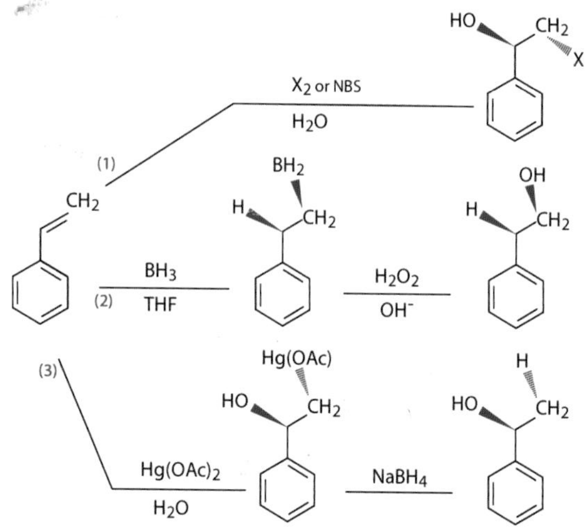

2. **Reduction of carbonyl compounds:** An alcohol can be prepared through the reduction of an aldehyde, ketone, carboxylic acid or ester. Aldehydes are converted into primary alcohols and ketones are converted into secondary alcohols in the presence of reducing agents $NaBH_4$ or $LiAlH_4$ (also symbolized as LAH or LithAl). Since $LiAlH_4$ is more powerful and more reactive than $NaBH_4$, it can be used as a reducing agent for the reduction of carboxylic acids and esters to give primary alcohols (see ORG 6.2.2).

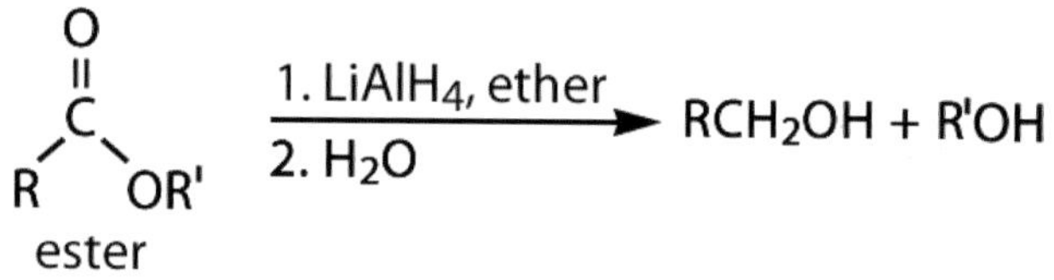

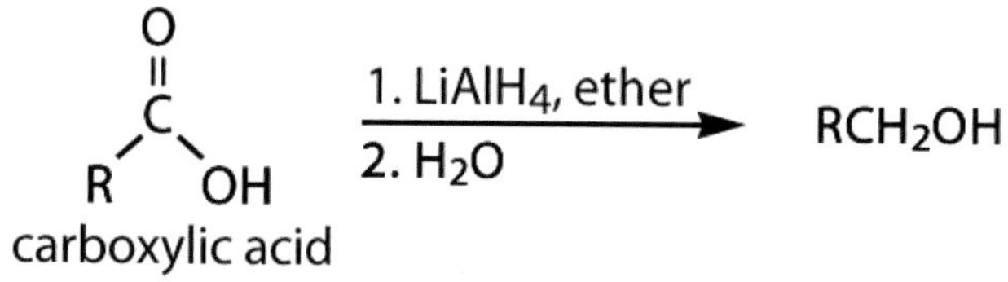

3. **Addition reaction with Grignard reagents:** Grignard reagents (RMgX) react with carbonyl compounds to give alcohols. Grignard reagents are created by reacting Mg metal with alkyl (aryl or vinyl) halide.

$$R\text{-}X + Mg \longrightarrow RMgX$$

A number of different alcohol products can be obtained from Grignard reactions with formaldehyde, other aldehydes, ketones or esters. A carboxylic acid does not give an alcohol product because, instead of addition reaction, the carboxylic acid reacts with the Grignard reagent giving a hydrocarbon and magnesium salt of the acid.

• <u>Formaldehyde</u>: Primary alcohol

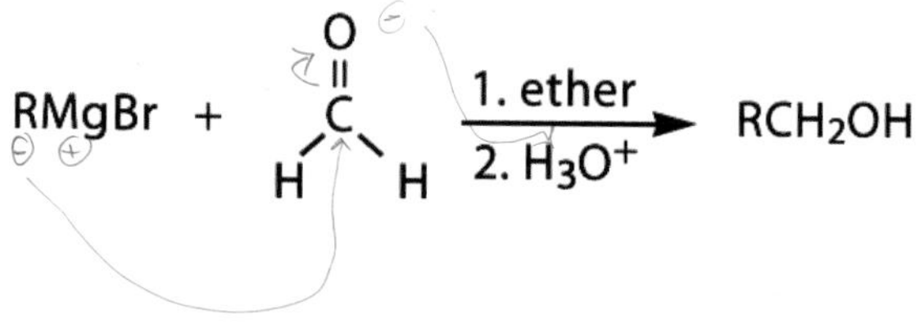

- Aldehyde: Secondary alcohol

RMgBr + [aldehyde structure: O double bond C, H and R'] $\xrightarrow[\text{2. H}_3\text{O}^+]{\text{1. ether}}$ [product: H, OH, C, R' R]

- Ketone: Tertiary alcohol

RMgBr + [ketone structure: O double bond C, R' and R''] $\xrightarrow[\text{2. H}_3\text{O}^+]{\text{1. ether}}$ [product: R, OH, C, R' R'']

- Ester: Tertiary alcohol

Two substituents from the Grignard reagent are added to the carbonyl-bearing carbon, giving a tertiary alcohol.

2RMgBr + [ester structure: O double bond C, R' and OR''] $\xrightarrow[\text{2. H}_3\text{O}^+]{\text{1. ether}}$ [product: R, OH, C, R' R] + R''OH

6.2 Important Reactions of Alcohols

6.2.1 Dehydration

Dehydration (= *loss of water*) reactions of alcohols produce alkenes. The general dehydration reaction is shown in Figure IV.B.6.1.

[reaction scheme:]
H, C–C, OH $\xrightarrow[\text{- H}_2\text{O}]{\text{+ H}^+}$ carbocation $\xrightarrow{\text{NaH}}$ C=C alkene

alcohol   carbocation   alkene

For the preceding reaction to occur, the temperature must be between 300 and 400 degrees Celsius, and the vapors must be passed over a metal oxide catalyst. Alternatively, strong, hot acids, such as H_2SO_4 or H_3PO_4 at 100 to 200 degrees Celsius may be used.

The reactivity depends upon the type of alcohol. A tertiary alcohol is more reactive than a secondary alcohol which is, in turn, more reactive than a primary alcohol. The faster reactions have the most stable carbocation intermediates. The alkene that is formed is the most stable one. A phenyl group will take preference over one or two alkyl groups, otherwise the most substituted double bond is the most stable (= *major product*) and the least substituted is less stable (= *minor product*).

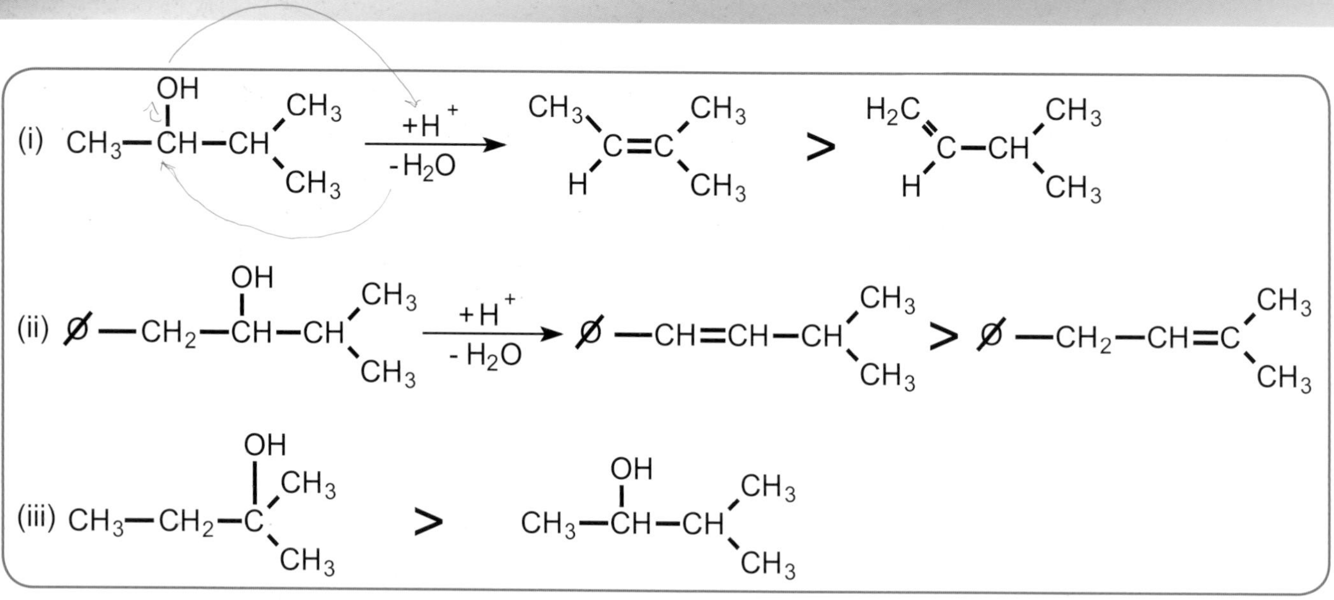

Figure IV.B.6.2: Dehydration of substituted alcohols. Major and minor products, respectively, are represented in reactions (i) and (ii). An example of a reactant with a greater reaction rate due to more substituents as an intermediate is represented by (iii). ϕ = a phenyl group.

6.2.2 Oxidation-Reduction

In organic chemistry, oxidation (O) is the increasing of oxygen or decreasing of hydrogen content, and reduction (H) is the opposite. Primary alcohols are converted to aldehydes using PCC or $KMnO_4$, under mild conditions (i.e. room temperature, neutral pH). Primary alcohols are converted to carboxylic acids using CrO_3 (the mixture is called a Jones'

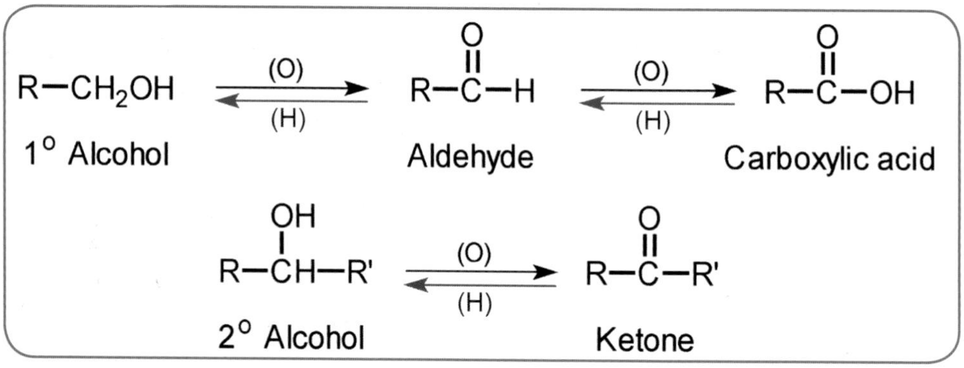

Figure IV.B.6.3: Oxidation-Reduction. In organic chemistry, traditionally the symbols R and R' denote an attached hydrogen, or a hydrocarbon side chain of any length (which are consistent with the reactions above), but sometimes these symbols refer to any group of atoms.

reagent), $K_2Cr_2O_7$, or $KMnO_4$ under abrasive conditions (i.e. increased temperature, presence of OH-). Secondary alcohols are converted to ketones by any of the preceding oxidizing agents. It is *very* difficult to oxidize a tertiary alcohol. Under acidic conditions, tertiary alcohols are unaffected; they may be oxidized under acidic conditions by dehydration and *then* oxidizing the double bond of the resultant alkene. Classic reducing agents (H) include $LiAlH_4$ (strong), H_2/metals (strong) and $NaBH_4$ (mild).

6.2.3 Substitution

In a <u>substitution reaction</u> one atom or group is *substituted* or replaced by another atom or group. For an alcohol, the –OH group is replaced (*substituted*) by a halide (usually chlorine or bromine). A variety of reagents may be used, such as HCl, HBr or PCl_3. There are two different types of substitution reactions, S_N1 and S_N2.

In the S_N1 (*1st order or monomolecular nucleophilic substitution*) reaction, the transition state involves a carbocation, the formation of which is the rate-determining step. Alcohol substitutions that proceed by this mechanism are those involving benzyl groups, allyl groups, tertiary and secondary alcohols. The mechanism of this reaction is:

(i) $R–L \rightarrow R^+ + L^-$
(ii) $Nu^- + R^+ \rightarrow Nu–R$

The important features of this reaction are:

- The reaction is first order (this means that the rate of the reaction depends only on the concentration of one compound); the rate depends on [R–L], where R represents an alkyl group, and L represents a substituent or ligand.

- There is a racemization of configuration, when a chiral molecule is involved.

- A stable carbonium ion should be formed; thus in terms of reaction rate, benzyl groups = allyl groups > tertiary alcohols > secondary alcohols >> primary alcohols.

- The stability of alkyl groups is as follows: primary alkyl groups < secondary alkyl groups < tertiary alkyl groups.

The mechanism of the S_N2 (*2nd order or bimolecular nucleophilic substitution*) reaction is:

$Nu^- + R—L \rightarrow [Nu----R----L]^- \rightarrow Nu—R + L^-$

There are several important points to know about this reaction:

- The reaction rate is second order overall (the rate depends on the concentration of two compounds); first order with respect to [R-L] and first order with respect to the concentration of the nucleophile [Nu⁻].

- Note that the nucleophile adds to the alkyl group by *backside displacement* (i.e. Nu must add to the *opposite* site to the ligand). Thus optically active alcohols react to give an <u>inversion</u> of configuration, forming the opposite enantiomer.

- Large or bulky groups near or at the reacting site may hinder or retard a reaction. This is called *steric hindrance*. Size or <u>steric factors</u> are important since they affect S_N2 reaction rates; in terms of reaction rates, CH_3^- > primary alcohols > secondary alcohols >> tertiary alcohols.

The substitution reactions for methanol (CH_3OH) and other primary alcohols are by the S_N2 reaction mechanism.

6.2.4 Elimination

<u>Elimination reactions</u> occur when an atom or a group of atoms is removed (*eliminated*) from adjacent carbons leaving a multiple bond:

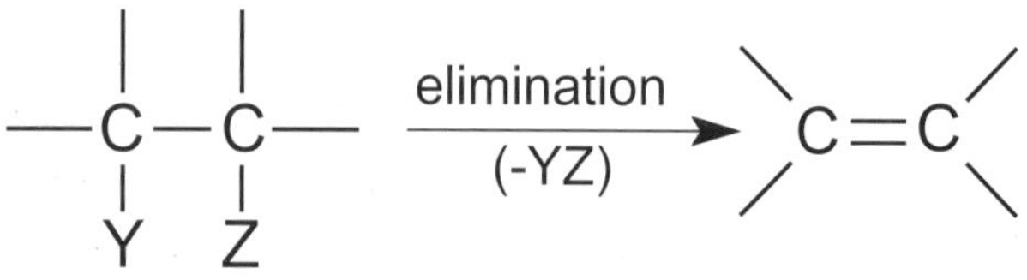

There are two different types of elimination reactions, E1 and E2. In the E1 (<u>E</u>limination, 1st order) reaction, the rate of reaction depends on the concentration of one compound. E1 often occurs as minor products alongside S_N2 reactions. E1 can occur as major products in alkyl halides or, as in the following example, to an alcohol:

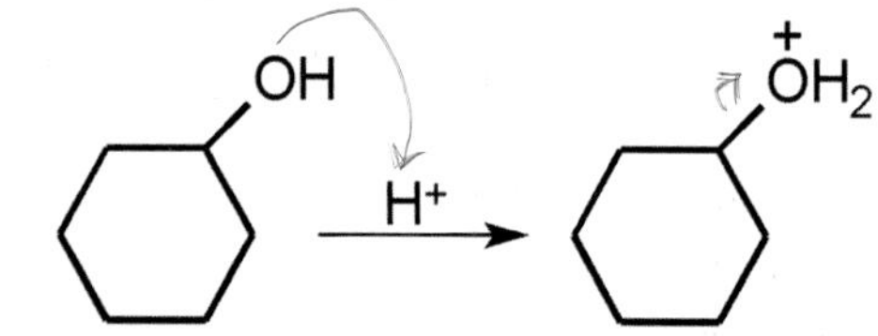

cyclohexanol

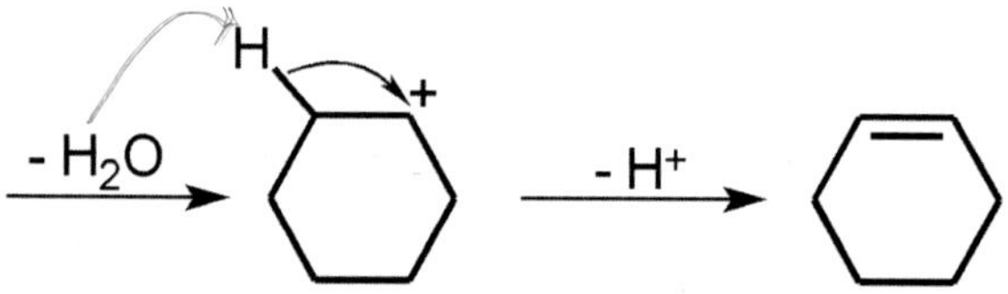

2° carbocation   cyclohexene

The acid-catalyzed dehydration of alcohols is thus an E1 reaction which yields the more highly substituted alkene as the major product. There is a carbocation intermediate formed during the preceding reaction, thus a tertiary alcohol will react faster and yield an alkene in a more stable way than a secondary or primary alcohol.

Secondary and primary alcohols will only react with acids in very harsh condition (75%-95% H_2SO_4, 100 °C). However, they will react with $POCl_3$ converting the −OH into a good leaving group to yield an alkene. This reaction takes place with an E2 mechanism.

In the E2 (<u>E</u>limination, 2nd order)

reaction the rate of reaction depends on the concentration of two compounds. E2 reactions require strong bases like KOH or the salt of an alcohol (i.e. *sodium alkoxide*). An alkoxide can be synthesized from an alcohol using either Na(*s*) or NaH (*sodium hydride*) as reducing agents. The hydride ion H⁻ is a powerful base:

$$R\text{-}OH + NaH \longrightarrow R\text{-}O^- Na^+ + H_2$$
sodium alkoxide

Now the alkoxide can be used as a proton acceptor in an E2 reaction involving an alkyl halide:

$C_2H_5O^-$ + ... 2-bromopropane

ethoxide   2-bromopropane

propene   ehanol

In the preceding reaction, the first step (1) involves the base (ethoxide) removing (*elimination*) a proton, thus carbon has a negative charge (*primary carbanion, very unstable*). The electron pair is quickly attracted to the δ^+ neighboring carbon (2) forming a double bond (note that the carbon was δ^+ because it was attached to the electronegative atom Br, *see* ORG 1.5). Simultaneously, Br (*a halide, which are good leaving groups*) is bumped (3) from the carbon as carbon can have only four bonds. {Notice that in organic chemistry the curved arrows always follow the movement of electrons}

The determination of the quality of a leaving group is quite simple: good leaving groups have *strong* conjugate acids. As examples, H_2O is a good leaving group because H_3O^+ is a strong acid, likewise for Br^-/HBr, Cl^-/HCl, HSO_4^-/H_2SO_4, etc.

A decision tree (substitution vs. elimination) is at the back of the book in the section Key Organic Chemistry Reaction Mechanisms.

6.2.5 Conversion of Alcohols to Alkyl Halides

Alcohols can participate in substitution reactions only if the hydroxyl group is converted into a better leaving group by either protonation or the formation of an inorganic ester. Tertiary alcohols can be converted into alkyl halides by a reaction with HCl or HBr. This reaction occurs in an S_N1 mechanism.

Primary and secondary alcohols do not react with HCl or HBr readily and are converted into halides by $SOCl_2$ or PBr_3. This reaction occurs in an S_N2 mechanism.

$$RCH_2OH + SOCl_2 \longrightarrow RCH_2Cl + SO_2 + HCl$$
$$RCH_2OH + PBr_3 \longrightarrow RCH_2Br + HOPBr_2$$

Go online to DAT-prep.com for chapter review Q&A and forum.

ALDEHYDES AND KETONES
Chapter 7

Memorize	Understand	Importance
* IUPAC nomenclature	* Effect of hydrogen bonds * Mechanisms of reactions * Acidity of the alpha H * Resonance, polarity * Grignards, organometallic reagents * Redox reactions	**1 to 3 out of the 30 ORG** DAT questions are based on content in this chapter (in our estimation). * Note that between 30% and 60% of the questions in DAT Organic Chemistry are based on content from 4 chapters: 1, 2, 5 and 6.

DAT-Prep.com

Introduction ▮▮▮▮

An aldehyde contains a terminal carbonyl group. The functional group is a carbon atom bonded to a hydrogen atom and double-bonded to an oxygen atom (O=CH-) and is called the aldehyde group. A ketone contains a carbonyl group (C=O) bonded to two other carbon atoms: R(CO)R'.

Additional Resources

Free Online Q&A + Forum

Video: Online or DVD

Flashcards

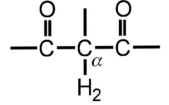

Special Guest

7.1 Description and Nomenclature

Aldehydes and ketones are two types of molecules, both containing the carbonyl group, C=O, which is the basis for their chemistry.

The carbonyl functional group is planar with bond angles of approximately 120°. The carbonyl carbon atom is sp^2 hybridized and forms three σ bonds. The C=O double bond is both stronger and shorter than the C-O single bond.

The general structure of aldehydes and ketones is:

$$
\begin{array}{cc}
\overset{\displaystyle O}{\overset{\displaystyle \|}{R-C-H}} & \overset{\displaystyle O}{\overset{\displaystyle \|}{R-C-R'}} \\
\text{Aldehyde} & \text{Ketone}
\end{array}
$$

Aldehydes have at least one hydrogen bonded to the carbonyl carbon, as well as a second hydrogen (= *formaldehyde*) or either an alkyl or an aryl group (= *benzene minus one hydrogen*). Ketones have two alkyl or aryl groups bound to the carbonyl carbon (i.e. the carbon forming the double bond with oxygen).

Systematic naming of these compounds is done by replacing the '–e' of the corresponding alkane with '–al' for aldehydes, and '-one' for ketones. For aldehydes, the longest chain chosen as the parent name must contain -CHO group and the -CHO group must occupy the terminal (C1) position. For ketones, the longest chain chosen as the parent name must contain the ketone group and give the lowest possible number to the carbonyl carbon. Common names are given in brackets:

$$
\underset{\substack{\text{ethanal}\\\text{(acetaldehyde)}}}{CH_3\overset{\displaystyle O}{\overset{\displaystyle \|}{C}}-H} \qquad \underset{\substack{\text{propanone}\\\text{(acetone)}}}{CH_3\overset{\displaystyle O}{\overset{\displaystyle \|}{C}}CH_3} \qquad \underset{\substack{\text{2-pentanone}\\\text{(methyl propyl ketone)}}}{CH_3\overset{\displaystyle O}{\overset{\displaystyle \|}{C}}CH_2CH_2CH_3}
$$

The important features of the carbonyl group are:

- Resonance: There are two resonance forms of the carbonyl group:

$$
\underset{\delta^+}{\overset{\delta^-}{R-\overset{\displaystyle O}{\overset{\displaystyle \|}{C}}-R'}} \longleftrightarrow \underset{+}{R-\overset{\displaystyle {}^-O}{\overset{\displaystyle |}{C}}-R'}
$$

- Polarity: Reactions about this group may be either nucleophilic, or electrophilic. Since opposite charges attract, nucleophiles (Nu^-) attack the δ^+ carbon, and electrophiles (E^+) attack the δ^- oxygen. In both of these types of reactions, the character of the double bond is altered:

$$
R-\overset{\overset{\displaystyle O\,\delta^-}{\displaystyle \|\,\delta^+}}{C}-R \quad E^+ \xrightarrow{\text{Electrophilic}}
$$

$$
\left[R-\overset{\overset{\displaystyle {}^+O\diagup E}{\displaystyle \|}}{C}-R \longleftrightarrow \underset{+}{R-\overset{\overset{\displaystyle O\diagup E}{\displaystyle |}}{C}-R} \right]
$$

$$
\overset{②}{Nu-}\overset{①}{\underset{\delta^+}{\overset{\overset{\displaystyle O\,\delta^-}{\displaystyle \|}}{R-C-R}}} \xrightarrow{\text{Nucleophilic}} R-\underset{Nu}{\overset{\overset{\displaystyle O^-}{\displaystyle |}}{C}-R}
$$

- **Acidity of the α-hydrogen**: The α-hydrogen is the hydrogen attached to the carbon next to the carbonyl group (the α-carbon). The β-carbon is the carbon adjacent to the α-carbon. The α-hydrogen may be removed by a base. The acidity of this hydrogen is increased if it is between 2 carbonyl groups:

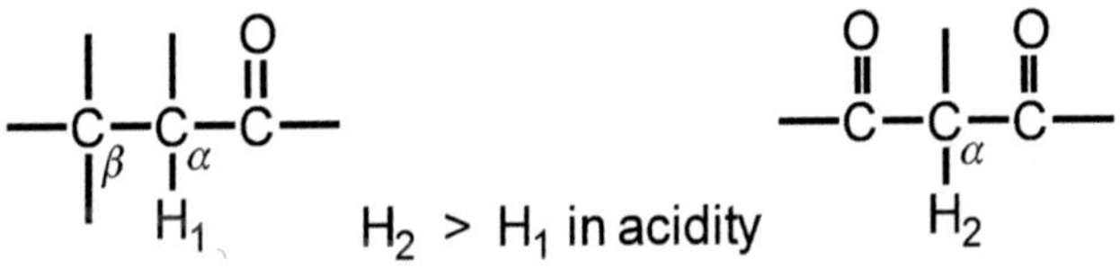

$H_2 > H_1$ in acidity

This acidity is a result of the resonance stabilization of the α-carbanion formed. This stabilization will also permit addition at the β-carbon in α-β unsaturated carbonyls (*those with double or triple bonds*):

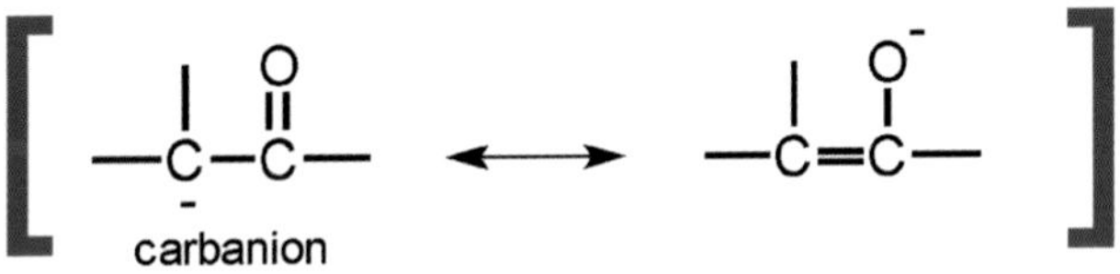

carbanion

resonance stabilization

Nu⁻

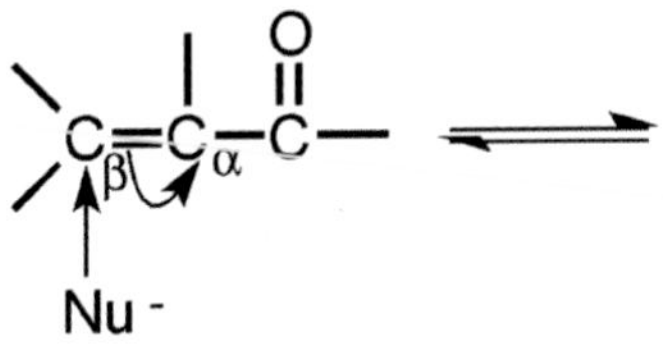

α, β unsaturated carbonyl

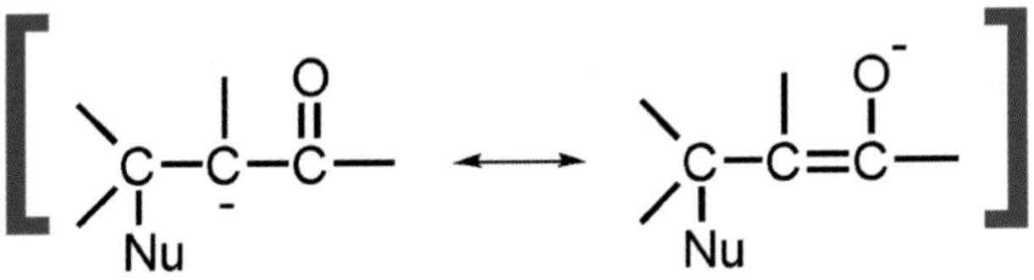

Note that only protons at the α position of carbonyl compounds are acidic. Protons further from the carbonyl carbon (β, gamma - γ, and so on, positions) are not acidic.

- **Keto-enol tautomerization**: Tautomers are constitutional isomers (ORG 2.1-2.3) that readily interconvert (= *tautomerization*). Because the interconversion is so fast, they are usually considered to be the same chemical compound. The carbonyl exists in equilibrium with the enol form of the molecule (enol = alk*ene* + alcoh*ol*). The carbonyl exists in equilibrium with the enol form of the molecule. Although the carbonyl is usually the predominant one, if the enol double bond can be conjugated with other double bonds, it becomes stable (conjugated double bonds are those which are separated by a single bond):

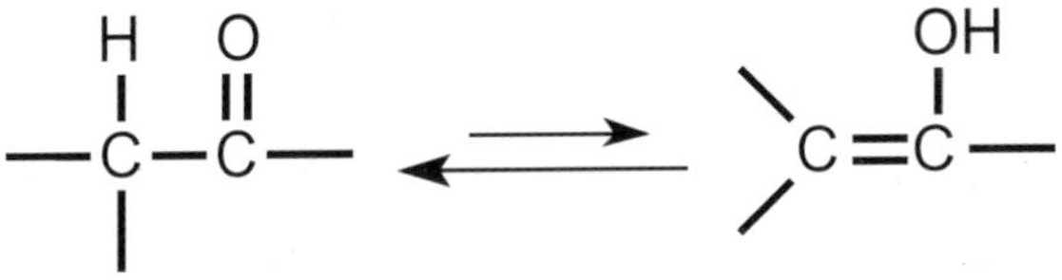

carbonyl   enol

- **Hydrogen bonds**: The O of the carbonyl forms hydrogen bonds with the hydrogens attached to other electronegative atoms, such as O's or N's:

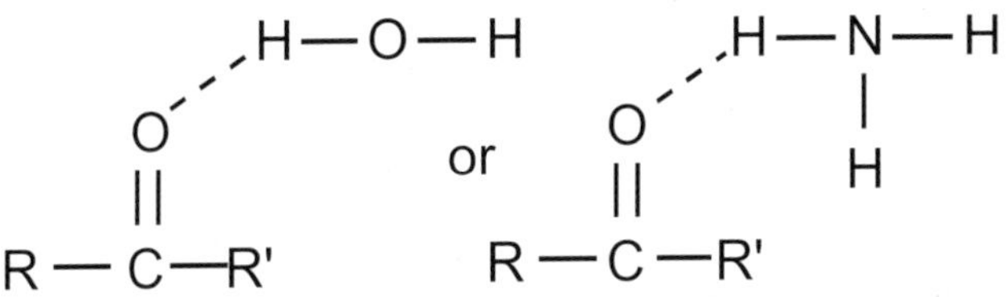

Since there is no hydrogen on the carbonyl oxygen, aldehydes and ketones do not form hydrogen bonds with themselves.

7.2 Important Reactions of Aldehydes & Ketones

7.2.1 Overview

Since the carbonyl group is the functional group of aldehydes and ketones, groups adjacent to the carbonyl group affect the rate of reaction for the molecule. For example, an electron withdrawing ligand adjacent to the carbonyl group will increase the partial positive charge on the carbon making the carbonyl group more attractive to a nucleophile. Conversely, an electron donating ligand would decrease the reactivity of the carbonyl group.

Generally, aldehydes oxidize easier, and undergo nucleophilic additions easier than ketones. This is a consequence of steric hindrance.

Aldehydes will be oxidized to carboxylic acids with the standard oxidizing agents such as $KMnO_4$, CrO_3 (Jones reagent), HNO_3, Ag_2O (Tollens' reagent). Ketones rarely oxidize. When the Tollens' reagent is used, metallic silver Ag is produced if the aldehyde functional group is present in a molecule of unknown structure, thus making it useful as a diagnostic tool. Therefore, the aldehyde will form a silver precipitate while a ketone will not because ketones cannot be oxidized to carboxylic acid.

There are several methods for preparing aldehydes and ketones. We have already seen ozonolysis (ORG 4.2.2) and the classic redox series of reactions (please review ORG 6.2.2). To add to the preceding is a reaction called "hydroformylation" shown for the generation of butyraldehyde by the hydroformylation of propene:

$$H_2 + CO + CH_3CH=CH_2 \longrightarrow CH_3CH_2CH_2CHO$$

Primary alcohols can be oxidized to yield aldehydes. The reaction is performed with the mild oxidation reagent PCC.

$$CH_3-CH_2-OH \xrightarrow[CH_2Cl_2]{\overset{+}{C_5H_5NH}[\overset{-}{CrO_3Cl}]\ (PCC)} CH_3-\overset{\overset{O}{\|}}{C}H$$

ethanol   ethanal

Secondary alcohols can be oxidized to yield ketones. These reactions are usually performed with PCC, Jones' reagent (CrO_3), and sodium dichromate.

Other reagents include: $K_2Cr_2O_7/H_2SO_4$ or CrO_3/H_2SO_4 or $KMnO_4/OH^-$ or $KMnO_4/H_3O^+$.

Alkenes can be oxidatively cleaved to yield aldehydes when treated with ozone (ORG 4.2.2).

Alkenes can be oxidatively cleaved to

yield ketones when treated with ozone if one of the double bond carbon atoms is di-substituted.

$$CH_3-\underset{\underset{CH_3}{|}}{C}=CH-CH_3 \xrightarrow[\text{2. H}^+]{\text{1. O}_3} CH_3-\overset{O}{\overset{||}{C}}-CH_3 \ + \ CH_3-\overset{O}{\overset{||}{C}}-H$$

Ketones can also be prepared by Friedel-Crafts acylation of a benzene ring with acyl halide in the presence of an AlCl$_3$ catalyst (ORG 5.2).

Hydration of terminal alkynes will yield methyl ketones in the presence of mercuric ion as catalyst and strong acids. The formation of an unstable vinyl alcohol undergoes keto-enol tautomerization (ORG 7.1) to form ketones.

$$R-C\equiv C-R \xrightarrow[\text{HgSO}_4]{\text{H}_2\text{O} + \text{H}^\oplus} \begin{bmatrix} \overset{R}{\underset{H}{\diagdown}}C=C\overset{\ddot{O}\cdot-H}{\underset{R}{\diagup}} \end{bmatrix}$$

addition   enol tautomer

$$\xrightarrow[\longleftarrow]{\text{tautomerization}} R-\underset{\underset{H}{|}}{\overset{\overset{H}{|}}{C}}-C\overset{\ddot{O}\cdot}{\underset{R}{\diagdown}}$$

keto tautomer

There are two classes of reactions that will be investigated: nucleophilic addition reactions at C=O bond, and reactions at adjacent positions.

The most important reaction of aldehydes and ketones is the nucleophilic addition reaction. A nucleophile attacks the electrophilic carbonyl carbon atom and a tetrahedral alkoxide ion intermediate is formed. The inter-

mediate can lead to the protonation of the carbonyl oxygen atom to form an alcohol or expel the carbonyl oxygen atom as H$_2$O or OH$^-$ to form a carbon-nucleophile double bond.

Aldehydes and ketones react with water in the presence of acid or base catalyst to form 1,1-diols, or gem-diols. Water acts as the nucleophile here attacking the carbonyl carbon.

$$CH_3-\overset{O}{\overset{||}{C}}-H \xrightarrow[\text{H}^+]{\text{H}_2\text{O}} CH_3-\underset{\underset{OH}{|}}{\overset{\overset{OH}{|}}{C}}-H$$

Aldehydes and ketones react with HCN to form cyanohydrin. CN⁻ attacks the carbonyl carbon atom and protonation of O⁻ foms tetrahedral cyanohydrin product.

$$CH_3-CH_2-\overset{\overset{O}{\|}}{C}H + HCN \rightleftharpoons CH_3CH_2\underset{\underset{CN}{|}}{\overset{\overset{OH}{|}}{C}}-H$$

propanal

$$CH_3-\overset{\overset{O}{\|}}{C}-CH_3 + HCN \rightleftharpoons CH_3\underset{\underset{CN}{|}}{\overset{\overset{OH}{|}}{C}}-CH_3$$

acetone

Reduction of aldehydes and ketones with Grignard reagents yields alcohols. Grignard reagents react with formaldehyde to produce primary alcohols, all other aldehydes to produce secondary alcohols, and ketones to produce tertiary alcohols.

$$\overset{\delta^-}{R'}-\overset{\delta^+}{Mg}X + R-\overset{\overset{O}{\|}}{C}-H(R) \xrightarrow{H^+} R-\underset{\underset{R'}{|}}{\overset{\overset{OH}{|}}{C}}-H(R)$$

$$\overset{\delta^-}{R'}-\overset{\delta^+}{Li} + R-\overset{\overset{O}{\|}}{C}-H(R) \xrightarrow{H^+} R-\underset{\underset{R'}{|}}{\overset{\overset{OH}{|}}{C}}-H(R)$$

$$R'-C\equiv C^-Na^+ + R-\overset{\overset{O}{\|}}{C}-H(R)$$

$$\xrightarrow{H^+} R-C\equiv C-\underset{\underset{HR}{|}}{\overset{\overset{OH}{|}}{C}}-H(R)$$

Reducing agents such as NaBH₄ and LiAlH₄ react with aldehydes and ketones to form alcohols (ORG 6.2.2). The reducing agent functions as if they are hydride ion equivalents and the H:⁻ attacks the carbonyl carbon atom to form the product.

LiAlH₄ or NaBH₄

7.2.2 Acetal (ketal) and Hemiacetal (hemiketal) Formation

Aldehydes and ketones will form hemiacetals and hemiketals, respectively, when dissolved in an excess of a primary alcohol. In addition, if this mixture contains a trace of an acid catalyst, the hemiacetal (hemiketal) will react further to form acetals and ketals.

An acetal is a composite functional group in which two ether functions are joined to a carbon bearing a hydrogen and an alkyl group. A ketal is a composite functional group in which two ether functions are joined to a carbon bearing two alkyl groups.

This reaction may be summarised:

$$R-\overset{\overset{\displaystyle O}{\|}}{C}-R' \quad + \quad R''OH \quad \underset{-H^+}{\overset{+H^+}{\rightleftharpoons}}$$

aldehyde (R' = H)   excess
or ketone (R' = alkyl)   alcohol

$$R-\overset{\overset{\displaystyle OH}{|}}{\underset{\underset{\displaystyle OR''}{|}}{C}}-R' \quad \underset{+H_2O}{\overset{+H^+/-H_2O}{\rightleftharpoons}} \quad R-\overset{\overset{\displaystyle OR''}{|}}{\underset{\underset{\displaystyle OR''}{|}}{C}}-R'$$

hemiacetal   acetal
or   or
hemiketal   ketal

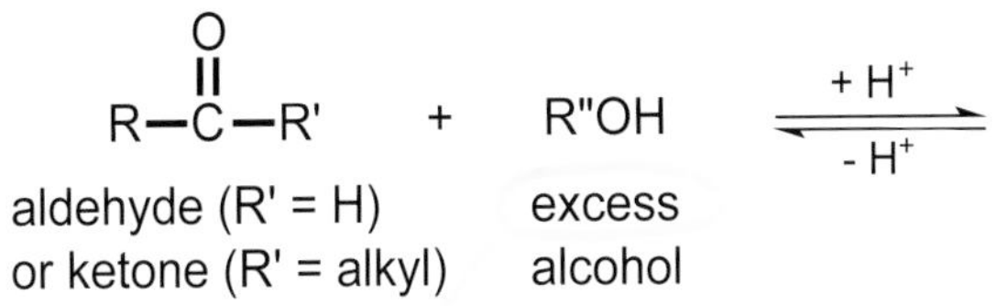

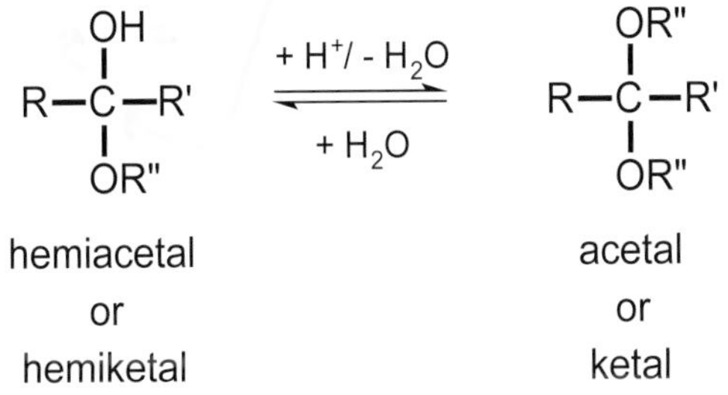

The first step in the above reaction is that the most charged species (+, the hydrogen) attracts electrons from the δ⁻ oxygen, leaving

a carbocation intermediate. The second step involves the δ⁻ oxygen from the alcohol *quickly* attracted to the current most charged species (+, carbon). A proton is lost which regenerates the catalyst, and produces the hemiacetal or hemiketal. Now the proton may attract electrons from -OH forming H_2O, a good leaving group. Again the δ⁻ oxygen on the alcohol is attracted to the positive carbocation. And again the alcohol releases its proton, regenerating the catalyst, producing an acetal or ketal.

Aldehydes and ketones can also react with HCN (hydrogen cyanide) to produce stable compounds called cyanohydrins which owe their stability to the newly formed C-C bond.

7.2.3 Imine and Enamine Formation

Imines and enamines are formed when aldehydes and ketones are allowed to react with amines.

When an aldehyde or ketone reacts with a primary amine, an imine (or Schiff base) is formed. A primary amine is a nitrogen

compound with the general formula $R-NH_2$, where R represents an alkyl or aryl group. In an imine the carbonyl group of the aldehyde or ketone is replaced with a C=N-R group.

The reaction may be summarised:

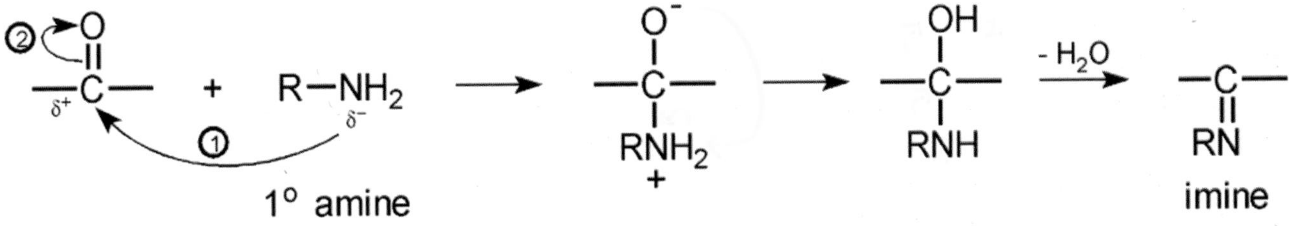

When an aldehyde or ketone reacts with a secondary amine, an _enamine_ is formed. A secondary amine is a nitrogen with the general formula R_2N-H, where R represents aryl or alkyl groups (these groups need not be identical).

Tertiary amines (of the general form R_3N) do not react with the aldehydes or ketones.

7.2.4 Aldol Condensation

Aldol condensation is a base catalized reaction of aldehydes and ketones that have α-hydrogens. The intermediate, an aldol, is both an _ald_ehyde and a _alcoh_ol. The aldol undergoes a dehydration reaction producing a carbon-carbon bond in the condensation product, an _enal_ (= _alk_en_e_ + _al_dehyde).

The reaction may be summarised:

The reaction mechanism:

An aldol can now lose H_2O to form a β-unsaturated aldehyde via an E1 mechanism.

7.2.5 Conjugate Addition to α-β Unsaturated Carbonyls

α-β unsaturated carbonyls are unusually reactive with nucleophiles. This is best illustrated by example:

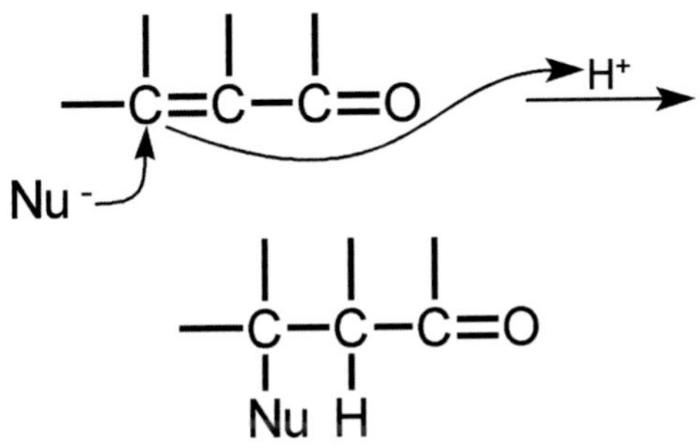

Examples of relevant nucleophiles includes CN⁻ from HCN, and R⁻ which can be generated by a Grignard Reagent (= RMgX) or as an alkyl lithium (= RLi).

For example:

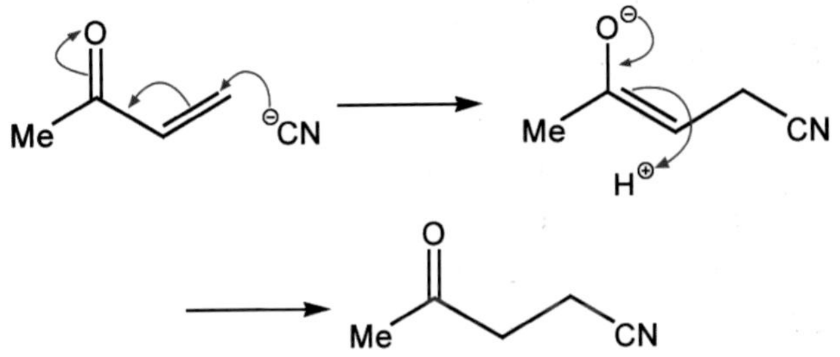

7.2.6 The Wittig reaction

The Wittig reaction converts aldehydes and ketones into alkenes. A salt is formed, followed by a ylide (A) which is a neutral compound, called the Wittig reagent, that eventually attacks the carbonyl carbon of the aldehyde (B) or ketone. This forms a four-membered ring intermediate (E) which decomposes to form the final product, a Z-alkene (G).

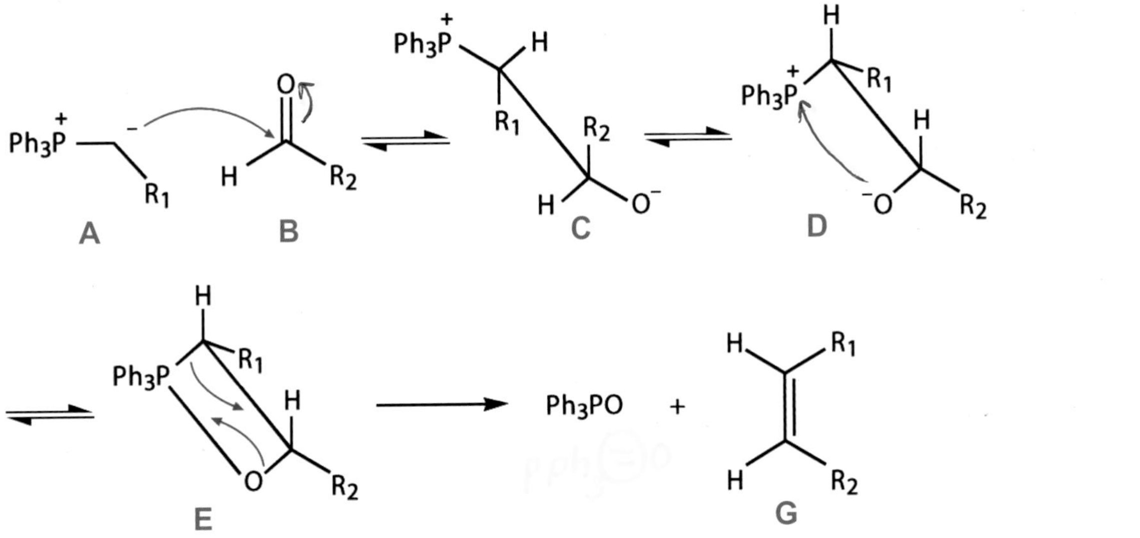

7.2.7 Reduction of Aldehydes and Ketones Revisited

We have already discussed reducing aldehydes and ketones to alcohols (ORG 6.2.2, 7.2.1; $NaBH_4$ and $LiAlH_4$, also symbolized as LAH). However, it is also possible to reduce aldehydes and ketones directly to alkanes using two principle methods:

1. **Clemmensen reduction:** Performed under acidic conditions:

2. **Wolff-Kishner reduction:** Performed in basic solution and only useful when the product is stable under basic conditions:

Go online to DAT-prep.com for chapter review Q&A and forum.

Acetal / Ketals

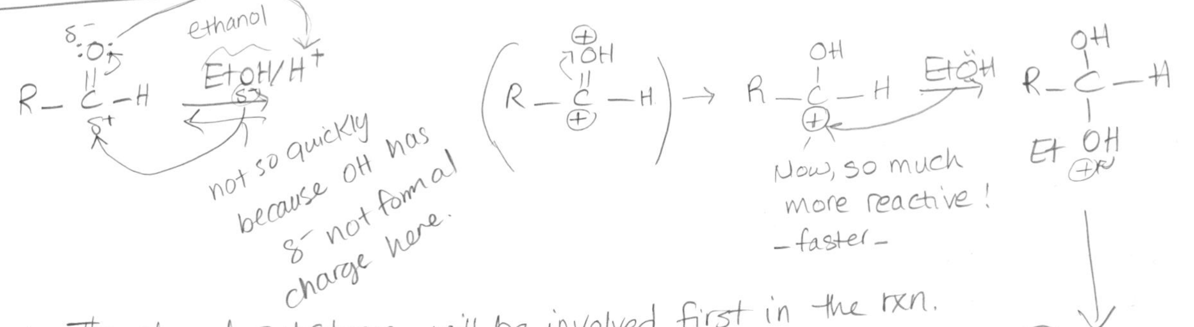

R—C—H ethanol EtOH/H⁺

δ⁻ :O:
     ||
R—C—H
     δ⁺

not so quickly because OH has δ⁻ not formal charge here.

$$\left(R-\overset{\oplus}{\underset{\oplus}{C}}-H \right) \rightarrow R-\underset{\oplus}{C}-H \xrightarrow{Et\overset{..}{O}H} R-\overset{OH}{\underset{Et\ OH}{C}}-H$$

OH
|
R—C—H
|
Et ⊕

Now, so much more reactive! —faster—

* The charged substance, will be involved first in the rxn.

Any rxn that is reproduced at the end and helps rxn faster.

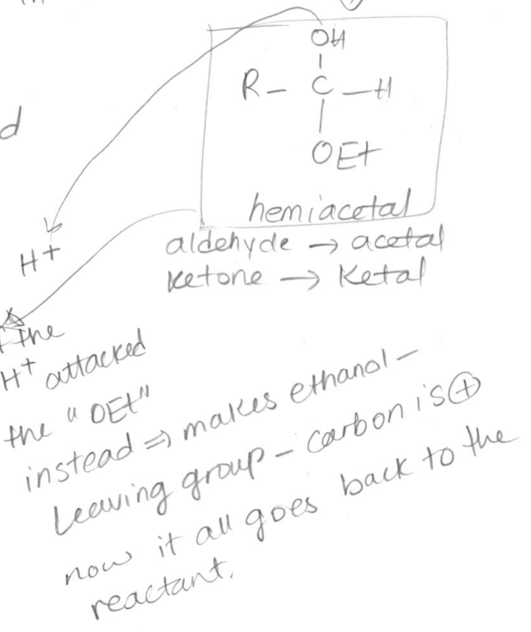

OH
|
R—C—H
|
OEt

hemiacetal
aldehyde → acetal
ketone → Ketal

H⁺

If the H⁺ attacked the "OEt" instead ⟹ makes ethanol — Leaving group — carbon is ⊕ now it all goes back to the reactant.

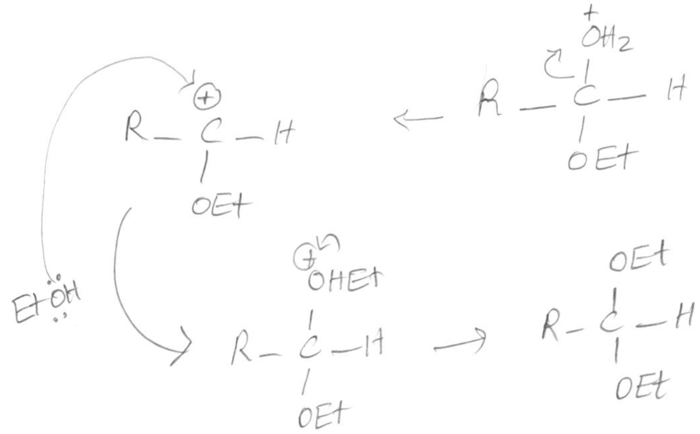

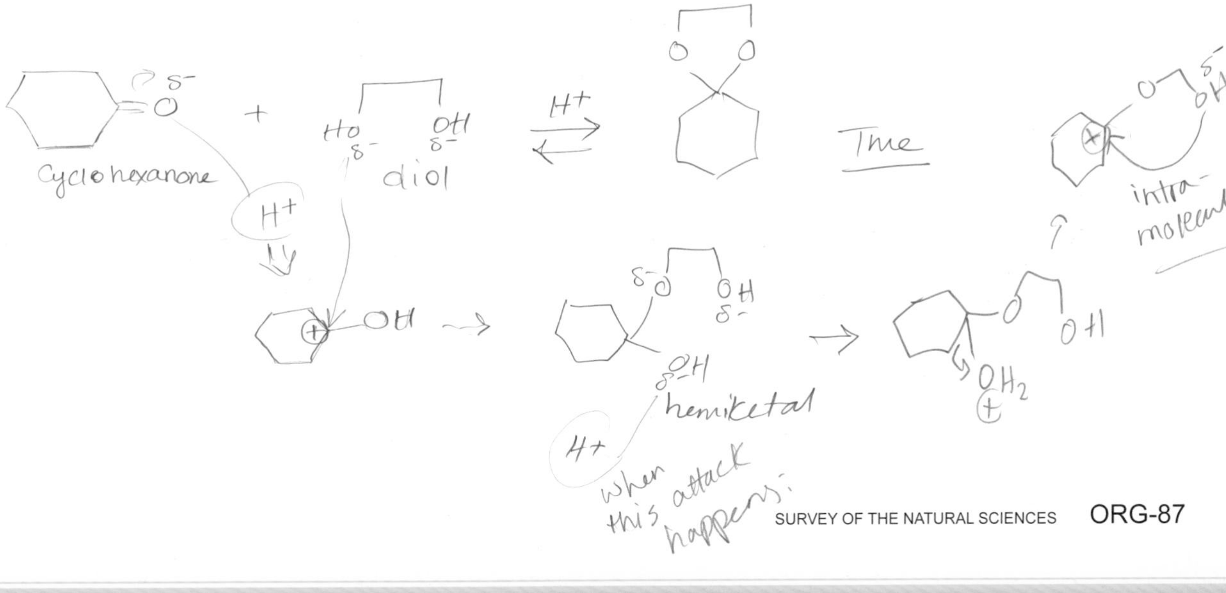

⊕
R—C—H
|
OEt

← R—C—H with ⁺OH₂ and OEt

Et ÖH

⊕OHEt
|
R—C—H   →   R—C—H with OEt / OEt
|
OEt

cyclohexanone + **diol** (HO— —OH) $\xrightarrow{H^+}$ (cyclic acetal)   _True_

intra-molecular

H⁺
⊕—OH →   hemiketal

H⁺ when this attack happens:

OH₂⁺

Memorize	Understand	Importance
* IUPAC nomenclature	* Hydrogen bonding * Mechanisms of reactions * Relative acid strength * Resonance, inductive effects * Grignards, organometallic reagents * Redox reactions	**1 to 3 out of the 30 ORG** DAT questions are based on content in this chapter (in our estimation). * Note that between 30% and 60% of the questions in DAT Organic Chemistry are based on content from 4 chapters: 1, 2, 5 and 6.

DAT-Prep.com

Introduction ▮▮▮▮

Carboxylic acids are organic acids with a carboxyl group, which has the formula -C(=O)OH, usually written -COOH or -CO$_2$H. Carboxylic acids are Brønsted-Lowry acids (proton donors) that are actually, in the grand scheme of chemistry, weak acids. Salts and anions of carboxylic acids are called carboxylates.

Additional Resources

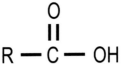

Free Online Q&A + Forum   Video: Online or DVD   Flashcards   Special Guest

8.1 Description and Nomenclature

Carboxylic acids are molecules containing the *carboxylic group* (carbonyl + hydroxyl), which is the basis of their chemistry. The general structure of a carboxylic acid is:

$$O$$
$$\|$$
$$R - C - OH$$

Systematic naming of these compounds is done by replacing the '–e' of the corresponding alkane with '–oic acid'. The molecule is numbered such that the carbonyl carbon is carbon number one. Many carboxylic acids have common names by which they are usually known (systematic names in italics):

O || H—C—OH	O || CH$_3$—C—OH	O || HO—C—OH
formic acid *methanoic acid*	acetic acid *ethanoic acid*	carbonic acid *hydroxymethanoic acid*

O   O
\|\| \|\|
HO—C—CH$_2$CH$_2$—C—OH

succinic acid
butanedioic acid

CO$_2$H

benzoic acid
same: *benzoic acid*

Low molecular weight carboxylic acids are liquids with strong odours and high boiling points. The high boiling point is due to the polarity and the hydrogen bonding capability of the molecule. Strong hydrogen bonding has a noticeable effect on boiling points and makes carboxylic acids boil at much higher temperatures than corresponding alcohols. Because of this hydrogen bonding, these molecules are water soluble. Carboxylic acids with more than 6 carbons are only slightly soluble in water, however, their alkali salts are quite soluble due to ionic properties. As well, carboxylic acids are soluble in dilute bases (NaOH or NaHCO$_3$), because of their acid properties. The carboxyl group is the basis of carboxylic acid chemistry, and there are four important features to remember. Looking at a general carboxylic acid:

- The hydrogen (H) is weakly acidic. This is due to its attachment to the oxygen atom, and because the carboxylate anion is resonance stabilized:

$$O$$
$$\|$$
$$R-C-OH \rightleftharpoons H^+ +$$

$$\left[\begin{array}{ccc} O & & O^- \\ \|\| & & \| \\ R-C-O^- & \longleftrightarrow & R-C=O \end{array} \right]$$

resonance forms

- The carboxyl carbon is very susceptible to nucleophilic attack. This is due to the attached oxygen atom, and the carbonyl oxygen, both atoms being electronegative:

$$\overset{\delta^-}{O}$$
$$\|\|$$
$$R-C-O-H$$
$$\delta^{++} \rightarrow \delta^-$$

② O
$$\|\|$$
$$R-C-O-H \longrightarrow$$
O
Nu⁻ ①

$$O^-$$
$$\|$$
$$R-C-O-H$$
$$\|$$
$$Nu$$

- In basic conditions, the hydroxyl group, as is, is a good leaving group. In acidic conditions, the protonated hydroxyl (i.e. water) is an excellent leaving group. This promotes nucleophilic substitution:

$$Nu^- \ + \ R-\overset{\overset{\textstyle O}{\|}}{C}-\overset{+}{\underset{\diagdown H}{\overset{\diagup H}{O}}}$$

$$\longrightarrow \ R-\overset{\overset{\textstyle O}{\|}}{C}-Nu \ + \ HOH$$

- Because of the carbonyl and hydroxyl moieties (i.e. parts), hydrogen bonding is possible both inter- and intramolecularly:

intermolecular (dimerization)

intramolecular

As implied by their name, carboxylic acids are acidic - the most common acid of all organic compounds. In fact, they are colloquially known as organic acids. Organic classes of molecules in order of increasing acid strength are:

alkanes < ammonia < alkynes < alcohols < water < carboxylic acids

In terms of substituents added to benzoic acid, electron-withdrawing groups such as $-Cl$ or $-NO_2$ inductively withdraw electrons and delocalize the negative charge, thereby stabilizing the carboxylate anion and increasing acidity. Electron-donating groups such as $-NH_2$ or $-OCH_3$ donate electrons and concentrate the negative charge, thereby destabilizing the carboxylate anion and decreasing acidity.

The relative acid strength among carboxylic acids depends on the inductive effects of the attached groups, and their proximity to the carboxyl. For example:

$CH_3CH_2-C(Cl)_2-COOH$ *is a stronger acid than* $CH_3CH_2-CH(Cl)-COOH$.

The reason for this is that chlorine, which is electronegative, withdraws electron density and stabilizes the carboxylate anion. Proximity is important, as:

$CH_3CH_2-C(Cl)_2-COOH$ *is a stronger acid than* $CH_3-C(Cl)_2-CH_2COOH$.

Thus the effect of halogen substitution decreases as the substituent moves further away from the carbonyl carbon atom.

8.1.1 Carboxylic Acid Formation

A carboxylic acid can be formed by reacting a Grignard reagent with carbon dioxide, or by reacting an aldehyde with $KMnO_4$ (*see* ORG 6.2.2). Carboxylic acids are also formed by reacting a nitrile (in which nitrogen shares a triple bond with a carbon) with aqueous acid.

Mechanisms to synthesize carboxylic acids:

- Oxidative cleavage of alkenes/alkynes gives carboxylic acids in the presence of oxidizing reagents such as $NaCr_2O_7$ or $KMnO_4$ or ozone.

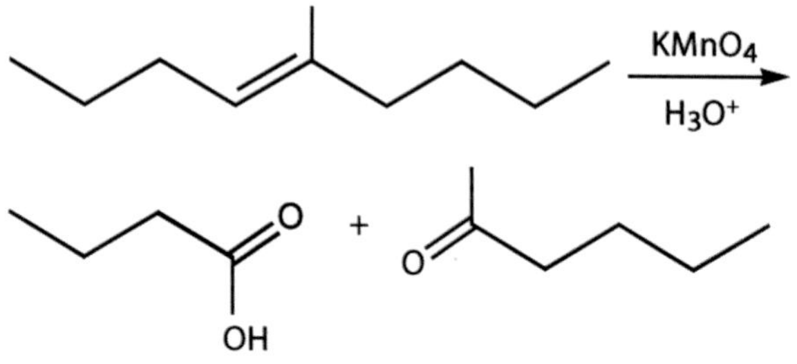

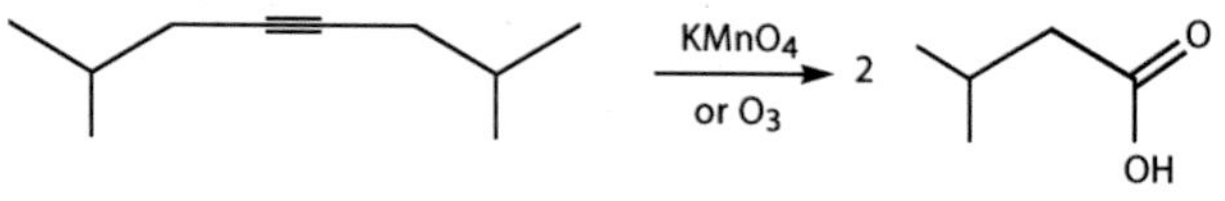

- Oxidation of primary alcohols and aldehydes gives carboxylic acids. Primary alcohols often react with an oxidant such as the Jones' reagent (CrO_3, H_2SO_4). Aldehydes often react with oxidants such as the Jones' reagent or Tollens' reagent $[Ag(NH_3)_2]^+$, also symbolized Ag_2O. Other

reagents include: $K_2Cr_2O_7/H_2SO_4$ or CrO_3/H_2SO_4 or $KMnO_4$.

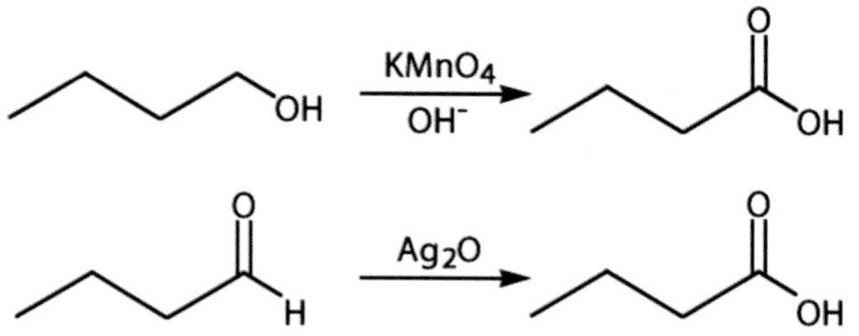

- Hydrolysis of nitriles, RCN, under either strong acid or base conditions can yield carboxylic acids and ammonia (or ammonium salts). Since cyanide anion CN^- is a good nucleophile in S_N2 reactions with primary and secondary alkyl halides, it allows the preparation of carboxylic acids from alkyl halides through cyanide displacement followed by hydrolysis of nitriles. Note that a nitrile hydrolysis reaction increases chain length by one carbon.

$$RCH_2X \xrightarrow{Na^{+-}CN} RCH_2C \equiv N \xrightarrow{H_3O^+} RCH_2COOH + NH_3$$

- Carboxylation of Grignards or other organometallic reagents react with carbon dioxide CO_2 to form carboxylic acids. Alkyl halides react with metal magnesium to form organomagnesium halide, which then reacts with carbon dioxide in a nucleophilic addition mechanism. Protonation of the carboxylate ion forms the final carboxylic acid product. Note that the carboxylation of a Grignard reagent increases chain length by one carbon.

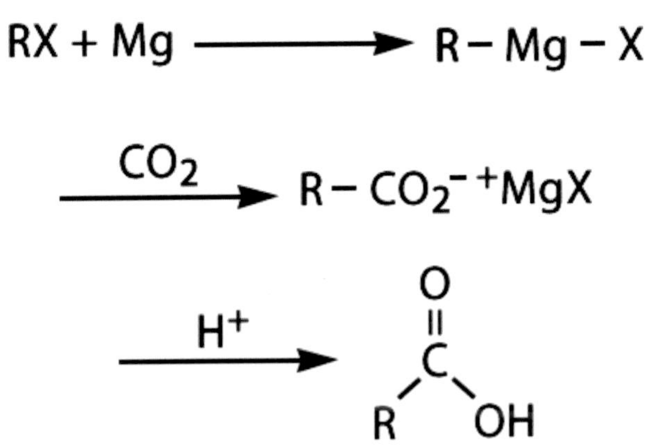

Grignard reagents are particularly useful in converting tertiary alkyl halides into carboxylic acids, which otherwise is very difficult.

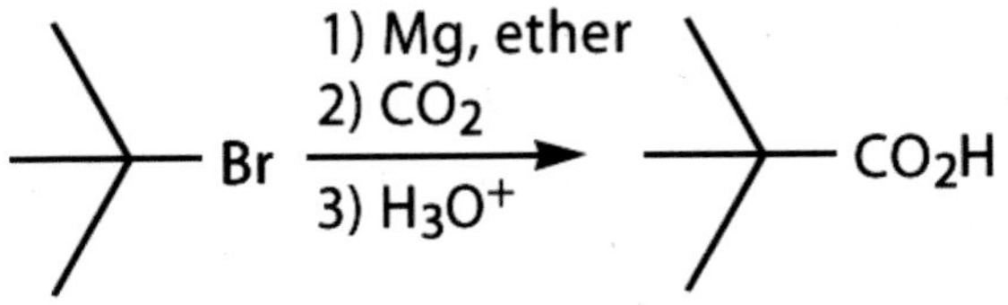

$$RX + Mg \longrightarrow R-Mg-X$$

$$\xrightarrow{CO_2} R-CO_2^- \, ^+MgX$$

$$\xrightarrow{H^+} \underset{R}{\overset{O}{\underset{}{\|}}} \overset{}{\underset{OH}{C}}$$

Tertiary halide with reagents: 1) Mg, ether 2) CO_2 3) H_3O^+ gives CO_2H product.

8.2 Important Reactions of Carboxylic Acids

Carboxylic acids undergo nucleophilic substitution reactions with many different nucleophiles, under a variety of conditions:

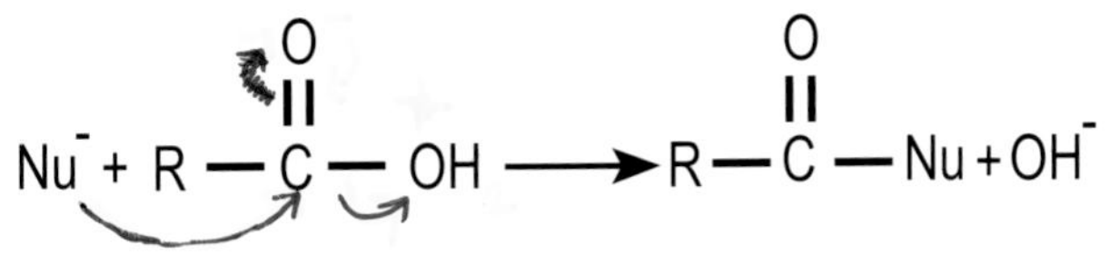

$$Nu^- + R-\overset{O}{\overset{\|}{C}}-OH \longrightarrow R-\overset{O}{\overset{\|}{C}}-Nu + OH^-$$

If the nucleophile is –OR, the resulting compound is an ester. If it is –NH$_2$, the resulting compound is an amide. If it is Cl from SOCl$_2$, or PCl$_5$, the resulting compound is an acid chloride.

The typical esterification reaction may be summarized:

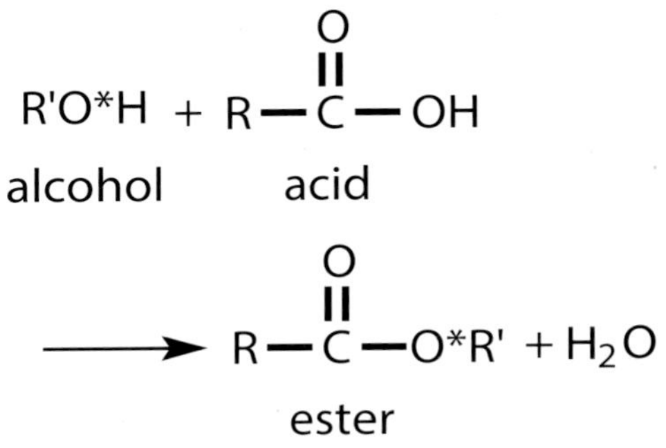

$$R'O^*H + R-\overset{O}{\overset{\|}{C}}-OH$$
alcohol   acid

$$\longrightarrow R-\overset{O}{\overset{\|}{C}}-O^*R' + H_2O$$
ester

Notice that an asterix* was added to the oxygen of the alcohol so that you can tell where that oxygen ended up in the product (i.e. the ester). In the lab, instead of an asterix (!), an isotope (CHM 1.3) of oxygen is used as a tracer or label.

The decarboxylation reaction involves the loss of the carboxyl group as CO_2:

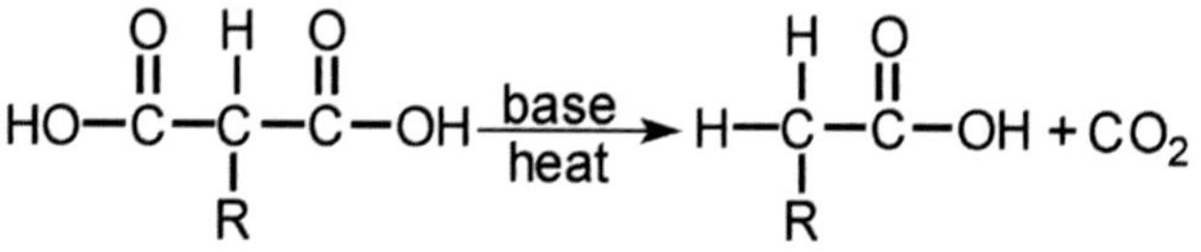

$$HO-\overset{\overset{\displaystyle O}{\|}}{C}-\overset{\overset{\displaystyle H}{|}}{\underset{\underset{\displaystyle R}{|}}{C}}-\overset{\overset{\displaystyle O}{\|}}{C}-OH \xrightarrow[\text{heat}]{\text{base}} H-\overset{\overset{\displaystyle H}{|}}{\underset{\underset{\displaystyle R}{|}}{C}}-\overset{\overset{\displaystyle O}{\|}}{C}-OH + CO_2$$

β – diacid

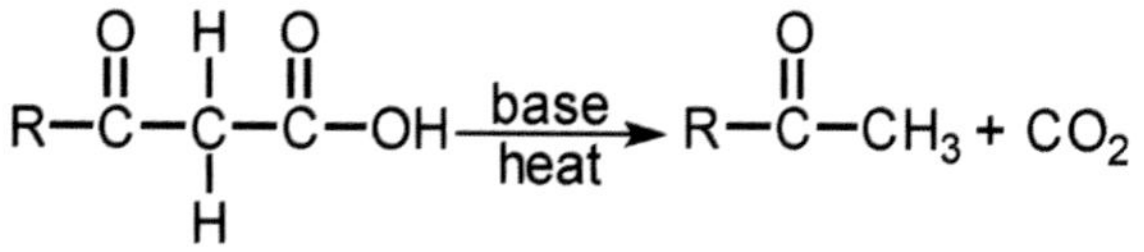

$$R-\overset{\overset{\displaystyle O}{\|}}{C}-\overset{\overset{\displaystyle H}{|}}{\underset{\underset{\displaystyle H}{|}}{C}}-\overset{\overset{\displaystyle O}{\|}}{C}-OH \xrightarrow[\text{heat}]{\text{base}} R-\overset{\overset{\displaystyle O}{\|}}{C}-CH_3 + CO_2$$

β – keto acid

$$LiAlH_4 + R-\overset{\overset{\displaystyle O}{\|}}{C}-OH$$

$$\longrightarrow R-CH_2-OH$$
alcohol

This reaction is not important for most ordinary carboxylic acids. There are certain types of carboxylic acids that decarboxylate easily, mainly:

- Those which have a keto group at the β position, known as β-keto acids.
- Malonic acids and its derivatives (i.e. β-diacids: those with two carboxyl groups, separated by one carbon).
- Carbonic acid and its derivatives.

Carboxylic acids are reduced to alcohols with lithium aluminum hydride, $LiAlH_4$, or H_2/metals (*see* ORG 6.2.2). Sodium borohydride, $NaBH_4$, being a milder reducing agent, only reduces aldehydes and ketones. Carboxylic acids may also be converted to esters or amides first, and then reduced:

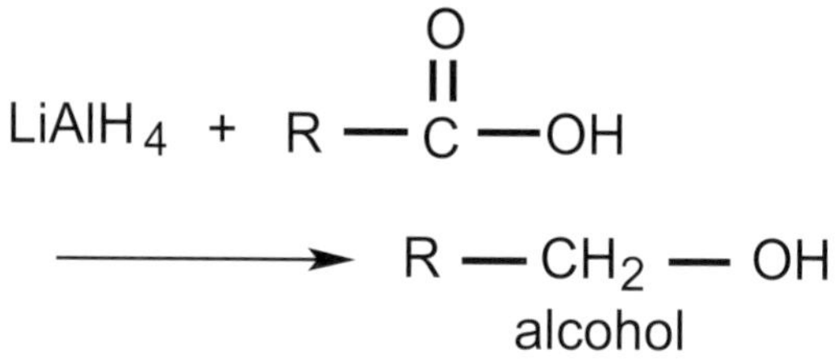

Carboxylic acids

$$-\overset{O}{\underset{\|}{C}}-OH \qquad \text{most acidic organic}$$

most acidic organic ———— next page

Carboxylic acids

* most acidic organic chemicals.   more acidic than alcohols.....
                           └ very stable base (resonance)

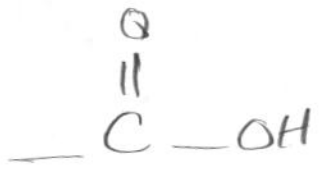

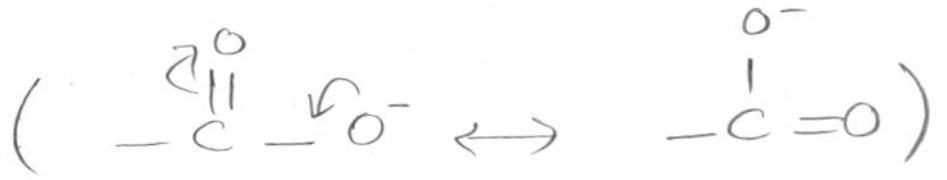

$$\underset{}{\overset{\overset{\displaystyle O}{\|}}{-C}}-OH$$

$$\left(\underset{}{\overset{\overset{\displaystyle O}{\|}}{-C}}-O^- \longleftrightarrow \underset{}{\overset{\overset{\displaystyle O^-}{|}}{-C}}=O \right)$$

Carboxylate anion.

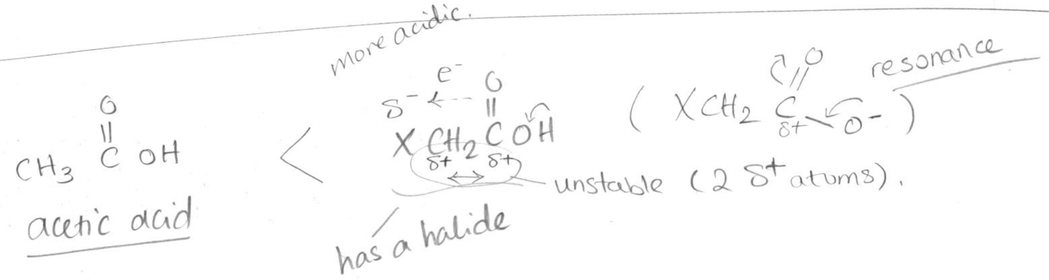

_____

                              more acidic.

$$\underset{\text{acetic acid}}{CH_3\overset{\overset{\displaystyle O}{\|}}{C}OH} \quad < \quad \overset{\delta^- \leftarrow \cdots \overset{\displaystyle O}{\|}}{X\underset{\delta+ \quad \delta+}{CH_2}\overset{}{C}\overset{}{OH}} \quad \left(XCH_2\overset{\overset{\displaystyle O}{/\!\!/}}{\underset{\delta+}{C}}-\overset{}{O^-} \right) \text{ resonance}$$

                                  unstable (2 δ⁺ atoms).
                   ↗
            has a halide

CARBOXYLIC ACID DERIVATIVES
Chapter 9

Memorize	Understand	Importance
• IUPAC nomenclature	* Mechanisms of reactions * Relative reactivity * Steric, inductive effects	**1 to 3 out of the 30 ORG** DAT questions are based on content in this chapter (in our estimation). * Note that between 30% and 60% of the questions in DAT Organic Chemistry are based on content from 4 chapters: 1, 2, 5 and 6.

DAT-Prep.com

Introduction ▮▮▮▮

Carboxylic acid derivatives are a series of compounds that can be synthesized using carboxylic acid. For the DAT, this includes acid chlorides, anhydrides, amides and esters.

Additional Resources

Free Online Q&A + Forum

Video: Online or DVD

Flashcards

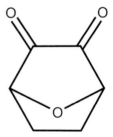

Special Guest

9.1 Acid Halides

The general structure of an acid halide is:

$$R-\overset{\overset{\displaystyle O}{||}}{C}-X \qquad X = Halide$$

These are named by replacing the 'ic acid' of the parent carboxylic acid with the suffix 'yl halide.' For example:

$$CH_3CH_2CH_2-\overset{\overset{\displaystyle O}{||}}{C}-Br \quad \text{Butanoyl bromide}$$

$$CH_3-\overset{\overset{\displaystyle O}{||}}{C}-Cl \quad \begin{matrix}\text{Acetyl chloride}\\\text{(ethanoyl chloride)}\end{matrix}$$

An "acyl" group (IUPAC name: alkanoyl) refers to the functional group RCO-.

Acid chlorides are synthesized by reacting the parent carboxylic acid with PCl_5 or $SOCl_2$. Acid chlorides react with $NaBH_4$ to form alcohols. This can be done in one or two steps. In one step, the acid chloride reacts with $NaBH_4$ to immediately form an alcohol. In two steps, the acid chloride can react first with $H_2/Pd/C$ to form a carboxylic acid; reaction of the carboxylic acid with $NaBH_4$ then produces an alcohol.

Acid halides can engage in nucleophilic reactions similar to carboxylic acids (see ORG 8.2); however, acid halides are more reactive (see ORG 9.6).

Acyl halides can be converted back to carboxylic acids through simple hydrolysis with H_2O. They can also be converted to esters by a reaction with alcohols. Lastly, acyl halides can be converted to amides ($RCONR_2$) by a reaction with amines.

9.1.1 Acid Anhydrides

The general structure of an acid anhydride is:

$$R-\overset{\overset{\displaystyle O}{||}}{C}-O-\overset{\overset{\displaystyle O}{||}}{C}-R$$

These are named by replacing the 'acid' of the parent carboxylic acid with the word 'anhydride.' For example:

$$CH_3-\overset{\overset{\displaystyle O}{||}}{C}-O-\overset{\overset{\displaystyle O}{||}}{C}-CH_3$$

acetic anhydride
(ethanoic anhydride)

$$CH_3-\overset{\overset{\displaystyle O}{||}}{C}-O-\overset{\overset{\displaystyle O}{||}}{C}-H$$

acetic formic anhydride
(ethanoic methanoic anhydride)

Anhydrides can be synthesized by the reaction of an acyl halide with a carboxylate salt and are a bit less reactive than acyl chlorides.

Both acid chlorides and acid anhydrides have boiling points comparable to esters of similar molecular weight.

9.2 Important Reactions of Carboxylic Acid Derivatives

- Nucleophilic acyl substitution reaction: Carboxylic acid derivatives undergo nucleophilic acyl substitution reactions in which a potential leaving group is substituted by the nucleophile, thereby generating a new carbonyl compound. Relative reactivity of carboxylic acid derivatives toward a nucleophilic acyl substitution reaction is amide < ester < acid anhydride < acid chloride. Note that it is possible to convert a more reactive carboxylic acid derivative to a less reactive one, but not the opposite.

- Synthesis of acid halides: Acid halides are synthesized from carboxylic acids by the reaction with thionyl chloride ($SOCl_2$), phosphorus trichloride (PCl_3) or phosphorus pentachloride (PCl_5). Reaction with phosphorus tribromide PBr_3 produces an acid bromide.

- Reactions of acid halides:

1. **Friedel-Crafts reaction:** A benzene ring attacks a carbocation electrophile -COR which is generated by the reaction with the $AlCl_3$ catalyst, yielding the final product Ar-COR.

2. **Conversion into acids:** Acid chlorides react with water to yield carboxylic acids. The attack of the nucleophile water followed by elimination of the chloride ion gives the product carboxylic acid and HCl.

3. **Conversion into esters:** Acid chlorides react with alcohol to yield esters. The same type of nucleophilic acyl substitution mechanism is observed here. The alkoxide ion attacks the acidchloride while chloride is displaced.

4. **Conversion into amides:** Acid chlorides react with ammonia or amines to yield amides. Both mono- and di-substituted amines react well with acid chlorides, but not tri-substituted amines. Two equivalents of ammonia or amine must be used, one reacting with the acid chloride while the other reacting with HCl to form the ammonium chloride salt.

5. **Conversion into alcohols:** Acid chlorides are reduced by LiAlH$_4$ to yield primary alcohols. The reaction is a substitution reaction of -H for -Cl, which is then further reduced to yield the final product alcohol.

Acid chlorides react with Grignard reagents to yield tertiary alcohols. Two equivalents of the Grignard reagent attack the acid chloride yielding the final product, the tertiary alcohol.

Acid chlorides also react with H$_2$ in the presence of Lindlar's catalyst (Pd/BaSO$_4$, quinoline) to yield an aldehyde intermediate which can then be further reduced to yield an alcohol.

6. **Synthesis of acid anhydrides:** Acid anhydrides can be synthesized by a nucleophilic acyl substitution reaction of an acid chloride with a carboxylate anion.

•   Reactions of acid anhydrides: The chemistry of acid anhydrides is similar to that of acid chlorides. Since they are more stable, acid anhydrides react more slowly.

1. **Conversion into acids:** Acid anhydrides react with water to yield carboxylic acids. The nucleophile in this reaction is water and the leaving group is a carboxylic acid.

2. **Conversion into esters:** Acid anhydrides react with alcohols to form esters and acids as in the following example with ethanoic anhydride.

3. **Conversion into amides:** Ammonia attacks the acid anhydride, yielding an amide and the leaving group carboxylic acid, which is reacted with another molecule of ammonia to give the ammonium salt of the carboxylate anion.

4. **Conversion into alcohols:** Acid anhydrides are reduced by LiAlH$_4$ to yield primary alcohols.

$$\underset{R\quad O\quad R}{\overset{O\quad\quad O}{CC}} \xrightarrow[\text{[H]}^-]{\text{LiAlH}_4} RCH_2OH$$

9.3 Amides

The general structure of an amide is:

$$R-\overset{\overset{\displaystyle O}{\|}}{C}-NR'_2$$

These are named by replacing the '-ic (oic) acid' of the parent anhydride with the suffix '-amide.' If there are alkyl groups attached to the nitrogen, they are named as substituents, and designated by the letter N. For example:

$$CH_3-\overset{\overset{\displaystyle O}{\|}}{C}-N\overset{\diagup C_2H_5}{\diagdown C_2H_5} \quad \text{N,N-diethylacetamide}$$

$$CH_3CH_2-\overset{\overset{\displaystyle O}{\|}}{C}-NH_2 \quad \text{propanamide}$$

Unsubstituted and monosubstituted amides form very strong intermolecular hydrogen bonds, and as a result, they have very high boiling and melting points. The boiling points of disubstituted amides are similar to those of aldehydes and ketones. Amides are essentially neutral (no acidity, as compared to carboxylic acids, and no basicity, as compared to amines).

Amides may be prepared by reacting carboxylic acids (or other carboxylic acid derivatives) with ammonia:

$$R-\overset{\overset{\displaystyle O}{\|}}{C}-OH + NH_3 + \text{heat} \xrightarrow{-H_2O} R-\overset{\overset{\displaystyle O}{\|}}{C}-NH_2$$

As well, amides undergo nucleophilic substitution reactions at the carbonyl carbon:

$$R-\overset{\overset{\displaystyle O}{\|}}{C}-NH_2 + NuH \longrightarrow R-\overset{\overset{\displaystyle O}{\|}}{C}-Nu + NH_3$$

Amides can be hydrolyzed to yield the parent carboxylic acid and amine. This reaction may take place under acidic or basic conditions:

$$\underset{\text{amide}}{R-\overset{\overset{\displaystyle O}{\|}}{C}-NHR} + H_2O \xrightarrow{H^+} \underset{\text{acid}}{R-\overset{\overset{\displaystyle O}{\|}}{C}-OH} + \underset{\text{amine}}{RNH_2}$$

$$\underset{\text{amide}}{R-\overset{\overset{\displaystyle O}{\|}}{C}-NHR} + H_2O \xrightarrow{OH^-}$$

$$\underset{\text{carboxylate}}{R-\overset{\overset{\displaystyle O}{\|}}{C}-O^-} + \underset{\text{amine}}{RNH_2} \xrightarrow{H^+} \underset{\text{acid}}{R-\overset{\overset{\displaystyle O}{\|}}{C}-OH}$$

Amides can also form amines by reacting with $LiAlH_4$.

Amides can also be converted to primary amines with the loss of the carbonyl carbon. This is known as a <u>Hofmann rearrangement</u>:

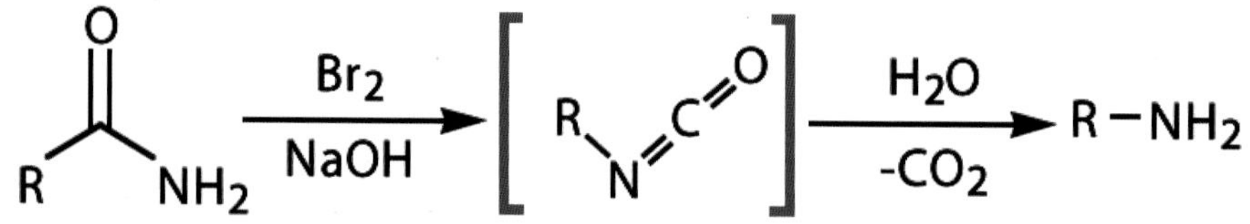

9.3.1 Important Reactions of Amides

Amides are much less reactive than acid chlorides, acid anhydrides or esters.

1. **Conversion into acids:** Amides react with water to yield carboxylic acids in acidic conditions or carboxylate anions in basic conditions.

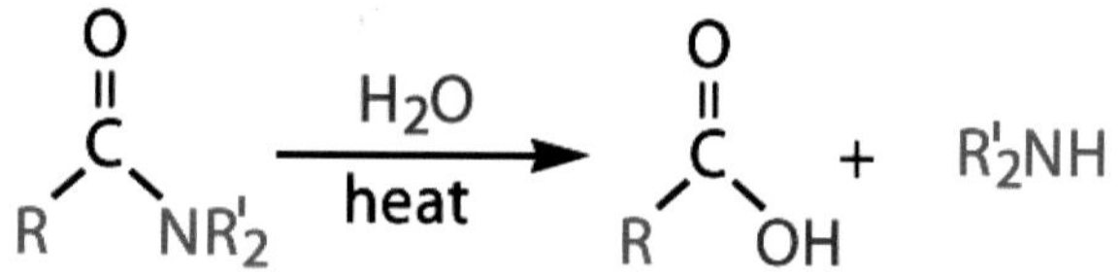

2. **Conversion into alcohols:** Amides can be reduced by $LiAlH_4$ to give amines. The net effect of this reaction is to convert an amide carbonyl group into a methylene group ($C=O \longrightarrow CH_2$).

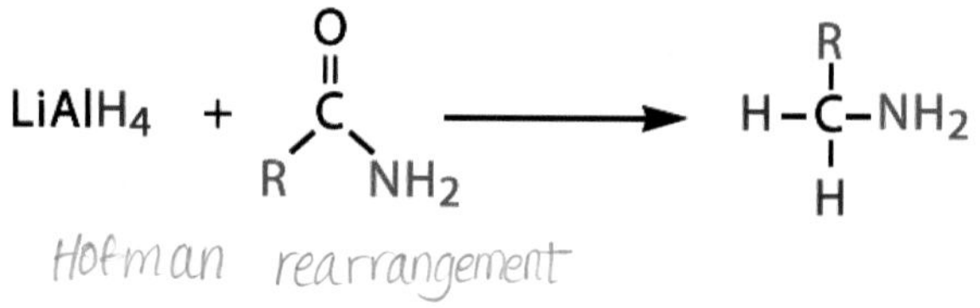

Hofman rearrangement

9.4 Esters

The general structure of an ester is:

These are named by first citing the name of the alkyl group, followed by the parent acid, with the 'ic acid' replaced by 'ate.' For example:

methyl acetate
(methyl ethanoate)

The boiling points of esters are lower than those of comparable acids or alcohols, and similar to comparable aldehydes and ketones, because they are polar compounds, without hydrogens to form hydrogen bonds. Esters with longer side chains (R-groups) are more nonpolar than esters with shorter side chains (R-groups). Esters usually have pleasing, fruity odors.

Esters may be synthesized by reacting carboxylic acids or their derivatives with alcohols under either basic or acidic conditions:

$$R'O^*H + R-\overset{\overset{\displaystyle O}{\|}}{C}-OH \longrightarrow R-\overset{\overset{\displaystyle O}{\|}}{C}-O^*R' + H_2O$$

alcohol   acid   ester

As well, esters undergo nucleophilic substitution reactions at the carbonyl carbon:

$$R-\overset{\overset{\displaystyle O}{\|}}{C}-OR' + NuH \longrightarrow R-\overset{\overset{\displaystyle O}{\|}}{C}-Nu + R'OH$$

Esters may also be hydrolyzed, to yield the parent carboxylic acid and alcohol. This reaction may take place under acidic or basic conditions.

$$R-\overset{\overset{\displaystyle O}{\|}}{C}-O^*R' \ + \ H_2O \ \xrightarrow{\ H^+\ }$$

ester

$$R-\overset{\overset{\displaystyle O}{\|}}{C}-OH \ + \ R'O^*H$$

acid   alcohol

Esters can be transformed from one ester into another by using alcohols as nucleophiles. This process is known as <u>transesterification</u>:

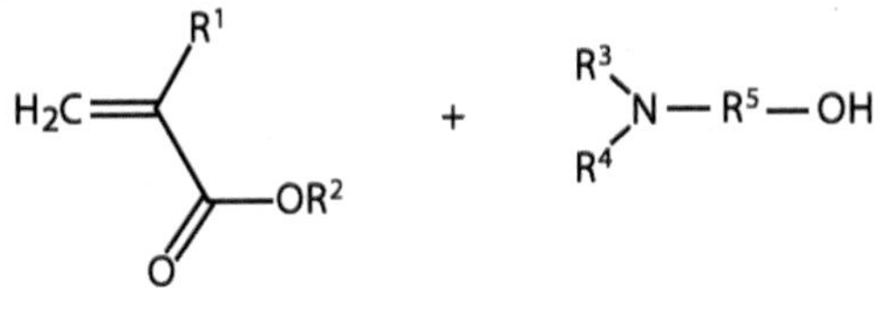

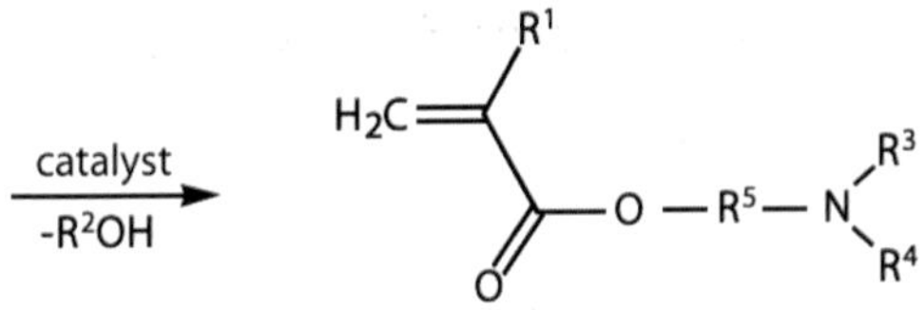

Another reaction type involves the formation of ketones using Grignard reagents. The ketone formed is usually only temporary and is further reduced to a tertiary alcohol due to the reactive nature of the newly formed ketone:

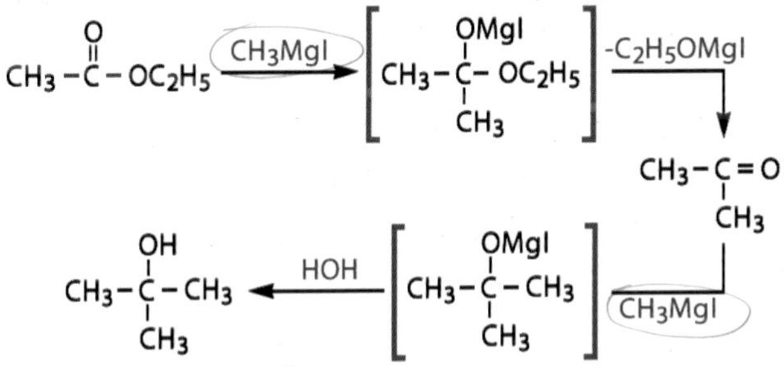

The Ester Bunny

NB: The Ester Bunny is NOT DAT material. In fact for you super-keeners: is the Ester Bunny a real ester? Find out in our Forum!

An important reaction of esters involves the combination of two ester molecules to form an acetoacetic ester (when two moles of ethyl acetate are combined). This is known as the <u>Claisen condensation</u> and is similar to the aldol condensation seen in ORG 7.2.4:

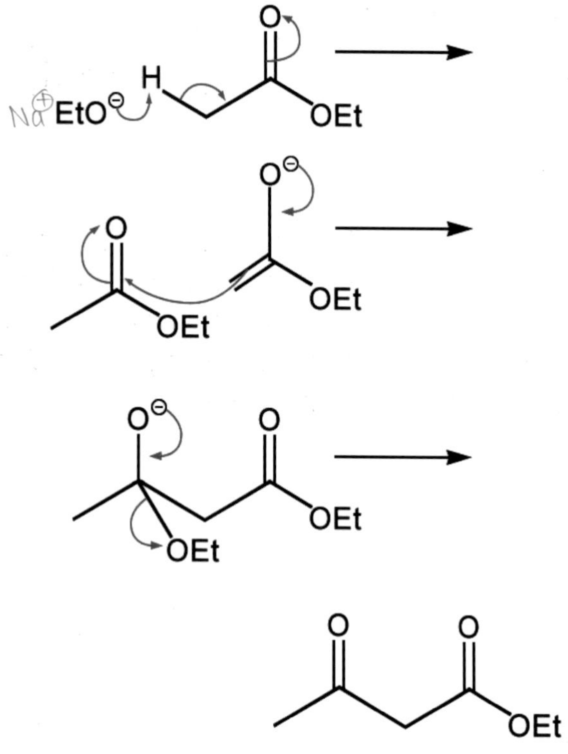

- <u>More reactions with esters</u>: Esters have similar chemistry to acid chlorides and acid anhydrides; however, they are less reactive toward nucleophilic substitution reactions.

1. **Conversion into amides**: Esters can react with ammonia or amines to give amides and an alcohol side product.

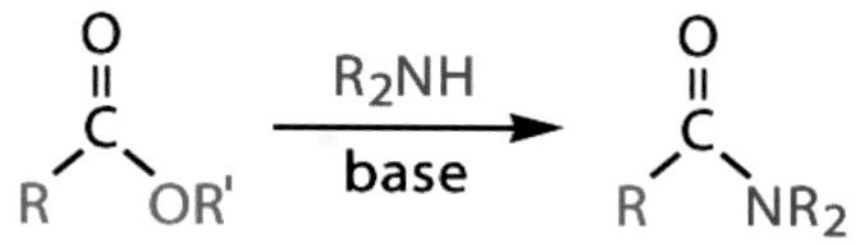

2. **Conversion into alcohols**: Esters can be easily reduced by $LiAlH_4$ to form primary alcohols. A hydride ion attacks the ester carbonyl carbon to form a tetrahedral intermediate. Loss of the alkoxide ion from the intermediate yields an aldehyde intermediate, which is further reduced by another hydride ion to give a primary alcohol final product.

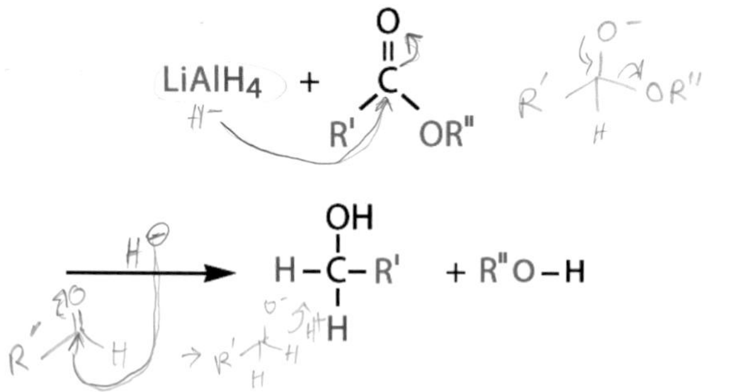

Esters can also be reduced to tertiary alcohols by reacting with a Grignard reagent (or alkyl lithium). Grignard reagents add to the ester carbonyl carbon to form ketone intermediates, which are further attacked by the next equivalent of the Grignard reagent. Thus two equivalents of the Grignard reagent (or alkyl lithium) are used to produce tertiary alcohols.

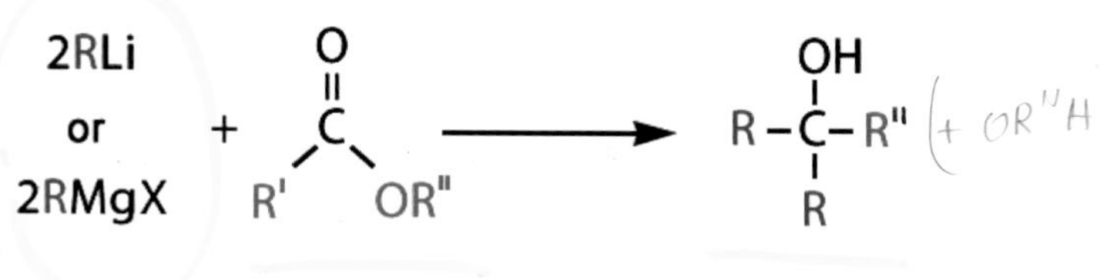

9.4.1 Fats, Glycerides and Saponification

A special class of esters is known as fats (i.e. mono-, di-, and triglycerides). These are biologically important molecules, and they are formed in the following reaction:

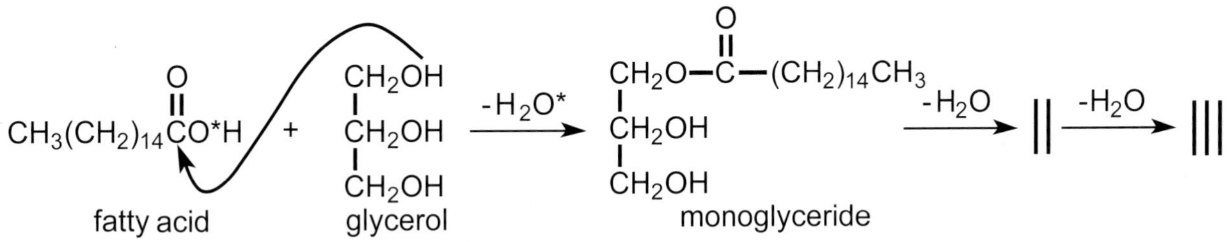

$$CH_3(CH_2)_{14}CO^*H \;+\; \underset{glycerol}{\begin{array}{l} CH_2OH \\ CH_2OH \\ CH_2OH \end{array}} \xrightarrow{-H_2O^*} \underset{monoglyceride}{\begin{array}{l} CH_2O-\overset{O}{\overset{\|}{C}}-(CH_2)_{14}CH_3 \\ CH_2OH \\ CH_2OH \end{array}} \xrightarrow{-H_2O} || \xrightarrow{-H_2O} ||| $$

fatty acid

Fatty acids (= *long chain carboxylic acids*) are formed through the condensation of C2 units derived from acetate, and may be added to the monoglyceride formed in the above reaction, forming diglycerides, and triglycerides. Fats may be hydrolyzed by a base to the components glycerol and the salt of the fatty acids. The salts of long chain carboxylic acids are called <u>soaps</u>. Thus this process is called *saponification*:

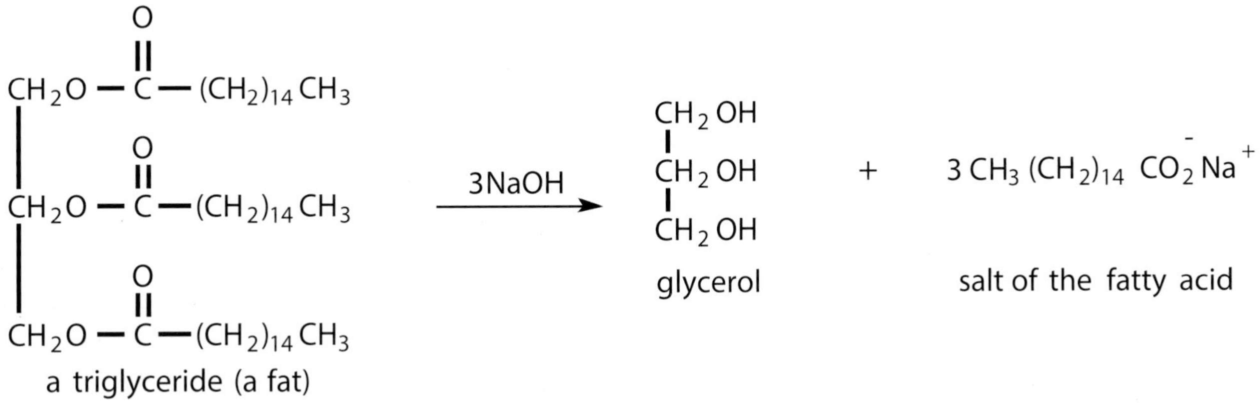

$$\begin{array}{l} CH_2O-\overset{O}{\overset{\|}{C}}-(CH_2)_{14}CH_3 \\ CH_2O-\overset{O}{\overset{\|}{C}}-(CH_2)_{14}CH_3 \\ CH_2O-\overset{O}{\overset{\|}{C}}-(CH_2)_{14}CH_3 \end{array} \xrightarrow{3NaOH} \underset{glycerol}{\begin{array}{l} CH_2OH \\ CH_2OH \\ CH_2OH \end{array}} \;+\; \underset{\text{salt of the fatty acid}}{3\,CH_3(CH_2)_{14}\,CO_2^{-}\,Na^{+}}$$

a triglyceride (a fat)

9.5 β-Keto Acids

β-keto acids are carboxylic acids with a keto group (i.e. *ketone*) at the β position. Thus it is an acid with a carbonyl group one carbon removed from a carboxylic acid group.

Upon heating the carboxyl group can be readily removed as CO_2. This process is called *decarboxylation*. For example:

$$R-\overset{\overset{\displaystyle O}{\|}}{C}-CH_2-\overset{\overset{\displaystyle O}{\|}}{C}-OH \quad \xrightarrow{\text{heat}} \quad R\overset{\overset{\displaystyle O}{\|}}{C}CH_3 \quad + \quad CO_2$$

$$\beta-\text{keto acid} \qquad\qquad\qquad\qquad \text{ketone}$$

9.6 Relative Reactivity of Carboxylic Acid Derivatives

Any factors that make the carbonyl group more easily attacked by nucleophiles favor the nucleophilic acyl substitution reaction. In terms of nucleophilic substitution, generally, carboxylic acid derivatives are more reactive than comparable non-carboxylic acid derivatives. One important reason for the preceding is that the carbon in carboxylic acids is also attached to the electronegative oxygen atom of the carbonyl group; therefore, carbon is more δ^+, thus being more attractive to a nucleophile. Hence an acid chloride (R-COCl) is more reactive than a comparable alkyl chloride (R-Cl); an ester (R-COOR') is more reactive than a comparable ether (R-OR'); and an amide (R-CONH$_2$) is more reactive than a comparable amine (R-NH$_2$).

Amongst carboxylic acid derivatives, the car- bonyl reactivity in order from most to least reactive is:

acid chlorides > anhydrides >> esters > acids > amides > nitriles

The reasons for this may be attributed to resonance effects and inductive effects. The <u>resonance effect</u> is the ability of the sub-stituent to stabilize the carbocation intermediate by delocalization of electrons. The <u>inductive effect</u> is the substituent group, by virtue of its electronegativity, to pull electrons away increasing the partial positivity of the carbonyl carbon.

Within each carboxylic acid derivative, <u>steric or bulk effects</u> also play an important role. The less the steric hindrance, the more access a nucleophile will have to attack the carbonyl carbon, and vice versa.

9.7 Phosphate Esters

Phosphoric acid derivatives have similar features to those of carboxylic acid derivatives. Phosphoric acid and mono- or di-phosphoric esters are acidic. Under acidic condition, these phosphoric esters can be converted to the parent acid H_3PO_4 and alcohols. To see the structure of phosphate esters, see ORG 12.5.5.

Go online to DAT-prep.com for chapter review Q&A and forum.

aryl or phenyl group.

spectator ion

$$ph - \overset{\overset{\ddot{O}\,\overset{-}{}}{|}}{\underset{\underset{\delta^{-}}{|}\overset{\delta^{-}}{OH}}{C}\,\overset{\delta^{+}}{\underset{}{}}\,\overset{\delta^{-}}{OCH_3}}$$

Tetrahedral intermediate — Extremely unstable

better leaving group than $\ominus$OH...

$$\rightarrow ph - \overset{O}{\overset{||}{C}} - OH + \overset{\ominus}{OCH_3}$$
carboxylic acid   (base)

only a partial $\ominus$ charge; no match for the formal charge of $\overset{-}{O}H$

acid + base → **Salt** + neutral compounds

$$ph - \overset{O}{\overset{||}{C}} - \overset{\ominus}{O}\,\,{}^{Na^{\oplus}} + HOCH_3$$
in solution

Chapter 10

Memorize	Understand	Importance
*IUPAC nomenclature	*S_N2 synthesis of ethers *Effect of substituent groups on phenols *Synthesis of oxiranes	**1 to 3 out of the 30 ORG** DAT questions are based on content in this chapter (in our estimation). * Note that between 30% and 60% of the questions in DAT Organic Chemistry are based on content from 4 chapters: 1, 2, 5 and 6.

DAT-Prep.com

Introduction ▢▢▢

Ethers are composed of an oxygen atom connected to two alkyl or aryl groups of the general formula R–O–R'. A classic example is the solvent and anesthetic diethyl ether, often just called "ether." Phenol is a toxic, white crystalline solid with a sweet tarry odor often referred to as a "hospital smell"! Its chemical formula is C_6H_5OH and its structure is that of a hydroxyl group (-OH) bonded to a phenyl ring thus it is an aromatic compound.

Additional Resources

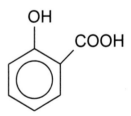

Free Online Q&A + Forum   Video: Online or DVD   Flashcards   Special Guest

10.1 Description and Nomenclature of Ethers

The general structure of an ether is R-O-R', where the R's may be either aromatic or aliphatic (= *containing only carbon and hydrogen atoms*). In the common system of nomenclature, the two groups on either side of the oxygen are named, followed by the word ether:

$$CH_3 - O - CH_3$$
dimethyl ether

$$CH_3 - O - \overset{\overset{\displaystyle CH_3}{|}}{C}HCH_3$$
methyl isopropyl ether

In the systematic system of nomenclature, the alkoxy (RO-) groups are always named as substituents:

$$CH_3 - O - CH_3$$
methoxy methane

$$CH_3 - O - \overset{\overset{\displaystyle CH_3}{|}}{C}HCH_3$$
methoxy isopropane

The boiling points of ethers are comparable to that of other hydrocarbons, which is regarded as relatively low temperatures when compared to alcohols. Ethers are more polar than other hydrocarbons, but are not capable of forming intermolecular hydrogen bonds (those between two ether molecules). Ethers are only slightly soluble in water. However, they can form intermolecular hydrogen bonds between the ether and the water molecules.

Ethers are <u>good solvents</u>, as the ether linkage is inert to many chemical reagents. Ethers are weak Lewis bases and can be protonated to form positively charged conjugate acids. In the presence of a high concentration of a strong acid (especially HI or HBr), the ether linkage will be cleaved, to form an alcohol and an alkyl halide:

$$CH_3 - O - CH_3 + HI \longrightarrow$$
$$CH_3 - OH + CH_3 - I$$

10.1.1 Important Reactions of Ethers

- <u>Williamson ether synthesis</u>: A metal alkoxide can react with a primary alkyl halide to yield an ether in an S_N2 mechanism. The alkoxide, which is prepared by the reaction of an alcohol with a strong base (ORG 6.2.4), acts as a nucleophile and displaces the halide. Since primary halides work best in an S_N2 mechanism, asymmetrical ethers will be synthesized by the reaction between non-hindered halides and more hindered alkoxides. This reaction will not proceed with a hindered alkyl halide substrate:

$$Na^+ {}^-OCH_3 + {}^{\delta+}CH_3 - I^{\delta-} \longrightarrow$$
$$CH_3 - O - CH_3 + Na^+ I^-$$

sodium cyclohexanoxide + CH₃I iodomethane (methyl iodide)

cyclohexyl methyl ether (methoxycyclohexane) + NaI

In a variant of the Williamson ether synthesis, an alkoxide ion displaces a chloride atom within the same molecule. The precursor compounds are called halohydrins. For example, with 2-chloropropanol, an intramolecular epoxide formation reaction is possible creating the cyclic ether called oxirane (C_2H_4O). Note that oxirane is a three-membered cyclic ether (epoxide).

Cyclic ethers can also be prepared by reacting an alkene with m-CPBA (meta-chloroperoxybenzoic acid) which can also form an oxirane:

cyclohexene

1,2-epoxycyclohexane (cyclohexene epoxide)

• Acidic Cleavage: Cleavage reactions of straight chain ethers takes place in the presence of HBr or HI (or even H_2SO_4) and is initiated by protonation of the ether oxygen.

Primary or secondary ethers react by an S_N2 mechanism in which I^- or Br^- attacks the protonated ether at the less hindered site. Tertiary, benzylic and allylic ethers react by an S_N1 or E1 mechanism because these substrates can produce stable intermediate carbocations. Please see the following mechanism:

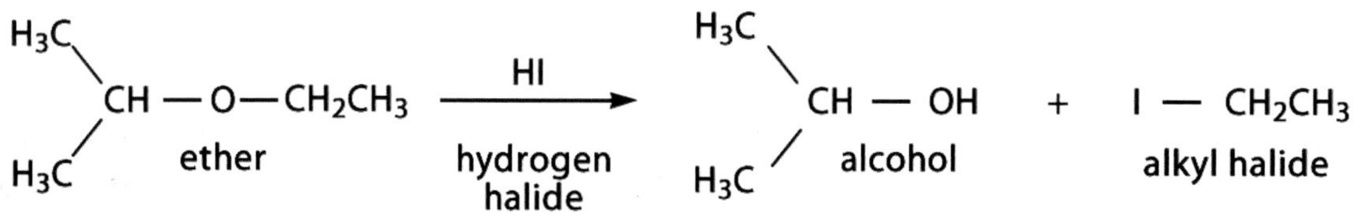
ether
HI
hydrogen halide
alcohol
alkyl halide

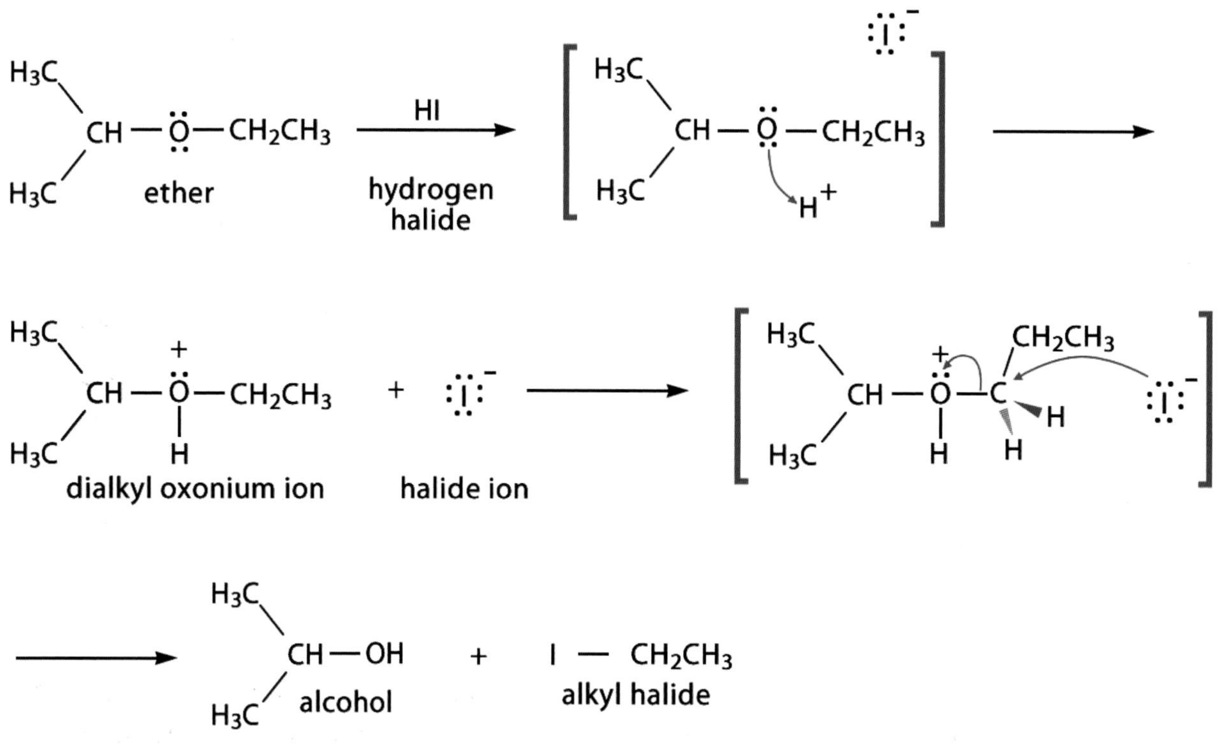
ether
HI
hydrogen halide
dialkyl oxonium ion
halide ion
alcohol
alkyl halide

10.2 Phenols

A phenol is a molecule consisting of a hydroxyl (–OH) group attached to a benzene (aromatic) ring. The following are some phenols and derivatives which are important to biochemistry, medicine and nature:

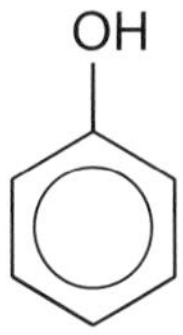

phenol

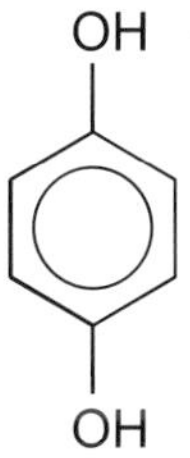

hydroquinone

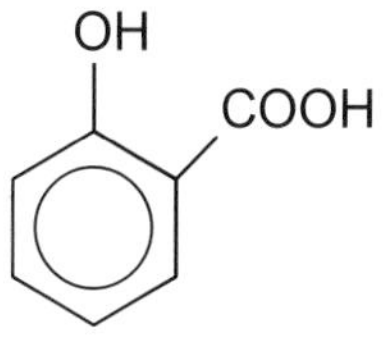

salicylic acid

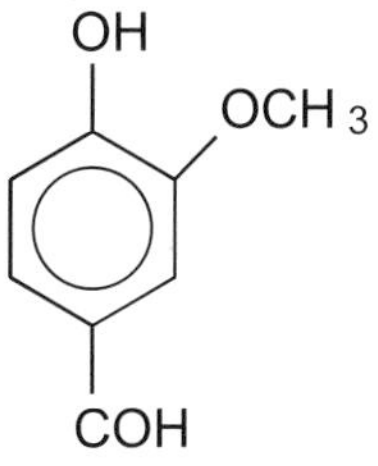

vanillin

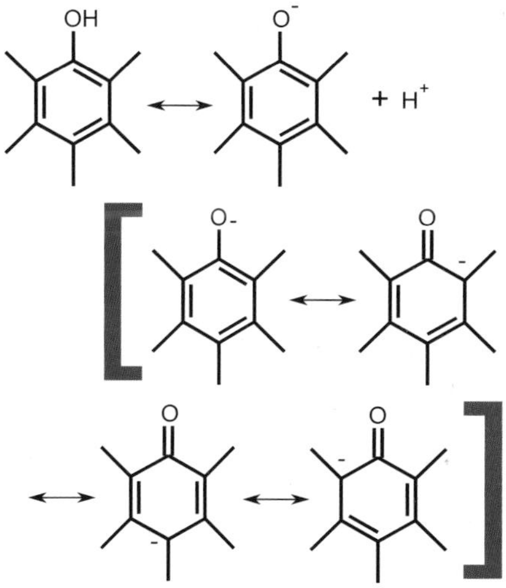

Substituent groups on the ring affect the acidity of phenols by both inductive effects (as with alcohols) and resonance effects. The resonance structures show that electron stabilizing (*withdrawing* or *meta directing*) groups at the ortho or para positions should increase the acidity of the phenol. Examples of these groups include the nitro group (–NO$_2$), –CN, –CO$_2$H, and the weakly deactivating o-p directors - the halogens. Destabilizing groups, such as alkyl groups, or other ortho-para directors, will make the compound less acidic. Phenols are ortho-para directors (see ORG Chapter 5).

Phenols are more acidic than their corresponding alcohols. This is due mainly to the electron withdrawing and resonance stabilization effects of the aromatic ring in the conjugate base anion (the phenoxide ion):

Phenols can form hydrogen bonds, resulting in fairly high boiling points. Their solubility in water, however, is limited, because of the hydrophobic nature of the aromatic ring. Ortho phenols have lower boiling points than meta and para phenols, as they can form intramolecular hydrogen bonds. However, the para and even the ortho compounds can sometimes form intermolecular hydrogen bonds:

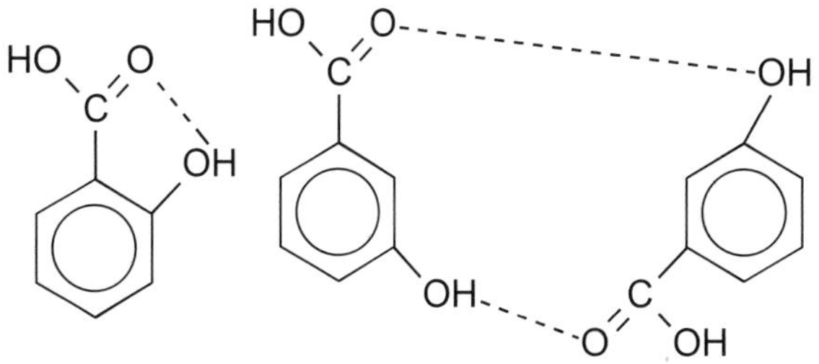

10.2.1 Electrophilic Aromatic Substitution for Phenols

The hydroxyl group is a powerful activating group and an ortho-para director in electrophilic substitutions. Thus phenols can brominate three times in bromine water as follows:

Go online to DAT-prep.com for chapter review Q&A and forum.

AMINES

Chapter 11

Memorize	Understand	Importance
* IUPAC nomenclature	* Effect of hydrogen bonds * Mechanisms of reactions * Trends in basicity * Resonance, delocalization of electrons * Aromatic amine chemistry	**1 to 3 out of the 30 ORG** DAT questions are based on content in this chapter (in our estimation). * Note that between 30% and 60% of the questions in DAT Organic Chemistry are based on content from 4 chapters: 1, 2, 5 and 6.

DAT-Prep.com

Introduction ▮▮▮▮

Amines are compounds and functional groups that contain a basic nitrogen atom with a lone pair. Amines are derivatives of ammonia (NH_3), where one or more hydrogen atoms are replaced by organic substituents such as alkyl and aryl groups.

Additional Resources

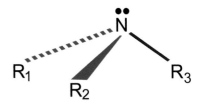

Free Online Q&A + Forum   Video: Online or DVD   Flashcards   Special Guest

11.1 Description and Nomenclature

Organic compounds with a trivalent nitrogen atom bonded to one or more carbon atoms are called amines. These are organic derivatives of ammonia. They may be classified depending on the number of carbon atoms bonded to the nitrogen:

Primary Amine: RNH_2
Secondary Amine: R_2NH
Tertiary Amine: R_3N
Quaternary Salt: $R_4N^+ X^-$

In the common system of nomenclature, amines are named by adding the suffix '-amine' to the name of the alkyl group. In a secondary or tertiary amine, where there is more than one alkyl group, the groups are named as N-substituted derivatives of the larger group:

$$CH_3 — CH — N — CH_2 — CH_3$$
N, N-methyl ethyl isopropylamine

In the systematic system of nomenclature, amines are named analagous to alcohols, except the suffix '-amine' is used instead of the suffix '-ol'.

When amines are present with multiple asymmetric substituents, they are named by considering the largest group as the parent name and the other alkyl groups as N-substituents of the parent:

N, N-dimethyl-2-butanamine

The $-NH_2$ group is named as an amino substituent on a parent molecule when amines are present with more than one functional group:

4-aminobutanoic acid

The bonding in amines is similar to the bonding in ammonia. The nitrogen atom is sp^3 hybridized (a common DAT question). Primary, secondary and tertiary amines have a trigonal pyramidal shape (CHM 3.5). The C-N-C bond angle is approximately 108°. Quaternary amines have a tetrahedral shape and a normal tetrahedral bond angle of 109.5°.

With its tetrahedral geometry, amines with three different substituents are considered chiral. Such amines are analogous to chiral alkanes in that the nitrogen atom will possess four different substituents - considering the lone pair of electrons to be the fourth substituent. However, unlike chiral alkanes, chiral amines do not exist in two separate enantiomers. Pyramidal nitrogen inversion between the two enantiomeric forms occurs so rapidly at room temperature that the two forms cannot be isolated.

11.1.1 The Basicity of Amines

Along with the three attached groups, amines have an unbonded electron pair. Most of the chemistry of amines depends on this unbonded electron pair:

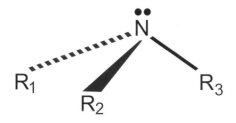

The electron pair is stabilized by the electron donating effects of alkyl groups. Thus the lone pair in tertiary amines is more stable than in secondary amines which, in turn, is more stable than in primary amines. As a result of this electron pair, amines are Lewis bases (see CHM 3.4), and good nucleophiles. In aqueous solution, amines are weak bases, and can accept a proton:

$$R_3N + H_2O \longrightarrow R_3NH^+ + OH^-$$

The ammonium cation in the preceding reaction is stabilized, once again, by the electron donating effects of the alkyl groups. Conversely, should the nitrogen be adjacent to a carbocation, the lone pair can stabilize the carbocation by delocalizing the charge.

The relative basicity of amines is deter-mined by the following:

- If the free amine is stabilized relative to the cation, the amine is less basic.
- If the cation is stabilized relative to the free amine, the amine is more stable, thus the stronger base.

Groups that withdraw electron density (such as halides or aromatics) decrease the availability of the unbonded electron pair. Electron releasing groups (such as alkyl groups) increase the availability of the unbonded electron pair. The base strength then increases in the following series (where Ø represents a phenyl group):

$$NO_2–Ø–NH_2 < Ø–NH_2 < Ø–CH_2–NH_2 < NH_3$$
$$< CH_3–NH_2 < (CH_3)_2–N–H < (CH_3)_3–N$$

Note that a substituent attached to an aromatic ring can greatly affect the basicity of the amine. For example, electron withdrawing groups (i.e. $–NO_2$) withdraw electrons from the ring which, in turn, withdraws the lone electron pair (*delocalization*) from nitrogen. Thus the lone pair is less available to bond with a proton; consequently, it is a weaker base. The opposite occurs with an electron donating group, making the amine, relatively, a better base (see ORG Chapter 5).

11.1.2 More Properties of Amines

- The nitrogen atom can <u>hydrogen bond</u> (using its electron pair) to hydrogens attached to other N's or O's. It can also form hydrogen bonds from hydrogens attached to it with electron pairs of N, O, F or Cl:

$$-N-H \cdots\cdots\cdots O-H$$

or

$$-\overset{..}{N}- \cdots\cdots -\overset{H}{\underset{O-H}{|}}$$

Note that primary or secondary amines can hydrogen bond with each other, but tertiary amines cannot. This leads to boiling points which are higher than would be expected for compounds of similar molecular weight, like alkanes, but lower than similar alcohols or carboxylic acids. The hydrogen bonding also renders low weight amines soluble in water.

- A <u>dipole moment</u> is possible:

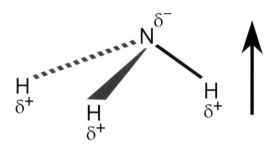

- The nitrogen in amines can contribute its lone pair electrons to activate a benzene ring. Thus amines are ortho-para directors.

- The <u>solubility of quaternary salts</u> decreases with increasing molecular weight. The quaternary structure has steric hindrance and the lone pair electrons on N is not available for H-bonding, thus their solubility is much less than other amines or even alkyl ammonium salts (i.e. $R-NH_3^+X^-$, $R_2-NH_2^+X^-$, $R_3-NH^+X^-$). Quaternary ammonium salts can be synthesized from ammonium hydroxides which are very strong bases.

$$(CH_3)_4N^+OH^- + HCl \longrightarrow (CH_3)_4N^+Cl^- + H_2O$$

Quaternary hydroxide   Quaternary salt

11.2 Important Reactions of Amines

- **Amide formation** is an important reaction for protein synthesis. Primary and secondary amines will react with carboxylic acids and their derivatives to form *amides*:

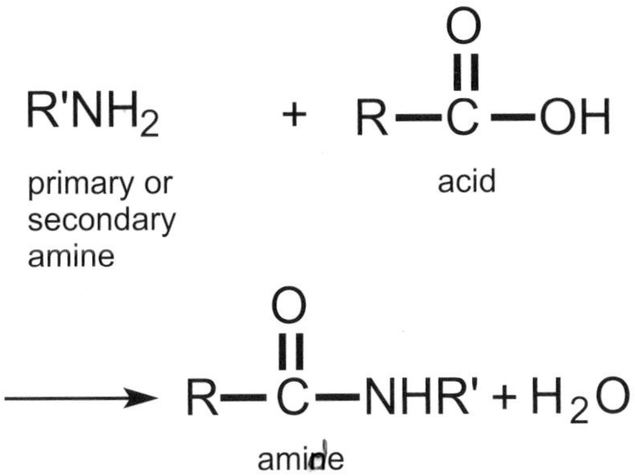

$$R'NH_2 \ + \ R-\overset{\overset{O}{\|}}{C}-OH$$

primary or secondary amine   acid

$$\longrightarrow \ R-\overset{\overset{O}{\|}}{C}-NHR' + H_2O$$

amide

Amides can engage in resonance such that the lone pair electrons on the nitrogen is delocalized. Thus amides are by far less basic than amines.

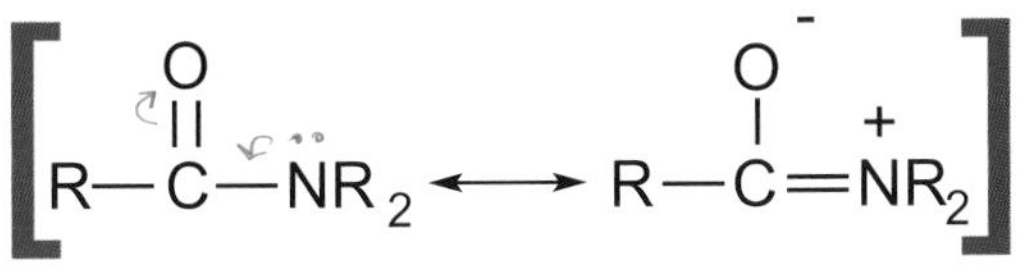

$$\left[R-\overset{\overset{O}{\|}}{C}-\overset{..}{N}R_2 \longleftrightarrow R-\overset{\overset{O^-}{|}}{C}=\overset{+}{N}R_2 \right]$$

As can be seen, the C–N bond has a partial double bond character. Thus there is restricted rotation about the C–N bond.

- **Alkylation** is another important reaction which involves amines with alkyl halides:

$$RCH_2Cl + R'\overset{..}{N}H_2 \longrightarrow RCH_2NH\,R' + HCl$$

1°, 2° or 3° amine

Both amide formation and alkylation make use of the nucleophilic character of the electrons on nitrogen.

Thus ammonia or an alkyl amine reacts with an alkyl halide to yield an amine in an S_N2 mechanism. Ammonia produces a primary amine; a primary amine produces a secondary amine; a secondary amine produces a tertiary amine; and tertiary amine produces a quaternary ammonium salt.

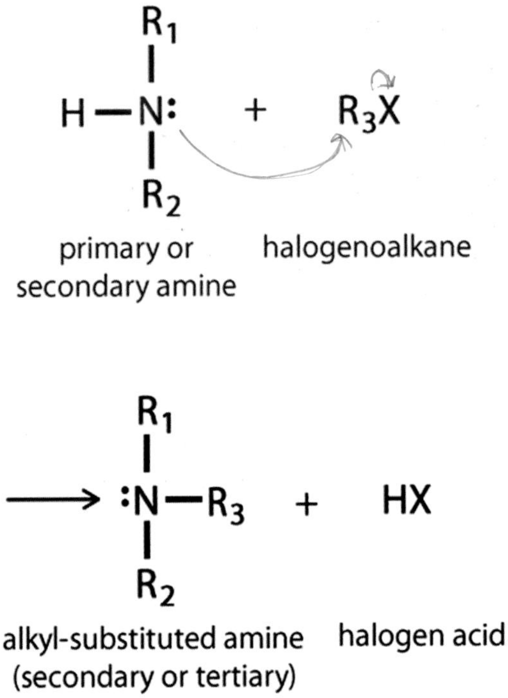

$$H-\overset{\overset{R_1}{|}}{\underset{\underset{R_2}{|}}{N}}: \ + \ R_3X$$

primary or secondary amine   halogenoalkane

$$\longrightarrow :\overset{\overset{R_1}{|}}{\underset{\underset{R_2}{|}}{N}}-R_3 \ + \ HX$$

alkyl-substituted amine   halogen acid
(secondary or tertiary)

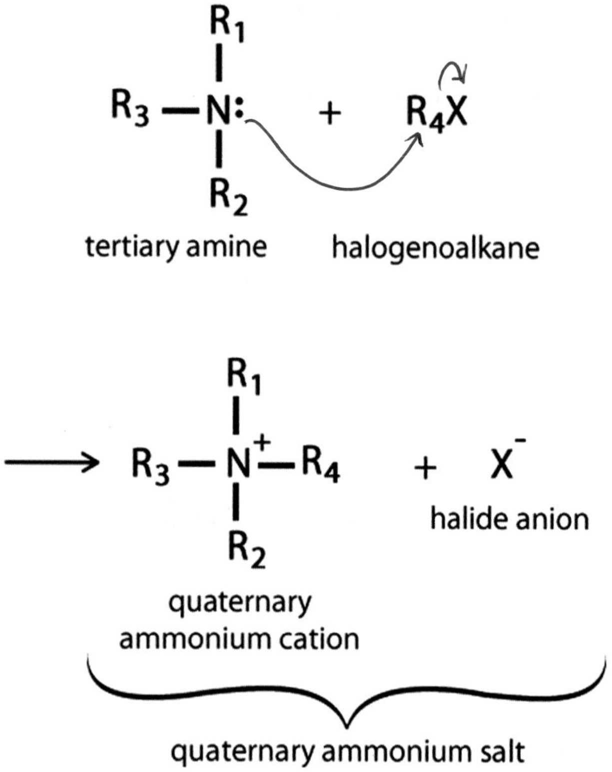

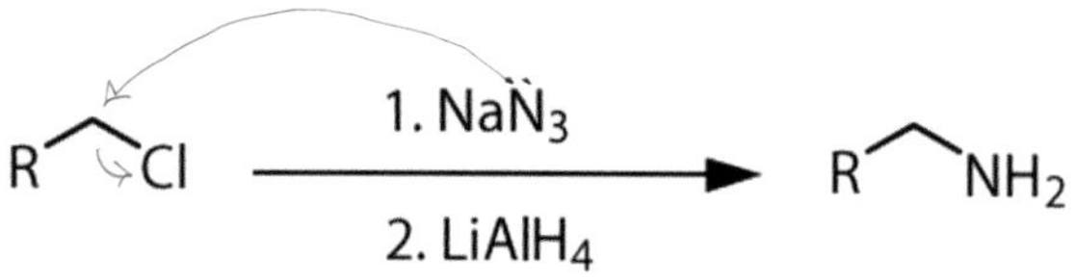

Gabriel amine synthesis occurs via a phthalimide ion displacing the halide from the alkyl halide followed by basic hydrolysis of the N-alkyl phthalimide yielding a primary amine.

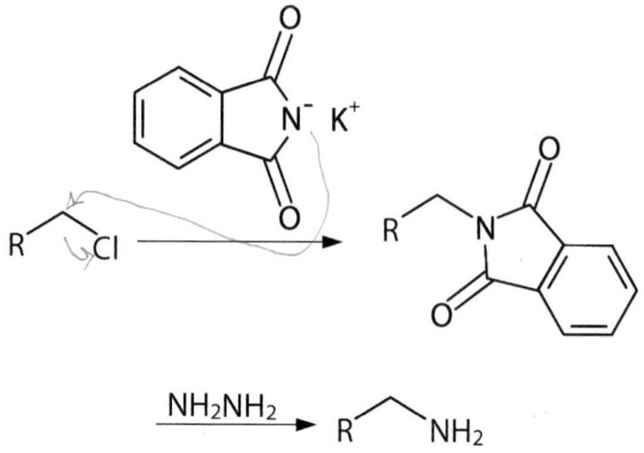

tertiary amine   halogenoalkane

quaternary
ammonium cation

quaternary ammonium salt

- **Reductive amination**: Amines can also be synthesized by reductive amination in which an aldehyde or ketone reacts with ammonia, a primary amine or a secondary amine to form a corresponding primary amine, secondary amine or tertiary amine.

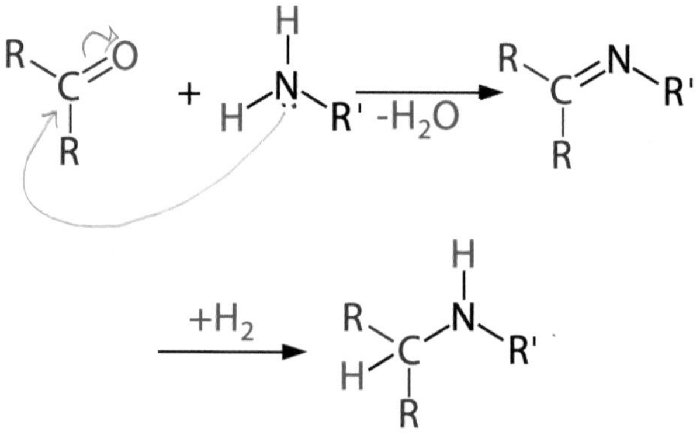

- **Gabriel synthesis**: Primary amines can also be obtained from azide synthesis and Gabriel synthesis in an S_N2 mechanism. The azide ion N_3^-, acting as a nucleophile, displaces the halide ion from the alkyl halide to form RN_3, which is then reduced by $LiAlH_4$ to form the desired primary amine.

- **Reduction of nitriles**: Nitriles can be reduced by $LiAlH_4$ to produce primary amines. This offers a way to convert alkyl halides into primary amines with one more carbon atom.

- **Reduction of amides**: Amides can also be reduced by $LiAlH_4$ to produce primary amines. Thus carboxylic acids can be converted into primary amines with the same number of carbon atoms.

Amides

$$R-\overset{O}{\underset{\|}{C}}-\overset{\cdot\cdot}{N}\big<\,^{R'}_{R''} \;\longleftrightarrow\; R-\overset{O^-}{\underset{\|}{C}}=\overset{+}{N}\big<\,^{R'}_{R''}$$

Actually :

$$R-\overset{O^{\delta-}}{\underset{|}{C}}\cdots N^{\delta+}\big<\,^{R'}_{R''}$$

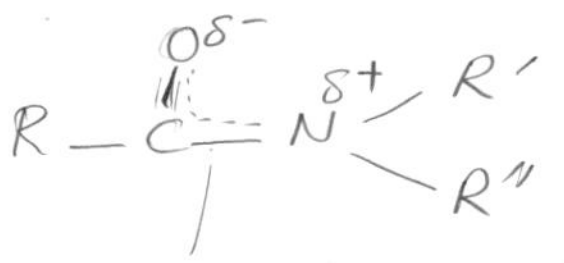

- restricted rotation – Partly delocolization.

- Lone pairs of Nitrogen are not freely available for bonding – lone pair involved in delocolization.

Best base?

a) $R-\overset{O}{\underset{\|}{C}}-\underset{\delta+}{NH_2}$ amide : Poor base

b) NH_3

c) $CH_3\,NH_2$ – more $\ominus$ | alkyl groups – somewhate e⁻-donating.

d) $(CH_3)_2\,NH$ – most $\ominus$ |

- Have to look for the δ⁻ or ⊖ w/ lone pair of e⁻ to be a good base (to accept a proton – as this is the definition of a base).

BIOLOGICAL MOLECULES
Chapter 12

Memorize	Understand	Importance
* Basic structures * Isoelectric point equation * Define: amphoteric, zwitterions	* Effect of H, S, hydrophobic bonds * Basic mechanisms of reactions * Effect of pH, isoelectric point * Protein structure * Different ways of drawing structures	**0 to 2 out of the 30 ORG** DAT questions are based on content in this chapter (in our estimation). * Note that between 30% and 60% of the questions in DAT Organic Chemistry are based on content from 4 chapters: 1, 2, 5 and 6.

DAT-Prep.com

Introduction

Biological molecules truly involve the chemistry of life. Such molecules include amino acids and proteins, carbohydrates (glucose, disaccharides, polysaccharides), lipids (triglycerides, steroids) and nucleic acids (DNA, RNA).

Additional Resources

Free Online Q&A + Forum   Video: Online or DVD   Flashcards   Special Guest

12.1 Amino Acids

Amino acids are molecules that contain a side chain (*R*), a carboxylic acid, and an amino group at the α carbon. Thus the general structure of α-amino acids is:

$$
\begin{array}{ccc}
& \text{O} & \\
& \parallel & \\
& \text{C}-\text{OH} & \\
\text{H}_2\text{N} \blacktriangleright\!\!\!-\!\!\!\blacktriangleleft \;\; & \text{C} & -\text{H} \\
& \mid & \\
& \text{R} & \\
\end{array}
\qquad
\begin{array}{ccc}
& \text{O} & \\
& \parallel & \\
& \text{C}-\text{OH} & \\
\text{H}-\!\!\!\blacktriangleright \;\; & \text{C} & \blacktriangleleft-\text{NH}_2 \\
& \mid & \\
& \text{R} & \\
\end{array}
$$

α-carbon

L - amino acid   D - amino acid

Amino acids may be named systematically as substituted carboxylic acids, however, there are 20 important α-amino acids that are known by common names. These are naturally occurring and they form the building blocks of most proteins found in humans. The following are a few examples of α-amino acids:

$$
\begin{array}{c}
\text{O} \\
\parallel \\
\text{C}-\text{OH} \\
\mid \\
\text{CH}_2 \\
\mid \\
\text{NH}_2 \\
\text{Glycine}
\end{array}
\qquad
\begin{array}{c}
\text{O} \\
\parallel \\
\text{C}-\text{OH} \\
\text{H}_2\text{N}-\text{C}-\text{H} \\
\mid \\
\text{CH}_3 \\
\text{Alanine}
\end{array}
$$

$$
\begin{array}{c}
\text{O} \\
\parallel \\
\text{C}-\text{OH} \\
\text{H}_2\text{N}-\text{C}-\text{H} \\
\mid \\
\text{CH}_2\text{OH} \\
\text{Serine}
\end{array}
\qquad
\begin{array}{c}
\text{O} \\
\parallel \\
\text{C}-\text{OH} \\
\text{H}_2\text{N}-\text{C}-\text{H} \\
\mid \\
\text{CH}_2\text{COOH} \\
\text{Aspartic acid}
\end{array}
$$

Note that the D/L system is commonly used for amino acid and carbohydrate chemistry. The reason is that naturally occurring amino acids have the same relative configuration, the L-configuration, while naturally occurring carbohydrates are nearly all D-configuration. However, the absolute configuration depends on the priority assigned to the side group (*see* ORG 2.3.1 *for rules*).

In the preceding amino acids, the S-configuration prevails (*except glycine which cannot be assigned any configuration since it is not chiral*).

The following mnemonic is helpful for determining the D/L isomeric form of an amino acid: the "CORN" rule. The substituents **CO**OH, **R**, **N**H$_2$, and H are arranged around the chiral center. Starting with H away from the viewer, if these groups are arranged clockwise around the chiral carbon, then it is the D-form. If counter-clockwise, it is the L-form.

Also note that, except for glycine, the α-carbon of all amino acids are chiral indicating that there must be two different enantiomeric forms.

12.1.1 Hydrophilic vs. Hydrophobic

Different types of amino acids tend to be found in different areas of the proteins that they make up. Amino acids which are ionic and/or polar are hydrophilic, and tend to be found on the exterior of proteins (i.e. *exposed to water*). These include aspartic acid and its amide, glutamic acid and its amide, lysine, arginine and histidine. Certain other polar amino acids are found on either the interior or exterior of proteins. These include serine, threonine, and tyrosine. Hydrophobic amino acids which may be found on the interior of proteins include methionine, leucine, trypto-

phan, valine and phenylalanine. Hydrophobic molecules tend to cluster in aqueous solutions (= *hydrophobic bonding*). Alanine is a nonpolar amino acid which is unusual because it is less hydrophobic than most nonpolar amino acids. This is because its nonpolar side chain is very short.

Glycine is the smallest amino acid, and the only one that is not optically active. It is often found at the 'corners' of proteins. Alanine is small and, although hydrophobic, is found on the surface of proteins.

12.1.2 Acidic vs. Basic

Amino acids have both an acid and basic components (= *amphoteric*). The amino acids with the R group containing an amino ($-NH_2$) group, are basic. The two basic amino acids are lysine and arginine. Amino acids with an R group containing a carboxyl ($-COOH$) group are acidic. The two acidic amino acids are aspartic acid and glutamic acid. One amino acid, histidine, may act as either an acid or a base, depending upon the pH of the resident solution. This makes histidine a very good

physiologic buffer. The rest of the amino acids are considered to be neutral.

The basic $-NH_2$ group in the amino acid is present as an ammonium ion, $-NH_3^+$. The acidic carboxyl $-COOH$ group is present as a carboxylate ion, $-COO^-$. As a result, amino acids are dipolar ions, or *zwitterions*. In an aqueous solution, there is an equilibrium present between the dipolar, the anionic, and the cationic forms of the amino acid:

$$H_3\overset{+}{N} - CH - CO_2H \underset{H_3O^+}{\rightleftharpoons} H_3\overset{+}{N} - CH - CO_2^- \underset{H_3O^+}{\rightleftharpoons} H_2N - CH - CO_2^-$$

Acidic (CH₃) — Neutral (CH₃) — Basic (CH₃)

Therefore the charge on the amino acid will vary with the pH of the solution, and with the <u>isoelectric point</u>. This point is the pH where a given amino acid will be neutral (i.e. have no net charge). For an amino acid with only one amine and one carboxyl group, the isoelectric point can be calculated from the average of the pK_a values of the 2 ionizable groups:

$$\text{isoelectric point} = pI = (pK_{a1} + pK_{a2})/2$$

For an acidic amino acid, the isoelectric point is the average of pK_a values of the carboxyl group and the additional carboxyl group on the side chain. For a basic amino acid, the isoelectric point is the average of pK_a values of the amino group and the additional amino group on the side chain.

Above the isoelectric point (basic conditions), the amino acids will have a net negative charge. Below the isoelectric point (acidic conditions), the amino acids will have a net positive charge.

As this is a common exam question, let's further summarize for the average amino acid: When in a relatively acidic solution, the amino acid is fully protonated and exists as a cation, that is, it has two protons available for dissociation, one from the carboxyl group and one from the amino group. When in a relatively basic solution, the amino acid is fully deprotonated and exists as an anion, that is, it has two proton accepting groups, the carboxyl group and the amino group. At the isoelectric point, the amino acid exists as a neutral, dipolar zwitterion, which means that the carboxyl group is deprotonated while the amino group is protonated.

12.1.3 The 20 Alpha-Amino Acids

1. <u>Nonpolar amino acids:</u> R groups are hydrophobic and thus decrease solubility. These amino acids are usually found within the interior of the protein molecule.

2. <u>Polar amino acids:</u> R groups are hydrophilic and thus increase the solubility. These amino acids are usually found on the protein's surface.

3. <u>Acidic amino acids:</u> R groups contain an additional carboxyl group. These amino

acids have a negative charge at physiological pH.

4. <u>Basic amino acids:</u> R groups contain an additional amine group. These amino acids have a positive charge at physiological pH. Note that asparagine and glutamine have amide side chains and are thus not considered basic (see ORG 9.3).

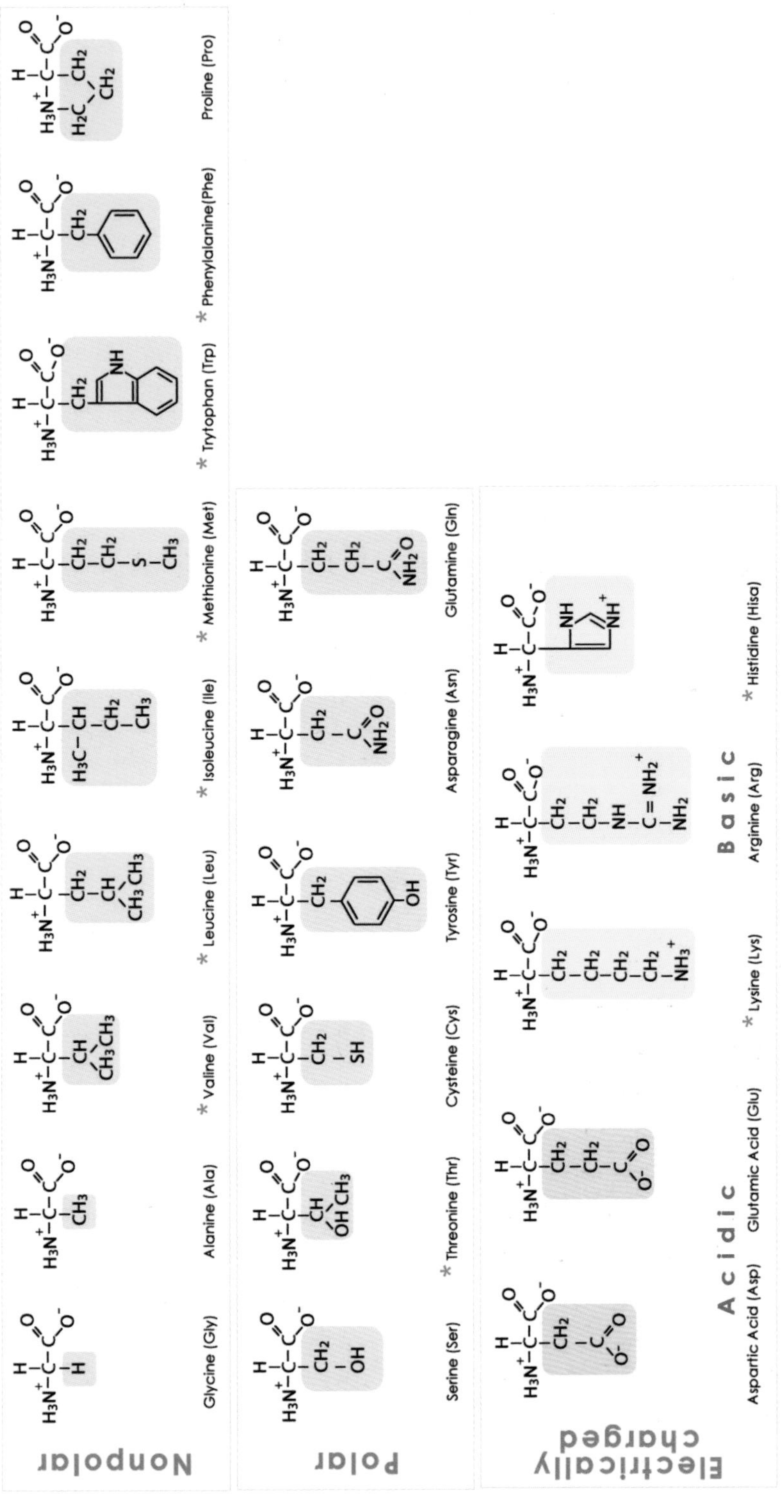

Figure 12.1.3 The 20 Standard Amino Acids. *9 essential amino acids.

12.2 Proteins

12.2.1 General Principles

Proteins are long chain polypeptides which often form higher order structures. Polypeptides are polymers of 40 to 1000 α-amino acids joined together by amide (*peptide*) bonds. These peptide bonds are derived from the amino group of one amino acid, and the acid group of another. When a peptide bond is formed, a molecule of water is released (*condensation = dehydration*). The bond can be broken by adding water (*hydrolysis*).

Since proteins are polymers of amino acids, they also have isoelectric points. Clas-

sification as to the acidity or basicity of a protein depends on the numbers of acidic and basic amino acids it contains. If there is an excess of acidic amino acids, the isoelectric point will be at a pH of less than 7. At $pH = 7$, these proteins will have a net negative charge. Similarly, those with an excess of basic amino acids will have an isoelectric point at a pH of greater than 7. Therefore, at $pH = 7$, these proteins will have a net positive charge. Proteins can be separated according to their isoelectric point on a polyacrylamide gel (*electrophoresis;* ORG 13.3).

12.2.2 Protein Structure

Protein structure may be divided into primary, secondary, tertiary and quaternary structures. The primary structure is the sequence of amino acids as determined by the DNA and the

location of covalent bonds (*including disulfide bonds*). Secondary, tertiary and quaternary structures all depend on primary structure.

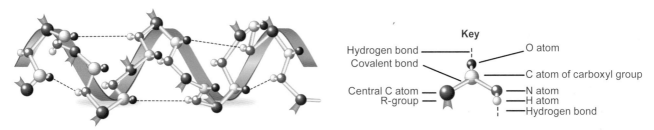

Key

Hydrogen bond ——————— O atom
Covalent bond ——————
——— C atom of carboxyl group
Central C atom ——— ——— N atom
R-group ——— ——— H atom
——— Hydrogen bond

Figure 12.2.2.1: Secondary Structure: α-helix. This is a structure in which the peptide chain is coiled into a helical structure around a central axis. This helix is stabilized by hydrogen bonding between the N-H group and C=O group four residues away. A typical example with this secondary structure is keratin.

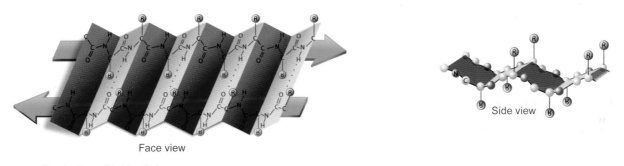

Face view

R = Amino acid side chain

Side view

Figure 12.2.2.2: Secondary Structure: Beta pleated sheet. Peptide chains lie alongside each other in a parallel manner. This structure is stabilized by hydrogen bonding between the N-H group on one peptide chain and C=O group on another. A typical example with this secondary structure is produced by some insect larvae: the protein fiber "silk" which is mostly composed of fibroin.

The <u>secondary structure</u> is the orderly inter- or intramolecular *hydrogen bonding* of the protein chain. The resultant structure may be the more stable α-helix (e.g. keratin), or a β-pleated sheet (e.g. silk). Proline is an amino acid which cannot participate in the regular array of H-bonding in an α-helix. Proline disrupts the α-helix, thus it is usually found at the beginning or end of a molecule (i.e. hemoglobin).

The <u>tertiary structure</u> is the further folding of the protein molecule onto itself. This structure is maintained by *noncovalent bonds* like hydrogen bonding, Van der Waals forces, hydrophobic bonding and electrostatic bonding. The resultant structure is a globular protein with a hydrophobic interior and hydrophilic exterior. Enzymes are classical examples of such a structure. In fact, enzyme activity often depends on tertiary structure.

The covalent bonding of cysteine (*disulfide bonds or bridge*) helps to stabilize the tertiary structure of proteins. Cysteine will form sulfur-sulfur covalent bonds with itself, producing *cystine*.

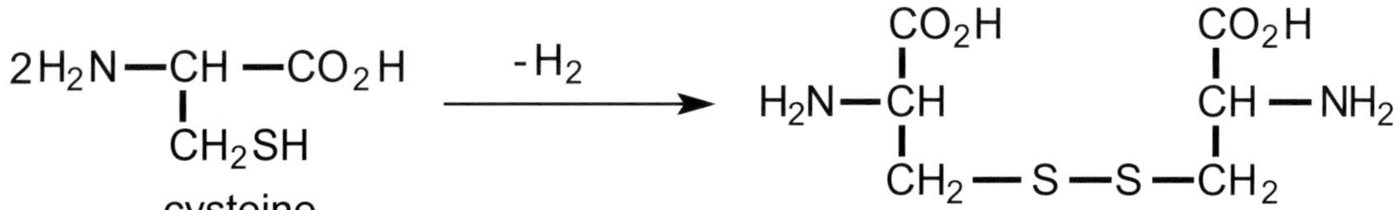

$$2H_2N-CH-CO_2H \xrightarrow{-H_2}$$

CH$_2$SH

cysteine

H_2N-CH ... CH$-NH_2$

CO$_2$H   CO$_2$H

CH$_2-S-S-CH_2$

cystine

The <u>quaternary structure</u> is when there are two or more protein chains bonded together by noncovalent bonds. For example, hemoglobin consists of four polypeptide subunits (*globin*) held together by hydrophobic bonds forming a globular almost tetrahedryl arrangement.

12.3 Carbohydrates

12.3.1 Description and Nomenclature

<u>Carbohydrates</u> are sugars and their derivatives. Formally they are 'carbon hydrates,' that is, they have the general formula $C_m(H_2O)_n$. Usually they are defined as polyhydroxy aldehydes and ketones, or substances that hydrolyze to yield polyhydroxy aldehydes and ketones. The basic units of carbohydrates are monosaccharides (sugars).

There are two ways to classify sugars. One way is to classify the molecule based on the type of carbonyl group it contains: one with an aldehyde carbonyl group is an *aldose*; one with a ketone carbonyl group is a *ketose*. The second method of classification depends on the number of carbons in the molecule: those with 6 carbons are hexoses, with 5 carbons are pentoses, with 4 carbons are tetroses, and with 3 carbons are trioses. Sugars may exist in either the ring form, as hemiacetals, or in the straight chain form, as polyhydroxy aldehydes. *Pyranoses* are 6 carbon sugars in the ring form; *furanoses* are 5 carbon sugars in the ring form.

In the ring form, there is the possibility of α or β *anomers*. Anomers occur when 2 cyclic forms of the molecule differ in conformation only at the hemiacetal carbon (carbon 1). Generally, pyranoses take the 'chair' conformation, as it is very stable, with all (usually) hydroxyl groups at the equatorial position. *Epimers* are diastereomers that differ in the configuration of only one stereogenic center. For carbohydrates, epimers are 2 monosaccharides which differ in the conformation of one hydroxyl group.

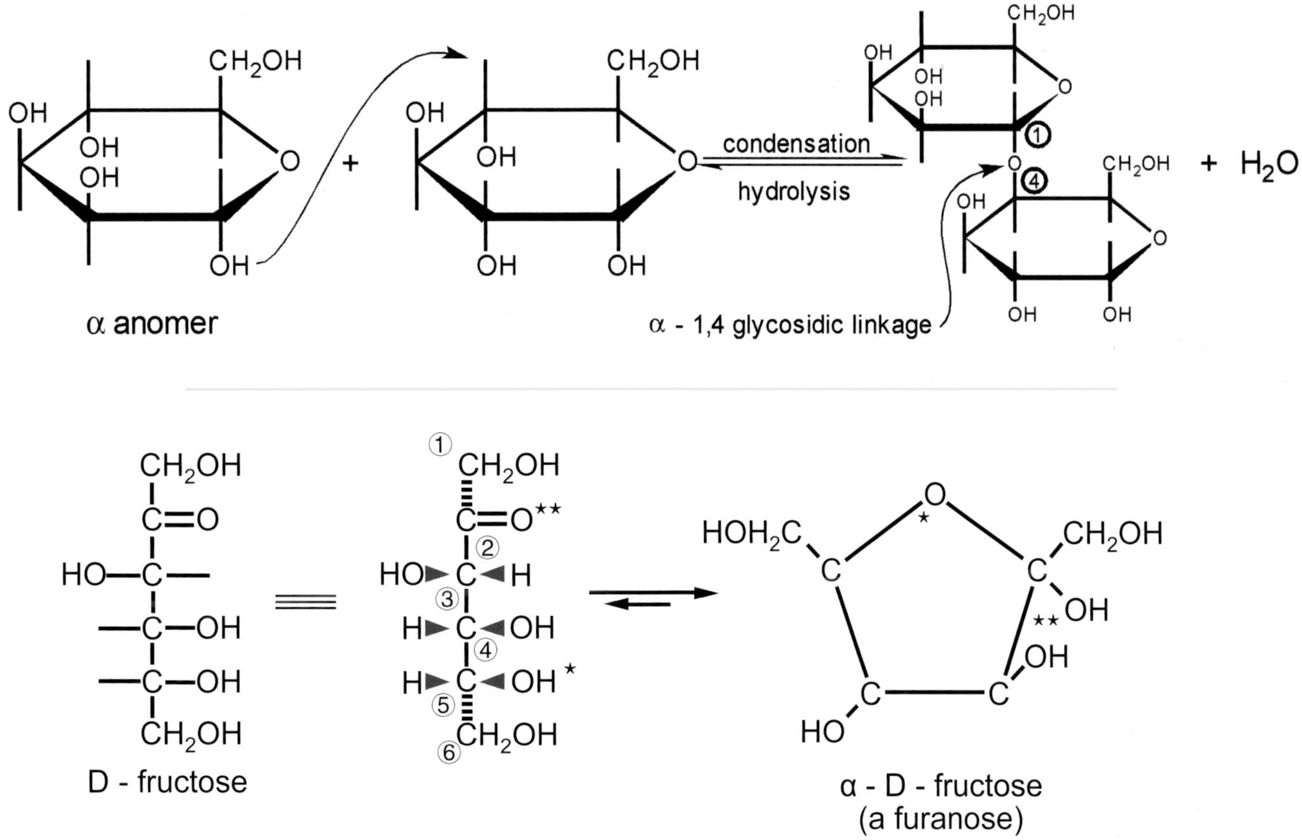

Figure IV.B.12.1 Part I: Names, structures and configurations of common sugars.

To determine the number of possible optical isomers, one need only know the number of asymmetric carbons, normally 4 for hexoses and 3 for pentoses, designated as n. The number of optical isomers is then 2^n, where n is the number of asymmetric carbons (ORG 2.2.2).

Most but not all of the naturally occurring aldoses have the D-configuration. Thus they have the same *relative* configuration as D-glyceraldehyde. The configuration (D or L) is *only* assigned to the highest numbered chiral carbon. The *absolute* configuration can be determined for any chiral carbon. For example, using the rules from Section 2.3.1, it can be determined that the absolute configuration of D-glyceraldehyde is the R-configuration.

The names and structures of some common sugars are shown in Figure IV.B.12.1.

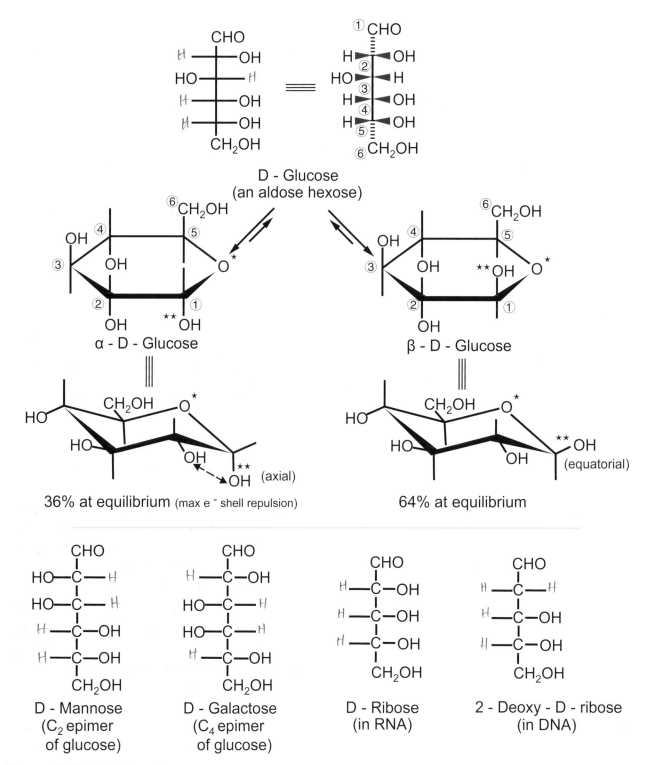

D - Glucose
(an aldose hexose)

α - D - Glucose

β - D - Glucose

36% at equilibrium (max e⁻ shell repulsion)

64% at equilibrium

D - Mannose
(C$_2$ epimer
of glucose)

D - Galactose
(C$_4$ epimer
of glucose)

D - Ribose
(in RNA)

2 - Deoxy - D - ribose
(in DNA)

Figure IV.B.12.1 Part II: Names, structures and configurations of common sugars. Though not by convention, H belongs to the end of all empty bonds in the diagrams above.

In the diagram that follows, you will notice a Fischer projection to the far left (*see* ORG 2.3.1). You will also find Fischer projections in the following pages since they are a common way to represent carbohydrates.

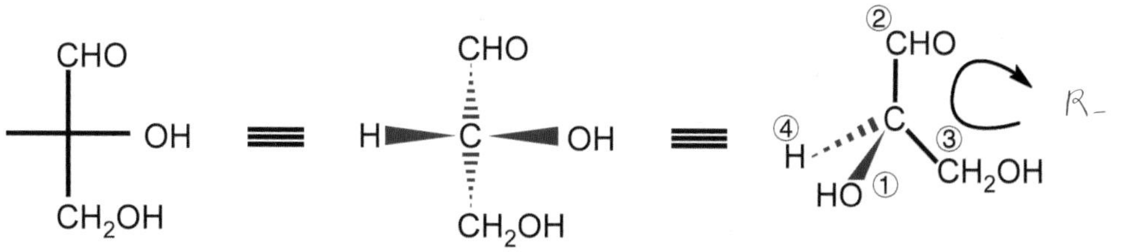

Fischer projection and 3-dimensional representation of D-glyceraldehyde, R-glyceraldehyde (*see* ORG 2.1, 2.2, 2.3 for rules).

12.3.2 Important Reactions of Carbohydrates

Hemiacetal Reaction

Monosaccharides can undergo an intramolecular nucleophilic addition reaction to form cyclic hemiacetals (see ORG 7.2.2). For example, the hydroxyl group on C4 of ribose attacks the aldehyde group on C1 forming a five-membered ring called furanose.

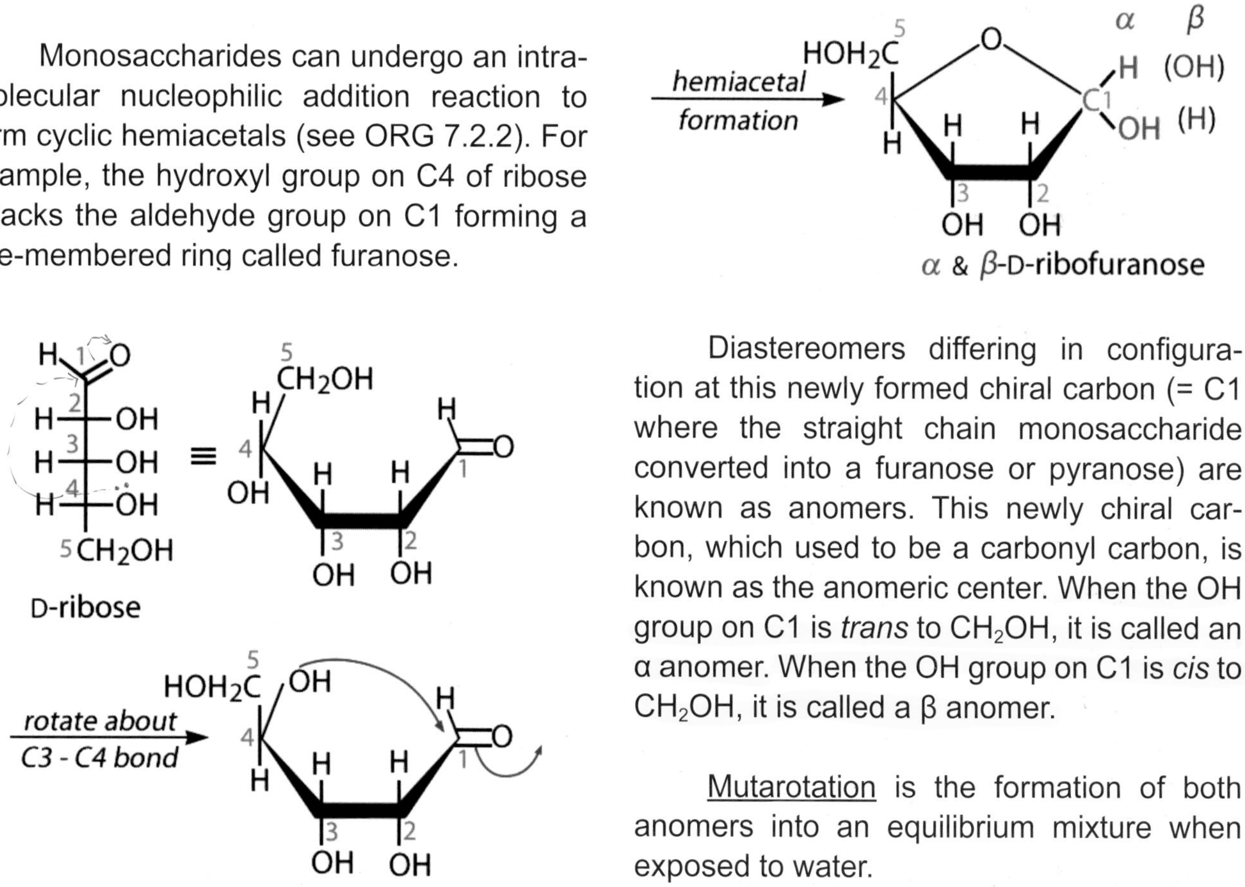

D-ribose

α & β-D-ribofuranose

Diastereomers differing in configuration at this newly formed chiral carbon (= C1 where the straight chain monosaccharide converted into a furanose or pyranose) are known as anomers. This newly chiral carbon, which used to be a carbonyl carbon, is known as the anomeric center. When the OH group on C1 is *trans* to CH_2OH, it is called an α anomer. When the OH group on C1 is *cis* to CH_2OH, it is called a β anomer.

Mutarotation is the formation of both anomers into an equilibrium mixture when exposed to water.

Glycosidic Bonds

A <u>disaccharide</u> is a molecule made up of two monosaccharides, joined by a *glycosidic bond* between the hemiacetal carbon of one molecule, and the hydroxyl group of another. The glycosidic bond forms an α-1,4-glycosidic linkage if the reactant is an α anomer. A β-1,4-glycosidic linkage is formed if the reactant is a β anomer. When the bond is formed, one molecule of water is released (condensation). In order to break the bond, water must be added (hydrolysis):

- Sucrose (common sugar) = glucose + fructose
- Lactose (milk sugar) = glucose + galactose
- Maltose (α-1,4 bond) = glucose + glucose
- Cellobiose (β-1,4 bond) = glucose + glucose

Ester Formation

Monosaccharides react with acid chloride or acid anhydride to form esters (see ORG 9.4, 9.4.1). All of the hydroxyl groups can be esterified.

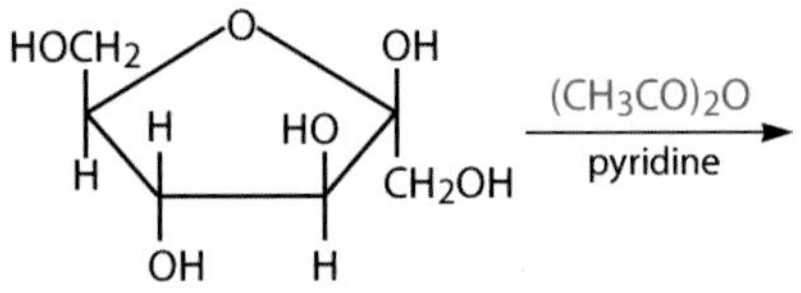

β-D-fructofuranose

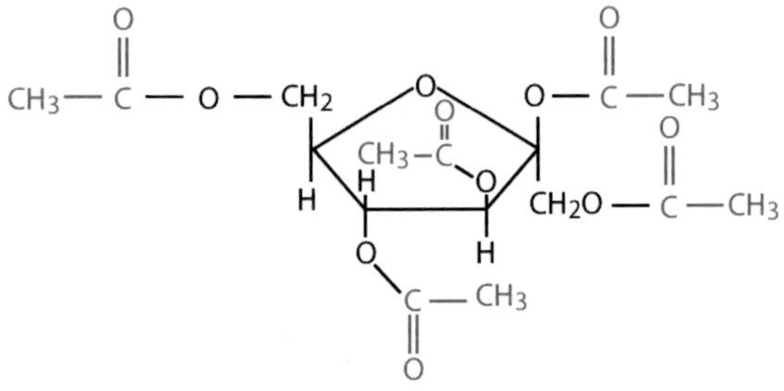

penta-O-acetyl-β-D-fructofuranoside

Ether Formation

Monosaccharides react with alkyl halide in the presence of silver oxide to form ethers. All of the hydroxyl groups are converted to -OR groups.

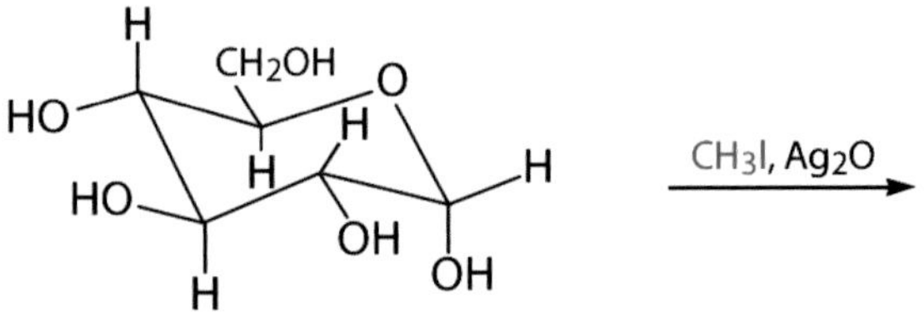

α-D-glucopyranose

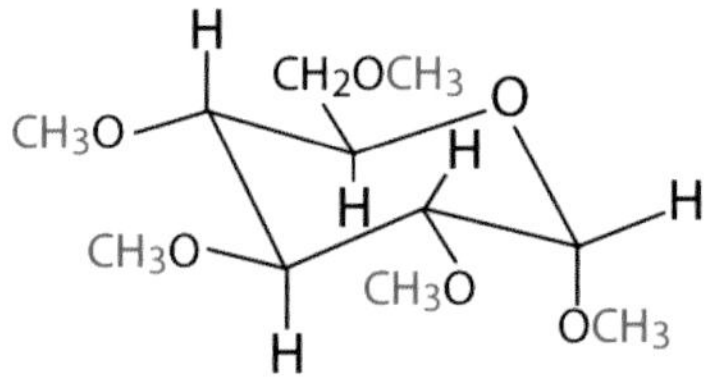

methyl 2, 3, 4, 6-tetra-O-methyl-α-D-glucopyranoside

Ether synthesis can also proceed using alcohols (see ORG 10.1):

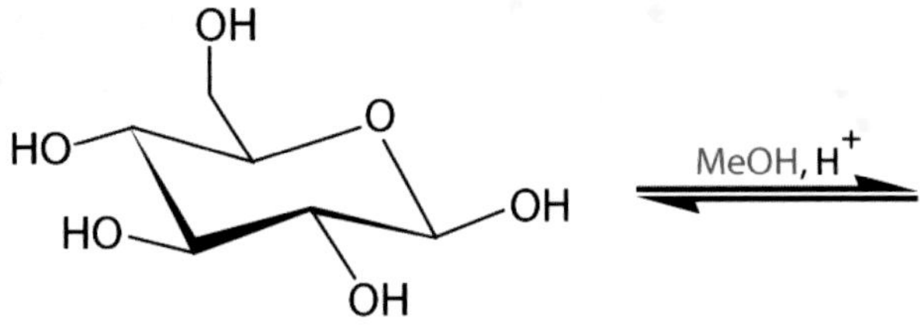

β-D-glucopyranose

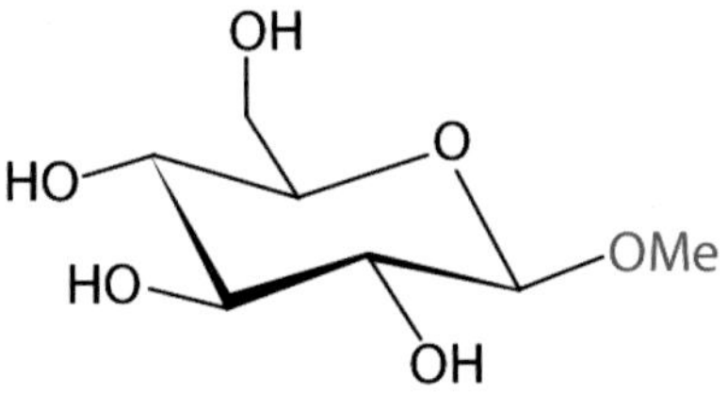

methyl-β-D-glucopyranoside

Reduction Reaction

Open chain monosaccharides are present in equilibrium between the aldehyde/ketone and the hemiacetal form.

Therefore, monosaccharides can be reduced by $NaBH_4$ to form polyalcohols (see ORG 6.2.2).

D-glucose   **D-sorbitol**

Oxidation Reaction

Again, the hemiacetal ring form is in equilibrium with the open chain aldehyde/ketone form. Aldoses can be oxidized by the Tollens' reagent $[Ag(NH_3)_2]^+$, Fehling's reagent $(Cu_2/Na_2C_4H_4O_6)$, and Benedict's reagent $(Cu_2/Na_3C_6H_5O_7)$ to yield carboxylic acids. If the Tollens' reagent is used, metallic silver is produced as a shiny mirror. If the Fehling's reagent or Benedict's reagent is used, cuprous oxide is produced as a reddish precipitate.

β-D-glucose   **open-chain form**   **gluconic acid (+ side products)**

When aldoses are treated with bromine water, the aldehyde is oxidized to a carboxylic acid group, resulting in a product known as an *aldonic acid*:

$$
\begin{array}{c}
\text{CHO} \\
\text{H}\!-\!\!-\!\text{OH} \\
\text{HO}\!-\!\!-\!\text{H} \\
\text{H}\!-\!\!-\!\text{OH} \\
\text{H}\!-\!\!-\!\text{OH} \\
\text{CH}_2\text{OH}
\end{array}
\;+\; \text{Br}_2 \;\xrightarrow[\substack{\text{CaCO}_3 \\ \text{pH 5-6}}]{\text{H}_2\text{O}}\;
\begin{array}{c}
\text{CO}_2 \\
\text{H}\!-\!\!-\!\text{OH} \\
\text{HO}\!-\!\!-\!\text{H} \\
\text{H}\!-\!\!-\!\text{OH} \\
\text{H}\!-\!\!-\!\text{OH} \\
\text{CH}_2\text{OH}
\end{array}
\;+\; \text{HBr}
$$

D-glucose (an aldose)   D-Gluconic acid (an aldonic acid)

Aldoses treated with dilute nitric acid will have both the primary alcohol and aldehyde groups oxidize to carboxylic acid groups, resulting in a product known as an *aldaric acid*:

$$
\begin{array}{c}
\text{CHO} \\
\text{H}\!-\!\!-\!\text{OH} \\
\text{HO}\!-\!\!-\!\text{H} \\
\text{H}\!-\!\!-\!\text{OH} \\
\text{H}\!-\!\!-\!\text{OH} \\
\text{CH}_2\text{OH}
\end{array}
\;\xrightarrow[\text{55-60}^\circ]{\text{HNO}_3}\;
\begin{array}{c}
\text{CO}_2\text{H} \\
\text{H}\!-\!\!-\!\text{OH} \\
\text{HO}\!-\!\!-\!\text{H} \\
\text{H}\!-\!\!-\!\text{OH} \\
\text{H}\!-\!\!-\!\text{OH} \\
\text{CO}_2\text{H}
\end{array}
$$

D-glucose (an aldose)   D-Glucaric acid (an aldaric acid)

Reducing Sugars/Non-reducing Sugars

All aldoses are reducing sugars because they contain an aldehyde carbonyl group. Some ketoses such as fructose are reducing sugars as well. They can be isomerized through keto-enol tautomerization (ORG 7.1) to an aldose, which can be oxidized normally. Glycosides are non-reducing sugars because the acetal group cannot be hydrolyzed to aldehydes. Thus they do not react with the Tollens' reagent.

12.3.3 Polysaccharides

Polymers of many monosaccharides are called <u>polysaccharides</u>. As in disaccharides, they are joined by glycosidic linkages. They may be straight chains, or branched chains. Some common polysaccharides are:

- Starch (plant energy storage)
- Cellulose (plant structural component)
- Glycocalyx (associated with the plasma membrane)
- Glycogen (animal energy storage in the form of glucose)
- Chitin (structural component found in shells or arthropods)

Carbohydrates are the most abundant organic constituents of plants. They are the source of chemical energy in living organisms, and, in plants, they are used in making the support structures. Cellulose consists of $\beta(1\rightarrow4)$ linked D-glucose. Starch and glycogen are mostly $\alpha(1\rightarrow4)$ glycosidic linkages of D-glucose.

Naturally, "triacyl" refers to the presence of 3 acyl subtituents (RCO-, ORG 9.1). <u>Lipids</u> are a class of organic molecules containing many different types of substances, such as fatty acids, fats, waxes, triacyl glycerols, terpenes and steroids.

Triacyl glycerols are oils and fats of either animal or plant origin. In general, fats are solid at room temperature, and oils are liquid at room temperature. The general structure of a triacyl glycerol is:

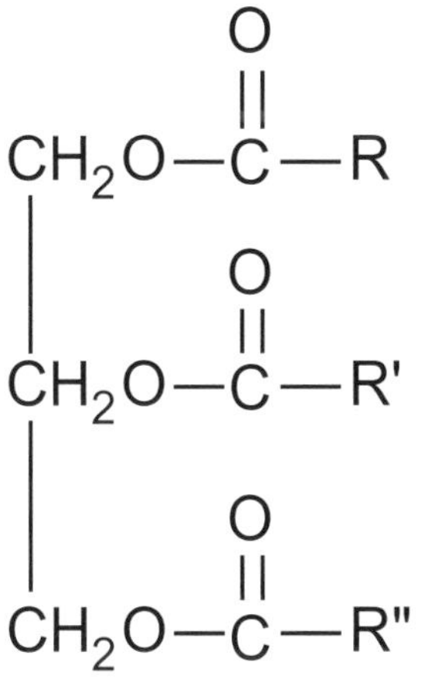

$$CH_2O-\overset{\displaystyle O}{\overset{\displaystyle \|}{C}}-R$$

$$CH_2O-\overset{\displaystyle O}{\overset{\displaystyle \|}{C}}-R'$$

$$CH_2O-\overset{\displaystyle O}{\overset{\displaystyle \|}{C}}-R''$$

The R groups may be the same or different, and are usually long chain alkyl groups. Upon hydrolysis of a triacyl glycerol, the products are three fatty acids and glycerol (*see*

ORG 9.4.1). The fatty acids may be saturated (= no multiple bonds, i.e. *palmitic acid*) or unsaturated (= containing double or triple bonds, i.e. *oleic acid*). Unsaturated fatty acids are usually in the *cis* configuration. Saturated fatty acids have a higher melting point than unsaturated fatty acids. Some common fatty acids are:

$$CH_3(CH_2)_{14}COOH$$
palmitic acid

$$CH_3(CH_2)_{16}COOH$$
stearic acid

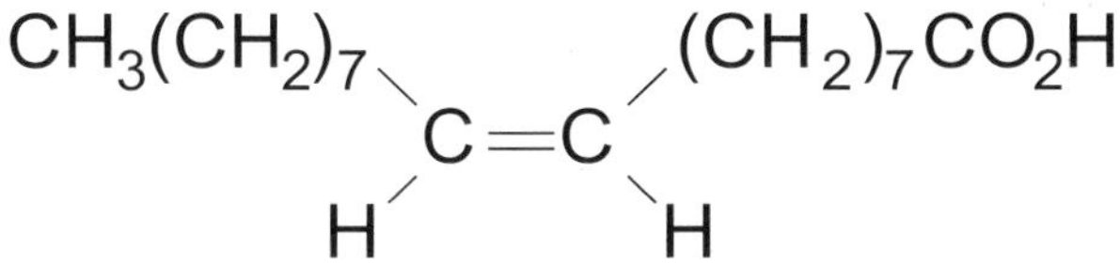

oleic acid

Soap is a mixture of salts of long chain fatty acids formed by the hydrolysis of fat. This process is called saponification. Soap possesses both a nonpolar hydrocarbon tail and a polar carboxylate head. When soaps are dispersed in aqueous solution, the long nonpolar tails are inside the sphere while the polar heads face outward.

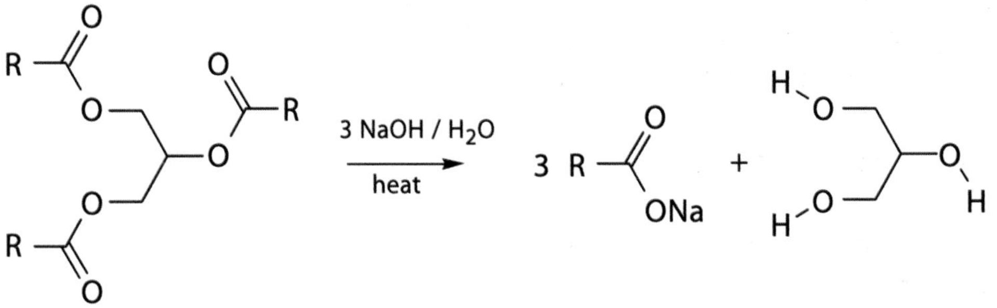

Soaps are surfactants. They are compounds that lower the surface tension of a liquid because of their amphipathic nature (i.e. they contain both hydrophobic tails and hydrophilic heads).

Of course, the cellular membrane is a lipid bilayer (Biology Chapter 1). The polar heads of the lipids align towards the aqueous environment, while the hydrophobic tails minimize their contact with water and tend to cluster together. Depending on the concentration of the lipid, this interaction may result in micelles (spherical), liposomes (spherical) or lipid bilayers.

Micelles are closed lipid monolayers with a fatty acid core and polar surface. The main function of bile (BIO 9.4.1) is to facilitate the formation of micelles, which promotes the processing or emulsification of dietary fat and fat-soluble vitamins.

Liposomes are composed of a lipid bilayer separating an aqueous internal compartment from the bulk aqueous phase. Liposomes can be used as a vehicle for the administration of nutrients or pharmaceutical drugs.

See BIO 20.4 for illustrations of a lipid bilayer, a liposome and micelles.

12.4.1 Steroids

Steroids are derivatives of the basic ring structure:

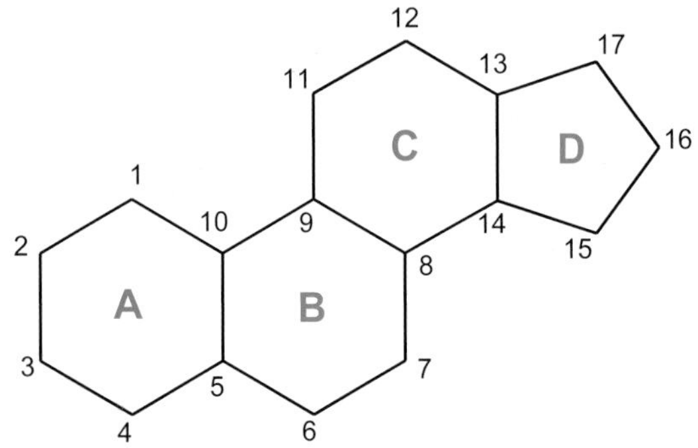

Estradiol
(an estrogen)

The IUPAC-recommended ring lettering and carbon numbering are as shown above. Many important substances are steroids, some examples include: cholesterol, D vitamins, bile acids, adrenocortical hormones, and male and female sex hormones.

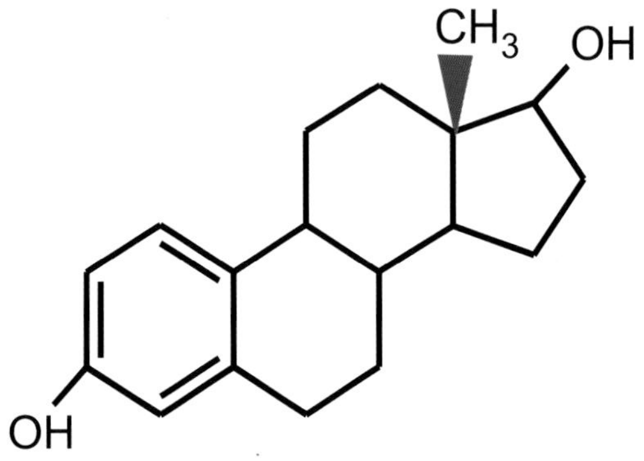

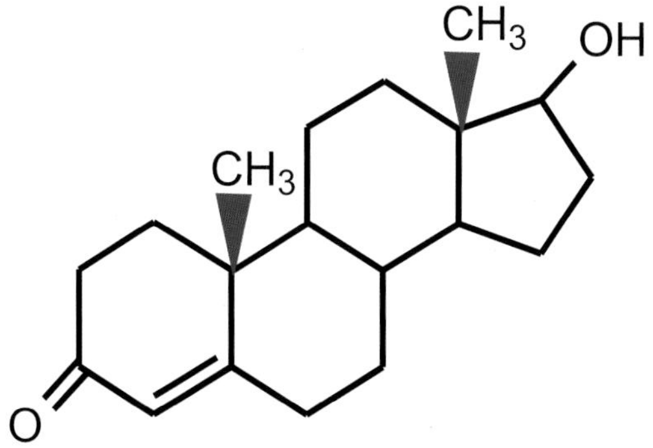

Since such a significant portion of a steroid contains hydrocarbons, which are hydrophobic, steroids can dissolve through the hydrophobic interior of a cell's plasma membrane. Furthermore, steroid hormones contain polar side groups which allow the hormone to easily dissolve in water. Thus steroid hormones are well designed to be transported through the vascular space, to cross the plasma membranes of cells, and to have an effect either in the cell's cytosol or, as is usually the case, in the nucleus.

**Testosterone
(an androgen)**

12.5 Phosphorous in Biological Molecules

Phosphorous is an essential component of various biological molecules including adenosine triphosphate (ATP), phospholipids in cell membranes, and the nucleic acids which form DNA. Phosphorus can also form phosphoric acid and several phosphate esters:

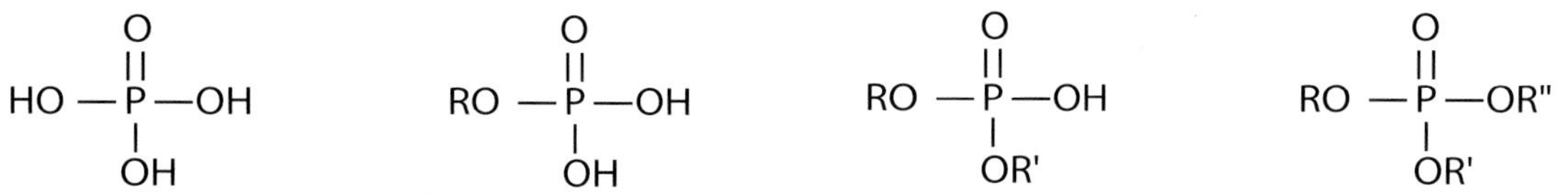

phosphoric acid

phosphate esters

A phospholipid is produced from three ester linkages to glycerol. Phosphoric acid is ester linked to the terminal hydroxyl group and two fatty acids are ester linked to the two remaining hydroxyl groups of glycerol (*see Biology Section 1.1 for a schematic view of a phospholipid*).

In DNA the phosphate groups engage in two ester linkages creating phosphodiester bonds. It is the 5' phosphorylated position of one pentose ring which is linked to the 3' position of the next pentose ring (*see* BIO 1.1.2):

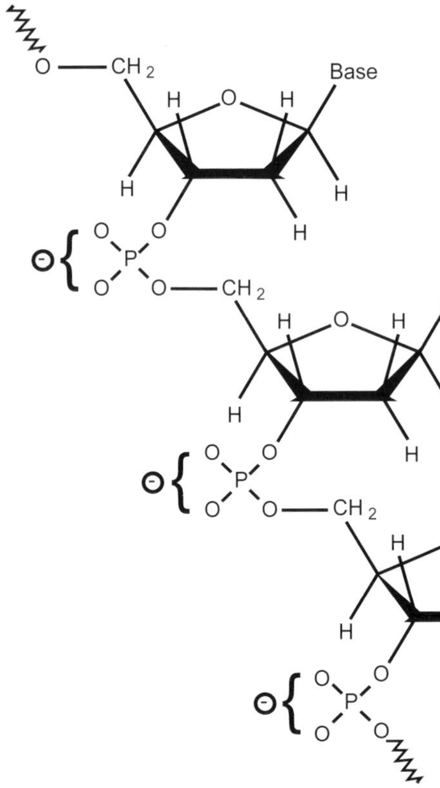

In Biology Chapter 4, the production of ATP was discussed. In each case the components ADP and P$_i$ (= *inorganic phosphate*) combined using the energy generated from a coupled reaction to produce ATP. The linkage between the phosphate groups are via *anhydride bonds*:

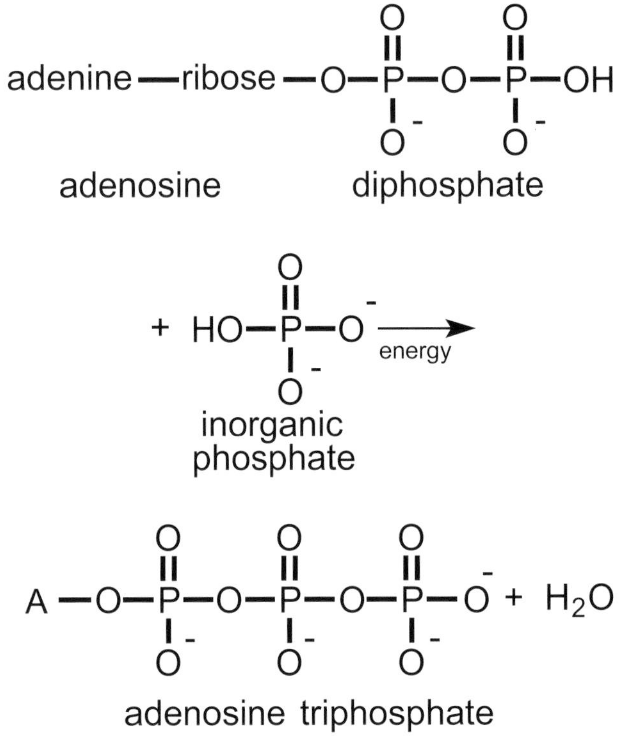

adenine —ribose

adenosine

diphosphate

inorganic phosphate

adenosine triphosphate

<u>Amino acids</u> α-hydrogen - slightly acidic.

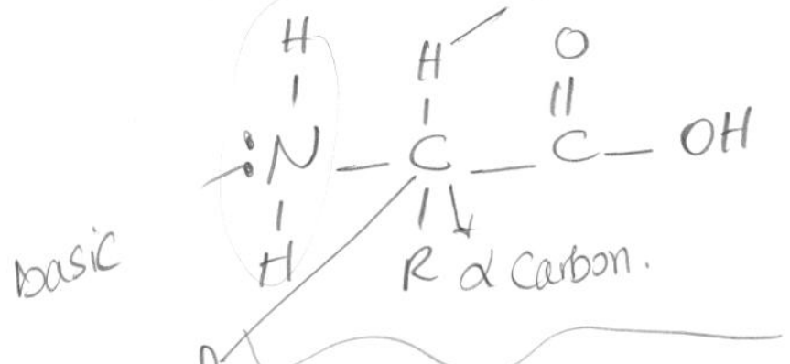

$$:N - C - C - OH$$

basic   α - amino acids.

R α Carbon.

chiral
- optically
active.

amphoteric - has both acid & base group / part.

— glycine is not optically active.

Zwitterion - Has $\overset{+}{N}H_3$ & $COO^{\ominus}$

)   (
              basic
now
acidic

Isoelectric point - $\dfrac{(COOH) + (NH_2)}{pK_a + pK_a'}{2}$ — parts of the molecule that would ultimately dissociate.

(

dipolar aa at which the molecule is ~~not~~ neutral.

PH below IP — more protons available — overall charge $\oplus$

" above IP - less "   " — " $\ominus$.

SEPARATIONS AND PURIFICATIONS
Chapter 13

Memorize	Understand	Importance
Definitions of the major techniques Interactions between organic molecules	* Different phases in the various techniques * How to improve separation, purification * How to avoid overheating (distillation)	**1 to 3 out of the 30 ORG** DAT questions are based on content in this chapter (in our estimation). * Note that between 30% and 60% of the questions in DAT Organic Chemistry are based on content from 4 chapters: 1, 2, 5 and 6.

DAT-Prep.com

Introduction

Separation techniques are used to transform a mixture of substances into two or more distinct products. The separated products may be different in chemical properties or some physical property (i.e. size). Purification in organic chemistry is the physical separation of a chemical substance of interest from foreign or contaminating substances.

Additional Resources

Free Online Q&A + Forum   Video : Online or DVD   Flashcards   Special Guest

Extraction is the process by which a solute is transferred (*extracted*) from one solvent and placed in another. This procedure is possible if the two solvents used cannot mix (= *immiscible*) and if the solute is more soluble in the solvent used for the extraction.

For example, consider the extraction of solute A which is dissolved in solvent X. We choose solvent Y for the extraction since solute A is highly soluble in it and because solvent Y is immiscible with solvent X. We now add solvent Y to the solution involving solute A and solvent X. The container is agitated. Solute A begins to dissolve in the solvent where it is most soluble, solvent Y. The container is left to stand, thus the two immiscible solvents separate. The phase containing solute A can now be removed.

In practice, solvent Y would be chosen such that it would be sufficiently easy to evaporate (= *volatile*) after the extraction so solute A can be easily recovered. Also, it is more efficient to perform several extractions using a small amount of solvent each time, rather than one extraction using a large amount of solvent.

The main purpose of filtration is to isolate a solid from a liquid. There are two basic types of filtration: gravity filtration and vacuum filtration. In gravity filtration the solution containing the substance of interest is poured through the filter paper with the solvent's own weight responsible for pulling it through. This is often done using a hot solvent to ensure that the product remains dissolved. In vacuum

Vacume

filtration the solvent is forced through the filter with a ~~vacuum~~ *Vacume* on the other side. This is helpful when it is necessary to isolate large quantities of solid.

Sublimation is a process which goes from a heated solid directly into the gas phase without passing through the intermediate liquid phase (CHM 4.3.1). Low pressure reduces the temperature required for sublimation. The substance in question is heated and then condensed on a cool surface (cold finger), leaving the non-volatile impurities behind.

Centrifugation is a separation process that involves the use of centrifugal forces for the sedimentation of mixtures. Particles settle at different rates depending on their size, viscosity, density and shape. Compounds of greater mass and density settle toward the bottom while compounds of lighter mass and density remain on top. This process is most useful in separating polymeric materials such as biological macromolecules.

Distillation is the process by which compounds are separated based on differences in boiling points. Compounds with a lower boiling point are preferably vaporized, condensed on a water cooler, and are separated from compounds with higher boiling points.

1. **Simple distillation** is used to separate liquids whose boiling points differ by at least 25 °C and that boil below 150 °C. The composition of the distillate depends on the composition of the vapors at a given temperature and pressure.

2. **Vacuum distillation** is used to separate liquids whose boiling points differ by at least 25 °C and that boil above 150 °C. The vacuum environment prevents compounds from decomposition because the low pressure reduces the temperature required for distillation.

3. **Fractional distillation** is used to separate liquids whose boiling points are less than 25 °C apart. The repeated vaporization-condensation cycle of compounds will eventually yield vapors that contain a greater and greater proportion of the lower boiling point component.

> **NOTE:** For an illustration of a standard distillation apparatus and to learn more about laboratory techniques and equipment, see General Chemistry Chapter 12.

13.2 Chromatography

Chromatography is the separation of a mixture of compounds by their distribution between two phases: one stationary and one moving. The mobile phase is run through the stationary phase. Different substances distribute themselves according to their relative affinities for the two phases. This causes the separation of the different compounds. Molecules are separated based on differences in polarity and molecular weight.

13.2.1 Gas-Liquid Chromatography

In gas-liquid chromatography, the *stationary phase* is a liquid absorbed to an inert solid. The liquid can be polyethylene glycol, squalene, or others, depending on the polarity of the substances being separated.

The mobile phase is a gas (i.e. He, N_2) which is unreactive both to the stationary phase and to the substances being separated. The sample being analyzed can be injected in the direction of gas flow into one end of a column packed with the stationary phase. As the sample migrates through the column certain molecules will move faster than others. As mentioned, the separation of the different types of molecules is dependent on size (*molecular weight*) and charge (*polarity*). Once the molecules reach the end of the column special detectors signal their arrival.

13.2.2 Thin-Layer Chromatography

<u>Thin-layer chromatography</u> (TLC) is a solid-liquid technique, based on adsorptivity and solubility. The *stationary phase* is a type of finely divided polar material, usually silica gel or alumina, which is thinly coated onto a glass plate.

A mixture of compounds is placed on the stationary phase, either a thin layer of silica gel or alumina on glass sheet. Silica gel is a very polar and hydrophobic substance. The mobile phase is usually of low polarity and moves by capillary action. Therefore, if silica gel is used as the stationary phase, nonpolar compounds move quickly while polar compounds have strong interaction with the gel and are stuck tightly to it. In reverse-phase chromatography, the stationary phase is nonpolar and the mobile phase is polar; as a result, polar compounds move quickly while nonpolar compounds stick more tightly to the adsorbant.

There are several types of interactions that may occur between the organic molecules in the sample and the silica gel, in order from weakest to strongest (see CHM 3.4, 4.2):

- Van der Waals force (nonpolar molecules)
- Dipole-dipole interaction (polar molecules)
- Hydrogen bonding (hydroxylic compounds)
- Coordination (Lewis bases)

Molecules with functional groups with the greatest polarity will bind more strongly to the stationary phase and thus will not rise as high on the glass plate.

Organic molecules will also interact with the *mobile phase* (= a solvent), or *eluent* used in the process. The more polar the solvent, the more easily it will dissolve polar molecules. The mobile phase usually contains organic solvents like ethanol, benzene, chloroform, acetone, etc.

As a result of the interactions of the organic molecules with the stationary and moving phases, for any adsorbed compound there is a dynamic distribution equilibrium between these phases. The different molecules will rise to different heights on the plate. Their presence can be detected using special stains (i.e. pH indicators, $KMnO_4$) or uv light (*if the compound can fluoresce*).

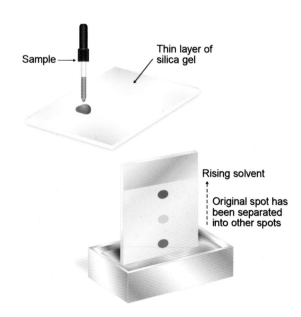

Figure IV.B.13.1: Thin-layer Chromatography.

13.2.3 Column Chromatography

Column chromatography is similar to TLC in principle; however, column chromatography uses silica gel or alumina as an adsorbant in the form of a column rather than TLC which uses paper in a layer-like form. The solvent and compounds move down the column (by gravity) allowing much more separation. The solvent drips out into a waiting flask where fractions containing bands corresponding to the different compounds are collected. After the solvent has evaporated, the compounds can then be isolated. Often the desired compounds are proteins or nucleic acids for which several techniques exist:

1. Ion exchange chromatography – Beads coated with charged substances are placed in the column so that they will attract compounds with an opposing charge.

2. Size exclusion chromatography – The column contains beads with tiny pores which allow small substances to enter, leaving larger molecules to pass through the column faster.

3. Affinity chromatography – Columns are customized to bind a substance of interest (e.g. a receptor or antibody) which allows it to bind very tightly.

13.3 Gel Electrophoresis

Gel electrophoresis is an important method to separate biological macromolecules (i.e. protein and DNA) based on size and charge of molecules. Molecules are made to move through a gel which is placed in an electrophoresis chamber. When an electric current is applied, molecules move at different velocities. These molecules will move towards either the cathode or anode depending on their size and charge (anions move towards anode while cations move towards the cathode. The migration velocity is proportional to the net charge on the molecule and inversely proportional to a coefficient dependent on the size of the molecule. Highly charged, small molecules will move the quickest with size being the most important factor.

There are three main types of electrophoresis:

1. Agarose gel electrophoresis – Used to separate pieces of negatively charged nucleic acids based on their size.

2. SDS-polyacrylamide gel electrophoresis

(SDS-PAGE) – Separates proteins on the basis of mass and not charge. The SDS (sodium dodecyl sulfate) binds to proteins and creates a large negative charge such that the only variable effecting their movement is the frictional coefficient which is solely dependent on mass.

3. Isoelectric focusing – The isoelectric point is the pH at which the net charge of a protein is zero (ORG Chapter 12.1.2). A mixture of proteins can be separated by placing them in an electric field with a pH gradient. The proteins will lose their charge and come to a stop when the pH is equal to their isoelectric point.

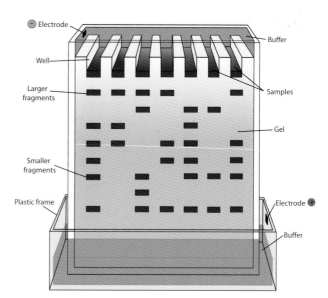

Figure IV.B.13.2: Gel Electrophoresis.

13.4 Recrystallization

Recrystallization is a useful purification technique. A solid organic compound with some impurity is dissolved in a hot solvent, and then the solvent is slowly cooled to allow the pure compound to reform or *recrystallize*, while leaving the impurities behind in the solvent. This is possible because the impurities do not normally fit within the crystal structure of the compound.

In choosing a solvent, solubility data (e.g. K_{sp} at various temperatures, etc.) regarding both the compound to be purified and the impurities should be known. The data should be analyzed such that the solvent would:

*   have the capability to dissolve alot of the compound (to be purified) at or near the boiling point of the solvent, while being able to dissolve little of the compound at room temperature. As well, the impurities should be soluble in the cold solvent.

*   have a low boiling point, so as to be easily removed from the solid in a drying process.

*   not react with the solid.

Go online to DAT-prep.com for chapter review Q&A and forum.

Protein Structure

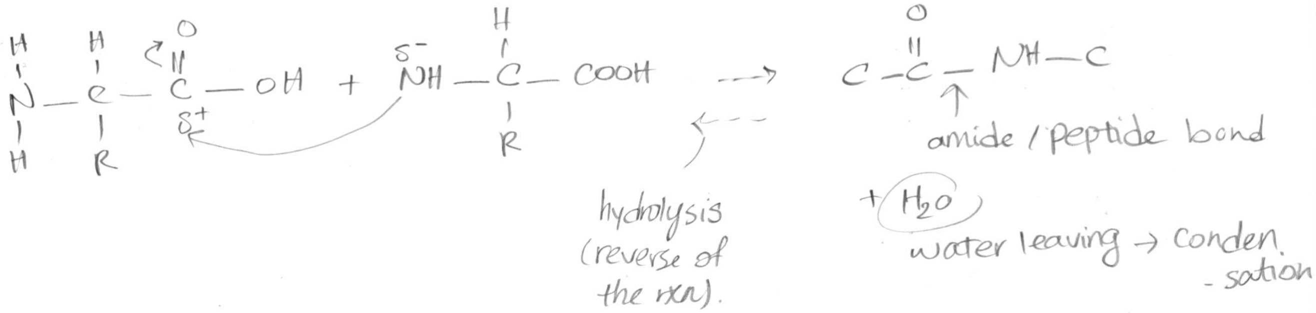

$$H_2N-\overset{H}{\underset{R}{C}}-\overset{O}{\underset{\delta^+}{C}}-OH \;+\; \overset{\delta^-}{N}H-\overset{H}{\underset{R}{C}}-COOH \;\longrightarrow\; C-\overset{O}{C}-NH-C$$

amide / peptide bond

hydrolysis
(reverse of
the rxn).

+ (H₂O)
water leaving → conden.
- sation

many peptide bonds - polypeptide.

protein
- 1° - order of aa (via covalent bonding)
- 2° - H-bonding (folding of protein) α helix / β-pleated sheets
- 3° - other electrostatic interactions (hydrophobic interactions.)
- 4° - like globular proteins.

* cystein (R group has a sulfur atom)
    bonding together: disulfide bond or disulfide bridges.
                                                    forming
                                                    a cystine

- phosphorous found in DNA / sulfur - protein.

SPECTROSCOPY

Chapter 14

Memorize	Understand	Importance
* Key IR absorptions * NMR rules	* Basic theory: IR spect., NMR * Very basic spectrum (graph) analysis * Deuterium exchange	**1 to 3 out of the 30 ORG** DAT questions are based on content in this chapter (in our estimation). * Note that between 30% and 60% of the questions in DAT Organic Chemistry are based on content from 4 chapters: 1, 2, 5 and 6.

DAT-Prep.com

Introduction

Spectroscopy is the use of the absorption, emission, or scattering of electromagnetic radiation by matter to study the matter or to study physical processes. The matter can be atoms, molecules, atomic or molecular ions, or solids.

Ex) CH₃—CH₂—CH₃   propane   — 2 enviroments

2:6(3+3) or 1:3   TMS

Additional Resources

of groups of peaks = # of hydrogen enviroment

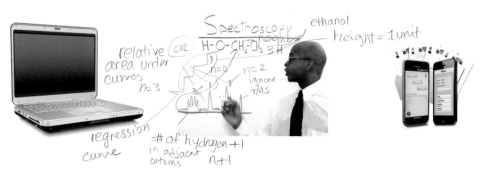

Free Online Q&A + Forum   Video: Online or DVD   Flashcards   Special Guest

14.1 IR Spectroscopy

In an infrared spectrometer, a beam of infrared (IR) radiation is passed through a sample. The spectrometer will then analyze the amount of radiation transmitted (= % *transmittance*) through the sample as the incident radiation is varied. Ultimately, a plot results as a graph showing the transmittance or absorption (*the inverse of transmittance*) versus the frequency or wavelength of the incident radiation or the wavenumber (= the reciprocal of the wavelength). IR spectroscopy is best used for the identification of functional groups.

The location of an IR absorption band (*or peak*) can be specified in *frequency units* by its wavenumber, measured in cm^{-1}. As the wave number decreases, the wavelength increases, thus the energy decreases (this can be determined using two physics equations which are not required content for the DAT: $v = \lambda f$ and $E = hf$). A schematic representation of the IR spectrum of octane is:

Electromagnetic radiation consists of discrete units of energy called *quanta* or *photons*. All organic compounds are capable of absorbing many types of electromagnetic energy. The absorption of energy leads to an increase in the amplitude of intramolecular rotations and vibrations.

Intramolecular rotations are the rotations of a molecule about its center of gravity. The difference in rotational energy levels is inversely proportional to the moment of inertia of a molecule. Rotational energy is quantized and gives rise to absorption spectra in the microwave region of the electromagnetic spectrum.

Intramolecular vibrations are the bending and stretching motions of bonds within a molecule. The relative spacing between vibrational energy levels increases with the increasing strength of an intramolecular bond. Vibrational energy is quantized and gives rise

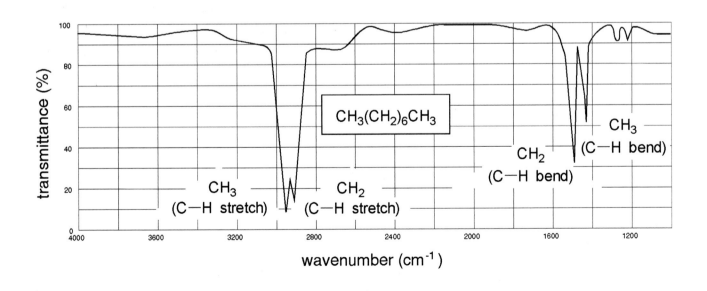

to absorption spectra in the <u>infrared region</u> of the electromagnetic spectrum.

Group	Frequency Range (cm^{-1})
Alkyl (C–H)	2850 – 2960
Alkene (C=C)	1620 – 1680
Alkyne (C≡C)	2100 – 2260
Alcohol (O–H)	3200 – 3650
Benzene (Ar–H)	3030
Carbonyl (C=O)	1630 – 1780
▶ Aldehyde	1680 – 1750
▶ Ketone	1735 – 1750
▶ Carboxylic Acid	1710 – 1780
▶ Amide	1630 – 1690
Amine (N–H)	3300 – 3500
Nitriles (C≡N)	2220 – 2260

Thus there are two types of bond vibration: stretching and bending. That is, after exposure to the IR radiation the bonds stretch and bend (*or contract*) to a greater degree once energy is absorbed. In general, bending vibrations will occur at lower frequencies (higher wavelengths) than stretching vibrations of the same groups. So, as seen in the sample spectra for octane, each group will have two characteristic peaks, one due to stretching, and one due to bending.

Different functional groups will have transmittances at characteristic wave numbers, which is why IR spectroscopy is useful. Some examples (*approximate values*) of characteristic absorbances are shown in the table.

The minimum frequencies that you should memorize for the DAT include the carbonyl and alcohol absorbances.

By looking at the characteristic transmittances of a compound's spectrum, it is possible to identify the functional groups present in the molecule.

Symmetrical molecules or molecules composed of the same atoms do not exhibit a change in dipole moment under IR radiation and thus absorptions do not show up in IR spectra.

14.2 Proton NMR Spectroscopy

<u>Nuclear Magnetic Resonance (NMR) spectroscopy</u> can be used to examine the environments of the hydrogen atoms in a molecule. In fact, using a (*proton*) NMR or

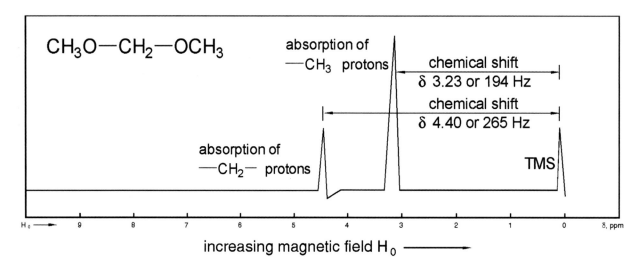

increasing magnetic field H_0 ⟶

^{1}HNMR, one can determine both the number and types of hydrogens in a molecule. The basis of this stems from the magnetic properties of the hydrogen nucleus (proton). Similar to electrons, the hydrogen proton has a nuclear spin, able to take either of two values. These values are designated as $+1/2$ and $-1/2$. As a result of this spin, the nucleus will respond to a magnetic field by being oriented in the direction of the field. NMR spectrometers measure the absorption of energy by the hydrogen nuclei in an organic compound.

A schematic representation of an NMR spectrum, that of dimethoxymethane is shown:

The small peak at the right is that of TMS, tetramethylsilane, shown here:

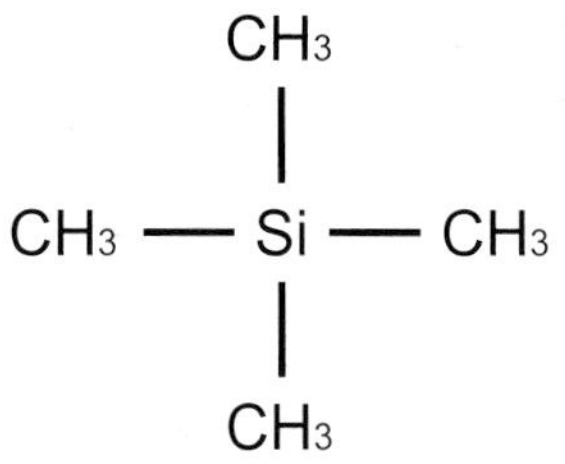

$$CH_3$$
$$|$$
$$CH_3 - Si - CH_3$$
$$|$$
$$CH_3$$

This compound is added to the sample to be used as a reference, or standard. It is volatile, inert and absorbs at a higher field than most other organic chemicals.

The position of a peak relative to the standard is referred to as its *chemical shift*. Since NMR spectroscopy differentiates between types of protons, each type will have a different chemical shift, as shown. Protons in the same environment, like the three hydrogens in $-CH_3$, are called *equivalent protons*.

Dimethoxymethane is a symmetric molecule, thus the protons on either methyl group are equivalent. So, in the example above, the absorption of $-CH_3$ protons occurs at one peak (*a singlet*) 3.23 ppm downfield from TMS. In most organic molecules, the range of absorption will be in the 0–10 ppm (= *parts per million*) range.

The area under each peak is directly related to the number of protons contributing to it, and thus may be used to determine the

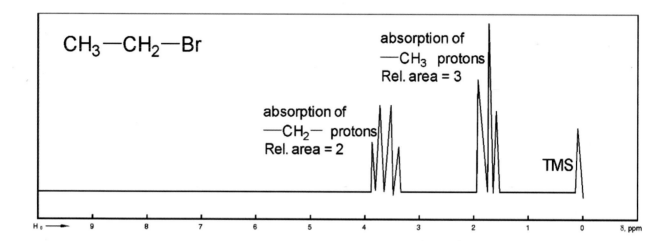

CH₃—CH₂—Br

absorption of
—CH₃ protons
Rel. area = 3

absorption of
—CH₂— protons
Rel. area = 2

TMS

H₀ ⟶ 9 8 7 6 5 4 3 2 1 0 δ, ppm

relative number of protons in the molecule. Accurate measurements of the area under the two peaks above yield the ratio 1:3 which represents the relative number of hydrogens (i.e. 1:3 = 2:6).

Let us now examine a schematic representation of the NMR spectrum of ethyl bromide:

It is obvious that something is different. Looking at the molecule, one can see that there are two different types of protons (*either far from Br or near to Br*). However, there are more than two signals in the spectrum. As such, the NMR signal for each group is said to be split. This type of splitting is called <u>spin-spin splitting</u> (= *spin-spin coupling*) and is caused by the presence of neighboring protons (*protons on an adjacent or vicinal carbon*) that are not equivalent to the proton in question. Note that the protons that are farther than two carbons apart do not exhibit a coupling effect.

The number of lines in the splitting pattern for a given set of equivalent protons depends on the number of adjacent protons according to the following rule: if there are n equivalent protons in adjacent positions, a proton NMR signal is split into $n + 1$ lines.

Therefore the NMR spectrum for ethyl bromide can be interpreted thus:

• There are two groups of lines (*two split peaks*), therefore there are two different environments for protons.

• The relative areas under each peak is 2:3, which represents the relative number of hydrogens in the molecule.

• There are 4 splits (*quartet*) in the peak which has relatively two hydrogens ($-CH_2$). Thus the number of adjacent hydrogens is $n + 1 = 4$; therefore, there are 3 hydrogens on the carbon adjacent to $-CH_2$.

• There are 3 splits (*triplet*) in the peak which has relatively three hydrogens ($-CH_3$).

Thus the number of adjacent hydrogens is $n + 1 = 3$; therefore, there are 2 hydrogens on the carbon adjacent to $-CH_3$.

The relative areas under each peak may be expressed in three ways: (i) the information may simply be provided to you (*too easy!*); (ii) the integers may be written above the signals (= *integration integers*, i.e. 2,3 in the previous example); or (iii) a step-like *integration curve* above the signals where the relative height of each step equals the relative number of hydrogens.

14.2.1 Deuterium Exchange

Deuterium, the hydrogen isotope ^2H or D, can be used to identify substances with readily exchangeable or acidic hydrogens. Rather than H_2O, D_2O is used to identify the chemical exchange:

$$ROH + DOD \rightleftharpoons ROD + HOD$$

The previous signal due to the acidic $-O\boxed{H}$ would now disappear. However, if excess D_2O is used, a signal as a result of HOD may be observed.

Solvents may also be involved in exchange phenomena. The solvents carbon tetrachloride (CCl_4) and deuteriochloroform ($CDCl_3$) can also engage in exchange-induced decoupling of acidic hydrogens (usu. in alcohols).

14.2.2 ^{13}C NMR

The main difference between proton NMR and ^{13}C NMR is that most carbon 13 signals occur 0–200 δ downfield from the carbon peak of TMS. There is also very little coupling between carbon atoms as only 1.1% of carbon atoms are ^{13}C. There is coupling between carbon atoms and their adjacent protons which are directly attached to them. This coupling of one bond is similar to the three bond coupling exhibited by proton NMR.

Signals will be split into a triplet with an area of 1:2:1 when a carbon atom is attached to two protons. Another unique feature of ^{13}C NMR is a phenomenon called spin decoupling where a spectrum of singlets can be recorded - each corresponding to a singular carbon atom. This allows one to accurately determine the number of different carbons in their respective chemical environments as well as the number of adjacent hydrogens (spin-coupled only).

14.3 Mass Spectrometry

Mass spectrometry (the former expression "mass spectroscopy" is discouraged), unlike other forms of NMR we have seen, destroys the sample during its analysis. The analysis is carried out using a beam of electrons which ionize the sample and a detector to measure the number of particles that are deflected due to the presence of a magnetic field. The reflected particle is usually an unstable species which decomposes rapidly into a cationic fragment and a radical fragment.

Since there are many ways in which the particle can decompose, a typical mass spectrum is often composed of numerous lines, with each one corresponding to a specific mass/charge ratio (m/z, sometimes symbolized as m/e). It is important to note that only cations are deflected by the magnetic field, thus only cations will appear on the spectrum which plots m/z (x-axis) vs. the abundance of the cationic fragments (y-axis). See the figure provided.

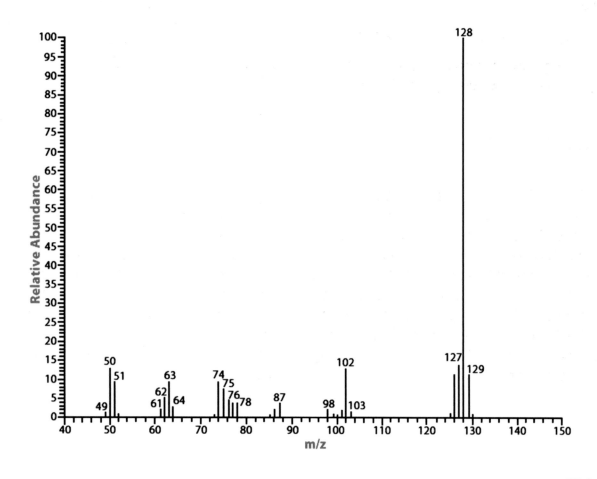

The tallest peak represents the most common ion and is also referred to as the base peak. The molecular weight can be obtained not from the base peak but rather from the peak with the highest m/z ratio, 129 in this case. This is called the parent ion peak and is designated by M^+. By looking at the fragmentation pattern, we can ascertain information regarding the compound's structure, something that IR spectroscopy is incapable of achieving.

Spectroscopy

• X-ray chrystrollography — Sample purified & then purified. Take x-rays and send to vessles....> diffraction patterns.
— DNA ⟹ Done by this.

IR — much less sample required.
Some rays absorbed: absorpence
" transmitted: transmittance → info for functional units

Units: cm^{-1} (wave length).

approximations ⎰* 1700 cm^{-1} for —C=O
⎱* 3300 cm^{-1} for —OH

NMR
Allows us to know # and type of hydrogens in a compound

Go online to DAT-prep.com for chapter review Q&A and forum.

KEY ORGANIC CHEMISTRY REACTION MECHANISMS

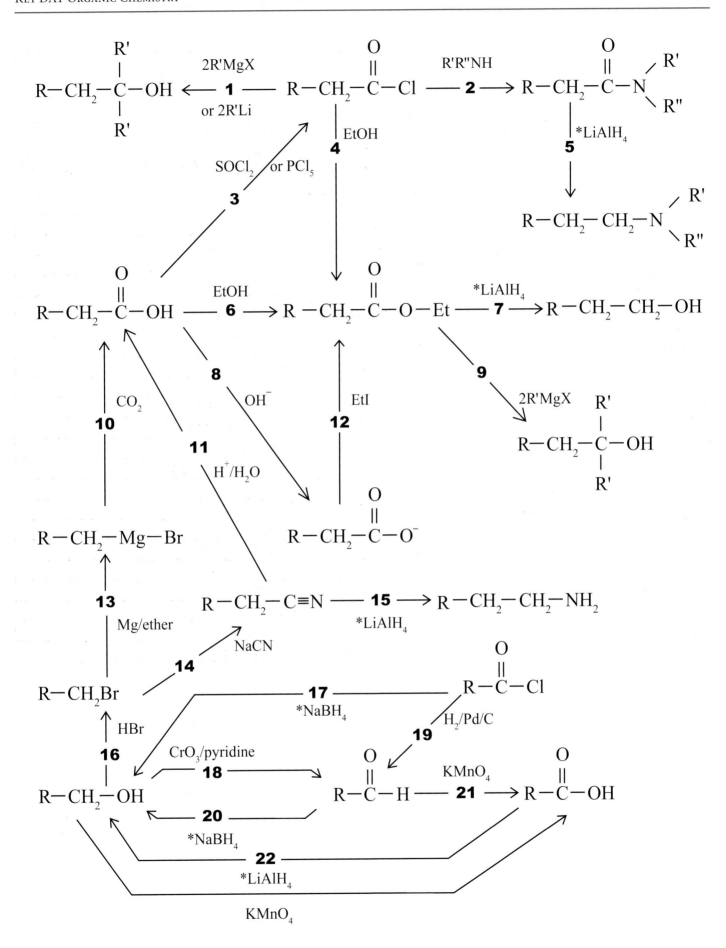

KEY

| R = alkyl | Et = ethyl | X = halide | R^-MgX^+ = grignard reagent | R^-Li^+ = alkyl lithium |

Grignard reagents and alkyl lithiums are special agents since they can create new C—C bonds.

*Reduction = addition of hydrogen or subtraction of oxygen. Mild reducing agents add fewer hydrogens/subtract fewer oxygens. Strong reducing agents add more hydrogens/subtract more oxygens. Cross-referencing to The Gold Standard DAT text.

Most reactions presented can be derived from basic principles (i.e. ORG 1.6, 7.1).

1) An acid chloride reacts with a grignard reagent to produce a tertiary alcohol. See ORG 9.1

2) An acid chloride reacts with a primary or secondary amine to produce an amide. See ORG 9.3 & 11.2.

3) A carboxylic acid reacts with $SOCl_2$ or PCl_5 to produce an acid chloride. See ORG 9.1.

4) An acid chloride reacts with an alcohol (e.g. ethanol) to produce an ester. See ORG 9.4.

5) An amide reacts with $LiAlH_4$ to produce an amine. See ORG 8.2, 9.3.

6) A carboxylic acid reacts with an alcohol (e.g. ethanol) to produce an ester. See ORG 8.2.

7) An ester reacts with $LiAlH_4$ to produce a primary alcohol. See ORG 8.2, 9.4.

8) A carboxylic acid reacts with base to produce a carboxylate anion. See CHM 6.3 & ORG 8.1.

9) An ester reacts with a grignard reagent to produce a tertiary alcohol. See ORG 9.4.

10) A grignard reagent reacts with carbon dioxide to produce a carboxylic acid. See ORG 8.1.1.

11) A nitrile reacts with aqueous acid to produce a carboxylic acid. Compare to ORG 10.1.1.

12) A carboxylate ion reacts with ethyl iodide to produce an ester. Compare to ORG 10.1.1.

13) An alkyl halide reacts with Mg/ether to produce a grignard reagent. Compare to ORG 10.1.1.

14) An alkyl halide reacts with NaCN to produce a nitrile. See ORG 6.2.3.

15) A nitrile reacts with $LiAlH_4$ to produce an amine. See ORG 8.2.

16) A primary alcohol reacts with HBr to produce an alkyl halide. Compare to ORG 10.1.1.

17) An acid chloride reacts with $NaBH_4$ to produce a primary alcohol. See ORG 8.2, 9.1.

18) A primary alcohol reacts with CrO_3/pyridine to produce an aldehyde. See ORG 6.2.2.

19) A acid chloride reacts with H_2/Pd/C to produce an aldehyde. See ORG 7.1 & 9.1.

20) An aldehyde reacts with $NaBH_4$ to produce a primary or secondary alcohol. See ORG 7.1, 8.2.

21) An aldehyde reacts with $KMnO_4$ to produce a carboxylic acid. See ORG 7.2.1.

22) A carboxylic acid reacts with $LiAlH_4$ to produce a primary alcohol. See ORG 8.2.

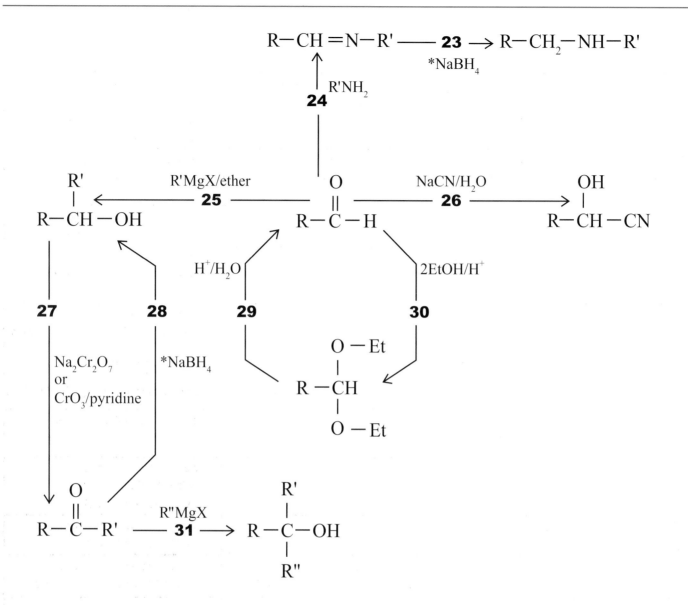

KEY
23) An imine reacts with NaBH$_4$ to produce a secondary amine. See 7.2.3, 8.2.
24) An aldehyde reacts with a primary amine to produce an imine. See ORG 7.2.3.
25) An aldehyde reacts with a grignard reagent and ether to produce a secondary alcohol. See ORG 7.1.
26) An aldehyde reacts with aqueous NaCN. See ORG 7.1.
27) A secondary alcohol reacts with Na$_2$CrO$_7$ or CrO$_3$/pyridine to produce a ketone. See ORG 6.2.2.
28) A ketone reacts with NaBH$_4$ to produce a secondary alcohol. See ORG 7.2.1.
29) An acetal reacts with aqueous acid to produce an aldehyde. See ORG 7.2.2.
30) An aldehyde reacts with an alcohol (e.g. ethanol) and acid to produce an acetal. Note that using with less EtOH/H$^+$, a hemiacetal will form. See ORG 7.2.2.
31) A ketone reacts with a grignard reagent to produce a tertiary alcohol. See ORG 9.1.

List of Common Reagents

Reagent	Comments	Reagent	Comments
$AlCl_3$ aluminum chloride	• Lewis acid • Friedel Crafts	Lindlar catalyst	• heterogeneous catalyst • syn reduction of alkynes to alkenes NOT alkanes
BH_3 borane	• Alkene hydroboration • anti - Markovnikoff	mCPBA meta - chloroperoxybenzoic acid	• epoxidation of alkenes • ketones to esters
CH_2N_2 diazomethane	• Converts carboxylic acids to methyl esters	Mg magnesium metal	• alkyl halide + Mg = Grignard
DCC N,N'-dicyclohexyl carbodiimide	• dehydrating agent for peptide couplings	$NaBH_4$ sodium borohydride	• mild reducing agent • aldehydes/ketones to alcohols
DIBAL -H diisobutylaluminum hydride	• reduces esters/nitriles to aldehydes	$NaIO_4$ sodium periodate	• strong ox. agent • cleaves vicinal diols to 2 aldehydes
DMF dimethylformamide	• polar aprotic (= no H+) solvent • facilitates S_N2	NBS N-bromosuccinimide	• brominations • radical subs. + electrophilic additions
DMSO dimethyl sulfoxide	• polar aprotic solvent • facilitates S_N2	NCS N-chlorosuccinimide	• chlorinations (similar to NBS)
$FeBr_3$ ferric bromide	• Friedel-Crafts • IUPAC: Iron(III)	O_3 ozone	• cleaves double bonds to aldehydes/ketones/acids (depends on workup)
HCN hydrogen cyanide	• makes cyanohydrins • weak acid	$Pb(OAc)_4$ lead tetraacetate	• strong ox. agent, cleaves diols • IUPAC: lead(IV) acetate
$Hg(OAc)_2$ mercuric acetate	• alkene • IUPAC: mercury(II) acetate	PBr_3 phosphorus tribromide	• alcohols to alkyl bromides • carboxylic acids to acyl bromides
K_2CrO_7 potassium dichromate	• mild oxidizing agent • alcohols to aldehydes/ketones	PCC pyridinium chlorochromate	• mild ox. agent • alcohols to aldehydes/ketones
$KMnO_4$ potassium permanganate	• strong oxidizing agent • i.e. hydroxylate alkenes	Pd/C palladium on carbon	• catalyst for hydrogenation i.e. of • unsaturated bonds
LDA lithium diisopropyl amide	• strong base • i.e. carbonyl to enolate	pyrrolidine	• cyclic 2° amine • aldol condensation forming enamines
Li lithium metal	• makes organolithium from alkyl bromide	R_2CuLi organocuprate Gilman reagent	• R replaces X in organic halides • 1,4-addition for unsaturated systems
$LiAlH(OR)_3$	• less reactive $LiAlH_4$ derivative • i.e. esters to aldehydes	$SOCl_2$ thionyl chloride	• chlorinations • i.e. makes acid chlorides
$LiAlH_4$ (LAH, LithAl) lithium aluminum hydride	• strong reducing agent • i.e. esters to alcohols	TsOH toluenesulfonic acid	• p-TsOH (PTSA): strong acid • TSO -, OTs: excellent leaving groups

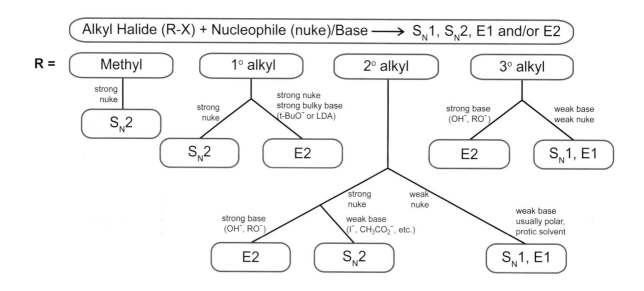

		S$_N$1	S$_N$2
S **U** **B** **S** **T** **I** **T** **U** **T** **I** **O** **N**	Mechanism	Two steps (carbocation rearrangements possible)	One step (= *concerted*)
	Rate law	Rate = k[R–X] (unimolecular, 1st order)	Rate = k[R–X][Nuke] (bimolecular, 2nd order)
	Stereochemistry	Loss of stereochemistry (racemization possible)	Stereospecific (inversion due to backside displacement)
	Substrate	Cation stability (benzylic > allylic > 3° > 2°) No 1° or methyl R$^+$ without extra stabilization.	Sterics (methyl > 1° > 2°) No S$_N$2 with 3°
	Nucleophile	Not Important	Strong/Moderate required •strong: RS$^-$, I$^-$, R$_2$N$^-$, R$_2$NH, RO$^-$, CN$^-$ •moderate: RSH, Br$^-$, RCO$_2^-$
	Leaving group	Very important (–OSO$_2$CF$_3$ > –OSO$_2$F >> derivatives of 4-toluenesulfonyl chloride >> –I > –Br > –Cl)	Moderately important (same trend as S$_N$1)
	Solvent	Polar protic (water, most alcohols, formic acid, HF, ammonia)	Polar aprotic (acetonitrile, DMF, HMPA, DMSO - dimethyl sulfoxide)

		E1	E2
E **L** **I** **M** **I** **N** **A** **T** **I** **O** **N**	Mechanism	Two steps (carbocation rearrangements possible)	One step (= *concerted*)
	Rate law	Rate = k[R–X] (unimolecular, 1st order)	Rate = k[R–X][Base] (bimolecular, 2nd order)
	Stereochemistry	Not stereospecific	Stereospecific (antiperiplanar transition state)
	Substrate	Cation stability (benzylic > allylic > 3° > 2°)	Alkene stability (3° > 2° > 1°)
	Base	Not important: usually weak (ROH, R$_2$NH)	Strong base required (RO$^-$, R$_2$N$^-$)
	Leaving group	Very important (same trend as S$_N$1)	Moderately important (same trend as S$_N$1)
	Solvent	Polar protic (water, most alcohols, formic acid, HF, ammonia)	Wide range of solvents
	Product ratio	Zaitsev's Rule (or Saytzeff's Rule): The most highly substituted alkene usually predominates. Hofmann Product: Using a sterically hindered base (i.e. t-BuO$^-$ or LDA), results in formation of the least substituted alkene (Hofmann product). High temperature favors elimination.	

CHAPTER 1: MOLECULAR STRUCTURE OF ORGANIC COMPOUNDS

1.2 Hybrid Orbitals

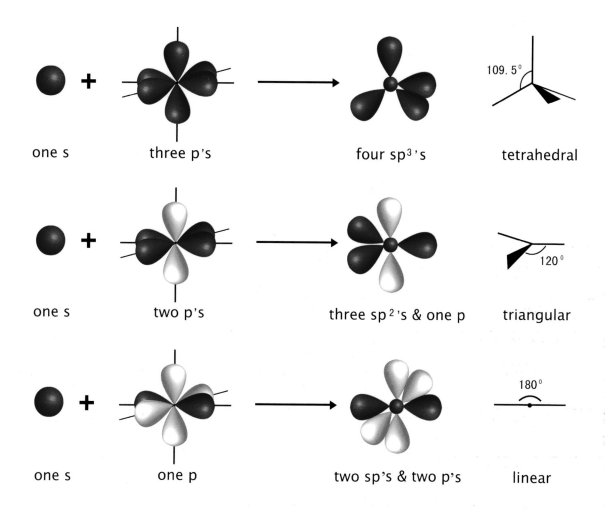

Figure IV.B.1.1: Hybrid orbital geometry

1.6 Ground Rules

"Like charges repel" and "opposites attract" are the basic rules of electrostatics. "Opposites attract" is translated in Organic Chemistry to mean "nucleophile attacks electrophile".

CHAPTER 1: STEREOCHEMISTRY

2.3 Absolute and Relative Configuration

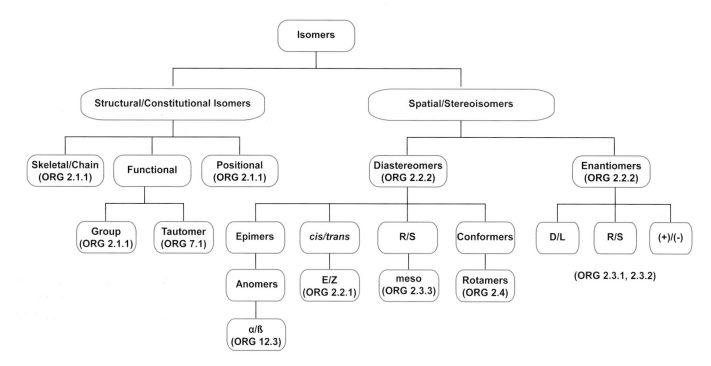

Figure IV.B.2.1.1: Categories of isomers.

2.4 Conformational Isomers

Common Terms

- dihedral angle: torsion (turning/twisting) angle
- gauche: skew, synclinal
- anti: trans, antiperiplanar
- eclipsed: syn, cis, synperiplanar,
  torsion angle = 0°

"anti" and "syn" are IUPAC preferred descriptors.

CHAPTER 3: ALKANES

3.1 Description and Nomenclature

C_1 = meth	C_5 = pent	C_8 = oct
C_2 = eth	C_6 = hex	C_9 = non
C_3 = prop	C_7 = hept	C_{10} = dec
C_4 = but		

3.3 Ring Strain in Cyclic Alkanes

The expected angles in some cyclic compounds can be determined geometrically: 60° in cyclopropane; 90° in cyclobutane and 108° in cyclopentane. Cyclohexane, in the chair conformation, has normal bond angles of 109.5°. The closer the angle is to the normal tetrahedral angle of 109.5°, the more stable the compound.

CHAPTER 4: ALKENES

4.2.1 Electrophilic Addition

Markovnikoff's rule is a result of this, and it states: *the nucleophile will be bonded to the most substituted carbon* (fewest hydrogens attached) *in the product. Equivalently, the electrophile will be bonded to the least substituted carbon* (most hydrogens attached) *in the product.* Markovnikoff's rule is true for the ionic conditions. Anti-Markovnikoff products are the major products under free radical conditions.

4.2.4 The Diels–Alder Reaction

The Diels–Alder reaction is a cycloaddition reaction between a conjugated diene and a substituted alkene (= the dienophile) to form a substituted cyclohexene system.

> Diene + dienophile = cyclohexene

All Diels-Alder reactions have four common features: (1) the reaction is initiated by heat; (2) the reaction forms new six-membered rings; (3) three π bonds break and two new C-C σ bonds and one new C-C π bond are formed; (4) all bonds break and form in a single step.

The Diels Alder diene must have the two double bonds on the same side of the single bond in one of the structures, which is called the s-cis conformation (s-cis: cis with respect to the single bond). If double bonds are on the opposite sides of the single bond in the Lewis structure, this is called the s-trans conformation (s-trans: trans with respect to the single bond).

s-cis diene   dienophile

Note that dienes can be divided into 3 classes, depending on the relative location of the double bonds:
1. Cumulated dienes, like allene, have the double bonds sharing a common atom.
2. Conjugated dienes, like 1,3–butadiene, have conjugated double bonds separated by one single bond.
3. Unconjugated dienes (= isolated dienes) have the double bonds separated by two or more single bonds. They are usually less stable than isomeric conjugated dienes.

CHAPTER 5: AROMATICS

5.1.1 Hückel's Rule

If a compound does not meet all the following criteria, it is likely not aromatic.

1. The molecule is cyclic.
2. The molecule is planar.
3. The molecule is fully conjugated (i.e. p orbitals at every atom in the ring; ORG 1.4).
4. The molecule has 4n + 2 π electrons.

If rules 1., 2. and/or 3. are broken, then the molecule is non-aromatic. If rule 4. is broken then the molecule is antiaromatic.

Notice that the number of π delocalized electrons must be even but NOT a multiple of 4. So 4n + 2 number of π electrons, where n = 0, 1, 2, 3, and so on, is known as Hückel's Rule. Thus the number of pi electrons can be 2, 6, 10, etc.

5.2 Electrophilic Aromatic Substitution

Aromatic halogenation:

benzene   halogen (X = Cl or Br)   halobenzene   hydrogen halide

Aromatic nitration:

Aromatic sulfonation:

Friedel-Crafts alkylation:

Friedel-Crafts acylation:

EDG	EWG	EWG: Halogens
activates the ring	deactivates the ring	weakly deactivating
O/P Directing	Meta Directing	O/P Directing
i.e. alkyl groups	i.e. nitro ($-NO_2$)	i.e. bromine
acid weakening	acid strengthening	acid strengthening
increase pKa	decrease pKa	decrease pKa

CHAPTER 6: ALCOHOLS

6.1.2 Synthesis of Alcohols

6.2.4 Elimination

CHAPTER 7: ALDEHYDES AND KETONES

7.2 Important Reactions of Aldehydes & Ketones

7.2.6 The Wittig reaction

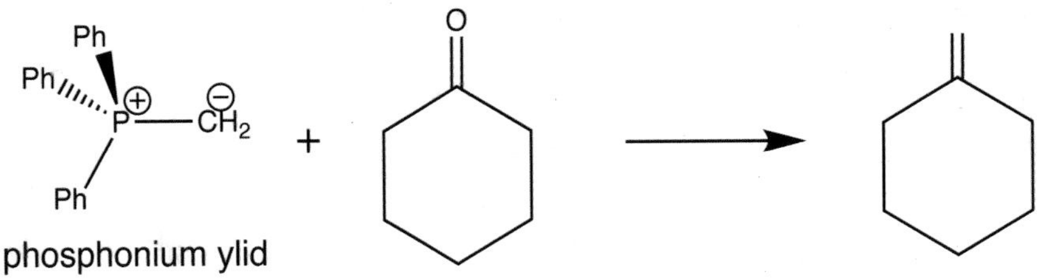

phosphonium ylid

CHAPTER 9: CARBOXYLIC ACID DERIVATES

9.4.1 Fats, Glycerides and Saponification

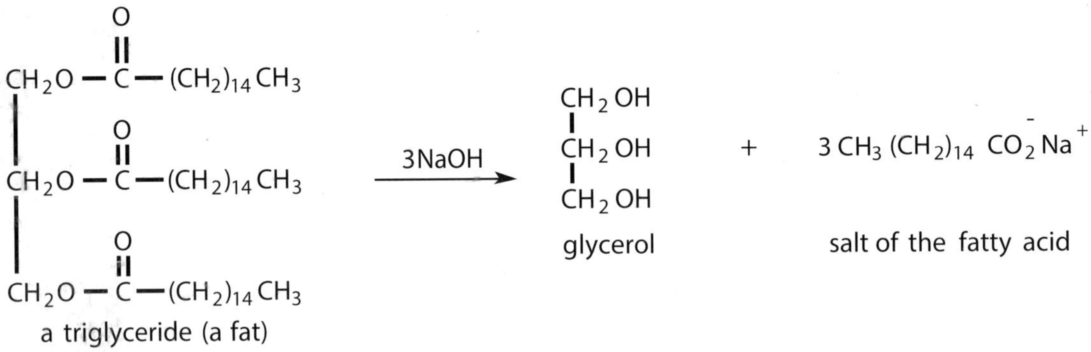

a triglyceride (a fat)

glycerol   salt of the fatty acid

CHAPTER 12: BIOLOGICAL MOLECULES

12.1 Amino Acids

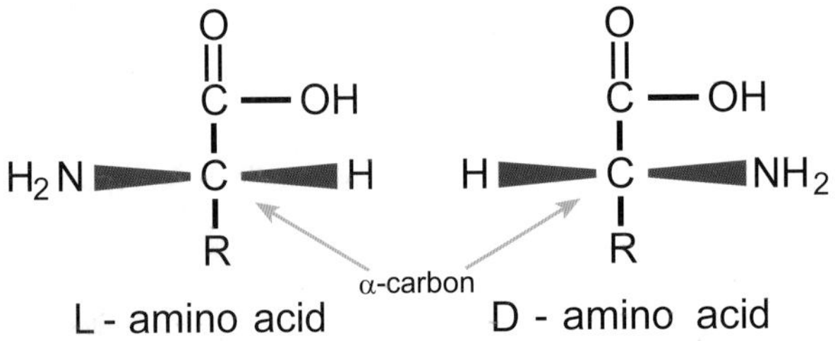

L - amino acid   D - amino acid

12.1.2 Acidic vs. Basic

$$\text{isoelectric point} = pI = (pK_{a1} + pK_{a2})/2$$

CHAPTER 14: SPECTROSCOPY

14.1 IR Spectroscopy

Group	Frequency Range (cm^{-1})
Alcohol (O–H)	3200 – 3650
Carbonyl (C=O)	1630 – 1780